Dress, Adornment, and the Social Order

Dress, Adornment, and the Social Order

EDITED BY

Mary Ellen Roach & *Joanne Bubolz Eicher*
University of Wisconsin   Michigan State University

John Wiley & Sons, Inc., New York · London · Sydney

Copyright © 1965 by John Wiley & Sons, Inc.

All Rights Reserved
This book or any part thereof
must not be reproduced in any form
without the written permission of the publisher.

10 9 8 7 6 5 4

Library of Congress Catalog Card Number: 65-19482
Printed in the United States of America
ISBN 0 471 72476 9

To Our Parents, Who Believed in Educating Daughters

Preface

Everywhere man adorns and dresses himself, and everywhere the nature of his attempts to modify his appearance is related to his social circumstances. This is a collection of readings concerned with the various relationships between the social order and adornment.

The reader will find that we have selected writings not only from academic disciplines such as cultural anthropology, economics, sociology, social psychology, and home economics but also from journalistic and popular sources. Some writings are classic statements; others are contributions selected from recently published books and journals; still others, from fairly obscure sources, have been chosen to illustrate points of view to which the editors wish to call attention. Some excellent selections readily available in paperback or reprint form have not been included but are noted in the supplementary readings and annotated bibliography.

We intend our book for students in a number of disciplines since the subject covered has long piqued the interest of individuals from diverse fields. It is especially directed to anthropologists, economists, home economists, psychologists, and sociologists interested in this aspect of human behavior. Costume historians should find it of interest for the light it throws on historical diversity and patterns of change in costume. Since writings on the socio-cultural aspects of dress and adornment are widely scattered, we believe that a reader that brings together a number of writings will relieve interested students of tedious searching. They can sample a variety of views by referring to one volume. On the other hand, we make no claim to complete coverage. The selections represent our orientation. As scholars interested in this area of study and research, we hope that provocative ideas included in the readings will stimulate students to make further investigation. It is for this reason also that we have included supplementary readings and appended an annotated bibliography of 529 items.

Following the introduction to the study of dress and adornment in Part One, the readings in this book are grouped under five major headings. The traditional topics of origins and functions of dress are presented in Part Two. Diversity in cultural patterns of dress is the theme in Part Three with special emphasis given to technical, aesthetic, moral, and ritualistic patterns. We consider observable relationships between dress and social organization, as exhibited by age and sex roles and the social structures of family, polity, economy, religion, and caste and class, in Part Four. The significance of clothing for the individual as a biological organism as well as a normal or deviant social self is developed in Part Five. Patterns of change and stability in dress and the related topic of fashion are discussed in Part Six. The readings for each part are preceded by comments which provide a framework for understanding and evaluating the selections. We have taken care to include in each major section reading materials which will provide opportunity for making crosscultural comparisons.

Acknowledgments

Many have helped us in editing and organizing this book. We are especially grateful to Elizabeth Nall, Gertrude MacFarlane, and Barbara Stowe for reading and commenting on the entire manuscript; to Vernon Allen, Charles Loomis, Arlene Ostermeier, and Mary Lou Rosencranz for critical comments on the overviews and organization; to Carl Eicher and Ruth Useem for the stimulation of their important and provocative suggestions and criticisms; to Elaine Found for assistance in proofreading and final polishing of the manuscript.

The bibliography could not have been compiled without the persistence and diligence of Eleanor Kelley, who bore major responsibility for the searching and sleuthing, which sometimes grew quite tedious.

Ideas and suggestions have been gleaned from a number of people including Helen Brockman, Wilbur Brookover, Howard Ehrlich, William Form, Duane Gibson, Charles Hughes, Iwao Ishino, Eleanor Mullikin, Frederica Neville, Beatrice Paolucci, Gregory Stone, and Arthur Vener. Support and encouragement have come from a number of other colleagues, especially our departmental chairmen, Mary Gephart and Emma Jordre.

Indispensable has been the assistance of such able people as Ellen Amman, Hazel Baxter, Margaret Faludi, Barbara Gibson, Carolyn Hammarsjkold, Suzanne Hendricks, Elizabeth Hill, Cletus Nwabia, Audray Remington, Ruth Sybers, Lillian Upcraft, Mary Ellen Wagner, Delores Weppner, Mildred Gahrsen, and Agatha Norton.

We are indebted to the Michigan State University Experiment Station for financial aid in compiling the bibliography. International Programs at Michigan State University is also acknowledged by the second author for support which has enabled her to make field observations in Nigeria and thereby strengthen theoretical points developed in our editorial comments.

The courtesy extended by authors and publishers for rights to reprint is acknowledged in appropriate footnotes.

Mary Ellen Roach
Madison, Wisconsin

Joanne Bubolz Eicher
Enugu, Nigeria

April, 1965

Contents

Part One ❀ Introduction to the Study of Dress, Adornment, and the Social Order — 1

Part Two ❀ Origins and Functions of Dress and Adornment — 5

    The Origins of Clothing
        RALPH BEALS AND HARRY HOIJER, 8
    What Shall We Wear?
        INA CORINNE BROWN, 9

Part Three ❀ Diversity in Cultural Patterns Related to Dress and Adornment — 11

    Clothing and Ornament
        E. ADAMSON HOEBEL, 15
    Technical Patterns, 28
    Clothing Materials
        RALPH BEALS AND HARRY HOIJER, 28
    The Eyed Needle
        M. D. C. CRAWFORD, 32
    Aesthetic Patterns, 34
    Ideals of Beauty
        HARRY C. BREDEMEIER AND JACKSON TOBY, 34

The Ideal Wife Is Shiny
ANONYMOUS, 35

Themes in Cosmetics and Grooming
MURRAY WAX, 36

Moral Patterns, 46

Nudity and Dress
ERNEST CRAWLEY, 46

Attitudes and Rationalizations Regarding Body Exposure
ERVING GOFFMAN, 50

Ritualistic Patterns, 53

Wedding Garments
ERNEST CRAWLEY, 53

Part Four 🎗 Social Organization and Dress   57

Age and Sex Roles, 64

On the Disappearance of Knickers: Hypotheses for the Functional Analysis of the Psychology of Clothing
GEORGE BUSH AND PERRY LONDON, 64

The Sexual Background of Dress
ERNEST CRAWLEY, 72

Adolescent Orientations to Clothing
ARTHUR M. VENER AND CHARLES R. HOFFER, 76

The Family, 82

Clothing and the American Family
MARY ELLEN ROACH, 82

Family Cycle
MILDRED TATE AND ORIS GLISSON, 86

Economy, 91

Clothing of Nigerian Cocoa Farmers' Families
R. GALLETTI, K. D. S. BALDWIN, AND I. O. DINA, 91

Factors Affecting Clothing Decisions
MILDRED TATE AND ORIS GLISSON, 97

Used-Clothing Sales in a Small City
GEITEL WINAKOR AND MARCELLA MARTIN, 105

Clothing Standards and Habits
FERDYNAND ZWEIG, 111

Ritual and Magic in the Control of Contagion
JULIUS A. ROTH, 117

Polity, 124

Clothes and Government
LAWRENCE LANGNER, 124

The New China
A. C. SCOTT, 127

First in Space—But Not in Femininity
AUDREY R. TOPPING, 135

Religion, 138

Sacred Dress
ERNEST CRAWLEY, 138

The Hasidic Community
SOLOMON POLL, 142

Caste and Class, 158

Stratification in a Prairie Town
JOHN USEEM, PIERRE TANGENT, AND
RUTH HILL USEEM, 158

Trend to Breakdown of Class Lines in Clothes
FREDERICK LEWIS ALLEN, 162

The Best-Dressed Poverty
MICHAEL HARRINGTON, 163

Men's Clothing and the Negro
JACK SCHWARTZ, 164

Clothing and Ornament
JOHN GILLIN, 174

Part Five ❀ Dress and the Individual 185

A Biological Organism, 191

The Differential Effects of Nudity and Clothing

on Muscular Tonus in Infancy
H. M. HALVERSON, 191

Thermal Comfort
RICHARD L. MEIER, 204

Why She Lives in a Space Suit
PRISCILLA JAQUITH, 210

Soft Suit Seen Safe for Lunar Surface Work
ANONYMOUS, 212

A Social Self, 214

Male and Female
EVELYN GOODENOUGH PITCHER, 214

Appearance and the Self
GREGORY P. STONE, 216

Identity Kits
ERVING GOFFMAN, 246

Perception of Self in Relation to Clothing
MARY S. RYAN, 247

Clothing and the Status Ratings of Men: An Experiment
THOMAS FORD HOULT, 250

The Matter of Clothing
MURRAY WAX AND ROSALIE WAX, 257

A Deviant, 265

Fashions of Royalty
CECIL BEATON, 265

The Mentally Ill and Management of Personal Front
ERVING GOFFMAN, 266

Therapy of Fashion
THEO K. MILLER, LEWIS G. CARPENTER, AND ROBERT B. BUCKEY, 269

Self-Tattooing Among Delinquents—A Research Note
JOHN H. BURMA, 271

The Clacton Giggle
ANONYMOUS, 276

Part Six ❀ Stability and Change in Patterns of Dress 279

        Custom, 287

            The Evolution of Garments
            JOHN C. FLUGEL, 287

        Law, 295

            Sumptuary Law
            ELIZABETH B. HURLOCK, 295

        Planned Reform Movements, 302

            Healthy Dress for Men
            ALFRED C. JORDAN, 302

        Culture Contact, 308

            Changes in Eskimo Clothing
            CHARLES CAMPBELL HUGHES, 308

            The Case of the Dying Kimono
            KEIICHIRŌ NAKAGAWA AND HENRY ROSOVSKY, 311

        Fashion and Fashion Leadership, 322

            Fashion: Identification and Differentiation in the Mass Society
            KURT LANG AND GLADYS LANG, 322

            The Arbiters of Fashion
            ELIZABETH B. HURLOCK, 346

ANNOTATED BIBLIOGRAPHY, 359

INDEX, 419

Part One

Introduction to the Study of Dress, Adornment, and the Social Order

FOR THOUSANDS OF YEARS the human species has invested much time, thought, and energy in dressing and adorning the human body. Using cosmetics, paints, and other additives, removing or dressing the hair, applying pressure as in bindings, deliberately mutilating the skin by cutting or piercing, covering himself with material trapping such as clothes or eye-catching accessories, man has achieved many modifications of the body's surface or contour. Several related terms connote these self-induced modifications. We speak of appearance, clothing, ornament, dress, adornment, cosmetics; and, wherever appropriate throughout this book, we shall use these terms interchangeably. Yet two of them, "dress" and "adornment," stand out as the most descriptive and inclusive and will be emphasized accordingly. Dress not only signifies the apparel worn by men and women but also refers to the *act* of covering the body with clothes and accessories. Although the two terms are synonymous, adornment stresses the aesthetic aspects of altering the body, whereas dress underscores the process of covering.

As social scientists, we have started with the general assumption of order in the universe and the corollary of orderliness in human behavior which can be described and understood. Use of the term "social order" reflects a belief in the patterning and predictability of human action, which includes the socio-cultural act of dressing and adorning the body.

The social order of a society encompasses (1) its cultural patterns, (2) its social organization, (3) its interacting individuals, and (4) a time dimension through which change and stablity can be examined. Adornment and dress are cultural products whose design and use are subject in a society to cultural patterning. Various social structures like family, economy, polity, religion, and caste or class compose the overall social organization. Associations of individuals with any of these structures may be made clear by clothing. As human beings within a society develop social selves, dress and adornment are intimately linked to their interacting with one another. These personal accouterments assist the individual in presenting his image and expressing himself. He can manipulate his appearance to fit his interpretation of a specific situation, adjusting to the variety of situations in which he finds himself. Since the social order proceeds through time, clothing, a material facility, may reflect change or stability in the society's nonmaterial aspects. Studying dress and adornment, we begin to realize that it is a study of man in relation to certain phases of the material world. This relationship is highly social because the material environment in which human beings live is one of the foremost achievements of mutual endeavor. Once created, this environment becomes the backdrop against which social interaction takes place. Firth summarizes the effects of material goods on social interaction as follows:

> They facilitate activity—like tools and transport; they crystallize and incorporate expenditure of effort; they serve as a reservoir of effort against future needs; they are the object of emotional attitudes. By their durability they give manifold links with the past, and so are perpetual conditioning factors to activity.[1]

It is obvious, however, that dress and adornment are neither exclusive factors in the determination of human behavior nor the only components of the material setting for interaction. Food, shelter, and many other elements contribute to the environment; like dress and adornment they

---

[1] R. Firth, *Elements of Social Organization*, London: Watts and Co. (1951), p. 42.

too serve multiple functions for man. Yet the portable character of clothing and associated decorative items make these highly visible and flexible in building the setting for behavior. Visually perceptible, they can, as a rule, be easily understood, more so than abstract, nonmaterial elements, such as beliefs, sentiments, and norms. Even if the motives behind the use of visible things remain obscure, it is possible to see how these objects may be manipulated and to place some interpretation on this activity. Understandings gained from the study of dress and adornment will cast light on the total picture of human behavior.

Supplementary Readings

The following general works and classic statements on dress and adornment are suggested: Bell (1947), Binder (1954, 1958), Carlyle (1921), Crawford (1940), Crawley (1931), Dearborn (1918), Flugel (1930B), Hiler (1929), Hiler and Hiler (1939), Hurlock (1929B), Langner (1959), Laver (1937, 1952), Merriam (1960), Rudofsky (1947), Veblen (1899), Webb (1907).

Part Two

Origins and Functions of Dress and Adornment

WHAT PROMPTED MAN to dress and adorn himself? Numerous attempts have been made to discover the motives for these actions. But motives are by nature subjective and difficult to isolate. Endeavors to describe the motives of prehistoric man automatically become conjecture. We can only speculate when dealing with the genesis of dress, as Crawley pointed out. He evaluated several traditional hypotheses on the origins of dress and made it clear that dress has many meanings, all of which do not represent reasons for its inception.[1]

The evidence for establishing the origins of clothing and ornament is limited. From archaeological findings come data to suggest that certain materials were used for decorating or covering the human body. The selection from Beals and Hoijer succinctly summarizes the scant informa-

---

[1] E. Crawley, *Dress, Drinks, and Drums*, edited by Theodore Besterman, London: Methuen and Co. (1931), p. 2.

tion available from archaeological sources but scarcely attempts to extrapolate beyond the few known facts.

Origins remain obscure. It seems logical, therefore, to recast the question from "what are origins" to "what are functions" of clothing? Many lists of functions have been offered with little agreement on a definitive list. It is apparent, however, that clothing does have multipurpose aspects. We propose two categories, expressive and instrumental, which can be used to analyze and include the innumerable, specific functions that clothing serves—and serves simultaneously.

The expressive function involves the emotional and communicative aspects of dress. Through dress one may express individuality by stressing unique physical features or by using unique aesthetics. Or through dress one may express group affiliation or the values and standards of the group. In an expressive sense, therefore, clothing divulges something about each human being—his beliefs, his sentiments, his status and rank, his place within the power structure. Hence where he fits into his society and how he relates to others composing it. Dress may symbolize ties to specific social groups such as family, social class, occupation, or religion.

Clothing may also be instrumental, involving rational use of dress in goal-directed behavior. Clothing may be utilitarian and protective; it may be used to attain desired rewards. Some rewards may be subtle, such as broad feelings of comfort and security. More specific rewards may be getting a job, winning friends, or finding a partner for marriage. The cliché "clothes make the man" suggests a common understanding in American society that clothing may be employed to change status, perhaps to move from one social class to another. The calculated use of special costumes at weddings, confirmation rites, and graduation exercises to herald changes in status and accompanying changes in the rights and privileges of those involved is instrumental in nature.

Clothing may also aid in transactions necessary for the attainment of other material and nonmaterial objectives. Thus, occupational dress or uniform may simply be necessary for routine work behavior which is basically directed toward acquiring money with which to buy the goods and services one desires. In this respect, factory regulations may force a worker to wear prescribed clothing to keep his job.

Both expressive and instrumental functions may be exhibited simultaneously by dress. For example, the ceremonial costumes and the functional or utilitarian uniforms may be expressive as well as instrumental if associated with feelings of group affiliation, awareness of self-importance, or attractiveness.

The excerpt from Brown includes references to several functions of dress and each of these may be classified as expressive, instrumental, or a combination of the two. It is obvious that adornment can be used for many specific purposes, depending on the time, the place, and the cultural situation.

Supplementary Readings

Statements on origins and functions of dress are included in the general works cited at the end of Part One. Other references are Benedict (1931), Bliss (1916), Bunzel (1931), Dunlap (1928), Harms (1938), Hawes (1942), Keesing (1958), Sanborn (1927), Thomas (1907), and Titiev (1959).

❀ The Origins of Clothing

RALPH BEALS AND HARRY HOIJER

The origins of both clothing and adornment are obscure; clothing and ornaments, unlike stone tools, do not survive in archeological deposits. From the fact that chimpanzees, at least in captivity, will deck themselves with strings and rags and smear paint on themselves, it has been suggested that adornment was employed early in human history. However, the first hint of such adornment does not occur until the mid-Paleolithic, where ochre, a pigment, is found frequently in Neanderthal burials.

Indirect evidence of clothing in the Mousterian epoch is found in the fact that Mousterian man lived in Europe during part of the Würm glaciation, and hence must have had some covering to protect himself from the cold. He also made scrapers of bone which may have been used, as nonliterates do today, to clean hides of fat and flesh and so prepare them for use as clothing.

In the Aurignacian period, the evidence for clothing is still stronger, for here are found the first eyed bone needles. These may well be taken as evidence of sewing and probably that skins were cut and shaped into garments. It is even likely, given the cold climate of parts of Europe during this period, that Aurignacian garments were tailored, like those of the present-day Eskimo. If so, this represents surely the earliest appearance of fitted garments and supports our earlier conclusion that tailored clothing developed first among hunting peoples living in the colder regions of the earth.

In the Solutrean and Magdalenian epochs, bone needles become far more frequent, and other artifacts of bone, such as a possible fastener shaped like a collar button, appear as well. All of this makes it fairly certain, despite the complete absence of any actual garments in archeological deposits, that Paleolithic man had achieved clothing possibly as early as the Mousterian and certainly by the Magdalenian, when the wearing of clothing must have been general.

Textile garments, however, are not known until the Neolithic, with the

Source: *An Introduction to Anthropology*, New York: Macmillan Co. (1959), pp. 383–384. Reprinted by permission of the publisher.

appearance of weaving. Remains from the Swiss lake dwellings afford positive evidence that flax was domesticated and its fibers used in weaving, and we find numerous examples of actual fabrics demonstrating a high technical skill. This clothing is not tailored, however, as was probably the case with at least some of the earlier Paleolithic skin garments. Positive evidence of tailored textile garments occurs first among the Chinese, who evidently acquired their clothing styles and techniques from their nomadic Mongol neighbors. During Roman times, tailored clothing was reported for the so-called "Barbarians" of northern Europe, but it did not come into general use in Europe until well after the beginning of the Christian era. Indeed, we know that the Romans resisted this innovation—at one time they even decreed the death penalty for those who wore trousers.

What Shall We Wear?

INA CORINNE BROWN

If we define clothing as anything applied to or put upon any portion of the body for any purpose, we shall need to include not only dress as we know it but also the dog-tooth necklaces worn by the Melanesian and the clay or paint with which the Australian aborigines and the Andaman Islanders decorate their naked bodies. Actually, whether much or little is worn, clothing may serve the demands of protection, modesty, and comfort; function as symbols of sex, age, occupation, status, or ritual condition; serve decorative purposes, or be used to attract the opposite sex. Most peoples use clothing for more than one of these purposes, and there is no people known to us who do not wear something that will fit under this broad definition of clothing.

Clothing as protection against weather is, in a sense, a portable shelter, and in the coldest parts of the world clothing is as necessary for survival as are houses. The loose, flowing robes of the desert nomad protect from heat and blowing sand. In tropical areas there is little need for clothing as shelter though in some areas rain hats are used and in other areas there may be need for protection from the sun or from thorns and briars.

Source: Understanding Other Cultures, Englewood Cliffs, New Jersey: Prentice-Hall (1963), pp. 25–26. Reprinted by permission of the publisher.

Most of the peoples of the world use dress also to conceal parts of the body in the interest of modesty. Many Westerners have judged the civilization of a people by the degree to which they have adopted Western-style garments; early missionaries often encouraged their converts to adopt Western dress and required that they cover their bodies when attending church. There is, however, no essential connection between clothing and modesty, since every society has its own conception of modest dress and behavior.

Almost everywhere clothing is used for decorative purposes, either to show off one's wealth or to enhance the good appearance of the wearer. In this category are decorations and ornaments, hair dressing, body painting, and various forms of body mutilation, such as tattooing and scarring. Clothing in this sense is an aesthetic expression.

Clothing as a symbol of sex, occupation, status, or ritual condition is also widespread. Almost all over the world clothing is used as a sex symbol, and taboos against persons of one sex wearing the garments appropriate to the other are found in many societies. In our own society, women may wear men's clothing but there is the strongest kind of feeling directed against the man who wears feminine attire. The use of military uniforms is both an old and a widespread custom, and numerous societies prescribe forms of dress or ornamentation for the married and the unmarried, the old, and the young. Priestly and kingly robes are badges of office and status, and special mourning garments are found in simple and sophisticated societies alike.

Part Three

Diversity in Cultural Patterns Related to Dress and Adornment

CULTURAL PATTERNS FOR DRESS may be similar or different from society to society, depending on the cultural configuration of each. Not only is there great variety from one society to the next in the resources available for solving basic problems of living, but there is also a wide range of ways in which these resources may be utilized to satisfy physical and sociocultural demands. Diversity in the human use of available resources to fulfill requirements for dress becomes dramatically evident as we compare societies; human beings have developed many ways of fabricating, designing, and wearing clothing.

The purpose of this section is to elaborate upon and give examples of cultural diversity in technical, aesthetic, moral, and ritualistic patterns connected with covering and adorning the body. Although these cultural patterns strongly influence the kind and amount of body covering and ornament, the effects of natural environment must not be overlooked. In some isolated, nonliterate societies, the natural environment seems to circumscribe the supply of raw materials available, whether from animal or vegetable source. Yet the presence of materials does not automatically lead to their utilization. Man needs knowledge and tools in order to exploit the raw materials of his natural environment in the manner prescribed by cultural patterns. Hoebel not only illustrates the diversity resulting from the interplay of aesthetic, moral, and ritualistic patterns with technology and the natural environment but he also refers to various functions of dress.

Technical Patterns

As man gains knowledge and learns to control and manipulate his environment technical patterns develop. The initial technological developments are usually associated with the procurement of food and water and the provision of protection through shelter and clothing. It is common to speak of the necessities of life as "food, clothing, and shelter."

In the production of clothing two basic types of technical knowledge are required. First, there must be some method for production of a pliable material capable of being shaped into clothing. Second, there must be some means of shaping this material into the three-dimensional form of clothing. A second selection from Beals and Hoijer illustrates how societies vary in selecting materials from their environments to be used in making pliable fabrics for clothes and also the different ways in which the fabrics may be produced or processed.

Although it seems like a small and insignificant invention, the eyed needle represents a vital step in man's conquest of his environment. Only after its invention could he shape and fit truly protective clothing that would allow him to migrate throughout the world and space. A key invention of this kind reminds us that the size and complexity of a technological element do not determine the degree of its impact on society. As Ogburn says:

> The extent of adjusting we do to a technological element is not closely related to its physical size, nor is the complexity of an element of technology an indication of the amount of adjusting we make.[1]

[1] W. F. Ogburn, "Technology as Environment," *Sociology and Social Research,* Vol. 41 (September–October, 1956), p. 4.

Crawford's article ties the invention of the eyed needle to Hoebel's preceding discussion of the world distribution of fitted and tailored clothing.

Aesthetic Patterns

Within any given society the range of designs for dress is limited by the aesthetic standards of the culture. Yet artistic expression is not entirely cultural in nature. It is also individualistic. Societies differ in degree as to which they encourage more—conformity to rigid cultural norms and practices in art or individual innovation in artistic expression.

Students of art sometimes distinguish between pure and applied art; but the acceptance of a broad definition of art, such as the one offered by Herskovits, eliminates undue concern with arbitrary divisions and permits us to view dress as part of the total aesthetic expression. Herskovits defines art as "any embellishment of ordinary living that is achieved with competence and has describable form."[2] Among all people the human body is readily accessible and a personally valued medium on which the individual can practice his artistic skill. Embellishment of the human being can be especially prominent as a form of aesthetic expression because decoration of the body is readily transportable. The individual can use his body as a portable art gallery constantly on display, subject not only to his own reactions but also to those of others.

The natural, unornamented body serves as the raw material for what Rudofsky called "body art."[3] This basic matter on which the artist exercises his skill is evaluated in its naked state according to each society's ideals for physical beauty.

If the naked body is unacceptable aesthetically it can be modified in a great number of ways in order to approach the aesthetic ideal. This alteration may be permanent or only temporary. For example it can be changed permanently by stretching, squeezing, tattooing, cutting, scarring, and even removing parts of the body form or surface. It can be modified temporarily by attaching objects or materials such as clothes or jewelry to the body or by applying cosmetics and paint. Bredemeier and Toby discuss the cultural bases of ideals for physical beauty, and "The Ideal Wife is Shiny" provides a further cross-cultural example for consid-

[2] M. J. Herskovits, *Man and His Works,* New York: Alfred A. Knopf (1956), p. 380.
[3] B. Rudofsky, *Are Clothes Modern?* Chicago: Paul Theobald (1947), p. 52.

eration. Wax, concerned mainly with ways of changing the body and physical appearance through the use of cosmetics and grooming, comments on how women strive to achieve ideals of physical beauty in America.

Moral Patterns

Cultural patterns are apparent in etiquette and morality connected with dress. Each society classifies clothing into proper and improper, right and wrong, and makes it evident that conventions and moral standards are universal. Individuals often enjoy choice and may even be unique in their dress, but in other circumstances the high value placed on modes of behavior with respect to appearance permits little variation in dress. Where choice is in order, the individual is under the influence of folkways of the society's manners and morals; where constraint prevails and violation of the expected pattern begets punishment, he is under the sway of society's mores. Departure from the norm in the *manners* of dress may be met with disapproval or disdain. Such departure from the *morality* norms may incur severe sanctions.

Several themes concerning the "rightness" or "wrongness" of clothing seem evident. In most societies some types of modesty reactions evolve. The individual may feel psychologically vulnerable if he lacks the material props to which he has become accustomed. In the selection previously cited, Hoebel illustrated how standards for modesty may vary from society to society.

Some societies regard wearing of specific clothing and adornment items as indicative of proper or improper deportment of self in relation to the opposite sex. Since procreation is essential to the continuity of a society, control of sexual relationships often commands a high value. Among the standards regulating action between the sexes, patterns for exposure or nonexposure of parts of the body may be considered symbolic of certain expected sex behavior. But what is accepted as sexually stimulating or symbolic of chastity in one society may not be tolerated in another society.

Crawley explores the relationships between nudity and dress, giving reasons for ceremonial nudity and for legal restrictions against nakedness. Goffman uses the term "body exposure" in discussing the "situational variability" that may occur in a society's definitions of proper and improper dress. He notes that a society may emphasize sensitivity to the appropriateness of a particular behavior situation rather than arbitrarily rule against body exposure at all times. Thus "modesty" within a culture, as well as cross-culturally, is relative to time and place. The "topless" phenomenon in women's dress of 1964 raised the question of a society's redefining situations in which partial nudity is acceptable.

Ritualistic Patterns

Although ritual is most frequently associated with magic and religion, it can refer to any culturally patterned activity that is taken seriously by the participant or participants. Anthropologists often divide ritual into two types, rites of passage and rites of intensification. The first refer to rituals that center on crises in the life cycle of individuals—birth, puberty, marriage, and death. These ceremonies indicate change from one status to another. The second refer to rituals that mark crises or occasions for the whole community, such as preparations for planting, harvesting, or war. These ceremonies bind the community together at a crucial time. New or special clothing is frequently associated with ritual. Crawley gives examples from several cultures of dress used for weddings, a rite of passage found in almost every society.

Supplementary Readings

Statements on various aspects of cultural diversity are included in many of the general works cited at the end of Part One. Other references are Biester (1952), Brown (1963), A. Ellis (1962), H. Ellis (1936), Hawes (1942, 1954), Heard (1924), Herskovits (1956), Ilfeld and Lauer (1964), Johnson (1959), Kroeber (1957), Miner (1956), Radcliffe-Brown (1933), Sullivan (1958), Sumner (1907), and Titiev (1959).

❀ Clothing and Ornament

E. ADAMSON HOEBEL

Man is a rebel against nature. He is prone to accept few things as they come. In all matters it is his irrepressible belief that by his tinkering he can improve upon them. His instrument is culture.

Source: Man in the Primitive World, New York: McGraw-Hill Book Co. (1958), pp. 239–251. Reprinted by permission of the publisher.

In all times and climes, man undertakes to effect what he vainly believes are improvements[1] upon his bodily appearance. His sartorial accomplishments, both primitive and civilized, are wonderful if not always beautiful to behold. The time and effort that have gone into painting, pricking, scarring, puncturing, and otherwise mutilating and deforming the human body for aesthetic and status reasons are beyond all calculation. We shall leave it to sociologists and economists to conjure up their guesses as to how many billion dollars are spent per year on clothes and cosmetics in this most advanced of civilizations.

The Naked Savage

People who wear little or no clothing are no contradiction to what has just been said. Be man ever so unclothed, he is never unadorned. If he wears not so much as a G-string, he certainly sports a nose, ear, or lip plug, or bears his tattoos or scarifications, or paints his face, or curls his hair, or cuts it off, or blackens his teeth, or knocks them out, or perhaps merely files them to a point.

The sense of modesty is merely a habit, not instinct. The discomfiture that is felt when one's sense of modesty is disturbed is a diffused neurophysiological upset of a large part of the nervous and organic system, shock-stimulated by a behavior situation that contrasts sharply with those to which a person has been intensely habituated. And of course, there is more than the element of mere habit in the total situation. There has also been a strong ideational indoctrination that penalties, social or supernatural, accompany any departure from the habituated pattern. Apprehension of dire consequences contributes much of the tone to fear and anxiety that colors the feelings of immodesty.

As late as 1936, old-timers among Comanche males felt acutely uncomfortable and indecent if they thoughtlessly went out without a G-string, even though fully clothed in American store pants and shirt.

A favored tale among anthropologists is that of Baron von Nordenskiold, who in his Amazonian travels undertook to purchase the facial plugs of a Botocudo[1] woman, who stood all unabashed in customary

---

[1] "The *Botocudo* owe their name to the large cylindrical wooden plugs worn by men and women alike in the ear lobes and lower lips. These cylinders, of light wood (*Chorisia ventricosa*), were 3 to 4 inches (7.6 to 10 cm) in diameter and 1 inch (2.5

nudity before him. Only irresistible offers of trade goods at long last tempted her to remove and hand over her labrets. When thus stripped of her proper raiment, she fled in shame and confusion into the jungle. After all, the close identification between the Botocudo as a person and the *botocudo* as a plug is such that to become unplugged is most un-Botocudo.

Such circumstances make it perfectly clear that the use of clothing does not rise out of any innate sense of modesty, but that modesty results from customary habits of clothing or ornamentation of the body and its parts.

Among primitive peoples the use or nonuse of clothing is more or less functional, although not wholly so. People who dwell in the tropical rain forests tend to get along with a minimum of clothing. This is true in Africa, the Americas, and Oceania. Generally, however, the men wear some sort of a pubic covering, a suspensory or supporter. It is hardly necessary to seek magical reasons for the widespread use of this device, as was done by the early anthropologist Waitz,[2] and after him by Sumner.[3] Notions of mystic shielding of the male sex organ from evil influences are more likely to be secondary developments. Certainly, the conspicuous coverings of gleaming shells, gourds, bark, hide, cloth, or grass do not serve to divert attention but rather to attract it.

An alternative to the rigid sheath is a small apron of leather, grass, or cloth worn in front, or fore and aft, or between the legs and about the waist. Such a garment is frequently worn by women as well as men. It is the basic, and often the only, bit of clothing for most primitive peoples.

When warmth is needed, something more must be added. Most races of mankind are so relatively hairless as to need artificial insulation. Hence, we rob the animals of their hairy covering—skin and all. The trapper flays the beast and prepares the hide, the tailor shapes it, and the lady of fashion slips the skins of animals over her own when she makes her winter excursions. Wool coverings are also produced at the expense of animals, but not necessarily by lethal methods.

Shoshones weave rabbitskin robes, as did the early prehistoric Basket Makers. African Bushmen provide themselves with skin cloaks. The Yahgan of Tierra del Fuego wore a small sealskin, sea-otter, or fox cape as the sole protection against a nasty subantarctic climate—except for a

cm) thick. The ears were perforated at the age of 7 or 8, the lips a few years later." A. Métraux, "The Botocudo," in *Handbook of the Indians of South America*, Vol. 1, p. 534.

[2] F. T. Waitz, *Anthropologie der Naturvölker*, Vol. 6, pp. 575–576.

[3] W. G. Sumner, *Folkways*, pp. 432, 456.

small pubic covering worn by women. The Ona of the same area and the nearby Tehuelche sported longer and larger capes. The Tasmanians wore no proper cloak, but the men were given to draping and tying sundry strips of fur around their shoulders and limbs. For the most part, the Tasmanians smeared themselves with grease and red ochre as proof against cold, as did also the Fuegians. The Central Australians, like the Tasmanians, deviate from the norm of collectors and gatherers who live in the temperate zone in that they have no cloaks. They seem never to have hit upon the idea of wearing skin for clothing. For the men a conspicuous pubic tassel suspended from a belt of human hair plus arm bands of twisted fur suffice. A woman is dressed if she has a string of beads around her neck.

When we turn our attention once again to South America, we find that the fur mantle is worn by Patagonians and Indians of the Gran Chaco in inclement weather. The famous woven wool ponchos of the Andean Indians are undoubtedly a cultural elaboration of this more primitive covering.

In North America, the buffalo-hide robe of the Plains Indians was also a form of cape, a large one, later to be replaced by the trader's blanket, which is to this day the symbol of the conservative Indian, the "blanket Indian," who clings to the old ways. Even in rugged Northeastern Woodlands the draped robe was the chief item of winter clothing, besides leggings and moccasins. In the Southeastern states the natives went naked except for a loin cloth. When cold did sweep down from the north, they, too, cast on a loose robe or cape of fur.[4]

The Tailored Man

Tailoring, it may be seen from our remarks, was not one of the more widely esteemed human arts. Most of mankind, including such sophisticates as the Greeks and Romans, have done quite well without it. The feature that is unique about tailoring is that by means of sewing, clothing may be made more or less to fit the human frame. The very idea of tailoring is "fit," and "well-tailored" means more fit rather than less. In

---

[4] For a Detailed account of the clothing of Southeastern Indians, see J. R. Swanton, "Southeastern Cultures," in Hoebel, Jennings, and Smith, *Readings in Anthropology,* pp. 117–122.

temperate and arctic climates it is functionally advantageous to have tailored clothes. The insulating efficiency of clothing is greatly enhanced by the closed, tubular effect of the tailored garment, which gives little room for the play of chilly breezes upon the body. In the tropical rain forest or torrid desert the very advantages of tailored clothing become its disadvantages.

Two factors, therefore, have combined to limit the pre-Columbian distribution of tailored clothing to Europe, northern Asia, and the northern half of North America: (1) selective adjustment to climatic factors; and (2) the fact that tailoring is an advanced technique, which the lowly Fuegians, who certainly could have used warm garments, were incapable of inventing for themselves.

That cultural improvements are not *ipso facto* beneficial is incidentally demonstrated in the debilitating effect of the introduction of European clothing among the Yahgan, of whom Cooper writes:

The clothing of the Yahgan seems to us utterly inadequate, given the climatic conditions—temperatures commonly around and well below freezing point in winter, high winds, frequent snow, hail, sleet, and cold rain—but in view of the seeming role played in their decline by introduced European clothing and their relative good health prior thereto, perhaps their clothing was reasonably well-adapted to the environment.[5]

In this case, we would observe that it is not so much that their clothing was reasonably well adapted (which it was not) as that they were physiologically reasonably well adapted to a *specific* environmental situation. The adjustment was more biological than cultural. The introduction of tailored European clothing and other elements was a cultural modification that so altered the total environment of the Yahgans as to disturb disastrously the biological balance between them and their physical world. Inexorable extinction apparently stalks them.

This, of course, has been a common consequence of culture contact when very primitive peoples find their environment drastically unsettled by incursive elements emanating from a suddenly presented, unlike, and higher culture.

To return to the problem of the distribution of tailored clothing, it originally was made among the arctic and subarctic peoples of Siberia and

[5] J. M. Cooper, "The Yahgan," in *Handbook of South American Indians*, Vol. 1, p. 87.

North America and the ancient Chinese. The distribution in North America, as Wissler pointed out,[6] was coterminous with the distribution of caribou; in Asia the association was coterminous with the reindeer. Although the Northwest Coast Indians could easily have adopted the tailoring technique (they did sew boxes together), they did not do so. The northern bison hunters of the Plains did, however, make loosely tailored shirts and dresses of the modified poncho type.

Real tailoring is done by the Eskimos and Indians of the Canadian woods. Coats are fitted with genuine sleeves and necks. Eskimo garments with the fur turned in and the outer skin dyed and decorated are not only functional but aesthetic.

The diffusion of tailoring in prehistoric times raises several unsolved problems. Did it spread from the ancient civilization of China to the Siberian barbarians, thence east and west? Or did the primitive skin workers of northern Asia develop it, whence it came to the Chinese?

The westward diffusion into Europe proper did not occur until a number of centuries after the conquests of Caesar. And finally, since the bursting of the confines of Europe in modern times, when tailored clothing became the symbol of the European conqueror, human creatures in all parts of the world have now enclosed their bodies in suits and dresses. The lovely tapa sarong of the Polynesian has given way to the missionary's Mother Hubbard. But lo, our parents having "civilized" the Polynesian out of the sarong, we moderns have taken its charms for our own.

Shoes and Hats

A properly dressed American woman never goes to church or afternoon tea without shoes and hat. The upper and nether extremities must be covered. Shoes and hats, like tailored clothing, may be functional—or mere status symbols.

Among primitives footgear is more common than headgear. The status functions of headgear can be served readily enough by hairdos. The protective functions of hats are also notably less important than the protective function of shoes.

Here again, the physical environment is an important factor in influenc-

[6] C. Wissler, *The American Indian*, p. 62.

ing the adoption or nonadoption of an element of material culture.

The problem of fabricating a foot covering that will stand up under the wet rot of the tropical jungle is practically insoluble. Even our best efforts with all the resources of science were not very satisfactory in the South Pacific campaigns of the Second World War. Jungle primitives prefer to go barefoot. An unshod foot dries more quickly and comfortably than one encased in a soaking and muddy moccasin. For this reason the highly sophisticated Indians of the Northwest Coast rain forest went barefoot, even in southern Alaska.

The simplest footgear is a piece of hide folded about the foot. When tailored, it becomes a moccasin of the type made famous by North American Indians. Further development of this form produces the boot. The so-called "Arctic boot" is an adjunct of true tailoring. This is not at all surprising, since anyone skilled enough in cutting and sewing to make a boot is *ipso facto* skilled enough to tailor clothing, and vice versa. Further, the same climatic circumstances that lend to tailored clothes their functional value act likewise with respect to boots. People who have to plod around in snow and cold find high tops more comfortable. Who enjoys walking through snowdrifts in oxfords? However, we have learned in anthropology not to expect that necessity necessarily mothers invention. The Indians of the North American boreal forests (the Canadian woodlands), who make tailored clothing and are confronted with heavy snows, make moccasins instead of boots, in spite of the fact that the more northerly of these Indians have contact with boot-wearing Eskimos. The boot of the Eskimos, worn from Greenland to Alaska, was undoubtedly borrowed from the Siberian herders and hunters. It is quite definitely an Asiatic trait.

The high, thigh-length, Cavalier-style riding boots of the Tehuelche Indians of the Patagonian pampas (whence comes its name, "the Patagonian boot") is apparently a post-Columbian adoption. The early, horseless "foot Tehuelche" wore a kind of moccasin stuffed with straw.[7] Because of its association with the horse, a post-Columbian acquisition, the Patagonian boot is hardly to be considered an independent primitive invention. But it is interesting to note that similar boots were not adopted in the Amazon, where the natives still prefer to go barefoot, or in the Andean region, where the prehistoric sandal holds sway.

[7] J. M. Cooper, "The Patagonian and Pampean Hunters," in *Handbook of South American Indians,* Vol. 1, p. 144.

The sandal is the other type of primitive footgear that finds great favor. In its simplest form it is a piece of leather roughly fitted to the sole and held firm by thongs passing over the foot.

Sandals with woven fiber soles were very popular with prehistoric Southwestern and Great Basin Indians. Wissler noted that "in eastern North America moccasins were discarded when walking in the rain, in wet grass, or upon moist ground."[8] This was also true of the Incas with their rawhide-soled sandals, which would go soft and feel squishy when wet, then become hard and out of shape when dried. Wissler thought he detected a link between the wearing of sandals and the wearing of woven clothing in both the Old World, and the New. The fact is, however, that in prehistoric North America the production of woven sandals antedates the weaving of cloth by thousands of years. Such sandals are an aspect of basket making, not of textiles.[9]

The Hairdo

Concern with the coiffure is one of the most intense interests of mankind. We know not when the earliest prehistoric men and women first began to play with the cranial hair. Archaeological evidence from the Upper Paleolithic in Europe decisively demonstrates that Cro-Magnon man and his contemporaries laid great emphasis upon the female hairdo. In the Aurignacian statuette of the Venus of Willendorf, no facial features were carved by the artist. To him there was no interest in a pretty face. But the pattern of the hair style is meticulously incised.

This trait of the Venus of Willendorf in the Aurignacian epoch, more than 20,000 years ago, was not a mere accident but a strong feature of the culture, for a similar degree of care was lavished upon the hair pattern of the female head from the Grotte du Pape at Brassempouy.

All recent primitives, from those of the lowest cultures to the highest, treat the hair. Add to this the fact that all civilized people do likewise, and we see that here is another universal trait in human culture.

The trimming and arrangement of the hair is not merely a matter of decoration and ornamentation; in culture after culture, it serves to symbolize social position. The most basic status represented in the treatment of

---

[8] Wissler, *op. cit.*, p. 65.
[9] *Ibid.*, p. 64.

the hair is that of sex. Males and females within any given society almost without exception have different ways of fixing the hair. With us the symbolism is so strong that short-haired women are considered mannish and long-haired men effeminate.

Less universally, hair styles are used to indicate age status. Omaha Indian boys had their heads shaved close, with isolated tufts of hair left here and there. Men wore either their full head of hair lying loose, or they shaved it off, except for a continuous roach along the sagittal line. Likewise, it used to be that young girls in our society wore their hair down, until after adolescence they were privileged to put it up.

Among the Omahas the shaved head of the boys indicated more than just age status, for the patterns of the remaining tufts were different for the boys of each clan. "The cutting of the hair was done, it was said, in order to impress on the mind of a child, as in an object lesson, the gentes [patrilineal clan] to which a playmate belonged." [10] This selfsame practice is widespread among Sudanese West Africans. There the pates of children are divided into patterns of diamonds and squares formed by parting the hair and gathering it into tightly tied tufts. In Africa, the various patterns indicate different social affiliations. In America, some of the styles can frequently be seen on small children among American Negroes, who have long since lost all vestiges of African clan organization; the practice apparently [11] expresses no more than a style convention that is but a survival of the old practice. A definitely New World symbolism has arisen among American Negroes in the matter of hair form. The passion for hair-straightening and kink-removing compounds among American Negroes reflects an identification of nonkinky hair with the social status of Caucasoids.

The varieties of hair decoration are so multifarious the world over that it is not possible to attempt a distributional summary here. Mention should be made of the localized Melanesian custom, particularly in New Ireland, of bleaching out black hair to a reddish orange with lime. This phenomenon confounded any number of American G.I.'s when they were first confronted with it in the South Pacific.

A closing comment on this subject would reemphasize the vital signifi-

---

[10] A. C. Fletcher and F. LaFlesche, *The Omaha Tribe* (Bureau of American Ethnology, Annual Report 27, 1911), p. 198.
[11] There has been no investigation into the possible functional significances of hair arrangements in American Negro children.

cance of the relation between hair treatment and formal social position. What is the meaning of the colloquialism, "They really let their hair down and had a good time"? Do we actually let down our hair? Only figuratively. What is let down are the customary restraints that keep us within our more cautiously preserved social roles. Let-down hair is ordinarily hidden from the public view, as is also the "uncensored" personality.

Cosmetics and Jewelry

Americans spend an estimated 700 million dollars on cosmetics in a normal year.[12] It is not the primitive but the universal man in us that accounts for this seeming extravagance. Viewed from the apex of a lofty asceticism, cosmetic aesthetics seem basely barbaric. Lotions, pastes, powders, pigments, and synthetic essences to alter the texture, color, feel, and smell of the external surfaces of the human body are neither primitive nor civilized. They are the universal cultural responses to the basic human need for favorable response. They are designed to heighten the stimulus intensity of the physical presence of one person upon the touch, smell, sight, and perhaps taste of others. The others are usually of the opposite sex, but not exclusively so. If personality is the social stimulus value of an individual, then cosmetics intensify personality.

Rouge is the most common cosmetic for two reasons: (1) red ochre (iron oxide) occurs in many places and is readily procurable; and (2) red is the primary color with the longest wavelength perceptible to the human eye, the color with the greatest natural stimulus value. When mixed with grease, it may be harmlessly applied to the human body. Yellow, black, blue, and white are the other favored colors.

Body painting among primitive peoples is for the most part limited to special occasions. Such occasions are, of course, usually ritual and ceremonial. They are events out of the ordinary, and painting changes the individual from an ordinary person to a man of distinction. War paint is usually linked to magical potency and serves less to frighten the enemy than to bolster the faint heart of its wearer. Thus, much of primitive cosmetic practice takes on symbolic values.

[12] J. Gunther, *Inside U.S.A.*, p. xii.

The trouble with paint and cosmetics, as every woman knows, is that its application is not lasting. The solution hit upon by many peoples is tattooing.

In North America, light tattooing runs from the Eskimos down the West Coast and into South America. The two high centers of the art, however, were Polynesia and Japan. Curiously, the status associations of tattooing in Polynesia and the civilized world are just reversed. With us soldiers and sailors in the lower ranks, longshoremen, and unskilled laborers are the persons who usually get themselves tattooed. For persons of higher status, it is definitely *déclassé*. But within the lower classes it serves as a symbol of masculinity and toughness. In Polynesia, the higher the social status, the fuller the tattooing. It extended over face, body, and limbs; in some overenthusiastic cases even to the tongue. The process was long drawn out and painful, but socially rewarding.

The technique of tattooing is to puncture the skin with needles carrying an indelible dye—usually carbon black. This posed a problem for Negroes and the Australian blackfellows. No white dye for tattooing was ever discovered by them. The solution hit upon in Africa and Australia is to incise the skin instead of puncturing it. Then by rubbing ashes, grit, or other irritants into the wounds scar tissue can be encouraged to form, so that a series of raised lumps remain in a permanent visible pattern.

In Central Australia cicatrization or *scarification,* as the process is called, is a part of the adolescent initiatory rites for boys. The patterns are simply parallel rows of lines on the chest and back, but they are absolutely necessary to manhood. So important are they as symbols of manhood that individuals voluntarily repeat the operations in later life to keep their scars large and fresh.

In Africa, scarification among the Congo Bantus is usually part of the initiatory rite. The designs are in some instances elaborate geometric patterns.

German corps (fraternity) students and university men give great kudos to dueling scars. Reputedly they have great sex appeal. A wound that does not fester and leave a glaring scar is a dead loss. So important are the duel-born scarifications that German impostors have been known to slash themselves with a razor and rub in salt to leave the impression that they, too, bear the scars of honor.

Decorative Deformations and Mutilations

Tattooing and scarification are only superficial ornamental embellishments impressed upon the body. Piercing of the nasal septum, the lips, or ears, so that sundry bones, feathers, shell, wood, or metal ornaments may be shoved through them, extends from the most primitive to highly civilized peoples. The invention of the screw and spring clip has only recently obviated the need for ear puncturing among our own ladies, who find the functionally atrophied external ear a convenient appendage from which to dangle pretty baubles.

Incas, in South America, and Bagandas, among others in Africa, gradually extend the ear lobes to receive thin disks as much as 6 to 8 inches in diameter. Inca nobility wore disks of gold. Baganda women, with their huge lip labrets, are familiar to all circus sideshow visitors.

Separation of the cervical vertebrae and extension of the neck in ringed brass collars by Burmese women is another familiar distortion.

Cranial deformation was much esteemed as a mark of beauty by various Northwest American Indian tribes (viz., the Flatheads of Idaho) and also by the Incas and other Andean peoples, who bound a flat board against the frontal region of the head of a baby in the cradleboard in order to produce a recessed forehead and a high, peaked occipital. Binding with cloth to produce long heads was also practiced.

Circumcision and subincision are not so much mutilations for ornamentation as they are mystical and status operations. The one is the removal of the foreskin of the penis; the other a slitting of the skin and urethra along the length of the male sex organ. Among the Central Australians they symbolize masculinity in a male-dominated and ideologically masculine society; like scarification, the operations (often fatal) are performed without anesthesia and with flint knives on adolescent boys as a part of initiation into manhood. Most African tribes also circumcise at adolescence, and for similar reasons. Circumcision is an absolutely required status mark of the Islamic male and orthodox Jew.

Filing or knocking out of incisor teeth occurs in scattered distribution from Australia up through Melanesia and Indonesia, and over into Africa. Prehistoric Europeans and American Indians spared themselves this mark of distinction. Of all the decorative blemishes imposed by man upon himself this is perhaps the most foolish. Scarification, tattooing, and circumcision may be painful, but except as they cause death through infection, they do not inhibit the healthy functioning of the body. The deliberate destruction of the teeth does just that.

Yet, as has been shown throughout this discussion, what is lost physically is gained socially. Mind triumphs over matter. No matter if the psychic satisfactions are not rational. The need that is met is elemental. The fashion and jewelry industries, the cosmetic manufacturers and purveyors, the beauticians, all may rest secure that their services have a future—as long as all mankind's.

Summary

The sense of bodily modesty is a habit and not an instinct. Human beings cover, decorate, or mutilate their bodies for a variety of reasons, chief among which are status identification (symbolic advertising of social position), protection against inclemency of climate, real or imagined self-beautification or enhancement, and magico-religious requirements.

Technical Patterns

✿ Clothing Materials

RALPH BEALS AND HARRY HOIJER

Both animal and vegetable products are extensively used in the manufacture of clothing. The simplest article of clothing—and perhaps the first to be used by men—is probably the robe or untailored cloak made from the skin of a large animal. Even this simple garment, however, requires considerable processing, for an untreated or raw hide becomes stiff and hard as soon as it dries. The skin must first be thoroughly scraped to remove the fat and flesh which adhere to it. Then it must be softened. Among some peoples, the hide is softened only by mechanical techniques, such as alternately wetting and beating the hide until it is flexible. The Eskimos soften even large hides by chewing them bit by bit until they are suitable for clothing. Mechanically softened hides, however, are not permanently cured, for if they become wet again the whole process must be repeated or the hide dries as stiff and hard as one which has not been treated.

Better curing is achieved by rubbing the hide with fatty or oily substances while it is being manipulated mechanically. Animal fats, such as brains and marrow, are widely used for this purpose, though urine and dung may also be employed. The result is, of course, a pliable but very oily skin, which remains soft only as long as the oil remains. Nevertheless, many hunting peoples possess no better technique for curing hides, and still manage to produce cured skins quite effective for the making of clothing.

The best curing technique—called tanning—is to treat the hide with vegetable substances that contain tannic acid. The bark of oak or willow trees, soaked in water, is adequate for this purpose; hides thoroughly

Source: An Introduction to Anthropology, New York: Macmillan Co. (1959), pp. 374–378. Reprinted by permission of the publisher.

worked in such solutions are quite unaffected by water and remain pliable even after repeated wettings. True tanning, as opposed to curing with animal fats, is limited to the Old World and to the technologically more advanced cultures of Europe, North Africa, and parts of Asia.

In cold climates, robes made from the skin of a large animal may be improved by cutting, sewing, and shaping the skin so that it conforms more closely to the body. It seems probable that the first fitted garments were made of skins or furs by people living in a cold climate. At least tailored garments of skin were worn by nonliterate peoples throughout most of the northern hemisphere long before peoples of more complex cultures began to cut and fit garments of either skin or cloth. It is possible, too, that Paleolithic peoples living at the borders of the great glaciers made tailored skin clothing at least as early as the Solutrean, though there is of course no direct evidence of clothing remaining in archeological deposits.

Where only small animals are available, the production of clothing requires ways of combining the skins of several animals to make a single garment. Often the best and warmest furs come from relatively small mammals. In most places the solution is to sew skins together, but many North American Indians use a weaving technique. This is especially common in areas such as Utah and Nevada where the only numerous animals are rabbits. Rabbit furs are cut in strips and either twisted by themselves into a long furry rope or twisted about a cord. Cords are then strung on a framework or back and forth between two poles to form a warp, and the fur strings or fur-covered cords are used as a weft in a simple weaving technique. The result is a soft, warm robe or blanket rather than a fitted garment.

Another way of utilizing animal materials for clothing is to employ the hair or wool. A central Asiatic people, probably the ancestors of the present Mongols, developed the technique of felting. In one method, wool or hair is combed out and placed in layers on a mat. Water is sprinkled on the material and the mat rolled up as tightly as possible. It then may be beaten with a stick, but more commonly is rolled back and forth for several hours between two lines of women. At the end of this time the hairs or wool fibers have become thoroughly matted. After patting, stretching, and sometimes repeated rolling, the resulting felt is light, warm, and durable. It may be cut and sewn, and is employed not only for garments and headgear but for boots, tent covers, and rugs. The first technologically advanced people to use felt were apparently the Chinese. Today we employ felt mainly for hats, but considerable credit for the success of the Russian winter campaigns against the Germans in World War II must be attributed to the Russian use of felt boots or inner boots which provided an ideal protection against frostbitten feet.

The hair of dogs, buffalo, goats, and other long-haired animals is used by some nonliterate peoples to make woven garments. The hair is usually twisted into a cord by rolling it on the thigh with the palm of the hand, and then is woven into blankets, robes, and other articles of clothing. The Indians of British Columbia made the famous Chilkat blanket from the hair of the mountain goat. Plains Indians sometimes use dog or buffalo hair to produce small fabrics. Usually, though, peoples who use hair do little weaving or possess only primitive weaving techniques. Wool is the only really satisfactory animal fiber for weaving.

Wool-using is mainly confined to Old World peoples who possess domesticated sheep. The first employment of wool seems to have occurred in the Neolithic period, but, as early sheep had little wool, extensive use of the material did not come until varieties of sheep had been developed with more abundant coats. In the New World the Peruvian Indians secure wool from several types of native American camels, the llama, the alpaca, and the vicuña. Often wool is used to embroider designs upon a cotton fabric rather than for weaving itself. In the Old World, camel hair is sometimes woven, but our so-called camel's hair coats are usually made of llama wool. Wool-weaving requires of course the possession of the loom.

Simple clothing of unprocessed vegetable fibers is illustrated by the grass skirt made in certain parts of Oceania. This garment consists only of long grasses tied to a waist band or cord. Similar garments are also made of willow bark which has been beaten to produce long bunches of fibers.

In most cases, however, vegetable materials, like those derived from animals, require considerable processing before they can be made into clothing. An example is found in bark cloth, which is probably the most widespread of all vegetable materials used for clothing. A suitable spongy bark—that of fig and paper mulberry trees is best—is stripped off in layers and soaked in water to make it pliable. Then three layers of bark are laid out on top of each other on a flat anvil—often of stone—with the grain of the center layer lying at right angles to that of the other two. A mallet is then used to pound the bark until the fibers are matted tightly together. The pounding also thins out and widens the bark and makes it soft and pliable. Large pieces of bark cloth are made by pounding separate sections together or even by gluing them as we should glue separate sheets of paper into a single larger piece. Designs may be added to bark cloth by employing mallets that have carved designs on their pounding surfaces. Bark cloth is often oiled or painted to preserve it.

Bark cloth was widely used in Oceania before the introduction of European trade cloth, and it is said that many Oceanic peoples revived the technique of making bark cloth—called *tapa* in the Malayo-Polynesian languages—when World War II prevented trade in European and American clothing materials. *Tapa* was so important to the aboriginal Oceanic peoples that they domesticated the paper mulberry tree, the bark of which produces an exceptionally fine fabric. Trees were planted in clumps so that they might grow with straight trunks and few branches. A special form of bark cloth, made of reeds pounded into flat strips and joined together, is the papyrus of ancient Egypt, which was used as a writing material.

Bark cloth is not very good material for cutting and sewing, and hence is found most often in relatively warm climates where close-fitting garments are not required. Bark cloth garments are usually made from a single rectangular piece of material, which is wrapped around the waist or chest as a sarong.

All other vegetable fiber clothing involves the technique of weaving. Bark fibers, such as those obtained from cedar bark by some American Indians, are occasionally woven into cloth. Extensive weaving, however, appears to be confined to relatively few vegetable fibers—flax, two kinds of hemp, and cotton in the Old World, and henequen (agave fiber or sisal hemp) and cotton in the New World. Peoples who use those fibers to weave cloth almost invariably cultivate the plant as well; weaving on an intensive level is found almost always among peoples who have domesticated plants. Nomadic gathering peoples, probably because weaving is a lengthy process that requires bulky and heavy equipment, only rarely make their clothing of woven fabrics.

The Eyed Needle

M. D. C. CRAWFORD

In the upper Paleolithic cultures of Central Europe, (the Aurignacian, the Solutrian and the Magdalenian), we come upon evidences of more complex sartorial techniques. Here we are dealing with modern man—physically and mentally our peer. He lived in the last ages of the ice, and was faced with the same problems that had faced his cruder prototype. The French scientists call these ages, "The Reindeer Ages,"—the period of the caribou. In other words, these people had large supplies of one kind of fur to use for clothing, and this led them to a somewhat more precise organization and a greater precision in tool making. These people are responsible, apparently, for one of the most brilliant composite inventions of the human intellect, that of the eyed needle, which draws the thread through the hole it pierces with its point. In their caves are found needles made from mammoth ivory, fine enough to sew almost any tailor-made garment of today. These people were artists, as the paintings on their cave walls and their carvings in bone and ivory indicate. They had a palette of sixteen colors, stored in hollow bones, and from the fineness of the needles, we may assume that they used the needles not only for sewing but also, perhaps, for decorative purposes. Undoubtedly, in these ages arises the modern tailor-made costume cut from furs, shaped and sewn to fit the human body and, conceivably, reaching a high degree of physical perfection.

Professor W. J. Sollas in his "Ancient Hunters and Their Modern Representatives," has suggested that certain Siberian tribes, such as the Koryak and the Eskimo, are at least cultural descendants of these last elegants of the Ice Age; and that the costumes of these primitive peoples of today are indications of proven and inherited skills. There are no finer tailored fur garments made anywhere in the world than among these people, and no source material of greater value to modern designers and dressmakers than are offered by collections of these garments. We may call to mind the fact that modern explorers in the Arctic and Antarctic

Source: Philosophy in Clothing, Brooklyn, New York: Brooklyn Museum (1940), pp. 10–13. Reprinted by permission of the publisher.

are forced to adopt this primitive type of clothing in order to live in these regions. More and more, as out-of-door winters attract us, we will find inspiration in these documents. They are the most perfect garments ever made for the bitter cold. It took men thousands of years to perfect them.

Man had been drifting over the surface of both the Old and the New World for untold millennia before he took to keeping records, and as he wandered he acquired and scattered "ideas"—tools, processes and products. One of the most interesting of these distribution problems is presented by the eyed needle. The oldest needles we know of were found, as I have said, in quantity in the upper Paleolithic caves thirty, perhaps forty, thousand years ago, together with toggles and buttons. Needles were known in Predynastic Badarian Egypt; in the silt of Neolithic Swiss Lake villages, and at least as early as the Shang period in China, traditionally 1760–1122 B.C. The eyed needle was and still is an essential tool in Siberia, and along the 5,000 miles of Arctic coast from Asia and Greenland—the home of the Eskimo. In the cultures of North America the eyed needle appears, and we find several highly developed forms in prehistoric Peru.

The eyed needle was invented, primarily, to aid the production of tailored, fitted and sewn garments. This has always remained its chief function. But it had other important, if secondary, uses. On the Northwest Coast an eyed needle of wood, three feet in length, was used to weave rush mats. The Woodland Indians of the Atlantic coast sewed bark and mats on the frames of their houses with a needle made of the "legge bone of a crane."

Neither the early Egyptians nor the Peruvians were tailors. Yet, in both of these cultures several forms of needles exist, evidently of local inspiration, even if the general idea was intrusive. In both cultures cloth was an important product, although more so in Peru than in the early Egypt. In both regions, the eyed needle was used for the decoration of cloth both in and out of the loom frames. Many of the finest Peruvian textiles, which we think of as the product of loom mechanism, are more easily comprehended as needle work.

Needles have been made of reindeer bone, of mammoth ivory, the walrus tusk, of drilled thorns, of wood, copper, bronze, silver, gold, iron and steel. To the basic principle of the needle and needle sewing nothing has been added for thousands of years.

Aesthetic Patterns

❀ Ideals of Beauty

HARRY C. BREDEMEIER AND JACKSON TOBY

These socio-cultural standards in terms of which members of a society mutually evaluate one another make social life predictable and thereby possible. But the existence of standards also implies that some people are found wanting. They are rejected by the community for not being beautiful enough or for belching at the wrong time. And, since these social standards are internalized even by the persons who are regarded as failures in terms of them, social rejection and self-rejection go hand in hand. Consider the relationship between personal appearance and a favorable self-assessment. Of course, every society has its own standard of physical pulchritude. There is a tribe in Africa, for example, where a woman's beauty is reckoned in proportion to her bulk. A girl who wishes to make herself attractive to the young men goes to the fatting house and gorges herself for weeks. When she waddles out, the tribal equivalent of the American "wolf" gives the tribal equivalent of the American whistle of appreciation. Such a standard of beauty seems strange to us because we like our women thin. Americans encourage girls to keep themselves from gaining what they consider "too much weight." From the point of view of this African tribe, however, American women are emaciated; and the American concept of dieting sounds unbelievable. Why should women in their right minds, women in a country which is the richest in the world, voluntarily starve themselves?

In short, the ideals of physical attractiveness of a society, any society, are arbitrary. A man who would be handsome in one country might be considered homely in another. Nevertheless, the standards of a given society

Source: Social Problems in America, New York: John Wiley and Sons (1960), pp. 17–18. Reprinted by permission of the publisher.

are stamped into the personalities of members of that society almost from birth. Americans, for instance, have definite notions of acceptable appearance: in terms of height, body build, profile, and skin condition. Hollywood did not invent these standards—although movies probably deserve credit (or blame) for narrowing the range of acceptable variation. Before Hollywood embodied our ideals and exhibited them to millions of people every week, homely women, short men, people with bad complexions or hooked noses had a better chance of escaping invidious comparisons.

The Ideal Wife Is Shiny

Height, average; skin, light or bronze and shiny; build, plump to fat.

These are the statistics which generally appeal to the rural African man in search of a wife, says a Boksburg engineer. But they are gradually being discarded for white standards. The engineer, Mr. Karl Hechter-Schulz, has made a study of tribal cosmetics for many years. He has investigated how primitive rural African women prepare and apply beauty aids to enable them to measure up to the "ideal."

"One of the most striking things," says Mr. Hechter-Schulz, "is the striving for a light complexion," according to the Rand *Daily Mail*.

"In cities the African woman is influenced by her white employer's beauty aids. But even the most unspoiled African women attempt to lighten their skins with colored clays and ochers. The lighter their skin, the more sought after they are."

To get the desired sheen on the skin Sotho women use melted butter.

Zulu women use animal fats—hippopotamus fat being the most highly prized. Fat from cats is never used because it is associated with witchcraft.

Bushman women chew *tsamma melo* pips to form a paste which is rubbed on the body as a cleanser and lubricant.

"African women are frequently force-fed before marriage to get them plump," said Mr. Hechter-Schulz. "This has a dual purpose. If a woman does not put on weight, the husband-to-be can claim it shows she is not healthy."

Source: *The Daily News*, Salisbury, Southern Rhodesia (July 8, 1963). Reprinted by permission of the publisher.

"Many African women use the leaves of a tree to develop the bust."

"When colored matter is applied to the skin of primitive women, it is not regarded as make-up in the Western sense of the word but signifies a special occasion."

"Herero women," said Mr. Hechter-Schulz, "make powdered rouge from the *kiaat* tree. Bushman women use rabbit fur as powder puffs."

"But even in rural areas today, the demand for white cosmetics and beauty creams is increasing. The demand for preparations which can be used to straighten the hair to resemble that of the white woman is just further evidence that the traditional African standard of beauty is being lost."

Themes in Cosmetics and Grooming

MURRAY WAX

This paper deals with some practices concerning highly conscious, social aspects of physical appearance, in particular the appearance of women.[1] These go under the names of "grooming" and "cosmetics," and they involve the manipulation of one's superficial physical structure so as to make a desired impression upon others.[2] The manipulations include bathing, anointing, and coloring the skin; cutting, shaving, plucking, braiding, waving, and setting the hair; deodorizing and scenting the body; coloring or marking the lips, hands, nails, eyes, face, or other exposed regions; cleansing, coloring, and filing the teeth; molding, restraining, and concealing various parts of the body; and so on.

As a class, these activities are universal among human beings. Some of the oldest artifacts discovered indicate the usage of cosmetics, for exam-

[1] For the past several years I have been intensively occupied in market research and am currently employed by a company that produces cosmetic and other items of personal care for women. The notions presented in this paper are derived from my research experience but, since the data and findings are the property of the client, cannot be offered in support of my arguments; the reader must judge validity by his own experience.

[2] Excluded from this paper but involved in the phenomena here discussed are certain other significant phenomena: gesture, facial expression, and demeanor as elements in the process of communication (*see* several articles by Erving Goffman) and physique, carriage, gait, and the development and tonus of the major muscles.
Source: *American Journal of Sociology*, Vol. 62 (May, 1957), pp. 588–593. Reprinted by permission of the author and publisher.

ple, the presence of red ocher in Cro-Magnon graves and the elaborate toilette sets of the Egyptians. The Bible relates varied instances of the use of cosmetics: Esther and the other maids being prepared for King Ahasuerus and the anointing of Jesus in Bethany.

The cosmetic and grooming practices of other peoples sometimes appear to us as peculiar or outrageous (e.g., lip-stretching, foot-binding, tattooing, head shaping, scarification), but in every case the custom can be understood as an attempt to modify or mold the superficial physical structure of the body into patterns considered attractive and appropriate to the status of the individual.

Apparently, there has been little analysis of the meaning of cosmetics by those in the sociological-anthropological profession.[3] Ethnographers have reported the tremendous variety of forms that personal ornamentation and grooming may take. More important, they have observed—and characterized as such—the association of patterns of dress and grooming with social status, noting how changes in dress and grooming are universally employed to denote the movement from one social status to another (infancy, childhood, sexual maturity, marriage, maternity, anility, death) or the assumption of special office (chief, priest, medicine man, Doctor's degree).

One of the main sources of literature on cosmetics and grooming is that of the moral critics. Throughout the recorded history of the West there have been repeated denunciations of the use of cosmetics. Isaiah's stern eschatology supplies the reader with both his attitude and a fair picture of how the sophisticated women of his time appeared:

In that day the Lord will take away the bravery of their tinkling ornaments about their feet, and their cauls, and their round tires like the moon,
The chains, and the bracelets, and the mufflers,
The bonnets, and the ornaments of the legs, and the headbands, and the tablets, and the earrings,
The rings, and the nose jewels,

[3] There is a literature, particularly in German, on the nature of physical beauty (*see*, e.g., Gustav Ichheiser, "The Significance of the Physical Beauty of the Individual in Socio-psychological and Sociological Explanation," *Zeitschrift für Völkerpsychologie und Soziologie*, 1928, a translation of which by Everett C. Hughes appears in Carl A. Dawson and Warner E. Gettys, *An Introduction to Sociology* [rev. ed.; New York: Ronald Press Co., 1935], pp. 749-53. This literature becomes relevant to the present problem to the extent that the analyst moves from considering "natural" beauty to considering the "artificial" creation or supplementation of physical beauty via cosmetics and grooming.

The changeable suits of apparel, and the mantles, and the wimples, and the crisping pins,

The glasses, and the fine linen, and the hoods, and the veils.

And it shall come to pass, that instead of a sweet smell there shall be stink; and instead of a girdle a rent; and instead of well set hair baldness; and instead of a stomacher a girding of sackcloth; and burning instead of beauty.[4]

(The prophet grants that the effect was "beauty.")

A more or less continuous line of critical commentary runs from the Old Testament through the medieval moralists to Shakespeare[5] ("The harlot's cheek beautied with plastering art")[6] and on to modern times. Evidently those who employed cosmetics were less vocal and less literary than their critics but equally persistent.

The themes of this criticism are, first, that women should be interested in more spiritual matters than the vanity of beautifying their physical appearance; second, that cosmetics make women more attractive to men and thus lead both parties from the path of virtue; third, that cosmetics are deceitful, inasmuch as they give women a better appearance than they natively have; and, fourth, a modern criticism,[7] that cosmetics are an instrument of the ubiquitous modern drive for conformity, in which all persons must look alike and act alike.

The Modern Use of Cosmetics

Some insight into the meanings of adornment, cosmetics, and grooming may be gained from three themes, expressed by opposing pairs of concepts: *casualness* and *control,* *exposure* and *concealment,* and *plasticity* and *fixity*. While these notions are not so clearly separable as might be required in a polished conceptual scheme—and, indeed, they may be but different aspects of the same theme—nonetheless, they will assist this preliminary study.

The brassière is a pointed illustration of the theme of exposure and concealment. On the one hand, the brassière is the principal one of several articles of clothing that serve to conceal the bosom from view. On the other

---
[4] Isa. 3:18–24.
[5] Gwyn Williams, "The Pale Cast of Thought," *Modern Language Review,* XLV (1950), 216–18.
[6] *Hamlet,* Act III, scene 1.
[7] Note on "Nails," *New Statesman and Nation,* XIV (1937), 245–46.

hand, the brassière makes the bosom more conspicuous, so that, even beneath several layers of clothing, the onlooker can appreciate the feminine form. Many brassières are designed with the purposes of exposing and emphasizing certain portions of the body and skin while concealing others.

The brassière also illustrates the theme of plasticity: it molds the bosom into forms that are considered attractive and elegant but that are found naturally, if ever, only among a few. Women differ in their emphasis on one or another of the opposing terms that compose a theme; for example, in discussing how they judged whether a brassière fitted, some said that they wished to feel a firm and definite, yet comfortable, lift, while others said that they made sure the garment fitted smoothly so that there would be no underarm exposure when they wore a sleeveless dress or blouse. Incidentally, the recent fashion in bosoms has called forth critical comment from social analysts in such terms as "infantilism" and "momism." On the other hand, the current ideal of the full yet high bosom is more mature and more sane than past emphases upon the flat chest and virginal torso.

The themes of concealment and control are pungently illustrated by the current emphasis on eliminating the odors of the body and its products. Bathing and even sterilizing the skin, reducing the rate of and absorbing perspiration, and personal and household sanitary techniques have spread widely throughout our society as devices for reducing human odor. Happily, the more old-fashioned *plastic* theme (which aims at the positive enhancement of body odor) has not been affected; the consumption of perfumes and scents seems to be increasing.

The demand for control of body odor seems to be experienced in several kinds of situations, primary among which is the enforced intimacy of heterosexual office work. In the office, people live with one another in close physical proximity for more of their waking hours than they do with their families. This minimizing of human odors may be interpreted as part of the attempt to minimize the physical being and to emphasize the social role and office. Office workers must strive to interact with each other in official roles, with a restrained personal interest, rather than as physical intimates. While physical intimacy between office personnel may occur, it is exceptional and contrary to the folkways. This does not deny to business its share of the sexual wickedness of the world but simply notes the restraints that seem automatically to be imposed when a small group of people must work hard together in the public eye.

The Permanent Wave as An Illustration

The way in which the motives for control and plasticity interlock and the efforts that women make to achieve the proper appearance are illustrated by modern "permanent"-waving customs. About two-thirds of the white women in the United States had their hair permanent-waved last year. For most of these women it was more or less habitual; they had had the operation performed several times during the year. Most permanent waves are given at home, using kits that cost only a few dollars. The successful merchandising of the home wave kit has put the waving process within the economic reach of the large majority of American women, and most of them have accepted the invitation.

On the face of it, the situation is peculiar. The cold-waving process, employing thioglycolate salts, is simple in principle, but, in practice, much depends on the skill and care with which the operations are performed and on the condition of the hair. Most women have experienced or seen cases of overprocessing that gave frizzy hair or of misprocessing that left no wave but dried the hair. Also, the waving process is unpleasant: while the odor of the waving lotion has been improved, the scent remains far from agreeable; the lotion is not kind to the skin; and the process is usually messy. Added to this is the uncertainty of the outcome.

When asked to describe what they seek, most women will answer, or accept the phrase, "A soft, natural wave." Since a majority of women have to go through the process just described in order to achieve this wave, it is difficult to agree that it is natural. But it has been a rather consistent cultural ideal of the West for some centuries that this type of wave is the natural and ideal kind of hair for women, while straight hair is natural and ideal to men. As a cultural ideal, it is as reasonable as many another, but it has little relation to sex-linked genes.

"Softness" of wave is likewise a loaded term. The student discovers painfully that a *soft wave* is by definition the kind of wave a woman wants, whether this be in fact the slightest of twists to the hair fibers or the most extreme rotation short of breakage. The soft wave is not an end in itself but only a proximate goal. Women wave their hair not merely for the wave per se but also because it gives them plastic control over their hair. Hair that is artificially or naturally curly has what women call "body" and may be arranged in an almost indefinite variety of coiffures. That curly hair thus becomes a plastic yet consciously controllable aspect of a woman's appearance is indicated by such expressions as "It will take a set" or "You can do something with it." [8]

Although they sound contradictory, plasticity and control actually require each other. Control is not possible unless there is some way to make a plastic arrangement or modification of the portion of the body, bringing it from a less to a more controlled state, and plasticity would be meaningless unless the rearrangement accomplished through plasticity could be fixed for some period of time.[9]

In permanent waving, women differ in their emphasis on sides of the plastic-fixed, casual-control themes. Some wish just enough wave to achieve some body and manageability and are fearful that too much curl will appear unnatural, that is, not casual. Others wish a wave that will enable them to keep their hair always neat and ordered; they do not want their hair to fly casually about. The firmer the wave, the easier it is to *manage* the hair and to keep it under control. Younger women constitute the largest market for loose, casual waves; older women, for tight, curly waves. Loose waves appear softer and more "feminine" but are more difficult to manage and can best be adapted to informal casual styles of grooming. Most women seek a compromise between the wave that is too soft to manage well and the wave that is so tight (controlled) that it appears unnatural or unfeminine, and many pursue the elusive goal of the soft wave and completely manageable hair.

Woman Makes Herself

Among some peoples the costume proper to the socially and sexually mature man or woman is relatively fixed. It may be a tattoo or a style of dress or of coiffure; but, whatever it is, it changes only slightly, if at all, unless the person moves into a distinctly different status. In the United

[8] In contrast, straight hair can be controlled but not so plastically. It can be imprisoned in a braid or a bun or cut so short that it is often considered unattractive or unfeminine ("the boyish bob"). Allowed to hang free, straight hair of any length is somewhat of a problem for its possessor and her intimates, although it can be beautiful.

[9] Hair sprays, which are a technique for applying a fixative, usually a lacquer—which is, incidentally, flammable—to hair which has been set, may change habits of hair care, but they do not substantially alter the present analysis.

States fixed dress and grooming are peculiarly distinctive of religious orders and some religious sects that cling to a stylized version of what was common and decent at the time that the sect or order was instituted.

Such fixity or rigidity of grooming practices is not characteristic of all peoples, and, particularly, it is not characteristic of the typical American woman, who, following the plastic theme, tends to view her body as a craftsman or artist views his raw material. This is the matter which she can shape, color, and arrange to produce an object which, hopefully, will be at once attractive, fashionable, and expressive of her own idividuality. Devices which increase her ability to mold her body (e.g., permanent waving) are received much as the *avant-garde* artist receives new techniques and modalities for his work.

The clearest expression of the (casual) plastic motif is afforded by the ideal of a girl in late adolescence. Continually experimenting with new styles of dress and grooming, she is in effect trying on this or that role or personality to see what response it will bring to her. She is most aware of new products and new styles, and she uses them to manipulate her appearance this way and that.

To some social observers, however, the teen-ager appears as the slave to fad and fashion and not as the experimenter. A more accurate formulation would be that the teen-ager follows fad and fashion—to the extent that she does, and not all do—because she is experimenting with herself and has not yet developed a self-image with which she can be comfortable. An older, more stable woman, who knows herself and her roles and how she wishes to appear, can ignore fad and follow fashion at a distance.

A clear expression of the conceal and control theme is given by the woman who is striving to eliminate her feminity and reduce herself to an *office*. She tries to minimize her natural shape, smell, color, texture, and movement and to replace these by impersonal, neutral surfaces. She is not opposed to cosmetics or grooming aids—indeed, she employs them vigorously for purposes of restraint and control—but she is critical of grooming aids when they are employed in the service of casual, exposed femininity. It is understandable that these types sometimes go with petty, bureaucratic authority, sitting as guardians of the organizational structure against the subversive influence of the less restrained of their own sex. It is interesting to compare these controlled women, who have reached the zenith of their careers, with the attractive girl who manipulates, rather than restrains, her appearance and employs it as an instrument for her upward mobility.

A different expression of plastic control, this time accompanied by a higher ratio of exposure, is afforded by those mature women who are engaged in the valiant battle against being classed as old. Our culture classifies old age as retirement from sexual, vocational, and even sociable activity, and the woman who is battling age is trying to prevent too early a retirement. She employs the techniques of grooming to conceal the signs of aging and to accentuate (and expose) the body areas where her appearance is still youthful. Some search hopefully for new techniques that will reverse the aging process in particular areas (e.g., "miracle" skin cream), others are shining examples of self-restraint and self-discipline (e.g., diet and exercise), and still others become virtuosos in the use of plastic devices of grooming (e.g., hair color rinses).

Interestingly, plastic control of grooming involves not only creativity but the application of the capitalistic ethic: beauty becomes the product of diligence rather than an inexplicable gift from the supernatural.[10] Thus, those with an interest in the elaboration of the grooming ritual (e.g., charm schools, cosmetic manufacturers, cosmeticians, beauty shops) issue advice that has a hortatory, even a moral, character. The woman is informed of the many steps she must take to maintain a "beautiful," that is, socially proper, appearance. She is praised when she fulfils every requirement and condemned for backsliding. It is ironic to compare this moral voice of modern society, with its insistence on perfect grooming, with the moral voice of the past as represented by Isaiah.

The Social Function of Grooming

There is also the social function of grooming, reported by the ethnographer: cosmetics and dress are often used to denote differences in status. So, in our society, cosmetics help to identify a person as a female of our culture and, generally speaking, as a female who views herself and should be treated as socially and sexually mature. The girl who wears cosmetics is insisting on her right to be treated as a woman rather than a child;

[10] Ichheiser notes that beauty may be "cultivated" or "denatured" and, further, that the socioeconomic position of the woman is important in facilitating or curtailing her access to the implements of cultivation (see Ichheiser's article cited above, n. 3). The mass-production society has reduced the differential due to socioeconomic position as far as access to cosmetic and personal care items is concerned. There remain significant differentials associated with ethnicity and income and perhaps most apparent in areas of aesthetic judgment (taste) and health so far as the present inquiry is concerned.

likewise, the elderly woman wearing cosmetics is insisting that she not be consigned to the neutral sex of old age.

To some critics modern grooming practices represent cultural demands for a high degree of conformity, but this is a view based on a limited study of the case and a limited knowledge of other cultures. Most societies have rather restricted notions of what are acceptable costumes for those who are socially and sexually mature. In this respect our society is less severe than most, and it is very unusual in the emphasis that it gives to individual expression in the designing of appearance. The woman who has the patience, the skill, and, most important, the eager and self-disciplined attitude toward her body can—even with limited natural resources—make of her appearance something aesthetically interesting and sexually exciting.

The question is sometimes raised, usually in the feature sections of newspapers: For whom does a woman dress—does she dress for men or women? We have observed that one indispensable kind of answer includes a reference to culture, or, more concretely, to the social situation. A woman dresses and grooms herself in anticipation of a *social situation*. The situations that require the most careful grooming are those in which her peers or social superiors will be present and which are not defined as informal (casual). The woman who is isolated from men who are her peers, for example, the suburban housewife, can "neglect her appearance." Her dress and grooming tend to be casual. When questioned, she replies defensively that she is "too busy" to worry about her appearance; but the career woman has far more demands on her time, newspaper feature editors notwithstanding. The point is that the career woman always has an audience of male and female peers alert to her appearance, while the housewife seldom has one.

It may seem as though the function of cosmetics and grooming in heightening the sexual attractiveness of one sex to the other has been neglected. This de-emphasis reflects the facts of the case, particularly as it is in modern society. Certainly, cosmetics and grooming practices are influential in courtship, and, moreover, novel practices seem to emerge within this relationship and spread to less sexualized areas of existence. (Thus it has happened that the grooming practices of courtesans have been adopted by respectable women.) But, while sexuality is thus basic to grooming, it cannot serve to explain grooming as a social activity any more than it can the American dating complex.

The function of grooming in our society is understandable from the perspective of *sociability,* not of *sexuality.*[11] A woman grooms herself to appear as a desirable sexual object, not necessarily as an attainable one. In grooming herself, she is preparing to play the part of the *beauty,* not the part of the erotically passionate woman. In this sense, cosmetics and grooming serve to transmute the attraction between the sexes from a raw physical relationship into a civilized *game.*

Some may carp at the game, feeling that activity should be functional and that beauty should therefore denote the superior female, the ideal sex partner and mother. Here the question becomes evaluative: Should cosmetics and grooming be judged as a form of *play,* engaging and entertaining its participants, or should they serve a nobler purpose? We leave Isaiah to confront the sculptor of the Cnidian Aphrodite.

CHICAGO, ILLINOIS

[11] Georg Simmel, "The Sociology of Sociability," translated from the German by Everett C. Hughes, *American Journal of Sociology,* LV (November, 1940), 254–61.

Moral Patterns

❀ Nudity and Dress
ERNEST CRAWLEY

When clothing is firmly established as a permanent social habit, temporary nudity is the most violent negation possible of the clothed state. Ceremonial nudity is a complex problem, but the idea of contrast, of an abnormal as contrasted with a normal state, may go far to explain many of its forms. At ceremonies of fumigation the Malay takes off his *sarong*.[1] Such cases are no doubt to be explained in the obvious way; the purificatory influence has more effect when the body is stripped of all coverings. But other examples of the practice are more obscure. In time of drought, Transylvanian girls strip naked when performing the ritual for rain.[2] In India the practice is regular.[3] To make rain, Kabui men go on the roof of a house at night, and strip themselves of all clothes. Obscene language is interchanged.[4] To induce rain to fall, Ba-Thonga women strip themselves naked.[5] Baronga women, to make rain, strip themselves of their clothes, and put on instead leaf-girdles or leaf-petticoats and head-dresses of grass.[6] At a festival of Sarasvatī, Bengali students danced naked.[7] A Gujarāt mother whose child is ill goes to the goddess's temple at night,

---

[1] W. W. Skeat, *Malay Magic* (1900), p. 269.
[2] E. Gerard, *The Land beyond the Forest* (Edinburgh 1888), ii. 40.
[3] *Panjab Notes and Queries*, iii. 41, 115; *North Indian Notes and Queries*, i. 210.
[4] T. C. Hodson, *The Nāga Tribes of Manipur* (1911), p. 172.
[5] H. A. Junod, "Les conceptions physiologiques des Bantou Sud-Africains et leurs tabous," *Revue d'ethnographie et de sociologie* (1910), i. 140.
[6] *Ibid., Les Ba-ronga* (Neuchatel 1898), pp. 412 ff.
[7] W. Ward, *A View of the History, Literature, and Religion of the Hindoos* (1817-1820), i. 72; *cp.* i. 130.

Source: *Dress, Drinks, and Drums*, edited by Theodore Besterman, London: Methuen and Co. (1931), pp. 111–117. Reprinted by permission of the publisher.

naked, or with only a girdle of *nim* (*Melia*) or *asopato* (*Polyalthea*) leaves.[8]

The principle in the above seems to be that a violent change in the course of Nature may be assisted by a violent change of habit on the part of those concerned. It is adaptation to the desired contrast by instituting a contrast in the officiators. The use of obscene language is, like nudity, a break with the habits of normal life. The use of leaf-girdles is probably no survival of a primitive covering, but merely a method of toning down the violence of the extraordinary state. Similarly, the idea of nakedness is often satisfied by the removal of the upper garment only. Ideas of fertility and outpouring as connected with leaves and with the genital organs are probably later.

The whole subject is illustrated by the following. The headman of certain New Guinea tribes becomes holy before the fishing season. Every evening he strips himself of all his decorations, a proceeding not otherwise allowed, and bathes near the location of the dugongs.[9] An Eskimo may not eat venison and walrus on the same day, unless he strips naked, or puts on a reindeer skin that has never been worn in hunting the walrus. Otherwise his eating gives pain to the souls of the walrus. Similarly, after eating walrus he must strip himself before eating seal.[10]

The principle of assimilation to special circumstances is here conspicuous. Possibly in the New Guinea example the later extension of the principle to assimilation by contact is involved.

Dress being, as will be more fully illustrated below, not only essentially a social habit, but one of the most distinctly social habits that have been evolved, the public removal of garments and nudity generally come under the regulation of custom and law. Dress, like other habits, is a second nature, and social inertia may fix it more securely; hence such curiosities of legalism as the pronouncement of Zoroastrian law, that it is a sin to walk with only one boot on.[11]

The sexual instincts of modesty and attraction give life to the idea of dress, and a balance is seldom exactly attained between them and legalism. In modern times the missionary movement has practically corrupted

---

[8] J. M. Campbell, "Notes on the Spirit Basis of Belief and Custom," *The Indian Antiquary* (1895), xxiv. 265.
[9] R. E. Guise, "The Tribes inhabiting the Mouth of the Wanigela River, New Guinea," *Journal of the Anthropological Institute* (1899), xxviii. 218.
[10] F. Boas, *Sixth Report on the North-Western Tribes of Canada* (1888), p. 584.
[11] *Pahlavi Texts* in *Sacred Books of the East*, v. 287.

many a wild race by imposing upon them, as the most essential feature of Christian profession, the regard for clothing developed in a cold climate among peoples inclined to prudery and ascetic ideals; hence a factitious sentiment of hypocritical decency. In other races, legalism has evolved similar conditions. In Uganda it is a capital offence to strip naked.[12] In most European countries "exposure of the person" is a criminal offence. The Roman Catholic Church taught, and still teaches in convent schools, that it is wrong to expose the body even to one's own eyes.[13] "Moslem modesty was carried to great lengths, insufficient clothing being forbidden. . . . The Sunna prescribes that a man shall not uncover himself even to himself, and shall not wash naked—from fear of God, and of spirits; Job did so, and atoned for it heavily. When in Arab antiquity grown-up persons showed themselves naked, it was only under extraordinary circumstances and to attain unusual ends."[14] Such ends have been illustrated above.

Such excess of the idea of decency renders still more powerful both the magical and the superstitious use of nudity and also its sexual appeal. In the sphere of art it may be the case that peoples accustomed to nakedness, like the Greeks, employ it as a regular subject for artistic treatment, but it does not necessarily follow that it is better understood than among peoples not so accustomed. It lacks the force of contrast. Similarly in the sexual sphere, both natural modesty and natural expansion may be enhanced by the artificial limitations of decency. In this respect dress plays an important part in social biology. By way of showing the contrast, the African and the European conditions may be sketched.

Of the Wa-taveita, Johnson remarks: "Both sexes have little notion or conception of decency, the men especially seeming to be unconscious of any impropriety in exposing themselves. What clothing they have is worn either as an adornment or for warmth at night and early morning."[15] Of the Wa-chaga he observes: "With them indecency does not exist, for they make no effort to be decent, but walk about as Nature made them, except when it is chilly, or if they wish to look unusually smart, in which cases they throw cloth or skins around their shoulders."[16]

[12] F. Ratzel, *History of Mankind* (1896–1898), i. 94.
[13] H. H. Ellis, *Studies in the Psychology of Sex*, iv. 32, quoting authorities.
[14] J. Wellhausen, *Reste arabischen Heidentums* (2nd edition, 1897), pp. 173, 195.
[15] Sir H. H. Johnston, "The People of Eastern Equatorial Africa," *Journal of the Anthropological Institute* (1886), xv. 9.
[16] *Ibid.*, xv. 11.

Among Englishmen, a race very observant of the decencies of civilization, Herrick is fairly typical. His attitude to sexual dress is thus described by Havelock Ellis: "The fascination of clothes in the lover's eyes is, no doubt, a complex phenomenon, but in part it rests on the aptitudes of a woman's garments to express vaguely a dynamic symbolism which must always remain indefinite and elusive, and on that account always possess fascination. No one has so acutely described this symbolism as Herrick, often an admirable psychologist in matters of sexual attractiveness. Especially instructive in this respect are his poems, 'Delight in Disorder,' 'Upon Julia's Clothes,' and notably 'Julia's Petticoat.' 'A sweet disorder in the dress,' he tells us, 'kindles in clothes a wantonness'; it is not on the garment itself, but on the character of its movement that he insists; on the 'erring lace,' the 'winning wave' of the 'tempestuous petticoat.'"[17] Herrick, of course, is dealing with the dynamic quality of dress, but its static meaning is hardly less explicit in the English and European mind.

The significance of dress as an expression of the body will be referred to below in the sexual connexion. Meanwhile the general idea thus illustrated may be regarded as the norm in modern civilization. Its opposite or complementary is the increased value given to legitimate nudity. A movement is even proceeding, particularly in Germany, but to a considerable extent in other countries also, for an extension of this individual privilege into a restricted and occasional social habit—the so-called *Nacktheit* movement.

Such tendencies coincide with the twofold attitude towards the human organism which dress has emphasized—regard for the body in itself and regard for its artificial extension. Periodic social phenomena accentuate one or the other aspect. The Spartan practice of nudity in athletics was based on a reasoned theory of health from exposure and of purity from knowledge. The Papuans have been said to glory in their nudeness, and consider clothing fit only for women. Temporary nudity, when in obedience to natural impulse, should be regarded not as a reversion,[18] still less as a survival of a primitive state, but as a rhythmical movement. The point is well illustrated by the use of nudity as a love-charm.

[17] H. H. Ellis, *op. cit.*, v. 45–46.
[18] As Schurr argues, *Philosophie der Tracht* (Stuttgart, 1891), p. 48.

✂ Attitudes and Rationalizations Regarding Body Exposure

ERVING GOFFMAN

Given the general level of tightness (or looseness) established in a situation, and the orderly changes prescribed in this regard, it is worth noting that the normative stability found in the situation may be due to the presence of guardians who informally or formally have the special job of keeping "order." Thus, we read of the *silentiarius,* the Roman slave whose job it was to regulate the noise level maintained by other slaves.[1] In our day, chaperones, referees, nursery-school teachers, judges, police, ward attendants, and ushers are among those who perform this function.

I want now to re-emphasize that when one thinks in terms of the looseness or tightness of situational orientation, and in terms of the dimensions and idiom through which this is exhibited, one has a means of passing a little beyond the rationalistic dicta by which we ordinarily account for our major explicit situational rulings.

Take, for example, our jumbled attitudes and rationalizations regarding body exposure. Instead of considering the amount or the parts of the body exposed, it might be more profitable to examine the *orientational* implications of exposure. The relative undress of a bathing suit is part of the whole looseness complex—which includes the way in which one handles one's voice and eyes as well as one's body—and it is this whole complex that is tolerated and even encouraged on the beach. (Why this complex should here be approved still remains a question, of course, but a slightly different one.) The relative undress of décolletage at balls may be appropriate for the opposite reason. The exposure of this much of the self would seem in part to be an appreciative acknowledgment that the participants are so tightly in step with the occasion as a whole, and so trustful of the good conduct of their socially homogeneous circle, that they can withstand this much temptation to undue mutual-involvement without giving in to it. (An extreme, here, is perhaps found in the morals-ruling in London, which permits nudes to appear on the stage providing they do

[1] H. Nicolson, *Good Behaviour* (London: Constable, 1955), p. 64.

Source: *Behavior in Public Places,* New York: Free Press of Glencoe (1963), pp. 211–213. Reprinted by permission of the author and publisher.

Diversity in Cultural Patterns Related to Dress and Adornment 51

not move while the curtain is up. Presumably the rigidity of their pose is such a strong mark of devotion and assimilation to the occasion as a whole that the license of nudity can be afforded them.[2]) Yet in almost any public situation in our society, a woman dressed only in an underslip, although completely covered by it, would be greatly out of place; for such attire implies that the wearer has not yet put on her situational costume, whatever it is to be, and is not in a position to honor her situational commitments, whatever they may be. Nudity in a nudist colony or a doctor's office, or on the posing platform in an art class, is manageable because here it is the garb that shows proper regard for the demands of the occasion. Logic would force one to claim that a woman's appearance in a slip on these occasions would be a gaffe; and, in fact, arrangements are sometimes made so that those who will properly appear nude will not first appear halfclothed and out of role. By the same logic one can understand how a model can appear half-clothed at a fashion show of underclothing, for this is the way she shows appropriate involvement within the situation, albeit in a special performer role. Thus, apparently, the formality of a dress-modeling establishment (and hence its "tone," the desirability of its street location, and the like) can be indicated by the care that models take not to wander around the floor, after a showing, in the slips they have shown.[3]

Exposure of self in situational déshabille may be condoned, of course, in the household, at least within certain limits. The point here is that certain close relationships may be defined as ones that give the related persons the license to let occasions decay when these persons are alone in each other's presence. Hence, when a visitor to the house accidentally witnesses a resident of the house in disarray, a minor relationship crisis occurs, which is due to the momentary but embarrassing implication that the witness is in a relationship to the observed that would warrant the lapsing of situational niceties between them.

Clothing conduct during crises and disasters can be similarly analyzed. At a hotel fire, guests in undress are tolerated, not, perhaps, because eyes are turned to more important things, but because participants are allowed to be so deeply immersed in the crisis that their undress can be taken as a sign of appropriate engrossment, and the undress of others felt as an

[2] A description of this practice is given by Hortense Calisher, "Bowlers and Bumbershoots at a Piccadilly Peepshow," *The Reporter,* October 4, 1956, pp. 33–36.
[3] Suggested by Eleanor Carroll.

insufficient stimulus, under the circumstances, to induce inappropriate mutual-involvement. When the fire is brought under control, and the crisis abates, when in fact the occasion is such that alienation from it is a more possible thing, undress once again becomes a threat to situational orientation, and survivors begin to become sheepish about their lack of clothing.

The argument here is that any state of dress is proper or improper only in terms of what other evidence is available concerning the individual's allocation of involvement and hence his orientation to the social occasion and its gatherings. Since dress carries much of the burden of expressing orientation within the situation, we can understand why such apparently petty matters of "mere" etiquette should be of concern. But given that this is the major reason why dress is important, we can expect and predict much variation in what will be defined as allowable dress. A male college student who enters the classroom in need of a shave and in trunks, or a female who enters with her hair in curlers, is nakedly showing lack of attachment to the behavior setting; but when an exam is being held, and all students in the exam hall are engrossed quite deeply in school work, having studied devotedly for the previous two weeks, then there is already sufficient sign of involvement in schooling, and thus the informalities of appearance I have mentioned may well be permitted, no longer being symbols of alienation. Similarly, an accountant or lawyer, with a downtown office, who attended to his clients dressed in an old sweater and no jacket would be considered to be disoriented in business situations and to the business world itself; the same man working overtime on Saturday afternoon can afford such laxness, however, because his mere presence in the office at an off hour is sign enough of regard for the work world.

Ritualistic Patterns

❀ Wedding Garments

ERNEST CRAWLEY

The sexual dress is at marriage intensified by the principle of affirmation, not of sexuality, but of personality. It is an occasion of expansion, of augmentation; as the social expression of the crisis of love (the culmination of human energy and well-being) it is precisely adapted. Often, for example, the pair assume super-humanity, and are treated as royal persons. A special and distinctive dress for the bride is a widely spread fashion. As a rule, the bride herself is supposed to make the dress. With marriage, housekeeping begins, and, as in Norway, Scotland, India, and elsewhere, the bride supplies the household linen, often including the personal linen of the husband. The variety of wedding dress is endless. Frequently each family supplies the other.

In North India the bride's dress is yellow, or red—colours which "repel demons." The Majhwār pair wear white, but after the anointing put on coloured clothes.[1]

English brides wear a white dress. So did Hebrew brides. Old English folklore directed that a bride must wear "Something old, something new, Something borrowed, something blue."[2] The Hindu bridegroom supplies the cloth for the wedding robes of the bride. The fact is (see below) that there is among the Hindus, not merely a dowry, but an interchange of gifts; furniture and clothes being the principal components. When presented, the clothes are put on; this forms a preliminary marriage cere-

---

[1] W. Crooke, "The Wooing of Penelope," *Folk-lore* (1898), ix. 125–126; *id., The Popular Religion and Folk-lore of Northern India* (new edition, 1896), ii. 28 ff.; *id., Tribes and Castes*, iii. 425.
[2] *Id.,* "The Wooing of Penelope," ix. 127–128.

Source: *Dress, Drinks, and Drums*, edited by Theodore Besterman, London: Methuen and Co. (1931), pp. 133–137. Reprinted by permission of the publisher.

mony.³ The gorgeous flowered embroidery, *phūlkāri*, of the Jāts is prominent in their wedding dress.

Magnificence, generally, is the characteristic of wedding garments throughout the world; white is frequent, as an expression of virginity. Red is often used, as an unconscious adaptation to the circumstances of expansion.

Special garments or specialized forms of garments are less common than "best clothes" and ornament. The Korean bridegroom-elect, often betrothed at the age of five, wears a red jacket as a mark of engagement.⁴ On the day before marriage the Roman bride put off the *toga prætexta*, which was deposited before the Lares, and put on the *tunica recta* or *regilla*. This was woven in one piece in the old-fashioned way. It was fastened with a woollen girdle tied in the knot of Hercules, *nodus Herculeus*.⁵ In European folklore an analogue is to be found in the true lovers' knot, the idea being a magical and later a symbolical knitting together of the wedded pair. The hair of the bride was arranged in six locks, and was ceremonially parted with the *cælibaris hasta*. She wore a wreath of flowers, gathered by her own hands.⁶

Some cases of investiture follow. On the wedding night the bride of the Koita people is decorated. Coco-nut oil is put on her thighs. She wears a new petticoat. Red lines are painted on her face, and her armlets are painted. Her hair is combed and anointed with oil, and in her locks are scarlet *hibiscus* flowers. The groom wears a head-dress of cassowary feathers; his face is painted with red and yellow streaks, and his ears are decorated with dried tails of pigs.⁷ The Hindu at marriage is invested by the bride's parents with the two additional skeins necessary to make the full complement of the *yajñōpavīta*, the sacred thread, of the married man.⁸ The Javanese bridegroom is dressed in the garments of a chief. The idea is "to represent him as of exalted rank." ⁹ The Malays term the

---

³ J. E. Padfield, *The Hindu at Home* (Madras 1908), p. 116.
⁴ H. S. Saunderson, "Notes on Corea and its People," *Journal of the Anthropological Institute* (1895), xxiv. 305.
⁵ Whittuck, "Matrimonium," *Dictionary of Greek and Roman Antiquities* (3rd edition, 1890).
⁶ *Ibid., loc. cit.*
⁷ C. G. Seligmann, *op. cit.*, p. 78.
⁸ J. E. Padfield, *op. cit.*, p. 123.
⁹ J. P. Veth, *Java* (Haarlem 1886–1907), i. 632–635.

bridegroom *rajasahari,* the "one-day king." [10] The dressing up of both bride and groom and all parties present, for the bridal procession of the Minangkabauers, is very remarkable.

The bridal veil, originally concealing the face, occurs in China,[11] Korea,[12] Manchuria, Burma, Persia,[13] Russia,[14] Bulgaria,[15] and in various modified forms throughout European and the majority of great civilizations, ancient and modern. In ancient Greece the bride wore a long veil and a garland. The Druse bride wears a long red veil, which her husband removes in the bridal chamber.[16] An Egyptian veil, *boorko,* conceals all the face except the eyes, and reaches to the feet. It is of black silk for married and white for unmarried women.[17] Various considerations suggest that the veil is in origin rather an affirmation of the face, as a human and particularly a sexual glory, than a concealment, though the emphasizing of maidenly modesty comes in as a secondary and still more prominent factor. The veil also serves as an expression of the head and the hair. These are also augmented by various decorations.

The wedding dress often coincides with, or is equivalent to, the grade-dress of the married. The *stola* as a badge of lawful wedlock was the distinctive garment of ancient Roman wives.[18] It was an ample outer tunic in design, and possibly is to be identified with the bridal *tunica recta.* Among the Hereros, after the wedding meal, the bride's mother puts upon the bride the cap and the dress of married women.[19] The "big garment," ear-rings, and the iron necklace distinguish Masai married women from girls.[20]

Further social stages are marked by distinctive dress, such as pregnancy,

---

[10] G. A. Wilken, "Plechtigheden en Gebruiken bij Verlovingen en Huwelijken bij de Volken van de Indischen Archipel," *Bijdragen tot de Taal-, Land- en Volkenkunde van Nederlandsch-Indië* (1889), xxxviii. 424.
[11] J. Doolittle, *Social Life of the Chinese* (New York 1867), i. 79.
[12] W. E. Griffis, *Corea* (1882), p. 249.
[13] J. Anderson, *From Mandalay to Momien* (1876), p. 141; J. H. S. Lockhart, "The Marriage Ceremonies of the Manchus," *Folk-lore* (1890), i. 489.
[14] W. R. S. Ralston, *The Songs of the Russian People* (1872), p. 780.
[15] S. G. B. St. Clair and C. A. Brophy, *A Residence in Bulgaria* (1869), p. 73.
[16] G. W. Chasseaud, *The Druses of the Lebanon* (1855), p. 166.
[17] E. W. Lane, *An Account of the Manners and Customs of the Modern Egyptians* (1846), i. 52.
[18] "Stola," *Dictionary of Greek and Roman Antiquities* (1890).
[19] J. Irle, *Die Herero* (Gütersloh 1906), pp. 106–107.
[20] A. C. Hollis, *The Masai* (Oxford 1905), p. 282.

motherhood, and, more rarely, fatherhood. As soon as a Wa-taveita bride becomes pregnant, "she is dressed with much display of beads, and over her eyes a deep fringe of tiny iron chains is hung, which hides her and also prevents her from seeing clearly." An old woman attends her, "to screen her from all excitement and danger until the expected event has taken place."[21] Among Cameroon tribes is found the custom of girls remaining naked until the birth of the first child.[22] The bride in South Slavonia used to wear a veil until the birth of the first child.[23] When the birth of twins takes place, the Herero parents are immediately undressed, previously to being specially attired. The detail shows the importance of immediate assimilation to the new state.

After childbirth the mother passes through a stage of recovery, of isolation, with her babe, often expressed by a costume. At its end she assumes the costume of normal life which has been temporarily suspended, or a special costume of her new grade of maternity.

[21] Sir H. H. Johnston, "The People of Eastern Equatorial Africa," *Journal of the Anthropological Institute* (1886), xv. 8–9; C. New, *Life, Wanderings, and Labours in Eastern Africa* (1874), pp. 360–361.
[22] Hutter, *Nord-Hinterland von Kamerun* (Brunswick 1902), p. 421.
[23] F. S. Krauss, *Sitte und Brauch der Südslaven* (Vienna 1885), p. 450.

Part Four

Social Organization and Dress

OBSERVABLE RELATIONSHIPS EXIST between patterns of dress and adornment and social organization. First, all societies are so organized that they have patterns of role differentiation based on age and sex, and ordinarily these social distinctions are reflected in dress. Second, roles associated with positions in the common social organizations of family, polity, economy, religion, and caste and class are often reflected in dress.

Age and Sex

Age and sex are ascribed on the basis of biological differences. However, the extent to which biology governs the pattern of behavior or roles associated with sex and age is neither clearly known nor agreed upon. On the other hand, social scientists widely agree that the culture strongly affects age and sex roles. The life of any individual necessarily follows a biologically determined cycle, and an individual is expected to occupy its successive stages. Even so, there are no universally assigned behavior patterns for specific stages. Between birth and death most societies distinguish childhood, adulthood, and old age, but even these periods differ in chronology. What should be noted is that different norms of behavior exist in all societies for each culturally determined stage in the cycle.

Distinctions in clothing appropriate for different age levels, however defined, are observable in most societies, and social unease often arises when systems of age symbolism are ignored. The Western teenage girl who wears a sleek, black evening dress instead of a bouffant pastel or the woman in her seventies who wears "short" shorts incurs social disapproval because each has violated the cultural norms for her age group.

In certain societal periods, age patterns for dress are more apparent than in others. After developing general hypotheses concerning changes in social roles and self-concepts, Bush and London try to account for what they consider decreasing distinctness of dress in twentieth-century America by investigating a particular age group, prepubescent boys. Their original hypotheses have wide applicability and call for future empirical and cross-cultural testing followed by critical evaluation.[1]

Dress is more clearly distinguishable with respect to sex than to age, although it is difficult to disassociate one from the other. Hard as it may be to generalize, the role assignments for the respective sexes often seem reflected in clothing. The use of trousers or short breech cloths by men often connotes the active role attributed to the male. In a perceptive treatment Crawley delineates the sexual dichotomy of dress. In a different kind of presentation Vener and Hoffer report the research procedure and results of a systematic study of adolescent American boys' and girls' attitudes toward clothing.

The Family

The family has the responsibility for regulating reproduction and for maintaining the socio-cultural system itself through protection, care, and

[1] The changing age structure in America encourages additional hypotheses concerning clothing. Sociologist Ruth Useem, for example, is intrigued by the implications for clothing research of the numerous age-grade distinctions in America and the high proportion of the aged. She asks what is the social significance of such fine distinctions as subteen, preteen, and teen in apparel.

training of the young. Not only physical preservation but also transmission of knowledge, ideologies, and values is vital. By socializing the young, the family passes along the ways of thinking and behaving that society considers human. With biological and cultural survival at stake, societies at all levels of complexity have some institutionalized form of the family.

Each individual ordinarily has many close ties to the family, and during the first years of his life, the family is the nearly exclusive agent of socialization. Roach emphasizes the strong influence of the American family on patterns of behavior related to clothing. In further analysis of the American family, Tate and Glisson point out how changes in activities affect handling of resources, such as clothing, at various stages in the family cycle. The family cycle is an important concept for us in further study of dress, for individuals within the family circle are affected by one another's action. Loomis suggested in the early 1930's that some families might be willing to take the bread off the table to clothe their children approaching marriageable age.[2]

The Economy

All societies have an economic organization. Even in simply organized societies, an age and sex division of labor exists and resources are utilized for production and consumption of goods. The economy determines the organization of production, consumption, and transfer of goods and services, including the personal consumption goods, apparel and ornament. These goods may symbolize position as consumer in the economy or position within the system of production in the economy. Some uniforms in particular signify the individual's position as producer. For example, witness the butcher's apron, the waitress's uniform, the mechanic's coveralls, the judge's robes, the surgeon's gown and mask.

The research data concerning styles, values, and trends in clothing consumption by families of cocoa farmers in Nigeria illustrate the link between families, as consuming units, and the economy. An analysis of factors affecting clothing consumption patterns of families in the American economy is provided by Tate and Glisson. Winakor and Martin

---

[2] C. P. Loomis, "The Study of the Life Cycle of Families," *Rural Sociology*, Vol. 1 (June, 1936), pp. 180–199.

60   Dress, Adornment, and the Social Order

report on purchase of used clothing. This method of acquisition may be more important than purchase of new clothing for some consumers. Two researchers, cited later,[3] who refer to used clothing are Schwartz in his discussion of American Negroes and Gillin in his analysis of Indians and Ladinos in Guatemala.

The reading from Zweig shows that dress may indicate position within the system of production and may therefore be tied to social-class position. Roth probes the meaning of status differentiation which exists in occupational clothing in the hospital. In a system of sharply defined statuses in which duties and privileges are clearly delineated, the visual symbolism and ritualistic use of the gown, cap, and mask signal rigidly prescribed and expected behavior. The coordination of a complex system of human interdependencies within the world of medical practice is thus facilitated.

The Polity

To maintain the social order, a society must solve the problem of regulation of power among individuals. In some societies, a simple system of authority arises; in others a complex governmental structure develops supported by regulations and laws.

Police and military organizations exist as effective means of maintaining order within any political system. Typically some sort of uniform or costume is required to remind the public of the force that stands ready for mobilization if the territory or authority of the legally instituted government is threatened from within or without. As emphasized in the reading from Langner these uniformed representatives of government are cogent reminders of the power of the political organization.

Association between political systems and patterns of dress can be shown dramatically in periods of abrupt social and political change when old patterns are abandoned and new patterns arise. The articles by Scott and Topping illustrate how austerity in dress symbolized the leveling of class that was the ideological promise of Communism on the mainland of China and Russia. Particularly interesting is the reassertion of aesthetic principles and the status incentive after the major crisis and readjustment have passed. Scott notes these kinds of reactions in China, and 1964 news releases underline similar trends in Russia. Indications are that Russian

[3] See Caste and Class.

women have increasing amounts of fashion goods available to them and that they are growing correspondingly more fashion conscious.

Religion

In his attempt to understand his universe, man often builds a system of religious or magic beliefs which particularly come into play during crises and times of uncertainty. Birth, puberty, marriage, illness, death, for instance, all signify moments of social readjustment which may require more explanation and support than secular sources give. Religion and magic offer balm in such periods of stress and also reinforce the continuity of group life.

In a basically secular world religious influence on dress and adornment is likely to be incidental for the general population and coercive only for the dedicated who join religious orders or the priesthood. Crawley, in another excerpt, comments on the methods whereby the priesthood, through religious garb, sets itself apart from the secular society.

The Hasidic community of Brooklyn, New York, has the characteristics of a quasi-theocracy in the midst of the highly secularizing surroundings and influences. Poll reports that the religious dress of the Hasidim serves many religious purposes. It is symbolic of their total subsociety within which religion is intertwined with all aspects of life.

Priestly dress serves primarily to differentiate the individual from the general society. Hasidic dress, on the other hand, not only indicates the individual's separation from the general society but also bolsters his position within his subculture and intensifies his identification with it.

Caste and Class

Caste and class systems grow within any societal organization as evaluations come to be placed on a variety of human roles and activities. Highest ratings are ordinarily given to roles considered of the most service to society. For example, roles associated with the preservation of human life, such as those of physician or medical man, tend to have a high value placed on them. On the basis of roles filled within various basic structures such as the family, political order, religious framework, and economy, plus personal or charismatic qualities and income or wealth, an individual acquires a place in a rank or class system. Any one of these classificatory alignments or characteristics may loom as most significant for his placement, and his garb may indicate this major relationship to others.

The term "class" implies a society in which mobility from level to level is fairly easy and marriage between members of different classes is possible. Social mobility in a class system is facilitated by the accessibility of economic resources and by mass production, which makes style-of-life symbols readily available to those who endeavor to move within the class system. "Caste" refers to a rigid stratification system in which mobility is not likely; individuals usually are born into, marry within, and stay within the caste for their lifetimes and thus provide the same stratification position for their children. Although societies are usually categorized as exhibiting either caste or class, it is possible for both to be found in one society. The United States is frequently given as an example containing both because of the castelike barriers between whites and Negroes.

A style-of-life symbolism that expresses the individual's position comes to be associated with either caste or class. Material possessions, including dress and adornment, are a recognizable part of this symbolism. Useem, Tangent, and Useem show how clothing fits in with the whole class system of external symbols in a small American community.

Allen suggests that visibility of social-class distinction on the basis of clothing symbols in America has decreased. The brief selection from Harrington extends the same theme by commenting that the availability of mass-produced clothing for even the poor in America blurs social-class lines and makes differences between classes difficult to see even though they still exist.

Generalizations concerning dress of American Negroes, sometimes described as being a caste within American society, are analyzed by Schwartz. Gillin describes the acculturative intertwining of Indian and European cultures in a castelike society in which each group has a distinctive mode of life. Clothing is a significant part of these modes.

Supplementary Readings

Statements on various aspects of social organization are included in a few of the general works cited at the end of Part One. Other references are Barber (1957), Coleman (1961), Ebeling and Rosencranz (1961), Form and Stone (1955), Gillin (1948), K. B. Hall (1956), Hostetler (1963), Hurlock (1955), Klitzke (1953), Lewis (1955), Lynes (1954, 1957), Myrdal (1944), Rosencranz (1962), Silverman (1945, 1960), Simon (1958), Stone and Form (1955, 1957), Tax (1963), Tumin (1952), Veblen (1894), and Winick (1963).

Age and Sex Roles

❁ On the Disappearance of Knickers:
Hypotheses for the Functional Analysis
of the Psychology of Clothing

GEORGE BUSH AND PERRY LONDON

Introduction

There are those of us for whom the rustling sound of corduroy has for many years been associated with memories of the almost indestructible knee-length trousers of our childhood. These memories, though not always pleasant, have gained enhanced value in recent years because of the disappearance of knickers from the American scene, a disappearance which, despite the fact that it occurred over a brief span of years (between the 1930's and early 1940's), passed relatively unnoticed and unremarked upon. Although the style of dress of women has changed frequently, markedly, and to the accompaniment of great public clamor, over the past half-century, the stability of dress of both men and children has been such as to lead one to think that any fundamental change in the dress styles of either would be an event rich in its psychological implications.

Whether or not this is the case, there seems to have been no widespread attempt to mine this field since the publication of *The Psychology of Clothes* by Flügel in 1930.[1] At about that time, psychological articles on and interest in this area disappeared, as quickly and quietly as did knickers, and except for sporadic studies based on limited clinical material, the field has remained quiescent.

[1] Flügel, J. C. Psychology of Clothes. London: Hogarth Press, 1930.
Source: *Journal of Social Psychology*, Vol. 51 (May, 1960), pp. 359–366. Reprinted by permission of the authors and publisher.

This article is an attempt to supplement previous work in this field by proposing in the form of hypotheses susceptible to more rigorous examination than is here attempted, a possibly more comprehensive and parsimonious explanation for changes in dress than is currently extant.

Theories of Origin

Early work in this field, which is comprehensively reviewed by Flügel,[2] was done mostly by anthropologists and sociologists, Westermarck[3] most notable among them. Their observations were seized upon by Ellis,[4] and incorporated into the first volume of his *Psychology of Sex*. All of this work is much concerned with explaining the origins of the use of clothing. This is attempted by deductions from function to origin, unhappily assuming that what "ruder" societies are, more civilized ones once were. Dunlap[5] has summarized the various origin theories proposed through 1926 under the headings of the Modesty, Immodesty, Adornment, and Protection theories. The first three, generally most popular, he dismisses as conflicting and improbable, and while accepting the protection theory in essence, limits it to protection from flying insects by the use of tassled or hanging clothing rather than protection from climate or rough terrain. Flügel has attempted to synthesize the Adornment and Protection theories by proposing that the original clothing articles were used for magical protection from harm.

Clothing Functions

Regardless of the validity of any of these theories with regard to *origins*, it is apparent that all of them describe *functions* of clothing. These may be subsumed under three headings: (*a*) Protection of the body against harm. (*b*) Concealment (or display) of parts of the body. (*c*) Differentiation (through decoration and adornment) of one individual or group from another.

[2] *Ibid.*
[3] Westermarck, E. The History of Human Marriage. London: Macmillan, 1891.
[4] Ellis, H. Studies in the Psychology of Sex. Philadelphia: Davis, 1900.
[5] Dunlap, K. The development and function of clothing. *J. Gen. Psychol.*, 1928, 1, 64–78.

Most theorists, including Dunlap and Flügel, believe that the most essential function of clothing has been that of differentiation, certainly in all graphically communicating societies. Veblen,[6] in his "conspicuosity" theories, has provided an excellent rationale for this insofar as leisure classes and the assimilation of their values in other classes is concerned, but the same hypothesis may be equally well employed to indicate that the use of clothing for differentiation cuts across several of the various possibilities for kinds of differentiation within a society or from one society to another.

Stereotypically oriented people, for example, still perceive various alien groups in terms of societal "uniforms." Such people anticipate Polynesians in sarongs and Eskimos in snowsuits, and few indeed have yet given up these notions as totally inadequate. Even without such overgeneralization, however, classes and castes are often quite legitimately differentiated on a clothing basis, sometimes by very simple means, such as the uniforms of soldiers *et al.* or the turned collars of Catholic clergymen. In already limited subgroups, moreover, such as the military, differentiations may be reflected by as little as the design of clothing insignia or as much as totally different colored and fitted uniforms.

Clothing Differences and Social Rôle

If we accept the assumption of the preeminence of differentiation among clothing functions, we might expect its use in this fashion to correlate highly with the *significance of the difference it makes within a culture,* so that the less important it is to differentiate people along a particular dimension, the less likely clothing will be the means of doing it. The importance for an individual then, of a given social rôle, as well as the intensity of his rôle taking (self-concept),[7] will frequently be reflected in his clothing. More broadly stated, we may hypothesize that *differences in modes of dress within a particular society are indicative of differences in social rôles and self-concepts of members of that society.*

To illustrate, let us return to the example of clergymen's dress. Roman Catholic priests, as opposed to Protestant ministers of most denominations, are easily differentiated from parishioners by their clothing. When

---
[6] Veblen, T. The Theory of the Leisure Class. New York: Macmillan, 1899.
[7] Cameron, N. The Psychology of Behavior Disorders: A Biosocial Approach. Boston: Houghton-Mifflin, 1947.

we explore the respective religious functions (social rôles) of these clergymen, we find that the difference in their dress is explicable by the above premise. In the Catholic conception, the priest is a divinely ordained representative of God, whose function allows his relatively direct intervention with divine forces on the behalf of his parishioners. This is not, on the whole, true of Protestant ministers, whose rôle is more nearly that of the wise leader than of one of superordinate position. Since this rôle differentiates him less from his parishioner than does that of the priest from his, it is less necessary for the difference to be implicitly stated through such obtuse means as clothing.

The reader may observe that this illustration, like its predecessor, is of a cross-sectional sort, i.e., concerns itself with a few of many concurrent social rôles. An equally significant source of information for the social scientist may lie in the possibility that social rôle and self-concept are also longitudinally reflected in clothing modes, so that *changes over a period of time,* in the clothing of any subgroup of society, may reflect changes both in the rôle attached to that group by society, and in its corollary, the self-concepts of the individuals composing the group. In the light of economic factors however, such as the provision by designers of new styles of clothes before old garments have worn out, this hypothesis must be more tenuously stated, to the effect that *changes in fundamental or enduring modes of dress in a society are indicative of changes in the social rôles and self-concepts of members of that society.*

Economic factors which provide frequent, minor style changes grossly out of proportion to utilitarian needs do, indeed, tend to muddy the waters of investigation of stable clothing changes. The very ability, however, of such changes to find markets, as well as the selectivity responsible for the success of one frill and failure of another, must be accounted for in terms of motivational determinants as well. In this connection, it is noteworthy that clothing designers have repeatedly pointed out that such psychological factors as aspirations and fantasies play a highly significant rôle in determining the extent to which clothing innovations meet with acceptance. Since aspirations and fantasies are intimately related to social rôle and self-concept,[8] one would expect a relationship between the frequency with which clothing styles vary in *any* direction and the stability of social rôles and self-concepts of the groups for which they vary.

The immense variability in the clothing styles of women and of adoles-

[8] *Ibid.*

cents, in conjunction with the indefiniteness of rôles assigned and conflicting demands made upon them in American culture,[9] illustrates the relationship between stability of dress and stability of rôle stated above. Converse illustrations of the identical relationship may be sought in the "conservative" dress of businessmen and three-cornered habiliments of infancy. These phenomena, we believe, lend themselves to generalization in the form of the following hypothesis: *The greater the variability of clothing styles in a society, the less well-defined and conflict-free are social rôles in that society* and, conversely, *the smaller the variability of clothing styles in a society, the more enduring, clearly defined, and conflict-free are the social rôles of individuals in that society.*

Testing the Hypotheses: Analysis of Knickers

One of the most difficult and persistent problems in the field of the psychology of clothing is that of subjecting hypotheses to empirical test. Unfortunately, the justification for many of the existing hypotheses in this area seems to lie mainly in their face validity rather than in extensive empirical validation. Furthermore, because of their lack of amenability to empirical test, it is doubtful if they can ever achieve anything more than face validity.

For this reason, we have attempted to present a series of hypotheses which lend themselves readily to repeated empirical test. By offering functional hypotheses, we feel, the study of correlative phenomena relevant to personality theory is encouraged, rather than the necessarily deductive search for constructs whose chief value may be historic. These hypotheses are themselves subject to further delimitation in terms of operational, quantifiable definitions. Prevalences or dearths of styles, for example, may be determined from samplings of mass communications media, such as the illustrations and advertisements of magazines and newspapers and the clothing worn on television, movies, and the legitimate theater, or from direct observations of what people are wearing under different circumstances and what shop windows are displaying. Social rôles may be measured in terms of income, dwelling types and costs, occupations, educational attainments, etc., as has already been so fruitfully begun by sociologists and cultural anthropologists.

[9] Horney, K. The Neurotic Personality of our Time. New York: Norton, 1937.

By way of illustration, we shall attempt, in the remainder of this article, to anecdotally apply the above hypotheses to the social rôle of the prepubescent boy as reflected in a fundamental change in his wardrobe.

Despite considerable overlap, it was possible, until the beginning of the Second World War, to distinguish most American boys younger than six or seven from those between the ages of seven and puberty, in that those in their preschool years generally wore shorts, while those in grammar school wore knickers. It was further possible to distinguish the prepubescent boy from the adolescent on a similar basis, namely the former's wearing of knickers and the latter's wearing of long trousers. The extent to which the receipt of one's first pair of long pants was associated with pubertal ceremonies, the anxious and pleasurable anticipation attending the first wearing of these pants, and the perception of this event as an affirmation of impending manhood, indicates the degree to which *differences in trousers were used as a means of differentiating one stage of development from another,* this change having something of the import of a *rite de passage.*

There were, incidentally, some noteworthy group differences in the wearing of knickers, primarily between urban and rural prepubescent boys. The farm boy, who was expected to assume considerable responsibility at an early age, rarely wore knickers. On those infrequent, relatively formal occasions when he did, he was expected to "mind his manners," that is, to conform to the social stereotype of his more "refined" city brethren. Within the urban community, children of the lower classes who, like the farm boy, assumed adult responsibility at an early age, began wearing knickers earlier than did children of the middle class and gave them up in favor of "longies" before puberty. We see here a demonstration of rôle differences extending even within one group, but still reflected in a clothing style.[10]

In recent years, however, trouser differences have become inadequate for distinguishing between boys of different age groups. By the middle 1930's, pre-school and prepubescent boys had taken more and more to wearing long pants, and around 1940 knickers were given up entirely. In

[10] Intragroup differences are partially accounted for by the American historical tradition of sans coulotte among rural dwellers and kneepants among members of the urban upper classes. Wearing of kneepants by children of various economic groups was originally perhaps, an attempt by their parents to emulate the upper classes, but the concept of "leisure," reflected in kneepants, has been translated as "non-productiveness" for children.

attempting to account for their disappearance at this particular time, we find two possible explanations. Though they may or may not be related in complementary fashion, the employment of either or both seems to reflect that, within recent years, a fundamental *change has taken place in the social rôle of the prepubescent boy.*

The first explanation is that there has come to be an increasing popular recognition and, possibly, acceptance of the emotional needs of children, particularly those of preschool and prepubescent age. This is reflected in such phenomena as the growth of the Mental Health movement, the popularity of psychology as a subject of school curricula, the growth of popular periodicals dealing exclusively with raising children, the sales of publications such as Spock's,[11] increased emphasis in teacher training on emotional aspects of development, and the broad popularization of the idea that psychological difficulties are at the roots of a whole host of familial and social maladies. The sum of such phenomena is that the Victorian ideal of children as small adults to be kept from underfoot has little popular status at present. Because of this increased favorable attention paid him, the prepubescent boy probably exists far less than previously in a psychological no-man's land between the joys and delights of childhood and the fancied prerogatives and maturity of adolescence, the age so aptly described by psychoanalysts as the latency period.

The second explanation involves the current increasing trend observed toward uniformity and conformity in our society.[12] This trend may be largely a function of the progressing dominance of middle-class values in America which, because of the enormous size of its middle class, and a national historic ideal of classlessness, is a suitable ground for the assimilation of all class values under a middle-class standard. The trend probably received significant impetus as a result of our entry into World War II, when it became necessary for the entire nation to focus upon the one great goal of defeating our enemies. In such circumstances, the luxuries of group differentiations are largely abandoned, and this relaxation of boundaries between socioeconomic groups may also extend somewhat to the developmental strata within each. The prepubescent boy was affected in such a way that he was expected to mature earlier, assume more responsibilities, and devote less time to living in a state of hibernation. This increasing trend to uniformity, at least in its initial phase, seems

[11] Spock, B. *The Common Sense Book of Baby and Child Care.* New York: Duell, Sloan and Pearce, 1945.
[12] Riesman, D. *The Lonely Crowd: A Study of the Changing American Character.* New Haven: Yale Univ. Press, 1950.

to have served the purpose of permitting him greater freedom as well.

The coexistence of the narrow range of clothing styles which, in the past, children were expected to wear, and the rôle of the prepubescent boy, which has been defined in terms of a latency period from Freud's time to our own, also appears to reflect a more than accidental relationship. Unlike the pre-school child, whose dress tended to change frequently with the development of his physical and psychological self, the prepubescent boy, who also passed through significant stages of physical development, formerly found himself simply wearing longer and longer knickers rather than differently styled trousers. When changes did occur, they came earlier to the preschool child than to the prepubescent one. In recent times however, as the prepubescent has been allowed to develop new rôles in some strata of society, old ones have not yet been relinquished in others. From the middle class "children should be seen and not heard" philosophy of an earlier day, we have progressed to a greater confusion of philosophies and expectations, so that the total variance of social stereotypes and expectations has markedly increased for this group. With some faithfulness, *variability in apparel of this group has increased with the decrease in the stability of common perceptions and expectations of it.*

Thus, the development of this one phenomenon over a period of time may be accounted for by the above proposed hypotheses. Many more changes than these have taken place, however, in the clothing of men, women, and children alike. As with knickers, these changes are in many cases demonstrably connected with changes in standards of acceptability and demands for achievement in our society, the implications of which go far beyond the use of clothing itself. Their study, we feel, presents the social scientist with a rich and relatively untapped field of investigation, from which significant structural psychological changes throughout society could be rapidly recorded and easily validated.

A further article, now in preparation, will deal with some of the rôle changes reflected in changes in modes of dress of American adults over the past several years.

Summary

This article presents a rationale for the formulation of three hypotheses for the analysis of the differentiation function of clothing in terms of the social rôles and self-concepts of wearers of particular articles. These are:

1. Differences in modes of dress within a particular society are indicative of differences in social rôles and self-concepts of members of that society.
2. Changes in fundamental or enduring modes of dress in a society are indicative of changes in the social rôles and self-concepts of members of that society.
3. The greater or smaller the variability of clothing styles in a society, the less or more respectively well-defined and conflict-free are social rôles in that society.

In illustration of the applicability of these hypotheses, an analysis of the differentiation function served by the wearing of knickers and the rôle changes of prepubescent boys which accompanied their disappearance was presented. A further article will attempt a similar analysis for changes in the habit of American adults.

✿ The Sexual Background of Dress
ERNEST CRAWLEY

The most distinctive social division is the permanent division of sex. Up to puberty this is more or less ignored, and the neutral quality of the previous stage is often indicated by the neutral connotation of the term "child," and by a neutral fashion of child-dress. It is natural that the growth and maturity of the primary sexual characters should give these a prominent place in the principles of the distinguishing garb, and that they should, as it were, mould the dress into adaptive forms. The idea of social sexuality is well brought out in the stories of children failing to distinguish girls from boys when nude. The adaptation of the distinctive feminine and masculine garments, skirt and trousers, to the activity of the respective sexes has already been referred to. The main idea of dress as a material expression in a social form of the psychical reflexes from personality, and, in this case, sexuality, has here particular prominence. To regard the affirmation, by means of dress, of primary sexual characters as intended to attract the attention of the other sex by adorning them is a superficial view. Such intention is secondary, though, of course, it has an

Source: *Dress, Drinks, and Drums,* edited by Theodore Besterman, London: Methuen and Co. (1931), pp. 126–132. Reprinted by permission of the publisher.

important social bearing. Goethe's remark is in point for the consideration of dress as an affirmation of personality: "We exclaim, 'What a beautiful little foot!' when we have merely seen a pretty shoe; we admire the lovely waist, when nothing has met our eyes but an elegant girdle."

Special cases of an intensification of sexual characters may be illustrated by the following. A type of female beauty in the Middle Ages represents forms clothed in broad flowing skirts, and with the characteristic shape of pregnancy. "It is the maternal function, . . . which marks the whole type."[1] The type possibly survived in "that class of garments which involved an immense amount of expansion below the waist, and secured such expansion by the use of whalebone hoops and similar devices. The Elizabethan farthingale was such a garment. This was originally a Spanish invention, as indicated by the name (from *verdugardo*, 'provided with hoops') and reached England through France. We find the fashion at its most extreme point in the fashionable dress of Spain[2] in the seventeenth century, such as it has been immortalized by Velasquez. In England hoops died out during the reign of George III, but were revived, for a time, half a century later, in the Victorian crinoline."[3] It is curious, but not exceptional to the view here expressed—it is, in fact, corroborative of it, because of the necessity of emphasizing feminine characters which is characteristic of the class—that this, like most other feminine fashions in dress, was invented by courtesans. The crinoline or farthingale is the culmination of the distinctive feminine garment, the skirt, as a protection and affirmation of the pelvic character.

Augmentation of the mammary character is similar. In mediæval Europe an exception is found in a tendency to the use of compressing garments. The tightening of the waist girth is a remarkable adaptation, which emphasizes at one and the same time the feminine characters of expansion both of the breasts and of the abdominal and gluteal regions. "Not only does the corset render the breasts more prominent; it has the further effect of displacing the breathing activity of the lungs in an upward direction, the advantage from the point of sexual allurement thus gained being that additional attention is drawn to the bosom from the respiratory movement thus imparted to it."[4] The development of the

[1] Marholm, quoted by H. H. Ellis, *Studies in the Psychology of Sex*, iv. 169.
[2] [But cp. A. Souza, *O Trajo popular en Portugal nos Seculos XVIIIe XIX* (Lisboa 1924).]
[3] H. H. Ellis, *loc. cit.*
[4] H. H. Ellis, *Studies in the Psychology of Sex*, iv. 172.

corset in modern Europe has been traced from the bands, or *fasciæ*, of Greek and Italian women. The tight bodices of the Middle Ages were replaced in the seventeenth and eighteenth centuries by whalebone bodices. The modern corset is a combination of the *fascia* and the girdle.[5]

In the sphere of masculine dress and the affirmation by its means of sexual characters, it is sufficient to note two mediæval fashions. The long-hose which superseded the barbarian trews and preceded the modern trousers emphasized most effectively the male attribute and social quality of energy and activity as represented by the lower limbs, the organs of locomotion. The *braguette,* or codpiece, of the fifteenth and sixteenth centuries is an example of a protective article of dress, originally used in war, which became an article "of fashionable apparel, often made of silk and adorned with ribbons, even with gold and jewels."[6] Its history supplies a modern repetition of the savage phallocrypt, and throws light on the evolution of the ideas of dress.

With regard to secondary sexual characters, sexual dress, itself an artificial secondary sexual character, carries on various adaptations. "The man must be strong, vigorous, energetic, hairy, even rough . . . the woman must be smooth, rounded, and gentle."[7] These characters are echoed in the greater relative coarseness and strength of fabric of masculine dress, and the softness and flimsiness of feminine. A somewhat greater darkness of women is a secondary sexual character; in this connexion a harmony is unconsciously aimed at; the tendency is for men to wear darker, and women lighter clothes. Women tend to "cultivate pallor of the face, to use powder," and "to emphasize the white underlinen."[8] The attraction of sexual disparity, so important in sexual selection, reaches its culmination in the matter of clothing, and "it has constantly happened that men have even called in the aid of religion to enforce a distinction which seemed to them so urgent. One of the greatest of sex allurements would be lost and the extreme importance of clothes would disappear at once if the two sexes were to dress alike; such identity of dress has, however, never come about among any people."[9]

---

[5] Léoty, *Le Corset à travers les âges* (Paris 1893), quoted by H. H. Ellis, *op. cit.,* iv. 172–173.
[6] H. H. Ellis, *op. cit.,* iv. 159; I. Bloch, *Beiträge zur Aetiologie der Psychopathia Sexualis* (Dresden 1902), i. 159.
[7] H. H. Ellis, *op. cit.,* iv. 208.
[8] *Ibid., loc. cit.,* quoting Kistemaecker.
[9] H. H. Ellis, *loc. cit.,* iv. 209.

The assumption of sexual dress at maturity raises the question of the original meaning of special coverings for the primary sexual characters. Their probable origin in an impulse towards protection against the natural environment has been suggested. When dress becomes more than a mere appendage and produces the reaction of an affirmation of personality, its meaning inevitably becomes richer. The decorative impulse and sexual allurement take their place in the complex. But the chief and the distinctively social factor is always that of affirming by a secondary and artificial integument the particular physiological stage which society transforms into a human grade of communal life. This is well illustrated by such facts as the frequent absence of the skirt, for example, until marriage, and, more significantly, until pregnancy or motherhood. In other cases, as in the frequent confinement of sexual covering to the mammary region, the principle is still logically followed. Thus, among many negro peoples, as the natives of Loango, women cover the breasts especially.[10] Nāga women cover the breasts only. They say it is absurd to cover those parts of the body which every one has been able to see from their birth, but that it is different with the breasts, which appear later.

The evolution of sexual dress involves some side issues of thought and custom which are not without significance.

The harmony between the ideas of sexual dress and its temporary disuse for natural functions is brought out in many customs and aspects of thought. The following is an instance. The Mekeo tribes of New Guinea have folktales of which the motive is that a man surprising a girl without her petticoat has the right to marry her. After any marriage it is still the custom for the husband to fasten ceremonially the bride's petticoat.[11] The ceremonial loosing of the virgin zone embodies similar ideas.

Savage folklore is full of stories connected with disparity of sexual dress. Difference of custom in different peoples leads to comment when coincidences occur. The Dinka call the Bongo, Mittoo, and Niam-Niam "women" because the men wear an apron, while the women wear no clothes whatever, getting, however, daily a supple bough for a girdle.[12] Sexual disparity, natural and artificial, has often led to speculation. Repudiating the sexual element, Clement of Alexandria argued that, the object of dress being merely to cover the body and protect it from cold, there is

[10] Pechuel-Loesche, "Indiscretes aus Loango," *Zeitschrift für Ethnologie* (1878), x. 27.
[11] C. G. Seligmann, *The Melanesians of British New Guinea* (Cambridge 1910), p. 363.
[12] G. Schweinfurth, *The Heart of Africa* (1878), i. 152.

no reason why men's dress should differ from women's.[13] The Nāgas of Manipur say that originally men and women wore identical clothes. The first human beings were seven men and seven women. "By way of making a distinction the man made his hair into a knot or horn in front; the woman behind. The woman also lengthened her waist-cloth, while the man shortened his." As a fact the *dhoti,* loincloth, is still the same for both sexes, though worn in different ways.[14] The waist-cloth differentiates in evolution very simply into either *dhoti* or skirt, both being fastened in the same way, and differing only in length.[15] It is probably a similar accident of national fashion that makes the "longevity garment" of the Chinese identical for both sexes.[16]

✽ Adolescent Orientations to Clothing

ARTHUR M. VENER AND CHARLES R. HOFFER

One of the characteristic elements of social life is the existence of numerous symbols or "signs" which serve to distinguish the social positions of individuals in a community. One of these "signs," clothing, is of crucial importance.

It provides the basis for the initial appraisal of a person's social standing, especially when the appraiser is not acquainted with the individual. It permits the stranger to determine the wearer's social position almost immediately, and thus facilitates communication with him. Also, it has been demonstrated experimentally, in recent years, that type of clothing plays an important part in shaping the nature of personal relationships.[1]

Research on the social aspects of clothing is not new. The Department of Sociology and Anthropology of Michigan State University has sponsored research pertaining to the social aspects of clothing in the Agricultural Experiment Station since 1950. This research provided substantial

[13] Clement of Alexandria, *Pædagogus,* ii. 11.
[14] T. C. Hodson, *op. cit.,* p. 15.
[15] *Ibid.,* p. 27.
[16] J. J. M. de Groot, *The Religious System of China* (Leyden 1892, etc.), i. 63.

[1] T. F. Hoult (June 1954), "Experimental measurement of clothing as a factor in some social ratings of selected American men," *American Sociological Review,* Vol. xix, pp. 324–328. Source: *Adolescent Orientations to Clothing,* Michigan State University Agricultural Experiment Station Technical Bulletin No. 270 (1959), pp. 3–4, 6–7, 26–28. Reprinted by permission of the authors and publisher.

proof that attitudes toward clothing constituted a significant element in social life.

The findings demonstrate that such factors as social class, sex, occupation, etc., are related to an individual's attitudes toward clothing and the use of it in his daily activities.[2,3] The previous research, however, dealt with adult married persons only. None of the studies pertained to the clothing behavior of adolescents.

Clothing behavior of adolescents nevertheless is often a source of much misgiving and puzzlement to parents. The actions of their children, in this respect, sometimes seem inconsistent, if not unreasonable. Yet it is an accepted principle in Social Science that human behavior of either adults or adolescents is rarely random and purposeless in nature. Rather, it is usually related to certain social and psychological influences which affect the behavior of the individual. Clothing behavior, i.e., the wearing of different kinds of clothing and orientation toward them, is subject to these same influences.

The general purpose of the research reported . . . is to study the attitudes of adolescents in relation to the selection and use of clothing. The research was designed to accomplish the following general goals:

1. To compare the degree of clothing awareness among a sample of adolescent boys and girls according to different social characteristics.
2. To ascertain the judgment of adolescents in different social categories with reference to how well they believe they are dressed.
3. To determine whom the adolescent considers important in evaluating the adequacy of his clothing behavior.

Three types of orientations to clothing manifested by adolescents were analyzed. In this study these included (1) clothing awareness—degree of "sensitivity" to clothing in social life, (2) clothing deprivation—an individual's judgment as to how well he is dressed, and (3) clothing influentials—persons who influence adolescent clothing behavior.

Variation in degree of clothing awareness was examined in terms of differences in (a) sex, (b) age-grade, (c) social class status and

[2] G. P. Stone and W. H. Form (March 1955), "Clothing inventories and preferences among rural and urban families," Mich. State Col. Agr. Expt. Sta. Tech. Bul. 246; (1957), "The local community clothing market: A study of the social and social psychological contexts of shopping," Mich. State Univ. Agr. Expt. Sta. Tech. Bul. 262.
[3] W. H. Form and G. P. Stone (June 1955), "The social significance of clothing in occupational life," Mich. State Col. Agr. Expt. Sta. Tech. Bul. No. 247.

related variables, and (d) conceptions of self. Some of these variables were used to explain differences in sentiments of clothing deprivation. Specific hypotheses were proposed involving these variables.

The limited data available related to clothing influentials did not permit the formulation of a specific, logically deduced, set of relationships. The focus here was centered around the problem: Do differences in age-grade, sex, and social class of adolescents affect the choice of persons they consider most important in evaluating their selection of clothing?

. . . .

A pre-test questionnaire was developed on the basis of information gathered from: (1) informal interviews, (2) direct observation of extra-curricular school activities, (3) compositions written on various themes, and (4) insights gained from other closely related substantive studies, especially those of Vener,[4] Silverman,[5] Ryan,[6] and Hurlock.[7]

Some of the themes participants were asked to write about were: "If you could dress like anyone you please, whom would you choose and why?" "What have been some of your most pleasant and unpleasant experiences with clothing?" "What has been your most embarrassing experience?"

The pre-test schedule was administered to approximately 200 10th and 12th grade boys and girls in the Flint school system. As a result of the pre-test, several of the items were revised, the wording of others was changed, and many of the items were re-arranged as they finally appeared in the schedule.

Several precautionary steps were taken in order to avoid potential bias in attitudes toward the questionnaire itself, or its specific content, which might have been transferred by classroom teachers and students. First, all classes in the selected sample of a specific school were given the question-

---

[4] A. M. Vener (June 1953), "Stratification aspects of clothing importance," unpublished Master's thesis, Dept. of Sociology and Anthropology, Mich. State Col.

[5] S. S. Silverman (1945), *Clothing and appearance: Their psychological implications for teen-age girls,* New York: Bureau of Publications, Teachers College, Columbia Univ.

[6] M. S. Ryan (Sept. 1952), Psychological effects of clothing, Part I, "Survey of the opinions of college girls," Cornell Univ. Agr. Expt. Sta. Bul. 882 (July 1953); Psychological effects of clothing, Part II, "Comparison of college students with urban students, boys with girls," Cornell Univ. Agr. Expt. Sta. Bul. 898 (August 1953); Psychological effects of clothing, Part III, "Report of interviews with a selected sample of college women," Cornell Univ. Agr. Expt. Sta. Bul. 900.

[7] E. B. Hurlock (1929), "Motivation in fashion," *Archives of Psychology,* No. 111; *Adolescent Development* (1955), New York: McGraw-Hill Book Co., Second Edition.

naire at precisely the same time. And secondly, no staff member of any of the schools was involved in its administration.

A total of 782 12th, 10th, and 8th grade boys and girls in the Lansing school system filled out the questionnaire. For the purposes of this investigation, an over-all representation of the student population was not necessary. The aim was to obtain an adequate number of representatives of certain groups in order that statistical comparison might be made. Specifically, in the selection of the sample, the goal was to obtain adequate representation by grade and sex. Table 1, below, shows the distribution of the sample population by these two groups.

Table 1 Distribution of the sample population by grade and sex

Grade	Boys	Girls	Totals
12th	105	120	225
10th	147	149	296
8th	138	123	261
Totals	390	392	782

All but one of the schools in the Lansing system were sampled.[8] The questionnaire was answered by selected home room sections. It was established that the principal criterion for assigning students to home room sections was that of alphabetical order. Therefore, sections were selected in each school which contained students whose surnames fell within the entire alphabetical range. All decisions as to which home room sections were to be included in the sample were made entirely by one of the writers.

. . . .

Findings which are statistically significant concerning areas of clothing awareness and of clothing deprivation are briefly summarized as follows:

1. Girls demonstrate greater clothing awareness than boys.
2. Girls who participate more in organizational activity, i.e., belong to more organizations and hold some official position in these organizations, tend to demonstrate greater clothing awareness.

[8] This school was recently consolidated into the Lansing school system and was in the process of reorganization. Hence it was decided that data from its pupils might not be typical or representative.

3. Girls who are more socially confident tend to be less aware of clothing.
4. Boys and girls who are more other-directed tend to be more aware of clothing. For girls only the statistical significance of the association and degree of association of these variables is much greater.
5. Boys and girls in higher grades tend to express sentiments of high clothing deprivation less frequently than those in the lower grades.
6. Boys and girls whose fathers are in occupations of higher status tend to express sentiments of high clothing deprivation less frequently than those whose fathers are in occupations of lower status.
7. Boys and girls who participate more in organizational activity tend to express sentiments of high clothing deprivation less frequently than those who are low participators.
8. Boys and girls who demonstrate more social confidence tend to express sentiments of high clothing deprivation less frequently than those who are not as socially confident.
9. Boys who are more aware of clothing tend to express sentiments of high clothing deprivation less frequently than those who are not as aware of clothing.

The relationship of grade, social class membership, and differences in sex with the relative tendency to refer to two highly important persons, "mother" and peers, in clothing selection decisions was also investigated. The statistically significant findings were:

1. Boys and girls in the lower grades tend to refer to "mother" more frequently than do those in the higher grades.
2. Girls tend to refer to "mother" more frequently than do boys.
3. Girls in the lower grades tend to refer to their peers more frequently than do girls in the higher grades.

Since no group differences were observed among 8th, 10th, and 12th grade students in respect to clothing awareness, it seems evident that by early adolescence the individual has already been made conscious of the importance of clothing in social life. As already stated, if a valid instrument which measured clothing awareness could be developed to include individuals of younger, pre-adolescent, age-grade status, it would be of some value to learn at what point differences in clothing awareness begin to occur. It is likely that the age-grade which represents a significant increase in the relative degree of awareness of clothing also represents a stage where a qualitatively higher level of social maturation has been reached.

No relationship between clothing awareness and the social class variables was found. As a possible explanation of this lack of relationship, it was suggested that youth culture may not be oriented toward the value of clothing in the same manner as that of the broader, community culture. Participation in the youth subculture may obviate some of the influences that social class status might have on clothing awareness.

The negative relationship of clothing deprivation with clothing awareness and age-grade status (i.e., the higher the feeling of clothing deprivation, the less the clothing awareness and the lower the age-grade), was an interesting finding. This could be viewed as an adjustive, integrative mechanism for the person involved. The hypothetical example of this type of individual was given. He is a lower class individual who expresses sentiments of high clothing deprivation and who does not possess the requisite purchasing power to acquire sufficient clothing to ease this feeling of deprivation. Such a situation would become intolerable if this feeling were intensified by an increasing sensitivity to clothing. Extreme frustration and possible disorganization of the personality might well be the result of too wide a discrepancy between what the person has and what he desires.

In respect to . . . clothing influentials, it was found that an adolescent's mother and his peers were highly important persons in decisions dealing with dress selection, while his father was of relatively little importance. Also, older brothers and sisters prove to be significant persons for those adolescents who had older siblings in their family.

Youths most frequently choose their peers as the type of person they aspire to emulate in their pattern of dress. Mass-media—Hollywood, television, and sports celebrities also have some impact upon adolescent dress behavior. However, it was concluded that those persons with whom an adolescent interacts on a personal, intimate basis, exert relatively greater influence upon his clothing behavior than those with whom his interaction is of an impersonal, more formal nature.

And finally, it was observed that 12th graders as a group tended to refer less frequently to specific other persons in their responses to the clothing referral items than did the individuals in the lower grades. It was therefore suggested that by the time the youth reaches the 12th grade, approved rules related to dress behavior have become habitual.

The Family

❀ Clothing and the American Family

MARY ELLEN ROACH

Since life for the individual ordinarily begins within the family and since he is in very close contact with this family during his formative and most receptive years, the family exists as a major agent of socialization. It is within the social setting of this primary group that the world begins to take on meanings that are likely to have lasting influence on the individual. With family members a main source of reference during his early years, a child's interpretations of the social situation will reflect those of the family group, particularly those of family figures whose positions are enhanced by age, size, or recognized authority. Parents necessarily stand as figures of greatest influence; but other family members, especially older ones, are also sources of reference.

Socialization within the family serves not only as a means of increasing solidarity within the family group but also within the larger society. In other words, since the family is a subdivision of a larger society, its system of values, norms, and sentiments will include those of the larger group, and it will act as a socializing agent for that larger group. Therefore, if the behavior of parents is patterned according to a dimension of the greater society like social class, it is anticipated that their children's activities and attitudes will be likewise patterned. Mead describes the manner in which the individual acquires the attitude of the whole community, that is, the generalized other, in this way:

If the given human individual is to develop a self in the fullest sense, it is not sufficient for him merely to take the attitudes of other human individuals

Source: Adapted from "The Influence of Social Class on Clothing Practices and Orientation at Early Adolescence: A Study of Clothing-Related Behavior of Seventh Grade Girls," unpublished Ph.D. dissertation, Michigan State University, (1960).

toward himself and toward one another within the human social process, and to bring that social process as a whole into his individual experience merely in these terms: he must also, in the same way that he takes the attitudes of other individuals toward himself and toward one another, take their attitudes toward the various phases or aspects of the common social activity or set of social undertakings in which, as members of an organized society or social group, they are all engaged.[1]

Of courses there are differences in the degree to which a family persuades the individual to conform to the ways of the general society. Sometimes nonconformity itself may be a value, and the individual in some families will be taught "to think more for himself" or "to be creative." In other cases, particularly among somewhat isolated subgroupings such as ethnic groups, perceptions of the world may be at odds with those of the general culture and socialization for general cultural values will be rejected for more acceptable subgroup values.

Although the family is widely recognized as a strong social influence on the individual, a number of factors may modify the socializing effects of the family. In the first place the fact that each individual is a unique organization of capacities rules out any complete uniformity in conditioning of individuals within the family group. Moreover, as a child grows and begins to be part of interactional situations outside the home, he comes into contact with an increasing number of influences. School mates, members of play groups, teachers, or other adults may act as socializing agents and may exert varying amounts of influence.

In addition, in American society an individual may find on achieving a certain age that group expectations for him have changed and that he must redefine his roles in order to maintain social acceptance. These new definitions may even mean shifts in loyalty and the redefining of roles in the light of norms of a new reference group. Such an age is adolescence. At this time group expectations change, behavior once sanctioned or rewarded is no longer appropriate, and new behavior patterns must be learned and internalized. It has frequently been assumed that the trend in America is for these new patterns to be acquired less within the family group and more within peer groups. If this assumption is accurate, quite discernible shifts in reference groups may be evident among individuals who are at the threshold of adolescence. Certain data from research re-

[1] G. H. Mead, *Mind, Self, and Society*, C. W. Morris (ed.), Chicago: The University of Chicago Press (1934), pp. 154-155.

ported by Bowerman and Kinch indicate that this is true.[2] They found for girls in grades four to ten that the greatest shift from family to peer orientation took place between the sixth and seventh grades. By the eighth grade there were more peer-oriented than family-oriented children in the sample they studied.

Further examination of their findings reveals, however, that a lowered orientation to family was not an inevitable change that took place in all adolescents. Instead it occurred only under certain circumstances, in this case when there was poor adjustment by a child to family members. In addition, their research suggested, although it did not explicitly make the point, that orientation to families or peers is not merely an either/or proposition but actually involves a rather complex system of identification whereby certain segments of behavior may be referred to one group and other segments to another. When commenting on the nature of this dual identification with peer and family groups by adolescents, another researcher, Rosen, emphasized that "significant others are not necessarily referents for all areas of the individual's behavior." [3]

Empirical studies concerning clothing cast light on the nature of the process by which various agents of socialization encourage the development of patterns of behavior structured along social-class lines. In the first place, certain studies substantiate that individuals are actually sensitive to the status symbolism of clothing. For example, Form and Stone,[4] Hoult,[5] and Douty,[6] in their separate studies, have shown that clothing is a criterion or symbol employed by individuals in assessing the status of others, particularly when the status determination being made is for anonymous others.

Further studies, concerned with clothing behavior of individuals at different age levels, suggest that the socialization effect of the family of

[2] C. E. Bowerman and J. W. Kinch, "Changes in Family and Peer Orientation of Children Between the Fourth and Tenth Grades," *Social Forces*, Vol. 36 (March, 1959), pp. 206–211.
[3] B. C. Rosen, "The Reference Group Approach to the Parental Factor in Attitude and Behavior Formation," *Social Forces*, Vol. 34 (December, 1955), pp. 139–140.
[4] W. H. Form and G. P. Stone, "Urbanism, Anonymity, and Status Symbolism," *American Journal of Sociology*, Vol. 62 (March, 1957), pp. 504–514.
[5] T. F. Hoult, "Experimental Measurement of Clothing as a Factor in Some Social Ratings of Selected American Men," *American Sociological Review*, Vol. 19 (June, 1954), pp. 324–328.
[6] H. I. Douty, "Influence of Clothing on Perception of Persons," *Journal of Home Economics*, Vol. 55 (March, 1963), pp. 197–202.

orientation may not be equally apparent in all stages of the life cycle. For adults,[7] significant relationships have been shown between social-class position and certain attitudes and practices associated with clothing. Similar patterning has been indicated for girls in middle childhood or preadolescent years. For adolescents, however, such consistency in socialization patterns has not been apparent. In studying certain behavioral patterns of seventh, eighth, and ninth grade girls, Deno [8] did find relationships between a very limited number of clothing practices and social class. On the other hand, Silverman's early study,[9] which touched briefly on the relationships between adolescent clothing behavior and social-class variables, failed to reveal associations between social-class level and the clothing behavior of girls of approximately the same age. In the area of attitudes, Vener's research [10] showed for adolescents of high school age that feelings of deprivation related to clothing were associated with social class while expressions of clothing awareness were not. Findings by Roach [11] also supported the position that social class is not always a highly relevant variable in the socialization of the adolescent for patterns of clothing behavior. Thus, although clothing behavior of adults and young children may be patterned along social-class lines, adolescent clothing behavior appears to be more variable, the implication being that reference for clothing behavior may be shifted from the family to the peer group at this age.

[7] W. H. Form and G. P. Stone, *The Social Significance of Clothing in Occupational Life,* Mich. State Univ. Agr. Expt. Sta. Tech. Bul. No. 247 (June, 1955); C. Gray, "Orientations to Fashion," unpublished master's thesis, Michigan State College (1953); M. L. Rosencranz, "Clothing Symbolism" *Journal of Home Economics,* Vol. 54 (January, 1962), pp. 18–22; M. L. Rosencranz, "A Study of Interest in Clothing among Selected Groups of Married and Unmarried Young Women," unpublished master's thesis, Michigan State College (1948); G. P. Stone and W. H. Form, *Clothing Inventories and Preferences Among Rural and Urban Families,* Mich. State Univ. Agr. Exp. Sta. Tech. Bul. No. 246 (March, 1955); G. P. Stone and W. H. Form, *The Local Community Market: A Study of the Social Psychological Contexts of Shopping,* Mich. State Univ. Agr. Expt. Sta. Tech. Bul. No. 262 (November, 1957); A. M. Vener, "Stratification Aspects of Clothing Importance," unpublished master's thesis, Michigan State College (1953).

[8] E. D. Deno, "Changes in the Home Activities of Junior High School Girls over a Twenty-Seven Year Period," unpublished Ph.D. dissertation, University of Minnesota (1958).

[9] S. S. Silverman, *Clothing and Appearance: Their Psychological Implications for Teen-Age Girls,* New York: Teachers College, Columbia University (1945).

[10] A. M. Vener, "Adolescent Orientations to Clothing: A Social-Psychological Interpretation," unpublished Ph.D. dissertation, Michigan State University (1957).

[11] M. E. Roach, "The Influence of Social Class on Clothing Practices and Orientation at Early Adolescence: A Study of Clothing-Related Behavior of Seventh Grade Girls," unpublished Ph.D. dissertation, Michigan State University (1960).

Although there is a suggestion that strong identification with peer groups may occur among adolescents, there is no indication that strong shifts away from the family of reference are inevitable. One reason for this may be that identification with peer groups may, on the one hand, imply blurring of social-class patterns of behavior; on the other hand, it may simply mean reinforcement of class patterns since clique mates are quite likely to share the same social class. Finally it is possible that differential socialization within various reference groups may result in certain aspects of the behavior of adolescents being patterned according to the social-class orientation of their families while other aspects may be more in harmony with peer-group norms. Speaking to the latter point, Newcomb asserts that actual membership groups may serve as both positive and negative reference groups for the same person. He uses the adolescent to illustrate his view in this way:

An American adolescent, for example, may share most of his family's common attitudes and may want his family to treat him as one who belongs and shares those attitudes. In such respects the family serves as positive reference group for him. But he may repudiate some of their common attitudes—toward church attendance, for example, or tobacco. With respect to these common objects his family serves as a negative reference group for him.[12]

Most commonly, Newcomb makes clear, negative reference implies positive reference to some other group, in the case of adolescents usually to peers.[13] Therefore, if the adolescent refers negatively to family norms for clothing, the group to which he may refer for this segment of his behavior may be his peers.

❀ Family Cycle

MILDRED TATE AND ORIS GLISSON

As the life of the individual is a cycle of growth, development, maturation, and decline, so too is the life of the family.[1] Clothing expenditures

[12] T. M. Newcomb, *Social Psychology*, New York: Dryden Press (1950), p. 227.
[13] *Ibid*.

[1] Myrtle B. McGraw, *Growth, A Study of Johnny and Jimmy*, D. Appleton–Century Co., New York, 1935, p. 4.
Source: *Family Clothing*, New York: John Wiley and Sons, (1961), pp. 16–19. Reprinted by permission of the publisher.

are unavoidably linked to these family cycles, each cycle having its characteristic pattern of clothing wants and needs. These family stages or cycles may be referred to as: (1) the beginning family, (2) the expanding family, (3) the contracting family, and (4) the family of later years.

The Beginning Family

The beginning family is launched when a young couple marries. It includes the childbearing phases of family life—pregnancies, infant and child care, and the preschool years. This period usually lasts from 7 to 10 years. The average couple will be relatively young when it leaves this stage, for the average mother today has her last child by the time she is 27 years of age.[2]

The first year or two of the beginning family is usually a childless period, with family expenses at their lowest. A small apartment will accommodate the couple; there are only two individuals to feed; and the chances are that the young man and woman brought clothing into the marriage sufficient, with limited additions, to carry them through the first years. At this time emphasis is usually placed upon the care of clothing already owned and routine replacements. Many couples find that these years are good for saving money to invest for later spending, or to buy durable goods or perhaps a home.

However, the family ship of fortune does not always sail a smooth and placid sea. It is not uncommon for the family to be launched while one or both are still in school. Thus the couple may end the first few years of marriage in debt, rather than with savings for emergencies or capital goods. Individuals entering into marriage bring attitudes, impressions, and expectations created throughout years of separate existence in a money-conscious world. Thus money and its use may have very different meanings to each party. Habits of spending and values associated with this spending may be far apart. A couple may find it difficult to move from individual plans of spending to a family plan.

The major increase in expenses from year to year for the beginning family will be in medical and hospital bills, food and clothing for the children, and additional household services. During this period the clothing expenditures of the father usually are low; however, those for the

[2] National Manpower Council, *Womanpower*, Columbia University Press, New York, 1957, pp. 10, 69, 169.

mother are of some importance. A pregnancy requires a special wardrobe. At the end of the pregnancy, many of the articles of clothing worn by the pregnant mother are no longer useful and must be replaced. Many of the articles of clothing worn by the young mother before the pregnancy are either out of style or too small after the childbearing period. Children added to the family bring about a pressure on housing space. Larger and more expensive living quarters are necessary and add to the cost of living. The beginning family stage has been labeled by Bossard and Boll [3] as the "budding stage," which they describe as follows:

Diapers and sterilizers, play pens and sitters, and assorted noises from seven to seven. The washing never stops. Privacy you've heard about but all day long the door of your room opens, the back door closes, the kitchen door opens. But the closet doors never quite close—bulging as the closets are with doll carriages and baseball bats, snowsuits and overshoes, soccer balls and skates. Before long, the sandlot pitcher becomes a menace to every fabric or painted surface he comes within two feet of. These are the years when mother answers to rotating calls for bottle washer, nurse, chief cook, policeman, referee, story teller, chauffeur. And father—well, father is a lucky man if *his* father remembered to tell him that this too shall pass, more quickly than he thinks.

The Expanding Family

The family moves into the expanding stage as the older children enter elementary school. These are the children's growing-up years. Current family expenses continue to increase from year to year, and at a more rapid rate than formerly. Food costs increase because there are more mouths to feed, and each mouth consumes more food. Clothing costs take an increasing share of the income. The older the child, the more expensive his clothes become. By this time, mother and father are in dire need of new clothes themselves, the cost of which must be added to that of the increasing needs for the school-age children. Expenses for school increasingly take their toll as the children get older.

Clothing expenditures rise fairly steadily as family size increases.[4] Not

---

[3] James H. S. Bossard and Eleanor Stoker Boll, "3 Wonderful Stages of Family Life," *House and Garden*, March 1959, pp. 66–67, 110.
[4] University of Pennsylvania, *Study of Consumer Expenditures, Income and Savings,* 1950, Wharton School of Business, Philadelphia, 1957; Vol. VI, *Summary of Family*

only does the expanding family of moderate or above average means tend to pay more for clothing, but it spends an increasingly larger proportion of the family income on this item. This does not mean, however, that there is increased spending for all family members. In every income group, clothing inventories and purchases for the parents decrease as the family gets bigger and its members grow older.

As expenses for food, clothing, and education gradually move up, pressures are put on the parents for a higher level of living to meet the standards of peer groups, both their own and those of their children. These pressures may be for bigger and better living quarters, more up-to-date house furnishings, a newer, or a second automobile, and more expensive recreation. By the time the children are in the latter years of high school, expenses for food, clothing, education, and entertainment have reached an all-time high. The family may receive some assistance from children's earnings in after-school and vacation work. However, most high school boys and girls use the money they earn to buy goods and services which they are unable to get from the family.

If the family's standard of living calls for a college education for the children, the next few years will entail even greater expenditures. Educational expenditures will probably be the largest item in the family budget. When children are in college, usually more money is spent on each of the children than on the mother and father combined.

The Contracting Family

After the children are grown, the average family reaches a plateau where parents enjoy a respite from the care and cost of child rearing and have the opportunity to make provisions for their retirement. This phase of family life has been referred to as the "recovery stage."[5] The only big expense that the average family may have for children during this period is in connection with marrying off of its daughters.

In the contracting family, parents usually increase their clothing expenditures. This change results from several factors. Oftentimes, the parents'

Expenditures for Clothing for Women and Girls, and Children under Two, p. 161; Vol. VII, *Summary of Family Expenditures for Clothing for Men and Boys, Clothing Materials and Clothing Services*, p. 160.

[5] Howard Becker and Reuben Hill, editors, *Marriage and the Family*, D. C. Heath and Co., Boston, 1942; "Money and Marriage," by Howard F. Bigelow, p. 385.

wardrobes have become threadbare or out of style during the years when children were finishing up high school and college. Complete replacement may be necessary. After the children leave home, parents have more freedom to travel, which increases the need for new clothing. Also, the mother and father frequently take a new interest in clothing, and it is amazing how their appearance improves. Although parents spend more on their own clothing during these years, the added expenditure for themselves does not equal the decrease in cost of living resulting from getting the children off of the family expense account.

The Family of Later Years

By the later years, most individuals have accumulated a standard wardrobe, and clothes are replaced only as they are worn out or the owner becomes tired of them. Since most elderly couples are retired or are approaching retirement, current expenses are relatively low and are scaled to what the reduced family income will permit. Food needs decrease, and the wear and tear on clothing is slight. Housing costs also decline. The family home may be paid for, leaving only the cost of upkeep. A small apartment may be more desirable than the larger house which was necessary when the children were at home.

The length of each of these stages in the typical cycle and the extent to which there is overlapping vary from family to family. These factors depend upon the age of the parents at the time of marriage, the time of the arrival of the first child, the number and spacing of children, and the amount and type of education provided for them.

Economy

❀ Clothing of Nigerian Cocoa Farmers' Families
R. GALLETTI, K. D. S. BALDWIN, AND I. O. DINA

Styles of Clothing

The Yoruba people attaches considerable importance to dress, and it is socially necessary for both men and women to be well attired not only on ceremonial occasions but also in much of their everyday life. For farm work and work in the home and village clothing may be reduced to a minimum and of the coarsest quality. But when the farmer and his wife are not working they lean to ample and elaborate costumes. These are predominantly of traditional patterns, suggesting influences from the parts of Africa farther north. European styles are not much favoured in the villages, except for men's working clothes.

There are various styles of clothing for men, some of which are connected with particular offices or dignities. The *buba*, a short tunic with wide sleeves, the *suliya*, which is wider and longer, and the *kaftani*, a long narrow gown, are worn with trousers (*sokoto*) and are usually made of imported cotton cloth, plain or printed: plush, velvet, artificial silk, and worsted materials may also be used. These garments are worn by all, whatever their age and status. So is the *danshiki*, which is a short sleeveless gown, usually made of locally woven cotton or the heavier imported textiles. The *agbada*, which is also made of locally woven cotton or a good class of imported cloth, is worn by elderly persons and the well to do: it is usually handsewn and carefully embroidered and when the material is rich and the workmanship of the highest class, as they are in the traditional robes of chiefs, the garments can be exceedingly handsome.

Source: Nigerian Cocoa Farmers, Oxford: Oxford University Press (1956), pp. 246–252. Reprinted by permission of the publisher.

The simplest *buba* and *sokoto* cost from 30s. upwards and the more elaborate robes from £10 to £25 according to the materials and embroidery. To be correctly dressed a man must also wear headgear, perhaps a cap of the same material as the dress, perhaps a fez or embroidered cap. Beaded caps are the insignia of *Obas*.

Styles for women are much the same for all ages and ranks. The usual attire is a wrapper (*iro*) worn with a blouse (*buba*), a cloth worn either around the waist or around the shoulders (*iborun*), and a headtie (*gele* or *oja*). The blouse is always made of imported cloth: the other garments may be of locally woven cloth or of imported cotton, artificial silk, or velveteen. The *gele* is ordinarily of the cloth called 'madras' after the celebrated 'Madras handkerchief,' characterized by bright colours and gay patterns.[1] The *oja* is usually of the same cloth as the wrapper, which is dyed in the fast native indigo dye with the traditional bold patterns in white. Abeokuta women are experts in this kind of dyeing and use imported white shirting material to dye wrappers not only for the greater part of the Western Region but also for the Yorubas resident in the Gold Coast.

Underwear is not always worn but men often use singlets and women chemises.

Value of Clothing

It has been estimated that of 150 million square yards of cotton textiles imported into Nigeria in 1950/1 59 million square yards valued at about £4.79 million were sold in the Western Region.[2] As the cocoa-producing areas are the wealthiest part of the Western Region it can be presumed that the average purchases per head in those areas exceeded by a fair margin the 9.3 square yards per head computed for the region as a whole. The value of the family wardrobe for many families exceeds the value of the family house and in all the areas in which the survey was conducted both the numbers of the garments and the estimated value were high

---

[1] In recent years much of the cloth used has been rayon and imported from Japan. Rayon headties are favoured by young girls.
[2] Prest and Stewart, *National Income of Nigeria*, 1950/1.

enough to suggest a fairly high expenditure over a considerable period. The male wardrobe was the larger part in every area except Ondo, though there are more women and girls per family.

Table 1 Total value of clothing in 776 families

Area	Male clothing	Female clothing	Total
	(a) Value per family (£)		
Abeokuta	81.0	56.4	137.4
Ibadan and Ijebu	86.9	68.1	155.0
Ife-Ilesha	84.4	66.3	150.7
Ondo	77.7	81.3	159.0
All areas	83.8	66.9	150.7
	(b) Percentage of total value		
Abeokuta	59.0	41.0	100
Ibadan and Ijebu	56.1	43.9	100
Ife-Ilesha	56.0	44.0	100
Ondo	48.8	51.2	100
All areas	55.6	44.4	100

Considering the difficulties of obtaining a complete statement of its wardrobe from each family and of making correct estimates of the value of old clothing, the uniformity of these results is rather striking. The figures cover 776 families in nineteen localities, about one in every two hundred cocoa-farming families, and the general average is probably a very reasonable approximation to the value of the average wardrobe. The distribution between families has not been worked out separately for clothing but the figures for the value of all durable goods (of which clothing accounts for 80 per cent) suggest that the distribution is unequal but less so than that of land. Though clothes afford an opportunity for the display of wealth and conspicuous expenditure, the Yoruba tradition of dress forces on even the poorer families a substantial expenditure on cloth and garments, so that the difference in income between the affluent and the struggling families is not fully reflected in their wardrobes.

The following tables summarize the information for the males and females in the 776 selected families.

Table 2   Clothing of males in 776 families

Article	Value per article	Value per male	Value per family	Number per male	Number per family
	(shillings)	(£)	(£)		
European style					
Coats	24.1	0.40	1.48	0.33	1.23
Trousers	18.5	0.62	2.29	0.67	2.48
Shirts	10.2	0.57	2.09	1.12	4.12
Underwear	4.9	0.24	0.89	0.98	3.63
Shorts	9.5	0.78	2.88	1.65	6.07
Shoes and sandals	17.6	0.48	1.77	0.54	2.00
African style					
Buba	14.0	1.89	6.96	2.69	9.91
Danshiki	17.5	1.31	4.83	1.50	5.52
Suliya	27.0	1.81	6.70	1.34	4.95
Kaftani	43.4	1.36	5.04	0.63	2.32
Agbada	75.8	5.79	21.37	1.53	5.64
Sokoto	18.7	3.52	13.00	3.77	13.93
Ibora and *iborun*	24.6	1.97	7.28	1.60	5.92
Fila	5.8	0.92	3.41	3.19	11.77
Bata	8.1	0.47	1.74	1.17	4.31
Other	—	0.55	2.04	—	—
Total value	—	22.68	83.77	—	—

The most numerous garments are the *sokoto, buba,* and headgear (*fila*), followed at some distance by shorts, used for work, and *agbada,* required for social occasions. In value the *agbada* and *sokoto* dominate, followed at a long interval by the cloths used for sleeping (*ibora* and *iborun*) and the *buba* and *suliya.* There are enough *bata* (African style slippers) to outfit all males with some kind of footgear, but English style shoes are much less common. The expensive items of the wardrobe are the long robes, but coats and trousers also require an outlay not inconsiderable in comparison with the family income.

The most numerous articles of women's apparel are the cloths, the *buba* or African style blouse, and the headties. Chemises are also possessed by a large proportion of the women. On the other hand shoes and slippers of any kind are rare. Most women go barefoot not only at home but also to market and their social occasions. The wrapper cloths predominate in value and the value of the headties is notable. The *iborun* is not ordinarily worn by young girls though it is needed for full dress occasions.

Table 3   Clothing of females in 776 families

Article	Value per article	Value per female	Value per family	Number per female	Number per family
	(shillings)	(£)	(£)		
European style					
Skirts	9.1	0.07	0.29	0.16	0.63
Blouses	12.9	0.16	0.64	0.25	1.00
Underwear	8.3	0.53	2.14	1.28	5.16
Frocks	10.6	0.28	1.13	0.53	2.14
Shoes and sandals	21.0	0.18	0.72	0.17	0.69
African style					
Buba	13.2	3.02	12.14	4.58	18.43
Iro and *Ibora*	24.5	7.03	28.28	5.75	23.12
Iborun	16.8	2.42	9.72	2.88	11.60
Fila and *Gele*	14.6	2.66	10.69	3.64	14.66
Bata	7.9	0.12	0.47	0.30	1.20
Other	—	0.18	0.72	—	—
Total value	—	16.65	66.94	—	—

Table 4   Value of clothing per person in different areas

	Abeokuta	Ibadan and Ijebu	Ife-Ilesha	Ondo	All areas
	\(a\) Value per person (£)				
Female clothing					
European style	2.07	0.80	1.11	1.37	1.22
African style	15.84	16.92	14.74	13.88	15.43
Total	17.91	17.72	15.85	15.25	16.65
Male clothing					
European style	4.59	2.57	2.22	4.04	3.09
African style	22.44	22.98	19.86	12.26	18.59
Total	27.03	25.55	22.08	16.30	22.68
	\(b\) Percentage of total value				
Female clothing					
European style	11.6	4.5	7.0	9.0	7.3
African style	88.4	95.5	93.0	91.0	92.7
Male clothing					
European style	17.0	8.4	10.1	24.8	12.7
African style	83.0	91.6	89.9	75.2	87.3

It is evident that for both men and women clothing of the foreign style is a minor part of the wardrobe. This is true for all areas, though in the Abeokuta province the influence of Lagos fashions seems to be shown in a higher proportion of foreign style clothing. To judge by the value of clothing per person the Abeokuta area is the dressiest and is followed by the Ibadan area. In the Ondo province wardrobes appear to be more largely composed of inexpensive local cloth.

In the Ondo area alone is the use of European style coats and trousers significantly above the general average and the use of Yoruba style robes by men significantly below it. In the Ondo and Abeokuta areas women have more European style frocks and underwear than in the central areas. The influence of adjoining provinces where less importance is attached to traditional styles may be felt in Ondo as the influence of Lagos is felt in Abeokuta. But we cannot explain a noticeable use of skirts and blouses in the Ife district.

Trends

Until the late 1920's or the early 1930's only literate Christian men and women or clerks in the cities wore European styles. Then these styles were widely adopted by literate people of every religion though older Muslims did not follow the fashion. Now a return to African styles is observable, which can be attributed mainly to a growth of nationalistic sentiment. To wear European styles is no longer a mark of advancement.

Some of the recent changes are due to increasing sophistication. In the 1920's women in the remote areas did not wear blouse or *buba,* but the spread of education and the influence of the people near the coast are causing it to be thought necessary to wear a *buba* out of doors even for ordinary occasions. The wearing of imported sandals is increasing, and fashionable wear, even for illiterate girls, includes the wrist watch!

In the choice of materials new tastes are spread not only by the importing firms, which study very carefully the appreciation of different patterns and qualities, but also by Yoruba textile dealers in Lagos, who prepare special designs to suit different ceremonial occasions and employ 'models' to set the standard. The increase of money incomes and real incomes in the post-war period has favoured the cultivation of new tastes.

The style of the traditional dress has not changed much, except that in the coastal areas the 'Gold Coast' style for women (*aganyin*) has found favour. But higher incomes have changed the pattern of purchases of imported textiles. Not only have more of them been bought but the more expensive kinds have been gaining ground: cotton prints and artificial silks have gained at the expense of the inferior unbleached, white, and coloured cotton piece goods. The proportion of rayon in the value of textile imports has risen from 8 per cent in 1938 to 14 per cent in 1950 and almost 28 per cent in 1952. Since the cocoa-producing areas have been the most prosperous, it is probable that most of the more expensive classes of textiles have been sold there. If the cocoa-producing areas continue to prosper, it is likely that the trend towards better fabrics will remain marked. The Yoruba styles lend themselves well to interpretation in rich and brilliant clothes, though in the past they were associated more with indigo-dyed hand-woven materials. Whether incomes are high or low there is little doubt that the Yorubas will spend more freely on their clothes than on any other needs after food and houses.

Factors Affecting Clothing Decisions
MILDRED TATE AND ORIS GLISSON

The clothing needs, desires, and demands of American families today are influenced by a multitude of circumstances. The American way of life has changed considerably from that of the days when clothing was either for dress or work, with somewhat worn-out representatives of each category serving as leisure clothing. Today's dress includes formal, semi-formal, informal, sport, casual, and work clothing. Within each category exists an ever-increasing number of designs and styles, all available in seemingly unlimited colors, textures, and fabrics.

Socio-Economic Factors Affecting Clothing

INCREASED INCOME

Increased personal and family income and the changed attitude about its use probably affect the family clothing picture today as much as any

Source: Family Clothing, New York: John Wiley and Sons (1961), pp. 10-16. Reprinted by permission of the publisher.

factors. There has been a startling growth of American middle-income and middle-rich classes during the last 30 years. Available statistics indicate that, on the average, the after-tax income of each American, when adjusted for price changes, is now two and a half times that income at the beginning of the twentieth century.[1,2] In 1929, fewer than 20 per cent of the families had annual incomes of $4,000 to $10,000. Now almost 50 per cent are in that range. Even if one adjusts for the change in the cost of living, there was an increase in the average real income of families of almost 47 per cent in 1955 over that in 1929.[3] This increase in family income is due in part to the increasing number of married women working outside the home.[4]

Research indicates that there is an important relationship between income and wardrobe content. As the income increases, the quantity of garments purchased usually increases, as well as the unit price paid for each item. The proportion of income spent on clothing changes very little, however. A study reported by the Institute of Home Economics in 1956[5] revealed that husbands in the income class of $4,000 to $5,999 buy 75 per cent more clothing a year than do the husbands of families with incomes of $2,000 to $3,999. The former also spend more than twice as much for their clothing. The quantity of garments for wives in the corresponding income groups does not increase as much as it does for the husbands, but the unit price paid for the wives' clothing increases at a higher rate. The inventories and purchases for children are less affected by income than are those for the adults.

Changing Status of Women

The importance of clothing in the family budget has been affected by women's employment. There are over 21 million women in paid employ-

[1] *Federal Reserve Bulletin Vol. 42,* No. 6, "1956 Survey of Consumer Finances," June 1956, pp. 559–569.
[2] United States Federal Reserve System, *Consumer Instalment Credit,* Part I, *Growth and Import,* Washington, D.C., 1957, p. 7.
[3] Frances Lomas Feldman, "A New Look at the Family and Its Money," *Journal of Home Economics,* Vol. 49, December 1957, p. 768.
[4] United States Department of Commerce, *Current Population Report,* U.S. Bureau of the Census, Series P-60, No. 27, Washington, D.C., April 1958, p. 7.
[5] Margaret L. Brew, Roxanne R. O'Leary, Lucille C. Dean, *Family Clothing-Inventories and Purchases,* Agricultural Information Bulletin No. 148, U.S. Department of Agriculture, Washington, D.C., April 1956, pp. 9, 21, 23.

ment in the United States today.[6] This number of employed women is more than a third of all women 14 years of age and over, and represents about one-third of the total labor force.[7] The number of women workers has increased very rapidly since 1940. Whereas the proportion of women in the labor force increased about 1½ per cent in the decade prior to 1940, since then the increase has been close to 5 per cent a decade. It is predicted that this rate of increase will continue for some years.

The type of women who work has also changed. Around 1900, 70 per cent of the working women were single, and 50 per cent were under 25 years of age. Today, one-half of the working women are married, and almost one-half are over 40. In addition, many of the married women who work have young children. Almost two out of every five mothers whose children are of school age are in the labor force.[8]

Today, at least nine out of every ten women work outside the home at some time during their lives, and they continue working for a much longer period of time than formerly. Around 1900, employed women continued working on the average of 11 years. Today's school girls may expect to spend 25 or more years in work outside the home during their lifetime.[9] Increasingly, they will remain in employment until they are 65 years of age.

One-fifth of the nation's income in the form of wages and salaries is earned by women. In 1955, this amounted to over 142 billion dollars. Families in which the wife goes out to work generally have higher incomes than those in which she does not work outside the home. In 1954, incomes of $5,000 or more were reported by 55 per cent of the unbroken families in which the wife worked, but by only 35 per cent of those in which the wife was unemployed.[10] The desire for higher incomes to meet mounting costs and increasing standards of consumption is undoubtedly an important factor in the rising employment of women.

Farm families seem to gain proportionately more than urban families

[6] United States Department of Commerce, *Current Population Report, Population Estimates,* Series P-25, No. 193, U.S. Bureau of the Census, Washington, D.C., February 11, 1959, p. 1.
[7] Roland R. Renne, "Womanpower and the American Economy," *Journal of Home Economics,* Vol. 49, February 1957, p. 83.
[8] National Manpower Council, *Womanpower,* Columbia University Press, New York, 1957, pp. 10, 69, 169.
[9] *Ibid.*
[10] United States Department of Commerce, *Current Population Report,* U.S. Bureau of the Census, Series P-60, *loc. cit.*

when the wife is employed. In 1954, farm families with women in the labor force had a median income 60 per cent larger than other farm families; urban families with wives employed had a median income 25 per cent larger than those in which the wife did not contribute.

Women's jobs are changing from unskilled and semiskilled manual work to clerical and sales employment, and increasingly greater numbers of women are employed in executive and managerial positions. Leaving the home to accept positions with more prestige value than manual labor affects the clothing needs and wants of women. These new positions require attractive, easily cared-for clothing, not only for the young girl but also for the middle-aged and older woman. Employed women spend more money for clothing than do unemployed women in all age and income classes. The level of income and education of the husband or head of the family appear to have little effect on the spending pattern of employed women. These factors are much more closely associated with the wife's income.[11]

The changing status of women in the United States is reflected as much in their educational advancement as in their increased employment. In 1890, only 4 per cent of all girls 17 years of age were being graduated from high school, whereas in 1956 better than 60 per cent were high school graduates. In fact, today more women than men complete high school.[12]

Similarly, the proportion of women in college has grown steadily during the last sixty years. Today, more than one-third of all bachelor and first professional degrees awarded are earned by women.[13] Within six months after graduation, 81 out of every 100 women college graduates will be at work. Even among the graduates already married or to be married in the immediate future—and one-third of today's girl graduates are in this category—about 70 per cent will be at work within a few months. Wives with more schooling are more likely to work away from home than those with less schooling. Better educated women also look for better quality when shopping for clothing. This practice has made the clothing retail field *quality*-conscious in its advertising and sale appeals.

[11] Ruth Jackendoff, *The Impact of Recent Economic Trends on Consumer Demand for Textiles,* an address to the Eastern Regional Conference of College Teachers of Textiles and Clothing in New York, November 1957.
[12] National Manpower Council, *loc. cit.*
[13] United States Department of Health, Education and Welfare, *Earned Degrees Conferred by Higher Educational Institutions 1957–1958,* Circular 570, Office of Education, Washington, D.C., 1959, p. 47.

Higher education appears to be associated not only with better personal appearance, but also with less satisfaction with dress.[14]

The American woman is a vital force in the social and economic development of today. This is a marked change from the past. Women today are responsible for most of the family spending in our 43 million family units. Estimates of personal and family expenditures controlled by women range from 60 to 85 per cent, or from 160 to 200 billion dollars annually.[15] Clothing retailing is designed to attract the woman of the house who is the buyer. Furthermore, the homemaker holds a position of prestige in the financial world. Many companies consider her a better financial risk than her husband. Her name on a bank note or a mortgage indicates that payments are more likely to be made[16] than if only her husband's name is used. Installment companies report that if the wife's name appears on the contract, the furniture, color TV, or the new car are far less likely to be repossessed. One of the country's largest personal loan companies has stated that a married woman as cosigner is its best security.[17] Thus the fact that women work and do the clothing shopping has probably had more effect upon the growing clothing credit transactions than any other factor.

Population Changes

The rapid population growth in the United States has affected the growth of the clothing industry. The United States population has grown from 123 million in the 1930's to approximately 180 million in 1960. It is expected to reach 243.9 million[18] by 1975. The very fact that these increasing numbers must be housed and clothed increases the demand for textile products.

The decreasing farm population is also a factor. Today only 12 per cent

---

[14] Katherine Burnette Hall, "A Study of Some of the Factors That Contribute to Satisfactions and Dissatisfactions in the Clothing of Ninety-Two Urban Low Income Families," Unpublished Doctor's Thesis, Pennsylvania State University, University Park, 1955.
[15] Harry A. Bullis, "Mrs. America—The Money Manager," *Vital Speeches*, Vol. 23, July 1, 1957, pp. 574–576.
[16] *Ibid.*
[17] *Ibid.*
[18] United States Department of Commerce, *Current Population Report*, U.S. Bureau of the Census, Series P-25 No. 187, Washington, D.C., November 10, 1958, p. 16.

of the families in the United States live on farms, as opposed to 28 per cent in 1920.[19] Urban and urban-oriented families have in the past spent more for clothing and textiles than have farm families.

The decreasing size of the family, accompanied by the increase in family income, makes possible more attention to clothing and textiles. The size of the average household in the United States decreased from 4.8 persons in 1900 to 3.4 in 1959.[20] At the same time the number of separate households increased from approximately 16 million to 51 million. By 1975, it is estimated that the number of households will exceed 65 million.[21] Not only are there two and a half times as many people to clothe today as in 1900, but there are over three times as many households to furnish with textile products.

Another factor affecting family clothing demands is the changing composition of the population. Increased longevity has resulted in a growing number of elderly people. Since 1900, the total population has more than doubled, but at the same time the number of people aged 65 and over has almost quadrupled. Senior citizens now number more than 14 millions, constituting one out of every 12 people in the United States. In another 20 years the number of older people will have risen to some 21 millions, or approximately one out of every ten Americans.[22]

Older persons spend less for clothing than do younger ones. For example, Lamale[23] found that urban single women with incomes of $2,000 to $3,000 after taxes, in 1950, spent $396 for clothing if they were under 25 years of age. With each successive age group, the amount spent for clothing decreased to the point where the women aged 65 to 75 years spent $153, and those 75 years and over spent only $82 annually for clothing.

Not only is the 65 and over age group increasing rapidly, but so are younger age groups. Whereas the total population of the United States increased 15 per cent between 1950 and 1958, the group under 5 years of age increased 21 per cent, those 14 to 17 years increased 27 per cent, and those 5 to 13 years of age increased over 40 per cent.[24] At the present time,

[19] United States Department of Commerce, *Statistical Abstracts of the United States*, 81st edition, U.S. Bureau of the Census, Washington, D.C., 1960, pp. 40, 42, 615.
[20] *Ibid.*
[21] *Ibid.*
[22] Everett E. Ashley, 3rd, "Housing for the Elderly," *Construction Review*, Vol. 4, March 1958, pp. 4–7.
[23] Helen Humes Lamale, "Changes in Expenditures of Urban Families," *Journal of Home Economics*, Vol. 50, November 1958, pp. 684–686.
[24] United States Department of Commerce, *Current Population Report, Population Estimates*, Series P-25, *loc. cit.*

approximately 36 per cent of the population is under 20 years and 21 per cent is under 10 years of age. The proportion of the clothing dollar going to clothe these younger citizens has been increasing at the expense of the adults' clothing allowances. As children become an even larger portion of the population, one may expect clothing demands to increase proportionately.

Family Location and Occupation

The clothing bought and the amount paid for it are partially determined by where a family lives. Urban families usually own more extensive and expensive wardrobes than do families living in rural areas.[25] It has been generally assumed that farm families are less fashionable in dress than city families. In 1941, the average farm family's expenditures for clothing were only 55 per cent as great as that of urban families. In 1955, farm families spent 87 per cent as much on clothing as did city families. As farm income has improved, and the communication between rural and city areas has increased through television, radio, and the printed word, the clothing of the farm family has come more nearly to approach that of the city family.

Farm families spend a larger proportion of their incomes on clothing and personal care than do urban families—17 per cent as compared with 12 per cent in 1955. This difference is due to two factors: (1) the farm family is larger, having approximately one and one-half times as many members as the urban family; and (2) farm income is lower.[26]

Regional differences in family clothing have lessened. In 1950, the Bureau of Labor Statistics Survey of Consumer Expenditures in 91 cities showed more similarities than differences among the various regions.[27] Except for the West, there was greater difference in the clothing spending pattern among city types within a region than between regions for the

---

[25] Brew, *loc. cit.*
[26] United States Department of Agriculture, *Farm Family Spending in the United States,* Agricultural Information Bulletin No. 192, Agricultural Research Service, Washington, D.C., June 1958, pp. 19–21.
[27] University of Pennsylvania, *Study of Consumer Expenditures, Income and Savings,* 1950, Wharton School of Business, Philadelphia, 1957; Vol. VI, *Summary of Family Expenditures for Clothing for Women and Girls, and Children under Two,* p. 161; Vol. VII, *Summary of Family Expenditures for Clothing for Men and Boys, Clothing Materials and Clothing Services,* p. 160.

same type of city. Families in the South spent less for clothing than did families in the North and West; however, they spent more for clothing services.

The geographic location in which a family lives affects the type of clothing worn. Climate is the major factor in clothing differences. The high cost of wool clothing needed in cold climates is usually offset by the necessity for frequent replacements of the lightweight, less expensive clothing used in warmer climates, where garments do not stand up well under the extreme heat, humidity, and repeated laundering and dry cleaning.

Finally, the kind and quantity of clothing purchased are influenced by the type of employment in which family members are engaged. If the father is a member of one of the professions, he will attach more importance to clothing than if he is a manual laborer.[28] Similar dress differences exist between semiprofessional workers and unskilled laborers. These class differences are expressed in increased inventories and annual purchases. The man who wears "work" clothes on the job owns and purchases about three-fourths as much clothing as the man whose occupation requires him to wear business suits.[29] Wives of businessmen also have higher clothing inventories and pay more for individual items.

Family Mobility

Families today are becoming increasingly mobile. One-fifth of the people in the United States change their place of residence in each year. Over half of the people have moved at least once in the last 5 years.[30] This of course includes some people who move frequently. Although the cost of moving generally causes the mobile family to acquire fewer possessions than families that are settled, it often spends as much for clothing. If the move is associated with higher income, the family members may have fewer but better clothes.

[28] United States Department of Agriculture, *Farm Family Spending in the United States*, loc. cit.
[29] Brew, *loc. cit.*
[30] United States Department of Agriculture, *Family Economics Review* (ARS 62–5), Institute of Home Economics, Agricultural Research Service, Washington, D.C., December 1958, p. 21.

Housing Changes

More all-purpose and nonseasonal clothing is being purchased by families today. This has resulted in part from the wide use of air conditioning—in houses, transportation facilities, and working areas. During the last 10 years, families have been constructing slightly larger but more compact houses, with greater emphasis upon storage space than formerly.[31] One might assume that more adequate storage space for clothing and textiles would stimulate family buying of clothing. There are, however, other factors which may have more influence than storage space. Since houses now are more adequately heated than formerly, warmth in clothing is less essential, and clothing need not be seasonal.

Consumer Credit

The use of consumer credit has produced a new way of life during the last several decades.[32] Many goods have been made accessible to those who do not have ready cash. This new way of life—buying today and paying tomorrow—suggests certain modifications of the traditional attitudes toward the use of money. This credit system has been a boost to the clothing industry and has helped the United States to win the title of the *best-dressed nation in the world.*

Used-Clothing Sales in a Small City

GEITEL WINAKOR AND MARCELLA MARTIN

The clothing that a family consumes within a given time period can come from several sources. The most thoroughly studied source is purchase of

---

[31] United States Department of Labor, "New Housing Characteristics in 1955 and Earlier Years," *Monthly Labor Review*, July 1956, pp. 796–804.

[32] United States Federal Reserve System, *Consumer Instalment Credit*, Part I, *Growth and Import*, Washington, D.C., 1957, p. 7.

Source: *Journal of Home Economics*, Vol. 55 (May, 1963), pp. 357–359. Reprinted by permission of the authors and publisher.

new clothing at retail stores. Garments may also be constructed at home or received as gifts. Clothing purchased in previous time periods and still remaining in the family inventory can provide a major source of clothing for consumption, because some articles of clothing last longer than one season. But some articles may be discarded by their original owners before they are fully worn out, particularly in a society where average income is high. Some of these used articles may then be acquired by other families through exchange, gift, or purchase.

Analyses of demand for houses and automobiles normally consider stocks and prices of secondhand units. Estimates of family well-being must take into account the large number of families who occupy used dwellings and drive used automobiles. Yet very little is known about the demand for used clothing relative to new clothing, or about the effect of used-clothing purchases on the clothing consumption of families.

Quantitatively speaking, used clothing is probably much less important than used dwellings, used automobiles, or even used household furnishings and equipment. Yet it may constitute a large part of the clothing supply of certain groups of families and may be an important supplement to the clothing of other families at certain stages in the family cycle. . . .

Goals of Study

We envisioned a consumer survey to find out who bought used clothing, what kinds of garments were bought, and how much was paid for them. However, when we talked with statistical advisers, two problems were evident. The first was that we lacked an appropriate vocabulary to use in preparing a questionnaire for consumers of used clothing. Second, for such a study a stratified sample would be more economical and effective than a random sample, but criteria for stratification were lacking.

Without previous research findings as a guide, our study of purchases of used clothing had to begin from scratch. It was decided to study used-clothing sales to develop a vocabulary and to learn about the availability of used clothing before interviewing consumers. The study was restricted to Ames, Iowa, a city of 27,000, because it appeared possible to describe the total used-clothing market within this area during a one-year period. The findings were not intended to apply to other cities, but our approach may provide a guide to researchers who wish to explore used-clothing sales in other areas.

Procedure

At the start, information about when and where used-clothing sales were held was obtained from conversations with local residents. As the study proceeded, classified advertisements in the local paper were read daily to locate sales. Sales were also advertised on a local radio program, on posters in supermarkets, and by announcements in church bulletins and organization newsletters.

The first step was to attend used-clothing sales and to make unstructured observations. In an effort to be inconspicuous, the observer wore clothing that was threadbare or faded and neutral in color. Notes of prices of garments at each sale were taken in a small notebook. Immediately upon leaving a sale, the observer recorded more detailed notes. As soon as possible, all notes were typed in a complete narrative form, following suggestions by Selltiz et al.[1]

With the information gained from these observations, a questionnaire was developed to be used in interviewing chairmen of used-clothing sales to learn more about the operation and procedure of sales. Questions were asked about the number of years each sale had been held; how sales were advertised; who donated the clothing that was sold; how and when clothing was collected, priced, and displayed; the types of garments that were most easily sold; and the disposal of unsold clothing.

Classification of Sales

From these interviews and from the unstructured observations, sales were then classified in two ways, by the nature of the sponsoring organization and by whether they were continuing or occasional sales. Some sales were sponsored by nonprofit organizations with all proceeds going to the organization. Others were conducted by seller-agents who re-

[1] C. Selltiz, M. Jahoda, M. Deutsch, and W. S. Cook. *Research Methods in Social Relations.* Revised one-volume edition. New York: Holt, Rinehart and Winston, Inc., 1961, p. 211.

turned a portion of the receipts to the owners of the clothing, retaining the rest for themselves. In a third type of sale, sponsored by the owner of all or part of the clothing for sale, all receipts were distributed to those who brought clothing to sell. Individuals or groups of individuals sponsored sales of their own garments in "clothesline" sales in their yards or homes. In general, organizations held sales as money-making projects, whereas individuals held sales to dispose of unneeded clothing.

A sale was classified as continuing if it was held regularly at least twice a month in a space not used for any other purpose. A sale held less frequently in a room used at other times for other purposes was classified as occasional.

All the sales in Ames, so far as is known, were managed by women, either working alone or in organized or informal groups. Organized groups included churches and sorority alumnae and service, social, and philanthropic organizations. Of the 12 active sorority chapters queried for this study, three each held one sale within the year. Among the 12 sorority alumnae organizations, four groups sponsored a total of five sales. Of the 96 social, fraternal, and service organizations in Ames, 13 held a total of 19 sales in the year of the study. Seven of the 31 Ames churches held 12 sales. These were all occasional sales. There were two continuing sales: one sponsored by an individual, one by an organization.

Characteristics of Sales

Sales were found to have some common characteristics, whatever the sponsoring organization or frequency of the sales. Sales were held throughout the year, with the majority in the spring and fall. Fridays and Saturdays were the most popular days. A sale that had a large selection of reasonably priced clothing, including a wide assortment of sizes for children and adults, was known as a "good" sale. Customers were usually waiting outside for such a sale to open. They made their selections quickly and silently, then carefully inspected each garment before buying.

The largest part of clothing at sales sponsored by organizations consisted of donations from members. Sometimes this was supplemented by unsold clothing left over from other sales and unsold merchandise from stores, although members of the organization did not always realize this.

Clothing was usually displayed on hangers on racks or iron pipes suspended from the ceiling. Garments were grouped into sections for men, women, and children. Within each section, clothing was further sorted by type of garment. Most garments were labeled with paper price tickets, although some items were unmarked. Shoes, hats, and purses were placed on tables. At some sales, large price signs were placed on tables; at other sales, items were marked individually. Few items were marked with size, because this information was usually not available to the worker doing the marking for the sale.

The most difficult part of conducting a sale, according to the women interviewed, was pricing the garments. Women with experience gained at other sales usually did the marking. There seemed to be definite limits on prices the customers were willing to pay for used clothing. Evidently the amount of wear remaining in a garment and whether it was still in fashion were more important than the original price. At an occasional sale, prices were cut before the end of the sale or, sometimes, when a customer bargained for a reduction. At a continuing sale, prices were cut only before a sale, never during a sale.

Ease of Selling Different Items

The 25 sale chairmen interviewed were asked to sort a group of 51 cards listing garments for men, women, boys, girls, and infants into five categories, depending on the ease with which each kind of garment sold. These categories were: (1) "usually sell very well," (2) "usually sell fairly well," (3) "sells," and (4) "hard to sell items." A fifth category, "not enough items at sale to know if they sell well," was used frequently by the chairman of small sales.

Infants' clothing was consistently ranked very easy to sell. Approximately half of the cards for boys' clothing were sorted into the first two categories. One-third of the girls' clothing cards were classified easy to sell. Men's clothing was rated as being harder to sell than other groups. No article of men's clothing was classified easy to sell by more than half of the women interviewed. There did not appear to be any consistent pattern in the rankings of garments for women. This could have been because some cards listed a fairly wide range of garments. For example, in an effort to limit the number of cards to be sorted, there was only one card representing all types of women's dresses. Several sale chairmen said that demand for out-of-season garments was limited. However, this was not apparent in the way they sorted the cards and further research would be necessary to test this statement.

Clothing not sold at one sale was saved for the next sale, donated to another sale in the community, or sent to such organizations as the Salvation Army or Goodwill Industries in Des Moines, Iowa.

Importance of Sales

Total receipts from sales of used clothing, as reported by the chairmen of sales sponsored by organizations in Ames, exceeded $8,000 in the year September 1, 1961, to August 31, 1962. It was not possible to estimate the total number of garments sold at the organized used clothing sales, although we would have liked to do so. The records of the sales did not provide this information, and the observer was not able to make counts without interfering with sale activities. No attempt was made to estimate the total receipts from informal clothesline sales held by individuals or groups of neighbors (a separate study would be needed to do this). These clothesline sales were more numerous than we had anticipated, and there was some evidence that they have been growing in number. Several organizations reported that they had ceased holding sales because of the increasing number of clothesline sales. We intend to continue observing local sales while going ahead with our original plan to study consumers of used clothing. It is our belief that used clothing may be sufficiently important to the clothing consumption of some groups of families that continued study is justified.

Although Ames is not a typical community, this study may provide a guide to those working in other cities. The questionnaire developed for interviewing sale chairmen could be adapted for other cities, with minor modifications made after observations of sales. The classification of sales developed here may also be applicable to other areas.

88 Clothing Standards and Habits
FERDYNAND ZWEIG

The clothing standards and habits of the workers are a fascinating subject of study. Clothes reflect our personality and at the same time they reflect environment. Personal and social factors are too closely interwoven to be separated.

Personal factors such as age, marital status, pastimes, education and upbringing, job and income level, individual desires and values, and physiological characteristics (especially circulation), the texture of the skin and general health, may be reflected in a man's clothing habits.

A man who wants to conform to the standards of the community will dress differently from a man who is anxious to assert himself and to express his own personality. A man who wants to please others or attract women will dress differently from a man who has developed a "don't care" spirit. A man who does not feel the cold will dress differently from a man who feels constantly cold, and a man with skin irritations will dress differently from a normal man.

Social factors also find expression in clothes. Taste, values, and desires are personal, but they are moulded, at least in part, by the social environment. The customs and standards of the group, the family, the district, of friends and work-mates, all have their influence. Advertising and salesmanship, conditions of work and opportunities for pastimes and hobbies, prices and wages, all influence our clothing standards and habits.

The first and chief distinction in clothing standards and habits is between age-groups. Young, middle-aged, and old men not only dress differently from one another, but spend a different proportion of their income on clothes. A young single man of 20 to 25 will spend nearly twice as much on clothes as a middle-aged man of, say 45 to 50, and three times as much as a man of 65 to 70. The clothes of a young man show a desire to attract women, to appear smart and attractive, the desire for excitement (shown in frequent changes and new clothes), and the desire for self-assertion (which has both sexual and economic sources). Those of an

Source: *The British Worker*, Harmondsworth, Middlesex: Penguin Books (1952), pp. 157–165. Reprinted by permission of the publisher.

older man show his gregarious instincts, the desire to conform to the views and habits of the group, the need for protection from cold and rain. A young man's clothes will be varied and sometimes extravagant, while those of an older man will be more drab and uniform. You will find great difference between the age-groups, whatever garments you choose for comparison—suits, underwear, gloves, or hats. Young men will more frequently wear a complete suit of the one material, while old men will be more inclined to wear oddments. Older men wear woollen vests, while young men wear cotton or rayon or none at all. Young men often wear raincoats, and older men woollen overcoats. Most young men wear nothing on their heads; older men caps, and some middle-aged men trilbies. Young men do not like to show they are workmen in their dress, and try to conform to the standards of the middle classes, while older men are content to be taken for what they are.

The fact that a man is married affects his clothing standards and habits in many ways. "You don't run after a bus when you've boarded it," one man remarked cynically to me. There is no need for him to look attractive; he no longer goes to dances, and will probably not go out as often as he used to. He had less money to spend because all his clothes must be bought with his pocket-money. His clothes will be better kept, dusted, and cleaned, and greater stress will be laid on comfort and respectability than on attractiveness. The wife's taste will often play a greater part than his own. "My wife doesn't like me to look too attractive," a man said to me.

The clothes of the workers are not often brightly coloured, extravagant, or showy. The great majority, even of young single men, prefer quiet respectable colours, preferably blue, brown, and grey.

Leisure time activities give rise to great differences in ways of dressing. A man dresses, in fact, according to his pastimes. A regular pub-goer will dress shabbily, a football player will dress better and have a sporty look about him, a man who is fond of dancing and cinemas will be very well dressed indeed, and will keep himself smart and neat. There is no doubt that the worst dressed is the regular pub-goer: firstly because he has little money to spare, secondly because rubbing shoulders in a smoky packed bar does not help to keep clothes at their best, and thirdly because there is a tradition that shabby clothes are worn by pub-goers. Cloth caps and mufflers are worn in pubs more than anywhere else; and even the crowds at dog-racing stadiums are better dressed than the regular pub-goers, chiefly because many race-goers are middle-class men, and secondly because those who win from time to time invest their "dividends" in good clothes.

With practice you can tell the way a man spends his evenings by the way he dresses. Whenever I met a very well-dressed young man, I was often right when I said to him: "You are interested in dances, shows, and films," and when I saw a man who looked completely abandoned I could see that he had no hobby at all and was a drunkard addicted to gambling.

Environment plays a big part in clothing traditions and standards. A docker's clothes are quite different from those of a Park Royal engineering worker. Dockers, navvies, heavy labourers, and road workers have their own traditional standards and habits which are different from those of factory workers and engineers, although the differences in what they wear in their leisure time are growing smaller. The same can be said about the standards and habits of different districts. Slum people have their own standards and habits, but here again the differences between them and the standards of others are less pronounced than they were.

Social status, as expressed in grades and wages, obviously determines clothing standards. Men in authority, foremen, inspectors, supervisors, black-coated workers, and men applying for better jobs have to wear better clothes than labourers, although the distinction is not as great as it used to be and is growing even smaller.

The part played by clothes in getting a job is very important. A man who is shabbily dressed becomes helpless, hopeless, and condemned to a gutter life. I remember an ex-hairdresser telling me that he could get a job if he had decent clothes. A labourer cannot find digs for himself unless he is decently dressed, and is condemned to living is hostels. The casual wards, which are now called rehabilitation centres, try to provide their inmates with suitable clothes so that they can get a job. One head of an institution in London told me that in most cases this is successful, but that a third of the men pawn or sell the clothes and when they have spent all, they come back in their ragged clothes to try the same thing over again.

All this applies primarily to clothes worn in leisure time and not to what is worn at work. That is a problem on its own and a very important one in the worker's life. The distinction between what is worn at work and what is worn at home is important in all classes, but in none so important as it is in the working class. The worker spends quite a lot on his working clothes, the wear and tear of which might be regarded as part of the cost of production. Work clothes are provided free in only a few trades such as transport and distribution which provide uniforms for their workmen. There are also firms which provide overalls and boiler-suits for their workers, but until now this has been exceptional, and more and more often the demand is heard that work clothes should be provided free by employers as part of the cost of production.

The clothing requirements of each job are, of course, different from those of every other. Coal-miners need safety boots, a large number of socks and pants, old trousers, and a jacket. The following figures were given to me by an experienced docker: "In a year I need two pairs of boots, four pairs of trousers, six shirts, six pairs of cotton vests, and twelve pairs of socks." Navvies, road workers, and other heavy labourers need boots, socks, and trousers most of all, but also vests, shirts, and jackets, if they have to carry loads on their backs. There are jobs in which five pairs of boots and six pairs of trousers a year are needed. Grease, oil, petrol, cement, asphalt, metal powders, starch, cotton cake, coke, coal, and fumes are all very injurious to working clothes; small accidents must be taken into account and the effect of constant handling of goods, machines, and tools. Factory workers need overalls and boiler-suits, although there are a great many who, feeling uncomfortable and tight in such garments or disliking the drab uniformity, never wear them. A man usually needs more work clothes than his worn-out home clothes can provide him with, so he has to buy them in second-hand shops or from his mates. The ability to stand hard wear is the most important consideration. Oddments of clothing are cheap and constantly replaced from the weekly wages, while leisure clothes are bought out of savings, windfalls from gambling, extras earned by overtime at week-ends, or any other occasional earnings. You often hear it said that a man who does not save has no clothes to wear in his leisure time, because in recent years they have become so expensive.

Most men have at least one best suit. Some wear their very best on Sundays and special occasions, and their second best for a change after work if they go out. "The Sunday suit used to be a special institution, it was specially cared for and kept clean. Things are different now," a man who worked in a tailoring business told me. Most men change at week-ends, but not all change on weekday evenings; it depends on their jobs and on their way of spending their leisure time.

The worker's ideas on clothes are definite and highly significant.

The worker does not believe in heavy clothes. "A lot of clothes don't make you feel warm," is a very common opinion. He is a firm believer in fresh air and exercise. "It isn't good for you to wear too many clothes, it's not natural," he says. The manual worker probably has a better circulation than a sedentary worker and does not feel cold as much. An outdoor worker is often more lightly dressed than a man working indoors, because his circulation is better. "Warmth comes from inside not from outside." "The more you wrap yourself up, the colder you feel. Good circulation is all that matters." This attitude is shown in the way the majority dress. Most workmen do not wear gloves in winter, and even on frosty days I have seen a great many men on outdoor jobs handling things with their bare hands. Young ex-Service men are more inclined to wear gloves than other workers.

Most young men do not wear anything on their heads and the tendency is to drop both the cap and the trilby. "The face and hands are meant to be uncovered, and you feel all right if you get used to it," they say.

On very cold winter nights in January and February I have seen in working-class districts about half the men in ordinary woollen coats, a third in raincoats and mackintoshes, about a tenth without any coat at all, and the rest in sports coats and leather jackets.

Service in the Forces has a very important effect on the clothing habits of the working classes because men get used to wearing certain garments, such as gloves, woollen overcoats, collars and ties, and woollen uderwear, and they continue to wear them in civilian life. Army life helps on the whole to reduce the distinctions in clothing standards between the classes.

Lack of ostentation is another characteristic of the workers' way of dressing. Smartness is not valued highly by the majority of them; on the contrary it is treated with suspicion. The worker thinks of a spiv as overdressed, wearing bright colours and over-padded shoulders; and a man who appears in the pub smartly dressed is taken for a "fiddler." The desire to conform is stronger in the working classes than it is anywhere else, and this is seen even in the way the young are dressed.

It may interest the reader to know that the best-dressed men among workers are foreigners, especially coloured workers; because by dressing well they can compensate for their sense of inferiority. I met coloured workers who spent half their wages on clothes, some spending as much as £120 a year buying enormous numbers of suits, shirts, shoes, ties, and coats, all in bright colours, and changing them constantly.

The coloured man says that a badly dressed "blackie" is taken for a beggar. The foreign worker, such as the E.V.W., also feels the need for self-assertion, especially if he has spent a long time in a concentration camp. He does not speak the language properly and does not know the ways of the country; so that, if he wants to be taken for someone, he must at least be well dressed. Sometimes national pride comes into it. Poles, especially ex-Service men, often say: "They mustn't think that we are a lousy lot. We must keep up our standards. A man can dress as he likes in his own country, especially if everyone knows him."

In the clothing standards of the workers the magnitude of the social changes in the last few decades can be seen more clearly than in anything else. Here are some workers' comments on the past:

A London policeman, a thoughtful man and a great admirer of Shaw: "Enormous progress has been made during the last forty years in every way. Before the 1914 war you could see little children, barefoot and in rags, begging from people in the street. Now they are all decently dressed and wearing shoes, and run happily around with ice-cream in their hands. This contrast shows best the changes in the last thirty years."

A general secretary of a mixed union of both craftsmen and labourers: "Forty years ago our national conferences looked like crowds of beggars, and I was the best-dressed man there. Now at our meetings most men are better dressed than I am. When I compare conditions now with those forty years ago, I am very hopeful. Don't believe the pessimists who say that there is no progress. This country is a workers' paradise compared with what it was thirty years ago."

A district secretary in a union on the north-east coast, an elderly man: "Men in my youth were dressed in dirty rags, and when man's clothes are ragged and dirty, his mind becomes ragged too. Cleanliness and intelligence, cleanliness and good manners, cleanliness and self-respect—they all go together."

A middle-aged workman from the East End: "When I was young the cockney wore a muffler instead of a collar. The more respectable ones wore a paper collar on Sundays, and if they were even more respectable a dicky with a 1½d. collar, and paper cuffs. All these dickies and paper collars and cuffs have disappeared completely, and mufflers are worn by only a few old men. In my days you could tell a workman by his dress, even on a Sunday, but you can't now. The funny thing is that the clothes standards of the working classes have risen considerably during the time of clothes rationing, not of course because of rationing, but because of full employment and good wages. In my days most workmen bought their clothes on the hire-purchase system, or by checks from special clothing clubs or 'diddle'm clubs' in the pubs; but nowadays most clothes are bought for cash, although the hire-purchase system is coming in again."

Social distinctions in clothing standards have certainly considerably lessened in the last thirty or forty years. In fact in a Sunday crowd you can hardly distinguish the working classes from the middle classes, especially in the age-group between twenty and thirty. The fondness for sports, and the belief in genuineness, have removed all the paper collars, dickies, and paper cuffs and they have given the working man more of a sportsman's appearance. The cloth cap, once a marked working-class feature, is disappearing except among some classes of workmen, such as navvies, heavy labourers, dockers, farmers, and road sweepers.

This tendency to drop all class distinctions in dress reveals what is going on in the worker's mind more than anything he says on the subject of class distinctions. There is no doubt that the clothing standards and habits of the working class have come considerably closer to those of the middle classes, the middle-class standards falling because of economic pressure, and the working-class standards going up.

Ritual and Magic in The Control of Contagion
JULIUS A. ROTH

Tuberculosis is a contagious disease. But just how contagious is it? In what ways and under what circumstances is it likely to be transmitted from one person to another? And what procedures are most effective for preventing its transmission? The answers to these questions are quite uncertain and TB specialists show considerable disagreement in the de-

Source: American Sociological Review, Vol. 22 (June, 1957), pp. 310–314. Reprinted by permission of the author and publisher.

118   Dress, Adornment, and the Social Order

tails of the manner in which they deal with these problems. These uncertainties leave the way open for ritualized procedures that often depend more on convenience and ease of administration than on rationally deduced probabilities. They also leave the way open for irrational practices that can properly be called "magic."

. . . .

Rank and Protective Clothing

A number of procedures are designed to protect the employees and patients within the hospital from spreading TB. One method, which has come into prominence in recent years, is the use of protective clothing—masks, gowns, and hair coverings—which the hospital personnel are supposed to wear when they come into contact with the patients or their effects. However, this protective clothing is often not worn. There is a definite relationship between the degree to which it is worn and the rank of the employee.

I recorded the wearing of surgical cap, gown, and mask by the nursing personnel of a VA hospital when entering a patient's room over a four-day period. The results are shown in Table 1.

Table 1   Wearing of protective clothing by nursing personnel in veterans administration hospital

	Times Entered Room	Cap	Gown	Mask
Nurses	56	100	57	75
Attendants	200	100	72	90

More detailed records were made of the use of protective clothing when entering patients' rooms in a state hospital that had a more complex nursing hierarchy. The record was made on ten different days, plus additional days for doctors and professional nurses in order to increase their very small number. The records were made on three different wards with different sets of personnel and were always for complete days to avoid the selective influence of certain work shifts or kinds of ward duties. Results are given in Table 2. The two instances of a doctor wearing cap and mask on recorded days (Table 2) both involved the same doctor—an assistant surgeon on a temporary assignment. His successor does not wear protective clothing.

Table 2 Wearing of protective clothing by doctors and nursing personnel in state hospital

	Times Entered Room	Percentages Wearing		
		Cap	Gown	Mask
Doctors	47	5	0	5
Professional nurses	100	24	18	14
Practical nurses	121	86	45	46
Aides	142	94	80	72
Students	97	100	100	100

As both of these tables show, the use of protective clothing is inversely related to occupational status level. The people of higher rank seem to have the privilege of taking the greater risks, particularly in the case of masks. The cap and gown are intended in part to prevent the spread of the disease to others; the mask is almost exclusively for the protection of the wearer.

It might be argued that the lower status employees should wear protective clothing relatively more often because they perform tasks which require more intimate contact with the patients and their effects. Thus, the aides and students do most of the work of collecting food trays and trash, making beds, washing furniture, picking up soiled towels. Certainly, this factor makes a difference, but it is not sufficient to account for the whole difference.

When we examine overlapping functions (those carried out by two or more levels of nursing personnel), differences, if any, are almost always in the direction of more frequent wearing of protective clothing by the lower-status employees. Table 3 gives the figures for the thirteen overlapping functions in which such differences occurred.

Why do persons with higher status wear protective clothing less often? For one thing, it is not considered necessary by people who know best.

Table 3 Wearing of protective clothing by state hospital nursing personnel while carrying out given functions *

	Times Entered Room	Cap	Gown	Mask		Times Entered Room	Cap	Gown	Mask
Take temperatures					**Bring in food trays**				
Professional nurses	26	19	54	46	Practical nurses	10	100	80	80
Practical nurses	24	79	63	71	Aides	21	100	100	81
Students	6	100	100	100	Students	20	100	100	100
Dispense medications					**Collect food trays**				
Professional nurses	7	28	14	0	Practical nurses	9	67	67	67
Practical nurses	15	87	40	40	Aides	17	94	100	94
Students	5	100	100	100	Students	14	100	100	100
Talk to patients when not performing a duty					**Serve drinking water**				
					Practical nurses	10	80	40	60
Professional nurses	11	18	0	0	Aides	11	100	82	73
Practical nurses	31	87	26	23	Students	3	100	100	100
Aides	29	86	52	55					
Students	5	100	100	100	**Give out supplies (tissues, tissue bags, etc.)**				
Distribute towels or linen					Practical nurses	11	82	73	91
					Aides	9	100	89	100
Professional nurses	2	0	0	0	Students	3	100	100	100
Practical nurses	6	100	67	67					
Aides	12	100	100	83	**Collect soiled towels & linen**				
Students	9	100	100	100	Practical nurses	7	43	29	57
Adjust blinds or windows					Aides	14	93	50	43
Professional nurses	3	33	33	0	**Give out refreshments**				
Practical nurses	4	75	25	25					
Aides	14	93	72	72	Practical nurses	4	100	0	25
Students	7	100	100	100	Aides	3	100	33	100
Distribute mail					**Collect trash**				
Professional nurses	5	0	0	0	Practical nurses	13	85	85	77
Practical nurses	3	67	0	0	Aides	27	93	85	78
Aides	6	83	33	33	Students	4	100	100	100

* Because the numbers of certain classes of personnel for some functions were very small, supplementary observations in addition to those given in Table 2 were made. These observations—which were always for complete days—have been included in this table. Doctors do not appear in this table because there was almost no overlap between their functions and those of the nursing personnel.

There is no good evidence that the systematic wearing of protective clothing makes any difference (even the person who planned and administered this program could cite no evidence showing its effectiveness) and people who know most about TB do not seem to consider it worth the trouble. Doctors, and to a lesser extent professional nurses, are, of course, most likely to recognize the probable futility of these procedures. The relative ignorance of the lower levels of ward employees makes it more likely that they will have doubts about whether it is safe to go without the protective clothing, especially on routine duties when they must enter patients' rooms repeatedly in a short interval. There are, of course, circumstances in which almost everyone would agree that the wearing of a mask and perhaps a gown was wise. It is the routine wearing of protective clothing for all contacts with patients that is generally rejected. Probably a more important factor is the likelihood that the employee can "get away with" a violation. A doctor need not worry about a "bawling out" for not protecting himself. A professional nurse might be criticized, but usually she is the highest authority on a ward. The chance of criticism increases down the scale. Students, who are new and unfamiliar with the situation (they put in four-week stints) and who worry about possible "demerits," wear protective clothing all the time in patients' rooms. Some ward employees, especially those of lower status, who are not "properly dressed" hurriedly don a mask and gown if they see the supervisor of the nursing education program on the floor.

Magic and the Tubercle Bacillus

Gauze or paper masks are rather difficult to breathe through. To make breathing easier patients and employees sometimes pull down the mask until their nostrils have a clear space. This, of course, destroys the point of wearing the mask and the mask then takes on the status of a charm necklace.

We can also find examples of institutional magic. In the state hospital patients are required to wear masks when they go to the first floor for a hair cut or for an x-ray and when they go to the eighth floor to see the social worker or the patient services director. They do not have to wear masks (and never do) when they go to the first floor for occupational therapy, to visit with their families, to attend socials or church services, or to see a movie, nor when they go to the eighth floor to the library and to play bingo. An examination of these two lists shows that patients must wear masks when they go somewhere on "business," but not when they go somewhere for "pleasure," even though they use the same parts of the building and come into contact with hospital personnel in both cases. The rules suggest that the tubercle bacillus works only during business hours.

Table 4 Wearing of protective clothing by practical nurses when carrying out duties and when "socializing" with patients

	Times Entered Room	Percentages Wearing		
		Cap	Gown	Mask
Carrying out duties	39	97	75	80
"Socializing"	23	91	17	9

The ward employee tends to wear protective clothing when carrying out her duties, but not when "socializing" with the patients. I kept a record over a short period of time on several practical nurses on the 3:00 to 11:00 P.M. shift. Table 4 shows the contrasts in their use of protective clothing. The nurses' contact with the patients was more prolonged and more intimate while socializing than while carrying out their duties. The average time spent in the room during this recorded period was less than half a minute for taking care of a duty and about three minutes for socializing. While giving out medicine or taking temperatures or bringing in food trays the nurses have very little close contact with the patients. While socializing, they often stand close to the patients, lean on their beds and other furniture, and handle their newspapers and other belongings. Logically, there is a greater need for the protective clothing—and especially the mask, which was hardly used at all—while socializing than while carrying out the routine duties.

Apparently, these nurses believe they need protection only when working. They remark that the gown, and more especially the mask, is a barrier to friendly intercourse.

Man's Laws and Nature's Laws

Rationally considered, the controls and protections used to check the transmission of TB should depend on an estimate of the probability of such transmission occurring under given conditions and in given circumstances. The problem for persons responsible for controlling the transmission of TB is to set their controls and protections at a level where a "reasonable" risk is involved. Admittedly, this is not easy because of the uncertain knowledge about transmission and susceptibility and public anxieties about the disease. Even if one were able to establish general rules for a "reasonable" level of control on the basis of present knowledge about the disease, putting these rules into practice would still be a major problem. To deal with this problem realistically, the controlling agents need a good understanding of the social organization of the hospital, the disease concepts of the personnel, and the patterns of administrative thinking on the part of supervisory persons.

The practices surrounding contagion control in a TB hospital represent an effort to make man's laws approximate the laws of nature, and when nature's laws are not well understood, man's rules are likely to be more or less irrational and their observance vacillating and ritualistic.[1]

---

[1] Professor Everett C. Hughes pointed out to me the implications of the use of the same word "law" for both the regularities of nature and the rules of conduct made by man.

Polity

⌘ Clothes and Government
LAWRENCE LANGNER

It is a startling thought that without the invention of clothing it would not be possible to develop the highly complex systems of governments with their armies, navies and police forces, which are now in existence all over the world. Yet this is obvious when we realize that all government is based on the domination of the population by an individual or small governing group which is, as we say, "clothed with authority." This authority is generally indicated by clothing.

Perhaps one of mankind's most ingenious uses of clothing is to employ it to demonstrate the authority of individuals or groups and to transform this authority into the power of government. This has been accomplished mainly by means of the uniform. The invention of the uniform has served many important social functions, including that of indicating police power as well as rank. The use of uniforms has often been supplemented or superseded by badges or insignia which may also serve the same purpose. The clothing which indicates the power of a ruling class usually undergoes a change if the power of this ruling class is taken over by another class. These various uses of clothing for purposes of government, as well as for some other purposes, will now be considered.

Since one of the primary purposes of clothes through the ages was to demonstrate the wearer's superiority, we may assume that one of man's first innovations was to use clothes to assist him in dominating others. The superior adornment and finery of the tribal chief which, added to his ability and prowess, enabled him to surpass in appearance the rest of the tribe, helped to produce the feelings of admiration, inferiority and sub-

Source: The Importance of Wearing Clothes, New York: Hastings House (1959), pp. 127–132. Reprinted by permission of the publisher.

mission among his followers which caused them to accept his leadership. The warrior, his body stained in unnatural hues, his face painted with frightening colors, his ornaments bristling with teeth or claws, his clothes of animal hides reminiscent of the strongest beasts of the forests, produced an effect which intimidated both friend and enemy. This form of terrorism found its counterpart in modern warfare in the clothing of the Prussian Death's Head Hussars and Hitler's terror-producing S.S. troopers. These inventions in clothing also enabled their users to disguise themselves as more powerful blood-thirsty creatures than their opponents or victims, and thus brought into play the power of fear to paralyze the defenses of their enemies.

Clothes were also of particular importance to indicate the stratification of society, and enabled the king with his crown jewels and magnificient robes, as well as the nobility, to show their superiority to the common man over whom they exercised authority. In their ceremonial robes, as members of the court, the nobility wore coronets or circlets on their brows, a minor or subordinate crown showing that the wearer was superior to "thee and me," but inferior to his liege lord, the king. In England the rank of the nobleman was further indicated by the number and size of the tines in his coronet, also an invention to distinguish one rank from another, while the robes and lengths of trains trimmed with one or more rows of ermine, according to the wearer's title, also served to indicate rank. The heads of the Fascist states, such as Hitler, Mussolini and Peron were also fond of dressing up to show their superiority, and adopted uniforms such as brown shirts, black shirts and many decorations to flaunt their brief authority to the world. Even in American political life, our Senators once had a habit of wearing large black hats and spreading coats. In giving expression to their position by their clothing, they were merely following the example of the Roman Senators, who wore a special kind of toga called a Laticlavan which lent dignity to their calling.

But government would never have been possible had it not been for the invention of the uniform, the apparel by which the government, whether it be that of a monarch, dictator or a democracy, indicates by its soldiers and police force its power over the masses. These uniforms distinguish the limbs of authority from the common herd and secure immediate obedience. Even in Communist countries where the use of distinguishing clothes for the governing hierarchy is absent, the uniformed police, and the soldiers and overdecorated officers of the Red Army who supply the force on which they must ultimately depend, are very much in evidence at all times, and there would be no government without them.

How governments depend on the use of uniforms in order to govern is shown by the following incident which I witnessed in the Unter der Linden in Berlin three days before World War I. The entire street was filled with a milling mob of Socialist workers demonstrating against Germany's going to war. A platoon of the Kaiser's Uhlans in full military regalia was thrown across the wide street. The sight of the soldiers in the uniforms which symbolized the power of the Kaiser was sufficient to cause the angry demonstrators to melt helplessly out of the street as the soldiers moved quietly forward sweeping them out of their way like a gigantic broom. The wearing of uniforms by large masses of the population was a particularly Germanic trait at the time, and was repeated in the events which led to World War II. It also made possible the famous hoax of *The Captain from Köpenick*. . . .

One of the two occasions when French soldiers landed on British soil since the Norman conquest occurred in Wales, at Goodwick near Fishguard Bay in the year 1797. The Welsh women, wearing their national costumes with red skirts and shawls and shiny high hats and carrying broom-sticks for muskets, lifted their skirts over their shoulders, showing their white thighs, and paraded like a regiment of soldiers on the sea front. The French, mistaking them for British soldiers in red-coat uniforms with white trousers, beat a hasty retreat to their ships, leaving their muskets behind them. These are still to be seen in a Welsh castle piled up in silent testimony to the fact that by Welsh women's wits and French fear of the British uniform, England was saved from invasion by Napoleon.

Another use of uniforms is to build up the *esprit de corps* of the men wearing them. The desirable feeling of belonging to a group which cherishes courage, honor, patriotism and other virtues, is produced by wearing the uniform of a given regiment whose members are comrades in war and peace.

Not only would it be impossible for governments to govern, but it would also be impossible to conduct warfare (other than guerilla warfare) without using clothes in the form of uniforms in order to distinguish friend from enemy. From barbarous times until today the uniform of the fighting man is regarded as a necessity, and there could be few wars without its use. A disarmament conference which resulted in a general agreement among the nations to prohibit the use of soldiers' uniforms as contrary to international law might possibly bring the world closer to universal peace than any other measure!

As a substitute for uniforms under conditions where there were none obtainable or usable, revolutionaries sometimes use other distinguishing symbols, such as colored arm bands. Badges and ornaments to distinguish the wearer have also been used for warlike purposes from time immemorial. For example, in the civil wars of England, red roses were used to symbolize the House of Lancaster, and white roses the House of York.

The invention of the uniform had significance other than to indicate the armed power of a government. Basically, the uniform was invented as a means to indicate the relationship of an individual to a group, such as members of the same tribe. So many are the uses of uniforms today that we tend to forget the origin of the word (uni-form: one form, all alike). *By wearing the uniform of a particular group, a man shows by his clothing that he has given up his right to act freely as an individual but must act in accordance with and under the limitations of the rules of his group.* From early times the livery of the servants or slaves, or the uniform of the soldier or policeman, have represented the submission of the individual to the rule of the chief, ruler, or commander. This use of the uniform has continued to modern times.

The New China

A. C. SCOTT

When the Communists came to power in China in 1949, they effected a revolution whose social and political repercussions were probably more startling in application than anything that had gone before in a thousand years; in nothing was this so outwardly marked as in the costume of the Chinese people. Almost overnight as it seemed, the nation was garbed in a dress whose sexless regimentation of style and shapelessness symbolized the liberation of a new national spirit according to Marxist theory, although to less politically perceptive eyes it appeared, however utilitarian, unnecessarily drab.

Source: Chinese Costume in Transition, New York: Theatre Arts Books (1958), pp. 92–101. Reprinted by permission of the author and publisher.

The Manchus also imposed new dress styles on the Chinese people when they came to power, but only on the official and governing classes and even so there was a great deal in the new costume which was derived from purely Chinese sources in the first place. Apart from this, women in general were left to dress as they had always done and this held true for everybody else provided they were not of Manchu race or held no official post. The Manchu costume reforms were designed to identify the new governing class only and symbolize their special position from the rest of society. Eventually the rest of society adapted official dress fashions to its own uses and this was only natural and typical of human nature.

The Communist dress reforms on the other hand were designed to symbolize a new form of government by proving that "the rest" no longer existed, society had been changed as a whole. Sartorial recognition of this fact commenced at the bottom instead of the top; the peasant and artisan were the most important members of society in the Marxist state and therefore everybody whatever his rank dressed like the peasant and artisan. But even Communist polemics are not proof against human nature when it comes to such personal matters as clothes, and from the perverse kind of dress exhibitionism which political regimentation induced among the Chinese people there has now been a swing away to more normal tendencies as we shall see.

During the long years that the Communist Party were in exile in China they prided themselves on wearing clothing which made no distinction in rank or sex and this was the position when they came to power, although by that time a certain standardization of pattern had been introduced into their uniform as against the more nondescript styles of their early years. It is interesting to compare a photograph of Mao Tse-tung taken in 1940 with one of today. The Chinese leader, somewhat tousled haired, wears the battered military style tunic, trousers, puttees and cloth topped Chinese style shoes which have formed the basic ingredients of Communist dress since the beginning, on his head is a soft and shapeless peaked cap after the style worn by Nationalist troops of those days. It is a somewhat different figure whose plump form smiles down from every hoarding and wall in China today, the puttees have gone and the trousers are creased, the jacket is basically the same in style but now made of smart barrathea cloth tailored and pressed while the cap has a less rakish air. The clothing of the revolutionary has become respectable and is now the formal dress of the political leader.

The uniform of the Communist armies which conquered China was not made of khaki but a cotton cloth of a harsh yellow green colour that was reputed to be due to the dyeing facilities peculiar to the Yenan district in which the Communists had their headquarters for so long. It consisted of high collared tunic, trousers with puttees and Chinese shoes or the rubber boots described in the last chapter. The cap, a soft peaked affair, was a little different in design from the earlier version copied from the one worn by the Chinese nationalist troops, being now not dissimilar to the type of cap worn as working dress by the G.I. in the technical branches of the American army. Apart from this the Communist troops wore tin hats of American and Japanese style and manufacture.

One of the less pleasing styles adapted by the East from the West is the cloth peaked cap, at its best it betokens informal country life, days of sport or else the everyday wear of industry, at its worst it can bestow on the wearer a peculiarly moronic appearance and it is the latter which sometimes seems to be the unhappy effect of official party head wear in Communist China. Judging by old photographs which are extant, a few Chinese seemed to have dallied with the European cloth cap style before the first world war. Curiously enough it was not only a male fashion for one or two actresses appear to have worn them, possibly inspired by the Western stage "dames". However, the cap never seems to have become a very widely used article of attire until the introduction of the rain wear described earlier, a waterproof coat with a softpeaked cap to match of unspeakable design. Such an outfit was very common in the streets of the cities after the last war and the cap's design, or lack of it, seems to have influenced the civilian cap worn in Communist China.

Once the Communist troops were established in the cities they had conquered, the civilian cadres made their appearance to take over administration and organize industry. Technicians, industrial workers and so forth were all clad in a cotton cloth uniform which, apart from the puttees, was more or less identical in every respect with the military uniform except that it was made of dark blue cloth. It was the same with the administrative uniform although this was grey in colour, the cap of the workers was similar to the military cap but it was blue while the administrative types appeared in a cap which was more akin to the rainproof style already mentioned, being somewhat flatter and with a less protuberant peak. Very soon changes were noticed in the dress of the population as a whole. Chinese students who in the past, either through poverty or merely the bohemianism of student life, had paid little attention to dress, were among the most enthusiastic innovators of the new and officially approved austerity cum untidiness in costume. Workers in official organizations, both clerical and manual, were soon in party uniform too and they, together with the students, quickly brought sartorial dullness to everyday life in town or countryside. Men and women wore exactly the same garments, dresses disappeared and the only thing that distinguished the sexes was the drooping hair worn straight to the shoulders or a severe, almost masculine bob, both styles being common to the women of Communist organizations. No directives were actually issued but it became tacitly understood by ordinary people that it was not patriotic to dress smartly, life was now a serious business and clothes were a frivolity out of keeping with the spirit of the times, women put away their smart *ch'i p'ao,* silk stockings and high heeled shoes and wore their shabbiest clothes, cosmetics were no longer used and jewellery disappeared. Those who found it difficult to forget human vanities could be sure of a public reprimand or lecture from some earnest young enthusiast dressed in the uniform of the day.

Economic, utilitarian and suitable for mass production, the drabness of the livery of the new state was succinctly justified by its creators. Revolutionary China was faced with the urgent necessity of making itself independent of others, there were production difficulties to be overcome including cloth shortages, the people were called upon to forego gaiety and face the tasks which lay ahead of them, the severe uniform was not meant to be beautiful or attractive but at least it represented clothes for everybody, it was a practical measure as well as an ideological symbol. There was a grim logic in it when seen from this rigid viewpoint which however sidestepped other factors. From the first it was obvious that ideological necessity in clothes must eventually be turned into a new cult, if society is forcibly deprived of its smart clothes it is only human that it overcomes this frustration by turning drabness into a mode and this is what happened in China. The leaders of the nation assisted this development on every important public and ceremonial occasion by wearing the new style which in their case became more respectable and better groomed as power was consolidated.

There was another side to it as well. It is noticeable that in any country and in any period women who are actively engaged with social and political reforms or feminist rights are rarely those blessed with the maximum physical attractions of their sex and may even be singularly lacking in them. There are possibly biological reasons for this although the writer has no scientific authority for the statement, but the visual facts are indisputable. Looking around in the early days of the Communist's seizure of power in China it was difficult not to feel that there had been ushered in a period of supremacy for the militant feminist such as had never occurred before. Those stern, bespectacled young women with the lank hair under the unspeakable caps gained a virtuous satisfaction not entirely ideological at seeing their more physically attractive contemporaries ordered into a state of sexless regimentation. That is not to say that every Chinese woman who became a supporter of the new government was unattractive, such was far from being the case, but those who were not had nothing to lose and everything to gain in the new movement, they had a part to play and somebody wanted them at last. They were a force that could not be ignored when considering the dress reforms of Chinese communism.

In a short space of time the standardization of clothing in China was completed, everybody throughout the land was attired in the blue or grey cotton, padded for winter use. The *ch'i p'ao* disappeared as did the long gown of the men together with their foreign style suits, even the actors and actresses who might have been expected to retain tradition if not smartness in dress went into the same dull uniform. Colour, gaiety and individuality vanished from the streets but the only protests came from outside China, inside the cult of the utilitarian nondescript was in full tide. Such a state of affairs was bound to have reactions in time especially when the new China became more firmly established and there were increased contacts with the outer world. Foreign visitors and delegations began to go to China in increasing numbers and China herself sent political and cultural missions to the West. In the case of the latter it was noticeable that the majority of the men wore Western style clothes and the women *ch'i p'ao* or at any rate more colourful and smarter wear than their people at home which seemed to indicate a certain sensitivity about clothing. Practically every foreign visitor who came to China, whether for or against the regime, agreed on one point, the dress of the Chinese people was colourless and depressing. Such criticisms were bound to add fuel to the feelings smouldering within the Chinese people themselves. Taking stock of the universal cult of drab utility in whose creation they had acquiesced, they must have felt that it paid no dividends for China to dress itself in such a joyless fashion when other countries, including even their East European friends, cultivated colour and traditional pattern in their clothes. Chinese women in particular began to resent their bondage to Marxist austerity and no doubt their resentment included those types of women who, because they themselves were unattractive, appeared unnecessarily vehement about uniform in the new state.

In the summer of 1955 the outer world first began to hear the Chinese people's own criticism about their dress. The criticism came to a head in a forum held by the *New Observer* of Peking to discuss clothes, this was in response to many letters received from its readers expressing the dissatisfaction from all quarters, the forum included artists, musicians, a poet, a woman trade union leader, journalists from a woman's magazine and a member of the Youth League together with the editor of the *New Observer* to open the discussion. The general opinion seemed to be that the time had come to do something about their national dress and bring back colour and beauty into people's lives. One member pointed out that many young people regarded being smartly dressed as a sign of backwardness, "as if," cried the member in his newly vocal indignation, "being progressive was dependent on wearing drab colours." A woman painter pointed out that although bourgeois people wear handsome clothes to show that they have plenty of money there was no reason why people in a socialist society should not dress nicely too. Another speaker remarked that they could not return to the past for styles, their present standard suiting was a combination of the style introduced by Sun Yat-sen and the uniform of the Peoples' Army, it belonged to recent history and should be reformed with present day life in mind. He then somewhat perversely contradicted himself by pointing out that the old style of costume worn by peasants was far more serviceable and economical for work in the fields. The present trend in which country people wore the ready-made uniform suits of the city workers was much less practical, the buttons came off and the seams split. A music critic on the forum advocated the return to the traditional gown for Chinese women whom he considered looked graceful and gentle when wearing it. He was opposed, as might be expected, by the woman trade union leader who vociferously disagreed that the traditional gown was either beautiful or graceful and was besides inconvenient to wear, although they wanted to abolish uniformity it must be done with new styles. The forum discussions finally ended with the resolution: "Artists should produce new designs and fashions should be discussed more in newspapers and journals. As a basis we should study peasant and national dress, everyone should try to help clear away the mental resistance to more varied cut and colour, then the people themselves will create new styles."

An amusing note was provided shortly after this forum had taken place when a Japanese mothers' delegation visited China and were asked for their impressions on reaching Hong Kong. They were unanimous in their statement that women in China did not care for dress but only meetings and work, they always wore the plainest clothes and never wore lipstick or cosmetics. The Japanese mothers evidently regarded this as an achievement of some worth yet four of their party were dressed in Chinese women's *ch'i p'ao*, not, let it be said, particularly successfully. The average Japanese housewive's figure is little suited to the Chinese gown.

The *New Observer* forum was the prelude to new developments which gathered momentum in Communist China. On February 2nd 1956, an announcement was made that the Chinese government had invited a group of East German tailors to visit Peking and teach Chinese tailors how to cut and stitch European clothes. A Hong Kong newspaper in its comments said: ". . . uniform may be a trifle less universal but uniformity will still prevail, though the selection of East German tailors of all people to teach the tailors of Peking forms a mystery not to be explained on such obvious grounds."

On March 1st 1956 came the announcement that Peking had held its first fashion show in a department store building when fifty of the shop assistants modelled some four hundred different dresses along lines of elegance, economy and comfort. "Prominently displayed," said Peking radio, "were short jackets, fur robes and spring wearing apparel." Representatives of government agencies and the Ministry of Culture were invited to see the show. By March 26th Peking radio announced that Chinese women would be wearing brightly coloured flowered print frocks by the spring and that fifty four thousand bales of printed calico had been turned out by Shanghai manufacturers. Then on April 1st came the announcement that a full scale fashion show had been held in the Palace of Culture in Peking in which one thousand kinds of material and five hundred different fashions were displayed, more than seventy-four thousand people visited the show within seven days.

Some of the designs from these first fashion shows were printed in the Chinese press. They were chiefly variations on the *ch'i p'ao* and *ao* styles of pre-Communist days, in one design the *ch'i p'ao* was a calf length garment with a full skirt, turn down collar and no sleeves and worn like a tunic over a blouse. The jackets or *ao* were shown with a low collar and front fastening, one with lapels being reminiscent of the styles of Ming days, in many of the designs the slit of the *ch'i p'ao* was turned into a pleat. New China appears to have decided that the *ch'i p'ao* is too valuable a fashion asset to be allowed to disappear altogether but seems intent on modifying its traditional cut, the high collared, close fitting version is frowned upon on the official grounds of inconvenience though there seems to be a certain puritanism in their concern for this fashion. One writer acting as an official apologist points out that the best style of *ch'i p'ao* is one which is loose and full in the skirt adequately covering the legs and the stomach, not every woman he points out has the same figure and those with short, muscular or fleshy legs, therefore, are not at a disadvantage when compared with their more fortunate sisters in wearing such a style. One has to admit the justice of the statement.

Although the traditional gown, or at anyrate its modified version, appears confirmed in a lingering survival in the New China it seems obvious that the print frock and blouse with skirt will replace it as universal garments of feminine attire. The tendency has been marked for some time and now that the Peking government has sanctioned the manufacture of colorful dress materials there is likely to be a wholesale adoption of these styles. A noticeable feature is the use of smocking, embroidery and coloured sashes which smack a great deal of the peasant styles of Eastern and Central Europe. A foreign visitor to Canton from Hong Kong recently commented on the gay skirts and dresses being worn by the women (April 1956) and the fact that he did not see anybody wearing the *ch'i p'ao* at all.

Little has been said about reforms in men's dress in China. The few new male styles that have been shown have consisted of nothing more interesting than sport jackets and slacks or Western style suits, indeed it is difficult to see what else there could be if the Chinese do not wish to return to their traditional dress, apart from this, so long as the leaders of China continue to wear their severe uniforms so long no doubt will they continue to give the lead in male fashions. Industrial civilization in the West standardized peoples' dress and the process is now happening in the East, particularly in China where it is ably assisted by political ideology. National costume is something that develops over a long period of time with the history of a particular country, it cannot be created overnight. The new China has written off much past history and with it her national dress, it will be many years yet before it has completely disappeared, but it is obvious that in creating something new to take its place, apart from a hotch potch of minor developments from various sources there can only be direct imitation of the West in basic clothing styles. It is a sobering thought to consider the whole of China dressed in tweeds and slacks or blouses and skirts but needs must when the twentieth century drives.

⚘ First in Space—But Not in Femininity
AUDREY R. TOPPING

While the world's first space woman, Valentina Tereshkova, was whirling through space, a 10-year-old Russian girl rushed over to a neighbor's apartment with news of a new baby sister named Valentina.

"All the girl babies born in the hospital except one are being called Valentina," she exclaimed.

To millions of Soviet women, Junior Lieutenant Tereshkova is a promise of the future. For a generation and a half, since the Revolution, Russian women have been torn between a drive for equality with men, a compulsion to prove their worth in building the glory of the state, and a desire to be feminine. Valya, as she is called here, represents Soviet women as the Kremlin pictures them when an ideal Communist society, still a dream of the future, becomes reality. She wears her hair in the latest, most popular, short, fluffy "kitten cut," but, to Soviet propagandists, her space feat is proof that Soviet women are on an "equal footing in work that calls for great courage, physical endurance and much knowledge."

. . . .

In the early years of the revolution, flushed with their new status of equality, Soviet women attempted to throw off all symbols of femininity. They wore loose, straight skirts, severe jackets with wide shoulders, coats resembling army greatcoats, high boots and red kerchiefs. It was almost a uniform. On the grounds that one should be free to work for the state,

Source: The New York Times Magazine (June 30, 1963), pp. 10-11, 44, 46. Reprinted with permission of author and publisher.

marriage was frowned upon and abortions were legalized. Any attempt to make oneself physically attractive was strictly "bourgeois."

When women had proved to themselves that they were equal to men, the desire to relax and be themselves began to kindle. In 1936, because of the drop in the birth rate, abortion became illegal and many couples who had been living together for years decided to get married.

In the late thirties, the first Soviet cosmetic industry was begun by Pauline Zemchugyna, wife of Vyacheslav Molotov, then Peoples Commissar of Foreign Affairs. Guided by her knowledge as a daughter of the privileged class before the Revolution, she distributed articles about the importance of beauty and taste, and urged women to be more feminine. (She was later exiled to Siberia by Stalin.)

Before Pauline could have much influence, the war came and women again played masculine roles. Many women fought side-by-side with men at the front; others, as guerrillas. There was a regiment of women bomber pilots who still have a yearly reunion at the Bolshoi Theater in Moscow.

More than 10 years of war and its terrible aftermath passed before women could begin to shake off their masculine trappings. The Government gave them little help. A miserable garment industry started producing inferior clothing with no style, and an inadequate cosmetic trade was begun. Although prices were ridiculously high, women who had not been able to buy for so long were ready to pay any price for the small things essential to women. It was not long before a female underground began producing and selling black-market lipsticks, brassieres, girdles and nylons to those who could pay. Bits of lace and face creams were sold at outrageous prices but the supply could not keep up with the demand. Some of the stuff was smuggled in from abroad, but most of it was manufactured underground.

In 1958, after such items had begun to appear on the open market, an official war was declared on speculators. Black-market factories were uncovered in Riga, Tashkent, Moscow and most of the other major cities of the Soviet Union. In the last six months a flood of women's foundation garments, many from East Germany, has eliminated a "panty underground."

By 1959, the Soviet woman's desire to look feminine was almost as great as her wish to be masculine had been 40 years earlier. Books such as "Meditations on Beauty and Taste" and articles on manners began appearing in the book stores and the controlled press. The House of Fashions in Moscow started putting on fashion shows three times a day. One could not buy the dresses shown, but patterns could be had for 15 cents. Sewing machines were plentiful, and industrious women could sew their own clothes.

Beauty salons began to spring up. There are more than 1,500 small hairdressing shops in Moscow, and one large beauty parlor that can handle 350 women a day.

Mrs. Maria Bodin, a smartly dressed blonde, is director of the Women's Salon. "Our standard of living is now at the point where we can focus more attention on ourselves," she says. "The first thing women want to do when they have time is to make themselves beautiful. We try to help them. The women here are very eager to improve their appearance. Many come in and just say, 'Please do something.' We try."

Prices are modest. A wash and set are 80 cents, but most women wash their hair at home and have only a set for 50 cents. A manicure is 40 cents, a facial and massage $1 to $1.50, and a pedicure $2.10. There are no appointments and one must wait one's turn. Usually it is a long wait, but on the day Valentina Tereshkova was launched into space any woman named Valentina was sent to the head of the line.

Women are beginning to be diet-conscious. It is no longer popular to be plump, although Russians definitely prefer a sturdier build than is fashionable in the West. Russian mannequins are not required to have the sleek, almost emaciated figures of French and American models. Their average height is now 5 feet 6 inches and their weight 125 pounds, compared with 1956 when the average mannequin was an inch shorter and 10 pounds heavier. However, at least one portly model is kept in every fashion show to appeal to the majority of women over 30.

Mannequins who go abroad to show clothes at Soviet exhibitions are trained to walk in the exaggerated style of Western models, but those modeling in Moscow are encouraged to be more natural. A beautiful brunette mannequin complained: "People in my country do not appreciate my profession."

Although Soviet women no longer consider that looking prettily feminine is all that "bourgeois," doing so is very difficult except for those in privileged and artistic circles. The average Soviet woman has a long way to go before she reaches the standard in America and Europe. Many are too busy attending to the necessities of life to care, and if they do care they cannot afford it.

Religion

❀ Sacred Dress
ERNEST CRAWLEY

The Dress of Sanctity

One of the longest and most varied chapters in the history of dress is that dealing with the garb of permanent sacred grades, priestly, royal, and the like, and of temporary sacredness, as in the case of worshippers, pilgrims, and victims. Some examples have been incidentally noticed; a brief reference to certain types must suffice here. In ancient India the ascetic had to wear coarse, worn-out garments, and his hair was clipped. The hermit wore skins or tattered garments—the term may include bark —or grass-cloth—and his hair was braided. The *Snātaka* wore clothes not old or dirty. He wore the sacred string. He was forbidden to use garments, shoes, or string which had been worn by others. The student for his upper dress wore the skin of an antelope or other animal, for his lower garment a cloth of hemp, or flax, or wool. He wore the girdle of a Brāhman, a triple cord of *Muñja* grass. A *Kṣatriya* wore as his cord a bow-string; a *Vaiśya* a cord of hemp.[1] The religious character of this caste-system renders the inclusion of the four last grades convenient.

Temporarily, in worship and on pilgrimage, the ordinary member of an organized faith assumes a quasi-sacerdotal character. For the *hajj* to Mecca the Musalmān must wear no other garments than the *iḥrām*, consisting of two seamless wrappers, one passed around the loins, the other over the shoulders, the head being uncovered. The ceremony of putting them on at a pilgrims' "station" is *al-iḥrām*, "the making unlawful" (of ordinary garments and behaviour and occupations). The cere-

---

[1] *The Laws of Manu*, vi. 44, 52, 6, 15; iv. 34–36, 66.
Source: *Dress, Drinks, and Drums*, edited by Theodore Besterman, London: Methuen and Co. (1931), pp. 159–164. Reprinted by permission of the publisher.

mony of taking them off is *al-iḥlāl,* "the making lawful." The *hajjī* shaves his head when the pilgrimage is over.[2] According to some, the *iḥrām* is the shroud prepared in the event of the *hajjī's* death.[3] More likely it is preserved and used as a shroud when he dies.

The most important item in the costume of Japanese pilgrims is the *oizuru,* a jacket which is stamped with the seal of each shrine visited. "The three breadths of material used in the sewing of this holy garment typify the three great Buddhist deities—Amida, Kawannon, and Seishi. The garment itself is always carefully preserved after the return home, and when the owner dies he is clad in it for burial."[4]

The dress of worshippers varies between "decent apparel" and garments of assimilation to the god or the victim or the priest. As in the case of Baal-worship, the garments were often kept in the shrine and assumed on entrance. In certain rites both Dionysus and his worshippers wore fawn-skins. The Bacchanals wore the skins of goats. The veil of the worshipper has been referred to. In the earliest Christian period a controversy seems to have taken place with regard to female head-dress during worship. In the modern custom the male head-dress is removed, the female is retained. Academies sometimes preserve the rule of a special vestment for worshippers, whether lay or priestly.

It has been noted that the dress of *jogleors,* troubadours, and *trouvères* was an assimilation to the sacerdotal.[5] From the same mediæval period comes the record of "singing robes."

Priestly Robes

The dress of the sacred world tends to be the reverse of the profane. Apart from the impulse—to be traced in the mentality of medicine-men—to impress one's personality upon the audience by the fantastic and the grotesque, there is here the expression of the fundamental opposition between natural and supernatural social functions. The garb of Tshi

---

[2] E. Sell, *The Faith of Islam* (2nd edition, 1896), pp. 279–289.
[3] Sir R. F. Burton, *Personal Narrative of a Pilgrimage to Al-Medinah and Mecca* (1898), i. 139.
[4] B. N. Chamberlain, "Notes on Some Minor Japanese Religious Practices," *Journal of the Anthropological Institute* (1893), xxii. 360.
[5] H. Spencer, *Principles of Sociology,* iii. 222.

priests and priestesses differs from ordinary dress. Their hair is long and unkempt, while the lay fashion is to wear it short. The layman, if well-to-do, wears bright cloth; the priest may wear only plain cloth, which is dyed red-brown with mangrove-tan. Priests and priestesses, when about to communicate with the god, wear a white linen cap. On holy days they wear white cloth, and on certain occasions, not explained, their bodies are painted with white clay. White and black beads are generally worn round the neck.[6] The Ewe priests wear white caps. The priestesses wear steeple-crowned hats with wide brims. Priests wear white clothes. Priestesses wear "gay cloths" reaching to the feet, and a kerchief over the breast.[7]

The survival of some antique mode often suffices, through various accidents and modifications, for the priestly garb, other than sacerdotal vestments. Thus, the *ricinium,* a small antique mantle, was worn by the *magister* of the *Fratres Arvales* and by *camilli* generally.

The history of the dress of the Christian priesthood is a striking example of this. Here also we find the principle of opposition to the lay-garb. The democratic and non-professional character of primitive Christianity may be seen in the fact that in A.D. 428 Pope Celestinus censured Gallican bishops who wore dress different from that of the laity. They had been monks, and retained the *pallium* and girdle instead of assuming the tunic and toga of the superior layman. It is curious that the social instinct towards differentiation of dress to mark differentiation of social function was resisted so long. But in the sixth century the civil dress of the clergy automatically became different from the dress of the country, since, while the laity departed from the ancient type, the clergy withstood all such evolution. Thus, in the Western Empire the clergy retained the toga and long tunic, while the laity wore the short tunic, trousers, and cloak of the Teutons, the *gens bracata.* Gregory the Great would have no person about him clad in the "barbarian" dress. He enforced on his *entourage* the garb of old Rome, *trabeata Latinitas.* This cleavage was gradually enforced, and from the sixth century onwards the clergy was forbidden by various canons to wear long hair, arms, or purple, and, generally, the secular dress.

[6] A. B. Ellis, *The Tshi-speaking Peoples of the Gold Coast of West Africa* (1887), pp. 123–124.

[7] *Id., The Ewe-speaking Peoples of the Slave Coast of West Africa* (1890), pp. 143, 146.

The characteristic garb of the Christian clergy, both civil and ecclesiastic, was the long tunic. Originally it appears to have been white. Then its evolution divided; the alb derived from it on the one side, the civil tunic in sober colours on the other. For the civil dress the dignified toga was added to constitute full dress; for use in inclement weather the *casula* or *cappa,* an overcoat (*pluviale*) with a cowl, was adopted. The last-named garment similarly divided into the ecclesiastic *cope,* and the civil overcloak. The long tunic still survives in three forms—the surplice, the cassock, and the frock coat. Its fashion in the last instance superseded the toga, which again survives in the academic gown.

The evolution of vestments is in harmony with the psychology of dress generally, and in many aspects illustrates it forcibly. With the vestment the priest puts on a "character" of divinity. By change of vestments he multiplies the Divine force, while showing its different aspects. The changing of vestments has a powerful psychical appeal. The dress is a material link between his person and the supernatural; it absorbs, as it were, the rays of Deity, and thus at the same time inspires the human wearer. The dress is accordingly regarded not as an expression of the personality of the wearer, but as imposing upon him a super-personality. This idea is implicit in every form of dress. Dress is a social body-surface, and even in sexual dress, military uniform, professional and official dress the idea that the dress has the properties of the state inherent in it is often quite explicit. Further, the dress gives admission to the grade. In particular cases of solemnity a dress serves to render the person sacrosanct. Thus the Australian messenger is sacred by reason of his red cap.[8]

A temporary sacred garment may even be used sacrificially. At the Zulu festival of the new fruits, the king danced in a mantle of grass or of herbs and corn leaves, which was then torn up and trodden into the fields.[9] In such cases there is perhaps a reverse assimilation of virtue from the sacred person.

[8] J. Fraser, *Aborigines of New South Wales* (Sydney 1892), p. 31.
[9] J. Shooter, *The Kafirs of Natal and the Zulu Country* (1857), p. 27; N. Isaacs, *Travels and Adventures in Eastern Africa* (1836), ii. 293.

The Hasidic Community
SOLOMON POLL

Social Stratification

The Hasidic community is stratified into six distinct social classes:

1. *Rebbes* (R)
2. *Shtickel Rebbes* (SR)
3. *Sheine Yiden* (SY)
4. *Talmidei Hachamim* (TH)
5. *Balebatishe Yiden* (BY)
6. *Yiden* (Y)

Social stratification in the Hasidic community is based primarily upon frequency and intensity of religious observance. "Frequency" relates to the number of religious performances in the course of a day. For example, a religious Jew upon awakening must rise immediately and be ready to serve his Creator before evil inclinations can prevail. He must wash his hands in a ritual manner, taking the vessel first in the right hand and then in the left; then he must spill the water with the left hand upon the right and then, in reverse, from his right hand upon the left, repeating this performance three times.[1] Similar ritualistic observances are performed throughout the day.

"Intensity" refers to the emotional manifestations, some of which may be observed during public ceremonies. A person who is intensely involved in his religious practices may shake his body during prayers, or he may pray longer or display during prayers certain mannerisms that are known as religious, symbolic gestures. The greater the number of rituals and the more intensely they are observed, the greater the esteem accorded a person. The rites, the rituals, and the elements necessary for these performances are prescribed by law. But the law does not indicate the mannerism, the body movement, the emotional ecstasy, the joy or sadness that accompany the performance. Since these expressions are not specifically

[1] *Code of Jewish Law, (Kitzer Shulhan Aruch)* compiled by Solomon Gansfried and translated by Hyman E. Goldin (New York: Hebrew Publishing Co., 1927), pp. 2–4.

Source: The Hasidic Community of Williamsburg, New York: Free Press of Glencoe (1962), pp. 59–69, 212–220. Reprinted by permission of the author and publisher.

prescribed, they are completely Hasidic in character. Social standing in the community is in direct proportion to the intensity of the performance.

Thus, the criteria by which the Hasidic community is stratified are not the same as in other American communities. Lineage, wealth, occupation, income, residence, morals and manners, and education operate differently. Such criteria do not determine status unless they are associated with ritualistic observance. For instance, if a person has wealth but the frequency and intensity of his observance is low, he will not rank high in the social order. Nor will a person who possesses the other characteristics ordinarily associated with high status rank high in the social structure if he is not also characterized by high frequency and intensity of ritualistic observance.

Social and economic characteristics are important determinants of position only if they are connected with ritualistic observances. If a person has wealth, it may be displayed only through luxuries that are Hasidic in character. A rich man may have two sinks, two stoves, or even two separate kitchens—one for meat and one for dairy products—so that he can observe the dietary laws more intensely. Or a wealthy man may have a more beautiful *shtreimel,* which is again an intensification of Hasidic observances. If one is educated in Jewish matters, he will rank high only if his education is used to intensify his Hasidic behavior. Education in itself, without Hasidic observances, has little status value. Occupation, income, and residence, too, carry status value only if they supplement intensive Hasidic behavior.

Considerable upward and downward mobility is found in the Hasidic community. At the very top is a nucleus composed of the *Rebbes,* whose religious observances, ritualistic behavior, and entire behavior are living examples to the community. Those persons closest to the *rebbes* also enjoy high status in the community and the further one is from this core, the lower his rank in the social scale. Thus, the more a person absorbs a *rebbe's* teaching and is absorbed by that teaching, the closer he moves to the upmost level. No one, except a *rebbe,* ever reaches the highest rank, nor do many people desire to, since the frequency and intensity of religious observance demanded of them would limit their enjoyment of worldly rewards. However, the less one observes the laws and the less intensely one performs the rituals, the lower the ranking he has within the social structure.

Downward mobility is characterized by a decreasing adherence to

Hasidic rituals and by less participation in Hasidic activities. Deviation from *any* Hasidic social and religious norm lowers prestige and initiates downward mobility.

At the bottom of the social structure are the *Yiden,* (literally, the "Jews"). They do not excel in wealth, in scholarliness, nor in intensive and frequent Hasidic behavior; therefore, no special adjectives accompany their category. However, if they are compared with non-Hasidic Jews, they are known as *Hasidishe Yiden*. But in the Hasidic group, the term *Hasidishe* is not applicable, since every member is a "Hasidic Jew." *Yiden* are Hasidic Jews who observe the Hasidic norms but who are not distinguished by the frequency and intensity of their religious behavior. Although they are at the bottom of the Hasidic social order, persons in this grouping outdo everyone outside of the Hasidic community in religious performance. In their own eyes, therefore, they are not the lowest of the low, but rather the lowest of the exalted. As one Hasidic Jew expressed it, "I would rather be the worst among religious Jews than the best among sinners."

Next in rank are the *Balebatishe Yiden* (literally, the "house-owning Jews"). They are the full-fledged community members who participate in most of the local affairs. They contribute generously to the Hasidic causes. They are known to be "well-off" and the frequency and intensity of their religious observance is higher than that of the *Yiden*. *Balebatishe Yiden* give more to charity and contribute more financially to Hasidic causes than anyone above them in social status. They are also learned but not enough so to be called scholars. Their wealth supplements their status because it is used to intensify Hasidic behavior.

The next social class is the *Talmidei Hachamim* (literally, the "students of the wise"), the learned men whose scholarliness complements intense Hasidic observance. Their observance is more frequent and intense than the observance of the *balebatishe Yiden* and *Yiden*. *Talmidei Hachamim* do not have professional religious positions; they are learned laymen. They have less wealth than the people who are beneath them in the status order, but their more intense religious behavior as supplemented by scholarliness places them in a higher rank. The mere fact that they spend much time studying is in itself considered an index of their intense religious observance.

Next are the *Sheine Yiden* (literally, the "beautiful Jews"). Their religious observance is more intensive and more frequent than that of those of lower rank. They become religious professionals such as teachers, instructors of Talmud, ritual slaughterers, circumcisors, and so forth. The original appointment as religious professionals results from their religiosity, and the performance of their duties increases the intensity and frequency of their observances. They cannot fail, therefore, to be of high rank in the community.

Next to the top are the *Shtickel Rebbes* (literally, "piece of *rebbe*" or "bit of *rebbe*" or "something of a *rebbe*") who are persons who recently came into the *rebbishe* ranks through their intensive Hasidic activity. They are not usually in direct line of descent from well-known *rebbes*, and if they are members of a famous lineage, the dynasty and its followers have already been inherited by someone else, perhaps by an older brother. *Shtickel rebbes* are young persons or relatively new arrivals in the community. Their followers tend to be those of older *rebbes* with whom the *Shtickel rebbes* are identified. *Shtickel rebbes* are religious practitioners whose authority is second only to that of a *rebbe*.

The *rebbes* are the top-ranking religious leaders, and their authority is inherited from their fathers or other close relatives.[2] It is believed ultimately to come from God. They are beyond question or reproach. They are recognized as the "most high who exceed, outdo, and outrank every other person in the entire world." Their entire behavior is thought to be ritualistic. Every move and mannerism is a form of religious worship. Their ritualistic observance is the most frequent and the most intense of all worshipers. Thus, the *rebbes* are the core of the community.

Each of these six classes in the Hasidic community has supplementary characteristics as shown in Table 1. Briefly, these are:

Table 1 The relationship of social rank and supplementary status characteristics in the Hasidic community

Descending Social Rank Order	Inheritance of Dynasty	Lineage	Professional Affiliation	Education	Wealth	Conformity
1. *Rebbes*	+	+	+	+	+—	+
2. *Shtickel Rebbes*	—	+	+	+	+—	+
3. *Sheine Yiden*	—	—	+	+	—	+
4. *Talmidei Hachamim*	—	—	—	+	—	+
5. *Balebatishe Yiden*	—	—	—	—	+	+
6. *Yiden*	—	—	—	—	—	+

+ = Positive   — = Negative   +— = Neutral

[2] Intensity of religious observance is a consistent criterion for social rank. Sons of *rebbes* who do not follow their fathers in matters of religion do not rank high. Their lineage would only supplement their individual religious observance.

The *Yiden* conform to the intense Hasidic religious performance that identifies and characterizes them as Hasidic Jews vis-a-vis observant non-Hasidic Jews.

The *balebatishe Yiden,* in addition, have wealth that they expend on Hasidic luxuries. These expenditures in themselves constitute religious observance.

The *Talmidei Hachamim,* though without wealth, are educated in religious matters and are considered learned laymen.

The *sheine Yiden,* besides having education, have a professional affiliation as "religious performers." They, too, lack wealth.

The *Shtickel rebbes* have education, professional affiliation, and some degree of kinship with a famous *rebbe.* A *shtickel rebbe* may or may not have wealth, and his wealth may be associated with the organization with which he is affiliated.

The *rebbes* have education, professional affiliation, and lineage, are identified with a dynasty and have inherited its followers. A *rebbe* may or may not have wealth; if so, it is closely connected with the organization of which he is an integral part.

Social stratification among the Hasidim has one especially interesting feature. The Hasidim are not only externally identifiable from members of the larger community, but they are also recognizable as members of a particular social stratum. Especially on the Sabbath and holidays, a Hasidic Jew can identify the social class of another Hasidic Jew by his dress. He feels that by wearing garments identifying him as a Jew he will be helped to refrain from coming into contact with sin. "Looking like a Jew with the image of God upon one's face" will serve as a barrier against acculturation and assimilation. As one Hasidic Jew expressed it, "With my appearance I cannot attend a theater or movie or any other places where a religious Jew is not supposed to go. Thus, my beard and my sidelocks and my Hasidic clothing serve as a guard and shield from sin and obscenity." [3]

The garments the Hasidic Jews wear today are considered by them to be the traditional Jewish garments which were once the apparel of all Jews. But because most of today's Jews imitate non-Jews, these garments are now exclusively Hasidic. The types of Hasidic clothing and the ways of looking Hasidic change from class to class. The extent of affiliation with Hasidism determines the particular kind of garments worn. The

[3] From the files of SFJ, 1956.

different types of Hasidic garments serve as identifying symbols of social rank.

The Hasidic garments vary from *zehr Hasidish* (extremely Hasidic) to *modernish* (modern). The less Hasidic men, that is, the persons whose religious performances are of less frequency and less intensity, wear *modernish* clothing. Though still recognizable as "Hasidic," these garments resemble those of western societies. Or these men wear western clothing that is turned into Hasidic clothing by Hasidic overtones; for instance, long-outmoded, double-breasted dark suits that button from right to left. The most observant wear *zehr Hasidish* clothing, and through this they are identified as persons of high rank. Their clothing alone indicates that the frequency and intensity of their observances have secured them high status. A person who wears *zehr Hasidish* clothing would be ridiculed if his behavior were not consistent with his appearance.

Thus, the only persons who wear "extremely Hasidic" garments are those whose behavior in frequency and intensity of religious observance coincides with the clothing they wear.

Gaining recognition in a higher social stratum is a gradual process effected by increasingly religious behavior. Individuals who display more intense religious observance are asked by the community or by the *rebbe* to put on more elaborate Hasidic garments to indicate their acceptance into a higher class. Requests to wear more Hasidic garments are also used to induce higher frequency and intensity of religious behavior. Once a person wears clothing symbolizing a higher status, the frequency and intensity of his behavior should be consistent with the type of garment he wears. It is assumed that wearing a garment symbolizing higher status will create a chain reaction of more and more intensified religious observance.

There are two major aspects to the external appearance of a Hasidic Jew. One is the Hasidic garment and the other is the *bord und payes,* the beard and side-locks. These status symbols vary with each social stratum as shown in Table 2.

Class 6, the *Yiden* (Y), has a minimum of the Hasidic status symbols. Chief among these are the dark, double-breasted suits that button from right to left.

Class 5, the *Balebatishe Yiden* (BY), has, besides some minimal Hasidic identifying symbols, the identifying status symbols of beard and

Table 2 The relationship of social rank and identifying status symbols in the Hasidic community

Descending Social Rank Order	(SZ)	(SB)	(K)	(BH)	(BP)	(SHI)
Class 1 (R)	+	+	+	+	+	+
Class 2 (SR)	−	+	+	+	+	+
Class 3 (SY)	−	−	+	+	+	+
Class 4 (TH)	−	−	−	+	+	+
Class 5 (BY)	−	−	−	−	+	+
Class 6 (Y)	−	−	−	−	−	+

Identifying Status Symbols:
- (SZ) *Shich and Zocken* (slipper-like shoes and white knee socks)
- (SB) *Shtreimel and Bekecher* (fur hat made out of sable and long silk coat)
- (K) *Kapote* (long overcoat worn as a jacket)
- (BH) *Biber hat* (large-brimmed hat made out of beaver)
- (BP) *Bord und Payes* (beard and side-locks)
- (SHI) Some Hasidic identity

Social Rank:
- (R) *Rebbe*
- (SR) *Shtickel Rebbe*
- (SY) *Sheiner Yid*
- (TH) *Talmidei Hachamim*
- (BY) *Balebatisher Yid*
- (Y) *Yid*

\+ = Positive   − = Negative

side-locks (BP). Some beards are never cut or trimmed and some side-locks are never cut or shaved, a symbol of still higher status.

Class 4, the *Talmidei Hachamim* (TH), besides having beard and side-locks, also wears a *Biber* hat (BH). This is a black, large-brimmed hat made out of beaver.

Class 3, the *Sheine Yiden* (SY), besides having the beard, side-locks and *biber* hat, also has the *Kapote* (K). The *kapote* is a long overcoat, usually black, worn instead of a jacket.

Class 2, the *Shtickel Rebbes* (SR), besides having the beard, side-locks, *biber* hat and *kapote,* has the *Shtreimel and Bekecher* (SB). The *shtreimel* is a fur hat made out of sable. The *bekecher* is a long Hasidic coat made of silk or silky material in which the pockets are in the back.

Class 1, the *Rebbes* (R), besides having the beard, side-locks, *biber* hat, *kapote, shtreimel* and *bekecher,* also has the *Shich* and *Zocken* (SZ). *Shich* are slipper-like shoes, and *zocken* are white knee socks into which the breeches are folded.

As the classes ascend in the social structure, more and more status symbols are associated with that particular class. Since wearing the status symbols is in itself a performance of religiosity, it is consistent with the social stratification of the Hasidic community. The *rebbes* are the only ones who, as a class and without exception, wear the *shich* and *zocken.* They also wear the symbolic *shtreimel* and *bekecher, biber* hat and *kapote,* and *bord und payes.* The *shtickel rebbes* are next in rank order, and while some of them do wear the *shich* and *zocken,* most do not. However, all the *shtickel rebbes* wear the other symbols—*shtreimel, bekecher, biber* hat and *kapote, bord und payes.* Likewise, some of the *sheine Yiden* may wear the *shtreimel* and *bekecher,* but most do not, and none wear the *shich* and *zocken.* All the other symbolic garments are worn. Next in order are the *talmidei hachamim,* some of whom may wear *kapotes,* and all of whom wear the *biber* hat, the *bord und payes.* The *balebatishe Yiden,* while some of them may wear higher status symbols, always have, as a class, the *bord und payes.* At the very bottom of the scale are the *Yiden,* all of whom have some Hasidic status symbols by which they are identified as Hasidic Jews.

Thus, in the Hasidic community, religion is the major criterion for social stratification. The frequency and intensity of religious behavior and the frequency and intensity with which one observes the rites and rituals of Jewish law in the course of the day are a major class index. Wealth, occupation, residence, and other social and economic characteristics only supplement one's status position. The external appearance of the members of this group may be conceived as status symbols by which members are identified with their social position. These external status symbols and the frequency and intensity of religious behavior must be parallel and consistent with each other. This *consistency* is a very important form of social control by which the group maintains and furthers its religiosity. It will be shown later that the major classification of the group's economic activities also falls within the class structure as outlined here. The economic activities, too, supplement the status position which has been gained through intensive religious observance.

The Manufacture or Sale of Nonreligious Articles

The category "manufacture or sale of nonreligious articles" includes all occupations connected with the manufacture and sale of articles that are not designated as or used for religious purposes. The manufacture and sale of nonreligious articles is usually directed toward the larger, non-Hasidic community, since these articles are secular in nature. However, in the Hasidic community, even these articles tend to assume semireligious characteristics. An example of such a semireligious article is the wig.

To clarify the semireligious nature of the wig, a short explanation of the Hasidic women's custom of head covering is necessary. The hair of a Hasidic woman must be cut off upon marriage. She is not allowed to wear her own hair uncovered, nor to display any part of her hair in public. Her head must be covered at all times. The "truly modest" Hasidic women do not even uncover their hair when they are alone. Covering one's hair even when in complete privacy is considered an act of chastity. To be able to observe this important ritual of "covering the head," and still appear in public, most Hasidic women wear a *sheitel* (wig), which gives the appearance of one's own hair. Even here, since the *sheitel* gives the appearance of real hair, the "most zealous of the zealous" Hasidic women consider the *sheitel* too modern. Instead of the *sheitel* they wear a headpiece that looks like a wig, except that it is made of some silky material, or they wear a turban. Thus, the headpieces or turbans of the "most zealous of the zealous" Hasidic women are not intended to create the illusion of human hair.

In itself the wig is a nonreligious item, but because the wearing of it in the Hasidic community serves a religious purpose, the *sheitel* maker is considered to be engaged in the manufacture of semireligious articles. It is important that the Hasidic woman beautify herself and make herself attractive to her husband, especially after her "clean days" and the ritual immersion following her menstrual period. Good grooming and an attractive *sheitel* are of utmost importance, so that the lure of the metropolis will have no influence on her husband. The wigs are combed, brushed, shampooed, styled, cut, and dyed by that important figure, the *sheitel macher*.

One *sheitel macher* advertises as follows:

Sheitelach

Order your wig from Esther's Beauty Salon
58 Lee Avenue, corner Ross Street,
Brooklyn, New York
You can get the most modern style and the most "natural look" and also have a better fitting. Made to order from the finest European hair. Also ready-made for sale in a large selection.
Call for appointment. ST 2-4323 [4]

Those Hasidic women who consider the use of the *sheitel* too modern cover their heads with turbans. Some of the women make these headpieces themselves, but the demand has now become great enough so that they are produced commercially. One manufacturer advertises at the various houses of worship with a handwritten and hand-drawn leaflet in which she calls to the attention of the community that:

> With the aid of God.
> Hasidic women!
> Turbans in all styles made to order by
> Mrs. Pollock.
> 80 South 10th Street, EV 7-6201 [5]

Like the *sheitel,* other articles made to accord with Hasidic norms are considered semireligious, because they serve religion. For instance, Hasidic women must wear clothing that covers their bodies properly. Dresses must have long sleeves and high necklines and are usually of a dark color. One dress shop advertises a sale of dresses that meet Hasidic requirements:

> Honig's Bargain Store
> 69 Avenue C, corner East 5th Street, New York
> Big sale of dresses with long sleeves
> Black and blue
> 20½, 18½, 14, 12
> Regular price $15.98—Sale price $2.50 [6]

Since covering the body is considered an act of chastity and a symbol of modesty, the dress of a Hasidic woman must cover her properly. She

---
[4] *Der Yid,* February, 1957. Translated from the Yiddish.
[5] From leaflet SH2. Translated from the Yiddish.
[6] *Der Yid,* November 2, 1956. Translated from the Yiddish.

must wear stockings at all times so that her legs will not be exposed to public view. The most zealous Hasidic women wear heavy-gauge stockings, not the sheer nylon ones that are considered to expose her legs. Only with these heavy-gauge stockings is she considered "truly modest" and proper. Thus, dry goods stores are actually selling semireligious items of Hasidic symbolism. The merchants refer to the long black stockings for women not as "long black stockings," but as "Hasidic stockings," indicating the religious significance of the merchandise. One merchant advertises the following:

You can obtain from us dry goods.

Baby equipment—children's things

Also children's and women's dresses with long sleeves, Hasidic shirts and underwear for men. We have just received imported Hasidic black, long stockings for women.

Best quality at low prices. Come and convince yourself.

Eliezer Waldman

147 Lee Avenue, Brooklyn 11, New York [7]

As discussed earlier, Hasidic men must wear "Hasidic garments," which are status symbols. The more Hasidic a person is, the higher the status he enjoys. The higher the status he enjoys, the more exclusively Hasidic garments he wears.

Thus, there are some Hasidic men who wear "extremely Hasidic garments" not only on the Sabbath and on holidays but also all week long. Others wear "extremely Hasidic garments" only on the Sabbath, and "less Hasidic garments" on weekdays. Still others wear "less Hasidic garments" on the Sabbath and holidays and *"modernish* garments" on weekdays. Finally, there are some who wear *"modernish* garments" all the time. Despite these differences, there is almost no one in the community who does not wear some Hasidic garment by which he can be externally identified as a Hasidic Jew.

One merchant advertises garments for *rebbes* and for laymen. He advertises various items of Hasidic clothing such as *bekechers, hapotas, halatin,* "chopped *kapotes,"* and even Prince Alberts. He also announces in his advertising that all the clothing he sells is guaranteed not to contain any *shatnes*. This advertisement reads as follows:

Rabbinical and *balebatishe* clothing.

[7] *Der Yid,* August 23, 1957. Translated from the Yiddish.

I announce to all my friends and customers that all sorts of clothing are available from me.

Best quality for very reasonable prices.

Silk *bekechers, kapotes,* table *chalatin,* chopped *kapotes,* Prince Alberts, wool and alpaca, long suits, overcoats, spring coats.

Special sale of Atlasin *bekechers,* 12 dollars.

We also make to order with the greatest punctuality all sorts of clothing. All clothing is guaranteed *shatnes*-free. With blessings to be inscribed and sealed into the Book of Life for good.

Gluck Clothing Store
210 Broadway, near Roebling Street,
Brooklyn, New York, EV 7–2004 [8]

At another time this merchant ran a special sale in honor of a Jewish holiday. He compared the regular prices to the sale prices, conveying to the community that his prices were reduced "in honor of the holiday." He offered silken *bekechers* and *chalatin,* special garments called "table *chalatin*" because they are worn at the holiday table. He also assured his customers that all his clothing was *shatnes*-free. This leaflet, which was hung in the various houses of worship, read:

SPECIAL SALE

In honor of the Holy Days that come to us for good.

With the help of God, May He be blessed, I announce to all my customers that I have received a great lot of beautiful double-breasted suits, overcoats, spring coats and winter coats made special from imported fine fabrics at amazingly cheap prices.

Suits: Regular price was $48.00, now only $35.90

Spring coats: Regular price was $42.00, now only $36.00

Winter coats: Regular price was $46.00, now only $39.80

Silken *bekechers:* special sale, $32.00

Table *halatin* in various beautiful designs: $9.90

Prince Alberts: $44.00.

We also make all garments to order very punctually by fine, first-class craftsmen for the cheapest prices.

All clothing is guaranteed *shantes*-free.

Our prices are greatly reduced in honor of the holiday.

Make your purchase in time so that we shall be able to satisfy you the best

[8] From leaflet CL3. Translated from the Yiddish.

way and fill all your requests. With blessings to be inscribed and sealed into the Book of Life for good.

[Signed] Moshe Mordechai Gluck
M. Gluck Clothing Corp.
210 Broadway, Brooklyn 11, New York
EV 7-2004 [9]

Still another merchant appeals not only to the "very Hasidic" with extremely Hasidic garments such as table *chalatin* and summer *bekechers* made of Persian silk, but also to the "less Hasidic" with *modernish* garments such as "long Hasidic tropical suits." He also advertises *bekechers* made of nylon, a typical example of how a traditional religion that opposes every possible move leading to secularism adopts technology as a means of furthering religiosity. The advertisement reads:

With the Aid of God

SUMMER SALE

Tropical suits, wool and Dacron, light as feathers, strong as iron, beautiful workmanship, half-lined with fine Bemberg lining. You buy quality for only $36.00.

Tropical suits from last season, sizes only 38 to 40, $25.00. Overcoats, topcoats, fine 100 per cent wool material, medium gray, dark gray, oxford gray, $42.00.

Long Hasidic tropical suits, $39.00. Table *chalatin* for the summer, $10.00. Summer *bekechers* made from Persian silk, special sale, $36.00. Long rayon jackets, practical in the country, $4.00. Luster topcoats, $18.00 and up.

Single-breasted tropical suits, very beautiful samples, Dacron and wool, $38.00. Single-breasted topcoats, navy and gray, 100 per cent wool, very fine quality, $39.00.

Nylon *bekechers*, $32.00. Light black summer pants, $6.50.

We make all sorts of clothing to order with the best workmanship. Satisfaction is guaranteed.

With honor,
[Signed] Roth & Wollner
145 Division Avenue, Brooklyn, New York
EV 4-4927 [10]

---

[9] From leaflet CL5. Translated from the Yiddish.
[10] From leaflet CL7. Translated from the Yiddish. Italics added.

It is not enough that a Hasidic Jew be identifiable by others through his external appearance; he must also have other identifying symbols that carry special meaning within his own group. Thus, his undergarments, as well as his outer garments, must meet Hasidic religious requirements. I was told that a religious functionary, who had all the qualifications for the position of a ritual slaughterer, was not hired in a Hasidic community in Europe because in the ritual baths people noticed that he was not wearing long underpants. It was assumed that if he wore shorts, he had gone too far astray in other religious matters. The truly Hasidic woman must wear a nightgown with long sleeves, regardless of seasonal change, since long sleeves are a sign of chastity.

The required Hasidic underwear is available at Gluck Brothers and Meyerowitz. They advertise the following:

In Honor of Passover

We are in a situation where we can serve you with the most beautiful double-breasted children's suits, in all sizes and colors. First-class fitting without alterations.

We have a large selection of children's and men's shirts. Also, right-to-left underwear, also long underpants, women's gowns with long sleeves, linen, bedding and other things for the home. Boys' and girls' polo shirts in various beautiful colors, and of the best quality.

With blessings for a kosher and happy holiday.

[Signed] GLUCK BROTHERS & MEYEROWITZ [11]

Proper observance of religion is a basis for competition in the Hasidic community. Some merchants try to show that their merchandise exceeds Hasidic requirements. Thus, they imply that they are "holier than thou," that they are aware of the Hasidic restrictions prescribed by the law, that they care lest their customers be exposed to the least possibility of transgression of the law. An illustration of this point can be seen in a clothier's advertisement. This clothier not only has a special department for all rabbinical and Hasidic clothing, he not only sells clothing that is free of *shatnes*, but he also guarantees that his customers will not wear *shatnes* even during the time of the fitting and thus not transgress the law prohibiting the wearing of *shatnes*. The advertisement reads:

---

[11] *Der Yid*, April 3, 1959. Translated from the Yiddish.

HOLIDAY SALE

The beautiful new clothing store of Roth & Wollner has prepared a big selection of all sorts of clothing such as: double-breasted suits, shirts, half-long and long overcoats, table *halatin, bekechers,* etc.

In the children's line, we have expanded our stock with husky sizes and also a beautiful selection of overcoats, sizes up to 20. Also very beautiful winter coats, lined with quilted cotton.

Special rabbinical department with all rabbinical and Hasidic clothing. Light table *chalatin,* special only ten dollars. All sorts of clothing are made to order also.

Stock of clothing is already tested for shatnes. You can be sure about shatnes even during fittings.

Visit us right away and you will walk out with the fullest satisfaction.

[Signed] CHAIM ROTH AND YONAH YITZCHAK DAVID WOLLNER
145 Division Avenue, Brooklyn 11, New York
Telephone: EV 4–4927

Cheapest prices

We wish to all our friends that they be inscribed and sealed in the Book of Life for good. [12]

One of the most significant status symbols among men in the Hasidic community is the *shtreimel,* made of sable, the average price of it is one hundred dollars. Anyone who wears such a hat is known as a *"Yid mit a shtreimel."* When a Hasidic man puts on a *shtreimel* for the first time (usually at his wedding), it is an indication that he commits himself to a Hasidic way of life, appropriate to one who wears this hat. The wearing of the *shtreimel* and the behavior expected of a person wearing it are simultaneous re-enforcements of the Hasidic norms. A person is expected to behave in a certain manner. When he does, the community permits him to wear a *shtreimel.* Then, because he has a *shtreimel,* he will not commit a breach of trust by not living up to those norms that govern behavior of a person wearing a *shtreimel.* Thus, wearing such a fur hat may identify a person as belonging to a certain status category; but it is not the fur hat itself that puts him there, it is his Hasidic behavior, with which he constantly justifies the wearing of the *shtreimel.*

Since the *shtreimel* is such an important Hasidic status symbol indicating one's religious behavior, it is considered a "religious item" and is

---

[12] *Hamaor,* March, 1957. Translated from the Yiddish. Italics the author's.

available at stores where other religious items are sold. Such hats are manufactured by a *shtreimel macher* (*shtreimel* maker), who usually has a large selection for sale. One advertises:

*"The Sabbatical Year Does Not
Let Go Until the End,"*

but a *shtreimel* you can buy right away so that you should have it by the beginning of the year. We have prepared, in honor of the holy days which should come to us for goodness, a large stock of beautiful sable *shtreimlach* for very cheap prices. Come as long as the stock holds out. You will be completely satisfied.

With blessings to be inscribed and sealed in the Book of Life for good.
The House of Trade and Manufacturer of *Shtreimlach*
Kepecs
80 Wilson Street, Brooklyn, New York [13]

The *shtreimel* is an exclusive Sabbath and holiday hat. People who wear a *shtreimel* on the Sabbath usually wear a *biber* hat on weekdays. Those Hasidic Jews who wear *biber* hats on the Sabbath too wear a large black hat on weekdays. These hats are considered Hasidic hats and are treated as semireligious articles. Selco Hatter advertises:

Hats

IN HONOR OF PASSOVER

The biggest selection of all sorts of Hasidic or modern hats. Prices from $5.95 to $20.00

Agency for Stetson hats.
Selco Hatter, Incorporated
337 Roebling Street, Brooklyn, New York
EV 8–6848 [14]

[13] *Hamaor*, July, 1958. Translated from the Hebrew.
[14] *Der Yid*, April 5, 1957. Translated from the Yiddish.

Caste and Class

✻ Stratification in a Prairie Town
JOHN USEEM, PIERRE TANGENT, AND

RUTH HILL USEEM

In this study, the two most distinct, polar strata are examined: the elite, locally referred to as "the Tops," live on top of a bluff on the east side of town; the low status group, called by Prairietoners "the Bottoms," are concentrated on the flats below the western portion of town.[1] From each of these two strata was drawn a sample of twenty-two families and the forty-four households were then interviewed. These samples covered about 25 per cent of Bottoms families and 50 per cent of Tops families.[2]

. . . .

As might be anticipated, differences in external symbols of status such as property and costume are considerable. Most of the Bottoms group live in two-room shacks without electricity and running water and with only

---

[1] A list of household heads was presented to ten persons in various strata of the population: a minister, a teacher, a banker, a businessman, a farmer, a "reliefer," a common laborer, a social worker, and two housewives of different social rank. These judges independently ranked the family heads in terms of their social position in the community. This procedure for delineating social classes is similar to that used by Edgar A. Schuler in his study, "Social and Economic Status in a Louisiana Hills Community," *Rur. Sociol.* 1940, 5:69–85; and George Lundberg, "Measurement of Socio-Economic Status," *Amer. Sociol. Rev.*, 1940, 5:29–39.

[2] The schedule used contained sections adapted from F. S. Chapin, *Measurement of Social Status by the Use of the Social Status Scale, 1933*, Minneapolis, 1933 and *A Social Participation Scale, 1937*, Minneapolis, 1938; from Emory S. Bogardus, "A Social Distance Scale," *Sociol. and Soc. Res.*, 1933, 17:265–271; from E. D. and M. B. Hinckley, "Attitude Scales for Measuring the Influence of the Work Relief Program," *J. of Psych.*, 1939, 8:115–124; and items added by the authors to elicit other information.

Source: *American Sociological Review*, Vol. 7 (June, 1942), pp. 332–333, 335–337. Reprinted with permission of the authors and publisher.

the bare essentials of household equipment. The mean score on Chapin's Living Room Scale is 27.41 with a range from 2 to 76.[3] Only six of this stratum own their homes and these have an average assessed valuation of $355. Although fifteen of the sample have cars, they were all bought second or third hand, average 12 years old, and four-fifths are Fords and Chevrolets. Heads of households own one suit of clothes and equally few other items of personal adornment which were bought several years ago and reflect rural standards of "presentability." Every Tops family is a home-owner and the average assessed value of property on which they live is $3,300. On Chapin's scale, the average for these families is 200.82.[4] In addition to the home in which they reside, many possess extensive farm and town properties secured by purchasing land lost through tax delinquencies and mortgage foreclosures during the last two decades.[5] Twenty of the twenty-two members of the elite sample own cars which average 1.25 years old and 60 per cent are in the higher price range, such as Packards and Buicks. Personal costumes are multiple in number and follow latest urban styles.

Formal education of the two groups stands in marked contrast. All but three of the upper stratum sample are college graduates, whereas the average grade completed by the lower class sample is the eighth, only three being high school graduates and none having attended college ($t = 11.29$). Paralleling this difference in educational attainments are tastes in reading and leisure time pursuits. The high ranking class pride themselves on their "cultural" interests and general knowledge of world events. To maintain this distinction, they buy numerous "best sellers" which are displayed in prominent parts of the living room, faithfully attend local

---

[3] Chapin found in his research with the scale that those whose score fell below 24 were so entirely lacking in the bare necessities of life as to be considered "destitute." The average for the entire lower stratum exceeds this by a scant three points, and twelve cases were found to be located below 24 points. Further, there were six cases in the 25–49 point category which Chapin designates as a "poverty, relief case" classification. Three more cases miss this grouping by the slim margin of but a single point, scoring 50. The remaining case, 76 points, is just barely ranked in the lower third of the "middle class" which ranges from 75–149 points.

[4] Eighteen of the sample rated in the "high class" which begins at 150 points. Three of the four cases which fell into the "upper middle class" had scores of 149. The remaining case was still in the upper third of the "upper middle class" with a score of 138 points. In short, 62 points separated the highest score of the Bottoms and the lowest score of the Tops. This difference is so obvious that a test of significance of difference is unnecessary.

[5] Many so dispossessed are now renters of the upper class.

"literary societies," subscribe to an average of six periodicals per family,[6] and more than half regularly receive newspapers from such distant cities as New York, Chicago, and Minneapolis. Bottoms people show little interest in the "arts" and would gain no prestige in their group through such activities. Only six of the sample are members of study clubs. Their reading material is confined to a few pulp magazines of the *True Stories* and westerns variety plus newspapers from the closest city.

Divergencies between the two classes are manifest in the vital processes of life itself. The mean age of death among the higher class during the past twenty years is 61.5 for men and 77.0 for women in contrast to 52.1 for men and 64.0 for women from the Bottoms.[7] Infant mortality is nearly twice as high in the latter class. The four local doctors report that imaginary ailments are far more common among upper class women and chronic, untreated sicknesses and malnutrition among the subordinate group. Likewise, the fertility of the two populations reveals a discrepancy; the ascendent class sample averages 2.27 living children and the lower class sample 3.86 ($t = 2.70$). The largest family in the Tops, is one with five children, while a third of the Bottoms families have that many or more offspring.

Lines of demarcation between classes are drawn more distinctly in the roles of women than of men. The latter tend to be impersonal in their interactions and associate more freely with members of the outgroup without losing status in the ingroup, whereas among the women, relationships are highly personalized. They are more alert to standings of individuals and more scrupulously conform to their class norms. The social distance between the two women's classes is far greater than between the two men's as measured by Bogardus' scale. Though none of the Tops wives are employed, all but two feel their social life is important for the business advancement of their husbands. Half of the Bottoms women work intermittently outside the home when employment is available and none regards her social life as having any bearing on her husband's status.

Upper class women are time conscious. Though they have few household duties because of hired help, mechanical appliances, and few chil-

---

[6] These include magazines of the *Reader's Digest, Good Housekeeping, National Geographic*, and *Fortune* varieties.

[7] These rates were compiled from local vital statistics records. Not included are those dying under five years of age. Since these figures are not a sample but represent the total universe, differences are significant without testing.

dren, many hours are absorbed in attending and preparing for social affairs, shopping for latest styles, going to beauty parlors, and participating in numerous clubs. There are ninety-five different "women's societies" composed almost exclusively of upper stratum women engaged in bridge playing and "cultural" activities.[8] Lower class women live more leisurely and without a sense of pressing social engagements. The limited size and content of their households means little effort spent in maintaining them. A self-respecting woman is expected to concentrate on rearing her children rather than on formal social affairs and to confine her social life to neighborly visiting. This difference in the tempo of life is indicated by the mean scores of the two groups on Chapin's Scale of Social Participation; the women of high rank had an average score of 20.36 as compared to 2.55 for the low ranking group ($t = 4.69$).[9]

Concern over personal appearance is far more extensive among upper class women. Over half the sample "diet" to preserve their figure in keeping with current fashion; none of the Bottoms women do. Tops women are more preoccupied with dress and current styles and are more critical of the costumes of their associates than are women of low status who neither discuss the matter often nor use dress as a criterion for the appraisal of others.

Although the process of ordering social position within the community is rarely discussed as a total pattern, it is all pervasive and involves both the intimate personal aspects of living as well as the most public and impersonal. Through gossip, invitations to affairs, membership in organizations, and other cues, positions in the social hierarchy are known to all. There is no doubt in the minds of Prairieton people regarding the class to which they belong and they also have no doubt about the social position of everyone else in the community.

[8] A similar pattern is noted in the study of a suburban area in an eastern state. See George Lundberg, Mirra Komarovsky and Mary Alice McIvery, *Leisure,* 177–179, New York, 1934. See also Robert S. and Helen M. Lynd, *Middletown in Transition,* 182, New York, 1937.
[9] Eleven of the lower group had scores of zero. The men's mean scores were 21.81 for those of high rank and 0.55 for those of low rank ($t = 6.19$).

Trend to Breakdown of Class Lines in Clothes
FREDERICK LEWIS ALLEN

Much more impressive, however, than the narrowing of the gap in *income* between rich and poor has been the narrowing of the gap between them in their *ways of living*.

For instance, consider the matter of personal appearance, remembering that in 1900 the frock-coated, silk-hatted banker and his Paris-gowned wife were recognizable at a distance, if they ventured among the common herd, as beings apart. Forty or fifty years ago the countryman in a metropolis was visibly a "hayseed"; the purchaser of inexpensive men's clothing was betrayed by his tight-waisted jackets and bulbous-toed shoes. Today the difference in appearance between a steelworker (or a clerk) and a high executive is hardly noticeable to the casual eye. Not long ago, at a tennis tournament, I sat two or three rows behind the chairman of the board of one of the most famous banking houses in the world, and looking at his veteran Panama hat and his ordinary-looking sack suit I wondered how many of the people about him would have guessed that he was anybody of great financial consequence. And there is many a man with an income in six figures (before taxes) and with thousands of employees who, though his suit may be a little better cut than those of most of the men about him on a New York subway train or a transcontinental plane, attracts no curious notice at all; he looks just about like everybody else.

As for women, the difference in appearance between the one who spends $5,000 a year on clothes and the one who spends only a small fraction of that is by no means as conspicuous as the difference between the woman who has good taste and the woman who lacks it. The fact that the wealthy woman has thirty dresses to the poor woman's three is not visible on the street, and the fact that her dresses are made of better materials and are better cut is observable only by the expert eye at close range. Fashion used to be decreed by Paris, imported by the most expensive dress shops, then modified by the more expensive American dress manufacturers, and finally—after an interval of six months to a year— modified still further, almost beyond recognition, by the manufacturers of

Source: *The Big Change,* New York: Harper & Bros. (1952), pp. 192–193. Reprinted by permission of the publisher.

cheap dresses. The process is now quicker and the differences much less sharp. Unless the poor woman is exceptionally poor—or indifferent—she like the rich woman has a permanent—probably in her case a home one. And women of every income group wear nylon stockings.

Consider for a moment a contrast with regard to those stockings. At the turn of the century silk stockings were a mark of luxury. In the year 1900, in a nation of 75 million people, only 155,000 pairs were manufactured. In the year 1949 the American sales of nylon stockings—considered by most people at least as fine as silk, if not finer—were not 155,000, but 543 *million* pairs: enough to provide every female in the country, from the age of fourteen up, with between nine and ten pairs apiece. How is that for an example of the dynamic logic of mass production, producing luxury for all?

A generation ago the great mail-order houses produced different clothes for the Western farmer's wife and for the city woman in the East; today there is no such distinction, and a friend of mine whose train stopped recently at a small Oklahoma town remarked that the girls on the railroad platform there were virtually indistinguishable in appearance from girls on Madison Avenue or Michigan Boulevard. It could almost be said nowadays that the only easily visible mark of wealth which a woman can put on is a mink coat.

At this point an explanatory word is in order. The trend that I am describing is not a trend toward uniformity. Among both men and women there is a great diversity in attire. The point I am making is that the diversity is more a matter of preference, or of custom among the members of a local or vocational group, than of economic class.

Does this trend toward the breakdown of class lines in clothes seem unimportant? I do not think it is. The consciousness that one is set apart by one's appearance is a great divider; the consciousness that one is not set apart is a great remover of barriers.

88 The Best-Dressed Poverty

MICHAEL HARRINGTON

Clothes make the poor invisible too: America has the best-dressed poverty the world has ever known. For a variety of reasons, the benefits of mass

Source: *The Other America,* New York: Macmillan Co. (1962), p. 5. Reprinted by permission of the publisher.

production have been spread much more evenly in this area than in many others. It is much easier in the United States to be decently dressed than it is to be decently housed, fed, or doctored. Even people with terribly depressed incomes can look prosperous.

This is an extremely important factor in defining our emotional and existential ignorance of poverty. In Detroit the existence of social classes became much more difficult to discern the day the companies put lockers in the plants. From that moment on, one did not see men in work clothes on the way to the factory, but citizens in slacks and white shirts. This process has been magnified with the poor throughout the country. There are tens of thousands of Americans in the big cities who are wearing shoes, perhaps even a stylishly cut suit or dress, and yet are hungry. It is not a matter of planning, though it almost seems as if the affluent society had given out costumes to the poor so that they would not offend the rest of society with the sight of rags.

Men's Clothing and the Negro
JACK SCHWARTZ

While the American standard of living comprises the basic needs of food, shelter and the like, a major component of this standard concerns the symbolic significance of the articles of consumption. In order to receive the full symbolic value of consumption, the individual is generally aware of the status generated by the consumed article. Status is acquired through the fulfillment of culturally defined patterns of consumption modified by personal interpretations.

Dress is a communication medium. Clothing can function as a communication medium in various ways for different groups and individuals. Clothing can hide bodily defects, suggest and stimulate personal gratification, and exaggerate physique. The consumption and status symbolization of men's clothing as it relates to one particular group, the Negro American, will be examined here. The lower economic position of the average Negro in the American class system does not, *per se,* provide sufficient information for predicting his patterns of consumption relative to those of

Source: *Phylon,* Vol. 24 (Fall, 1963), pp. 224–231. Reprinted by permission of the publisher.

whites. When a significant difference is observed in proportionate consumption and expenditure between Negroes and whites, an explanation for this phenomenon cannot be limited to strictly economic interpretations.

It is undeniable that within the American social structure groups do exist to whom status symbols are differentially denied. The professed democracy witnesses a system in which rewards and punishments, rights and duties, knowledges and advantages are unequally distributed between Negroes and whites. Whether it is called a class system or a caste system, it controls peoples' lives, and educates others in its ways and precepts.

But is it correct to refer to a segment of the population as the Negro population? Are there exclusive Negro clothing items? The grouping of any segment of the population must be based upon some diagnostic which distinguishes it from other social groups. With the passage of time and the continuous reference to these characteristics, real or imaginary, any one of the more bizarre features will become a synonym for the group. With the Negro American, according to Myrdal, one of these characteristics has been loud, flashy clothing.[1] Can this alleged characteristic be dismissed simply because of its promotion by the white majority seeking to justify its dominant position? What may appear as distortions of "average" American behavior and consumption patterns exist because Negroes generally live on the margin of American life. The very existence of a separate Negro community with its own institutions, according to Frazier, "is indicative of [the community's] quasi-pathological character, especially since the persistence of this separate community has been due to racial discrimination and oppression."[2] That the Negro has rarely been permitted to play a serious role in American life has forced him to develop those habits of behavior and consumption which satisfy the peculiar exigencies of an isolated community life. When the Negro community, or any other minority community, is denied access to many status symbols, it is forced to use compensatory devices to raise self-esteem, aid status symbolization, and cushion the traumatic effects of a subordinate position. Clothing is one of these available devices, along with cars, furniture, and housing. Being a more portable and relatively less expensive object of conspicuous consumption, clothing is more easily exhibited than other status symbols.

[1] Gunnar Myrdal, *An American Dilemma* (New York, 1944), p. 962.
[2] E. Franklin Frazier, *Black Bourgeoisie* (Glencoe, Illinois, 1957), p. 234.

Pre-Emancipation Styles

For the majority of slaves in the pre-emancipation United States, dress was of a strictly European or American nature, African styles having been largely forbidden or considered impractical by the overseers. The plantation field hands' clothing was coarse, poorly tailored, with shoes and hats furnished only during certain seasons, if furnished at all. The plantation owner's major consideration was the slaves' protection from the elements in order to preserve their commercial utility. The use of attractive clothing was usually limited to that time in the slave's life when he was exhibited for sale by the slave trader. Ottley reported that slaves were dressed in bright, showy clothes at sale time, and doused with whiskey. Pet dogs performing tricks would amble through the corrals diverting the thoughts of "the sorrowful blacks. Such up-to-date methods impressed the people of the time as being humane."[3]

The clothing provision of one large Southern plantation allotted each adult field hand seven yards of osnaburg, three of check and three of baize every October, the slaves themselves performing the cutting and sewing. A hat or cap was given each field slave; however, footwear is absent from the list of provisions.[4] Another owner gave each man two cotton shirts, two pairs of pants and a woolen jacket every year, and one pair of shoes, given in the fall. Headwear is absent from this record.[5]

Twilled red flannel shirts, Scotch caps, jeans and check shirts were also popular items, used almost exclusively by Negroes in slavery and afterward until their recent adoption by Ivy League upper-middle-class whites. One Negro writer bluntly states that:

They call it the Ivy look but ask any haberdasher worth his salt, and he'll tell you it really started in Harlem rather than Harvard . . . and naturally it wouldn't be exactly high fashion to admit it all began in Harlem. So Harvard gets the credit. Yet when the Negro's uninhibited contribution to the American way of life became so acceptable that jazz entered the concert halls, . . . it was just a matter of time before a Harvard lad would discover that a Harlem hustler's cap was . . . appropriate for hotrodding an MG.[6]

[3] Roi Ottley, *Black Odyssey* (New York, 1948), p. 127.
[4] Ulrich B. Phillips, *American Negro Slavery* (New York, 1952), p. 64.
[5] *Ibid.*, p. 266.
[6] Vincent Tubbs, "Those Crazy Caps," *Duke* (July, 1957), p. 21. *Duke* is no longer published.

The large servant staff of the plantation was dressed in elaborate livery and carefully trained to reflect the wealth of the master. The Negro servants rivaled the Southern gentlemen with powdered wigs, embroidered waistcoats, striped trousers and fancy silk handkerchiefs around their necks. The huge, well-proportioned black butler was attired in the morning with a swallow-tailed coat and silk knee breeches; in the evening he wore an embroidered silk jacket, a vest of faded lilac, silk stockings, shoes with silver buckles, and a powdered wig.[7]

The numerous field hands and house slaves observed the white man's dress when the master's family and friends were garbed in formal or recreational attire. Since they interacted more frequently with the Southern white bourgeoisie, the clothing emulation standard of Negroes was higher than that of lower-class rural whites. Within the Negro slave community, the house servants were the source of emulation for the more numerous field hands. The butler, maid and personal valet were in continuous contact with the white household, enjoying the best opportunities to emulate its manners and acquire its discarded clothing. Buckingham observed in 1835 that:

On Sundays when the *slaves and servants* are all at liberty after dinner, they move about in every thoroughfare, and are generally more gaily dressed than the whites. The young men among the slaves wear white trousers, black socks, broad-brimmed hats and carry walking-sticks; and from the bowings, curtseying and greetings in the highway one might almost imagine one's self to be at Hayti [*sic*] and think that the coloured people had got possession of the town and held sway while the whites were living among them by sufferance.[8]

Such a display may represent a release from the deep frustrations felt by many Negroes for the oppressive implications of racial prejudice. Davie feels that the emotionalism found in many Negro churches, and the excessive absorption in the pursuit of pleasure found in Negroes and other discriminated groups, represent a release of frustration. The clowning and the laughter, he says, are escapes "from the galling realities of [the Negro's] subordinate status."[9]

[7] Ottley, *op. cit.*, pp. 32–33.
[8] J. S. Buckingham, *Slave States,* II (London: Fisher & Son, 1842), p. 427. (Italics mine.)
[9] Maurice R. Davie, *Negroes in American Society* (New York, 1949), p. 442.

Status Compensation

The need for status compensation within the Negro sub-culture may also be greater with men than with women. Within the world of slavery, the woman as mother held the strategic position and the dominant role in Negro family life. The father could easily be transferred to other owners, but the mother rarely left her young offspring. While Negro men today are gradually assuming the traditional role of provider, like their white counterpart, the Negro woman in the family unit is likely to contribute a substantial proportion of the income and assume the larger share of family responsibility since employment is generally more widely available to her.[10]

The occupational differentiation of Negroes and whites, particularly in the South, offers one explanation for different clothing patterns. That most Negroes engage in or are candidates for productive labor means that work clothes are the dominant dress style. While ties and suits may be worn by Negro teachers, undertakers and the clergy in the South, says Lewis, the general Negro community is typically aware of the pressure from whites and dresses to communicate deference and humility. ". . . in telling of their approach to whites in a situation where he wanted something, [a Negro] will stress 'and I put my hat in my hand!' "[11]

The dress of the Negro entertainers influences a perception of "the Negro" diametrically opposed to that given by the lower classes. Negro stage personalities play a vital role in setting standards of emulation within the Negro community. They are of relatively high status since their profession involves a comparatively high degree of respect, interaction and acceptance by whites. Frazier contends that Negro entertainers, who often have a lower class background, exert a much greater influence upon the Negro middle class than white stage personalities exert on the white community.[12]

The use of hand-me-down clothing given by employers to Negroes, particularly poorly paid domestic service workers, also contributes to

[10] 46 per cent of Negro women were in the labor force in 1961 compared with 36 per cent of white women. (*Statistical Abstracts*, 1962, p. 218 based on *Current Population Reports* Series P-50, No. 66.)
[11] Hylan Lewis, *Blackways of Kent* (Chapel Hill, 1945), p. 62.
[12] Frazier, *op. cit.*, p. 127.

different dress patterns between Negroes and whites. Sterner's research of 1935–36 data indicates that hand-me-down clothing was more frequently worn by Negroes than whites in rural and lower income urban communities.[13] This practice adds as much to the occasional awkwardness of the Negro male's dress as does the limited selection which most clothing merchants stock in rural and semi-urban communities, particularly in the South. Ottley reported after World War II that throughout the South the emergence of a large class of serious looking, neatly dressed, intelligent Negroes had become increasingly apparent. The familiar rags and hand-me-downs, the scuffed, unlaced shoes, the improvised hats—all these and many other details had vanished.[14]

Anthropometry

Anthropometric differences between Negroes and whites also contribute to a need for clothing of differing dimensions. The research of Herskovits,[15] and Todd and Lindala [16] indicates the width of the head to increase and the length to decrease with increasing proportions of white ancestry, and the Negro male's foot is both longer and wider than whites'. Consequently, different hat and shoe sizes and shapes would be preferred by both groups; however, if social prestige via an association with white physical dimensions is desired by the individual Negro, consciously or not, he may seek those sizes and styles which do not correspond exactly with his body measurements, e.g., long, pointed shoes.

The difference in skin color is another contributing factor to dissimilarity in clothing color preferences between Negroes and whites, since certain colors and hues harmonize better with Negro than with white complexions.

---

[13] Richard Sterner, *The Negro's Share* (New York, 1943), p. 137. Also see Paul K. Edwards, "Distinctive Characteristics of Urban Negro Consumption" (unpublished Ph.D. dissertation, Harvard University, 1936), p. 109.
[14] Ottley, *op. cit.*, pp. 305–06.
[15] Melville J. Herskovits, *The Anthropometry of the American Negro* (New York, 1930), p. 187.
[16] Wingate Todd and Anna Lindala, "Dimensions of the Body: Whites and American Negroes of Both Sexes," *American Journal of Physical Anthropology*, XII, No. 1 (July, 1928), p. 98.

Expenditure

An empirical difference in proportionate expenditures for clothing between Negroes and whites is shown in the consumption of clothing. At all income levels over $1,000 in 1950, the proportion of total income spent for clothing by whites was relatively constant at all income levels, while the rate for Negroes—always higher than for whites—showed a steady increase with each succeeding income level. The proportion of total income spent for clothing by whites earning over $4,000 was 11.4 per cent, for Negroes 14.3 per cent.[17] When regions of the United States are compared, expenditure by Negroes for clothing is proportionately higher than that by whites in all regions.[18] That a greater proportion of the average Negro's total income is spent for clothing tells us nothing relative to the prices paid for individual garments by both groups. This difference can be explained by assuming that Negroes purchase either (1) larger quantities of the same or lower priced items, (2) smaller quantities of higher priced garments, or (3) neither. Since clothing is one of a limited number of channels for conspicuous consumption available to Negroes, it may be hypothesized that the inability to compete for "restricted-consumption" status symbols is compensated by the consumption of either higher priced garments or quantities of clothing in excess of that consumed by whites of comparable class or income.[19]

[17] Calculated from the *Study of Consumer Expenditures, Incomes and Savings*, VII (Philadelphia, 1957), pp. 31–35. For income levels over $4000 the N for whites was 3756, Negroes 176. For all income levels giving expenditure for total family clothing the N for whites was 9847, Negroes 1254.

[18] The mean per cent of total income after taxes spent for clothing by Negroes and whites respectively in large Northern cities was 12.8 per cent, 11.4 per cent; large Southern cities 13.1 per cent, 11.4 per cent; small Southern cities 14.0 per cent, 11.4 per cent; large Western cities 13.6 per cent, 10.9 per cent. Based on calculation from *ibid*. by Irwin Friend and Irving B. Kravis, "New Light on the Consumer Market," *Harvard Business Review*, XXXV (January, 1957), 112. Using an N for whites of 11,136, Negroes 1,294, the per cent of total income devoted to the following consumption categories by Negroes and whites respectively were: food 31.9 per cent and 29.5 per cent; housing 11.3 per cent and 11.5 per cent; clothing 13.6 per cent and 11.3 per cent. Negroes spent 7.2 per cent on furnishings; whites spent 11.9 per cent on automobile expenses. Of the first four articles of consumption for both groups, clothing ranks as the fourth largest expenditure for whites, second largest for Negroes.

[19] This same hypothesis can be made for other minority groups as well.

The Negro male's orientation toward individual garments may reflect the importance of the social aspects of the garment: in style and appearance, and a de-emphasis of the physical aspects: fit and comfort. He may also be expected to compensate for a less independent role in male-female relationships than his white counterpart by consuming, in larger proportions, those clothing items invested with sexual or personal gratification. Using one psycho-analytic interpretation of clothing symbols, the Negro male might be expected to consume items which help the individual's personality expansion, cathexis, and phallic gratifications. Diguises from Negroid anthropometric characteristics might also be sought through clothing. A sharply pointed, slim, high-fashioned shoe with thin soles and a delicate, supple fabric may serve these functions, as well as large Homburgs [20] with wide brims and deep, soft creases.

Content Analysis

In order to test these hypotheses, I compared men's clothing advertisements in Negro and white periodicals and examined haberdasheries in a large urban community with sizable Negro and white populations. The comparable periodicals were *Ebony* and *Life,* the urban community, Chicago.[21] These methods were used to try to determine how advertisers and small haberdashers communicate their knowledge and feelings about the Negro and white men's clothing markets. This is to say that the advertiser or haberdasher tailors his talk with his customers to fit his knowledge of their habits and desires.

[20] Soft felt hats with a creased crown and small creases on each side of the front of the hat.

[21] Randomly selected copies over the period 1947–56, with a .5 p for *Ebony,* a monthly, and .09 p for *Life,* a weekly. Sample size of *Ebony's* ads 499, *Life's,* 287. These periodicals were selected since both have national coverage, "slick" reproductions; Claude Hall, "The Negro Market," *Printers' Ink* (August 23, 1957), 238, maintains that *Ebony* occupies a position in the Negro community comparable to *Life.* The average income of *Ebony* readers, according to 1956 Daniel Starch Reports, was 165 per cent of the income of the average Negro according to *Statistical Abstracts,* 1957, p. 315 for 1955, Series P-60, Nos. 9, 19, and 23. The mean income of *Life* readers was 149 per cent of the national white income. For both periodical audiences we are dealing with those segments of Negro and white communities approximately equal in its economic distance from the mean community income. Ten per cent of *Life's* readers are Negro, 6 per cent of *Ebony's* readers are white. In the haberdasher study, 60 randomly selected stores in Chicago neighborhoods with 95 per cent either Negro or white populations were used.

In both the priced men's clothing ads in *Ebony* and the price tags in haberdasheries in urban Negro neighborhoods, the mean price of all garments was higher than in *Life* or white neighborhood stores.[22] Suits and jackets were the only clothing items not higher priced to Negro audiences; all other items—undergarments, hats, ties, shirts, slacks, stockings, shoes, overcoats and jewelry—were higher priced when shown in *Ebony* and men's clothing stores in Negro neighborhoods. The significance of these facts, particularly with hats and shoes,[23] seems to be that Negroes do spend more for most individual clothing items, on the average, than whites. Whether this phenomenon is occasioned by the desire of Negroes for personal gratification to compensate for a subordinate social role, or whether it represents the exploitation of a vulnerable minority by white merchants cannot be determined from this research.[24]

A content analysis of advertising copy in *Ebony* and *Life's* men's clothing ads was made to examine the hypothesis that the Negro man dresses more for style than for comfort. The proportion of copy stressing appearance, style and prestige was measured against expressions stressing durability of the garment, comfort and fit; e.g., "your friends will admire you with a new, smart looking suit" vs. "a comfortable, long-lasting, lightweight suit." The average *Life* ad stressed the physical qualities in 60 per cent of the copy, as compared with 42 per cent of the *Ebony* copy, strongly suggesting that the latter's advertisers conceive of the Negro male consumer as more concerned with the social advantages to be derived by wearing the advertised garment than with its physical comfort. If this accurately reflects a greater style consciousness among Negro men, it may represent either the greater desire to conform to vogue or the desire to stress individual eccentricity in dress, the former described as "smart," the latter "loud and flashy."[25] Though the definition of style as inter-

---

[22] Seventy-nine per cent of *Ebony's* ads were priced compared to 66 per cent for *Life*. Since fewer *Life* men's clothing ads were priced, this suggests that the advertisers in *Life* believe their audiences are less affected by price as such than do *Ebony* advertisers.

[23] Hat prices in Negro and white neighborhood stores respectively were $13.42(N = 130) and $9.22(N = 58), in *Ebony* and *Life* respectively, $16.52(N = 80) and $7.67 (N = 6)! Shoe prices in Negro and white neighborhood stores respectively were $17.21 (N = 148) and $14.63 (N = 75); in *Ebony* $16.75 (N = 207), in *Life*, $12.75 (N = 35).

[24] A mixture of both reasons is probably operating.

[25] The way *style* is defined by both groups represents a virgin field for communications research.

preted by the individual, Negro or white, is not suggested here, men's clothing is exhibited to Negroes in a verbal context where style, and not the physical qualities of the garment, plays the major role.

Men's clothing ads and haberdasher displays were used again to determine the clothing items popular with Negro and white audiences. Hats and shoes were found to be the two items exhibited most frequently to Negroes, and in proportions significantly exceeding that shown to whites,[26] suggesting the plausibility of psychoanalytic and anthropometric interpretations. Sharply pointed shoes and wide brimmed Homburgs were the shoe and hat styles chiefly shown to Negroes.[27] The shoe fabrics and leathers exposed to Negroes differed from those shown to whites by the popularity of real or imitation reptile, unborn calf, pony, polka-dotted calf and suede-reptile combinations. Sharply pointed shoes as well as those with delicate fabrics are not generally identified with productive labor but communicate the wearer's association with leisure activity. The average Negro, whose occupational history is mainly in non-professional jobs, may use these fabrics and styles to communicate a dissociation from the traditional working classes.[28]

Summary

This research has suggested that hats and shoes are exhibited to and presumably consumed in greater proportions by Negroes than by whites. Men's clothing advertised to Negroes is also higher priced than that shown to whites. Explanations for this phenomenon were made on the basis of the operation of clothing as cathectic objects, sexual and personal symbols of gratification, and anthropometric disguises. Since many Negroes are generally conceived as socially inferior, both by themselves and by whites, it was suggested that the individual Negro compensates

[26] Hats occupied 39.8 per cent of the display space in Negro neighborhood stores compared to 24.5 per cent for whites, with Ns of 142 and 63 respectively. 16.6 per cent of *Ebony's* men's clothing ads were for hats compared with 3.2 per cent for *Life*. Dress shoes were advertised in 57.7 per cent of *Ebony's* men's clothing ads compared with only 22.3 per cent in *Life*.
[27] Sharply pointed shoes composed 42 per cent of the shoes exhibited to Negroes, 6 per cent for Whites. Sixty-three per cent of the hats shown to Negroes were Homburgs, 8 per cent of those shown to whites.
[28] Strong racist attitudes in both Negroes and whites can operate in certain individuals, and it should not be inferred that all Negroes want to imitate whites.

for this position through clothing symbols. A position economically inferior to that of the Negro female may force Negro males to use those hats and shoes invested with sexually gratifying symbols.

Segregation has produced patterns of consumption originating with status differentiation but leading to repercussions in more subtle ways for the subordinate class. It has conditioned the pattern of consumption in such a way that the economic position of both groups is not necessarily the most significant factor for predicting these patterns. The evidence supported by status symbolism, anthropometry and a dynamic psychological interpretation appear to offer more valuable clues than economics to the understanding of clothing as an American cultural communication medium.

Clothing and Ornament

JOHN GILLIN

Each caste in San Carlos has its own typical costuming. Under certain conditions Indians wear patterns which belong to the Ladino, but Ladinos practically never wear the distinctively Indian elements of clothing.

Older informants say that Indian women in the community wove cloth up until about 1884 or 1885 at which time it is said that President Rufino Barrios ordered that women stop weaving. Previous to this time women did not wear blouses, but about 1885 began doing so upon the order of President Rufino Barrios. The material for the wrap-around skirt worn by women in those days is said to have been very coarse. According to older informants it was not resist-dyed (jaspe) of the type which is now used for women's skirts and made by Indians in the western part of Guatemala. In those days men also wore homespun clothes, according to accounts, consisting of shirts and short pants. The shirt was decorated with thin pink stripes (coloraditas) which ran perpendicularly. One ran down each sleeve and one around each cuff. One stripe ran down each side of the shirt. The pants came to just below the knee and had no fly. To

Source: *The Culture of Security in San Carlos*, New Orleans: Middle American Research Institute, The Tulane University of Louisiana (1951), pp. 34–39. Reprinted by permission of the publisher.

urinate a man had to pull up his trouser leg. One informant who was born in 1880 says as a small boy he can remember his grandfather wearing this kind of clothing although his father did not. This would seem to indicate that the style was going out or had gone out before 1880. Other informants, while they confirm this older pattern of men's clothing, are less precise about dates. Older informants can remember their mothers spinning. They say that a spindle with a gourd (tecomate) was used and that the loom was a belt loom. The older men think that cotton must have formerly been grown in the region, although I have found no one who has seen it growing in the township with his own eyes. Unfortunately, there are no records available which would bear upon this subject. At present, only one vestige of weaving is left among the Indians. This is the practice of weaving a tecoyal (P., šik'ap), a band about one-half inch wide and about five feet long which is wound into the hair for a marriage decoration. The thread is bought from traders but the tecoyales are made here by specialists.

The Indian woman when dressed in the native costume or vestido at the present time wears the following garments. The first and most conspicuous item is the wrap-around skirt or corte so arranged that it overlaps in front usually with the edge on the left side or near the left hip. The material is resist-dyed jaspe cloth made by footloom in the region around Quetzaltenango. The colors are mainly blue and green arranged in figures or small checks, stripes, and conventionalized representations of animals, etc. This general design and the type of weaving is familiar to students of western Guatemala.[1] The material is bought in the market in San Carlos from traveling Indian traders who carry the cloth on their backs or on pack donkeys. They also sell the girdles or belts which are likewise made of material woven on handlooms by Indians in the western part of the country. A good piece of skirt material is supposed to be five varas, or 165 inches long, and one vara wide. The upper part of the body is covered by a blouse of factory-made muslin, usually plain. The bottom ends of the blouse generally hang outside the belt and skirt although when dressed for ceremonial occasions the front edge of the blouse is usually tucked into the girdle for a horizontal space of about six or nine inches. The blouse has a yoke or breastplate, which is sewed around the neck forming a decorative feature, and also a collar. The yoke is usually shirred and trimmed with lace. Short sleeves ending above the elbow are

[1] See O'Neale, 1945, 24–27, 166.

sewed in as separate items of the blouse in such a way that they are puffed out over the shoulder. They are often provided with a tight band just above the elbow and are sometimes finished in lace. The lace is the manufactured article bought from traders. The cloth of the blouse, or camisa, may also be made of printed cotton or of solid colors. A few women wear rayon blouses.

The women usually decorate themselves with several necklaces. The most important beads are of glass and the most popular colors are red, white and blue. The beads are about the size of a pea. Coral and orange beads are also very common, and some women wear gold glass beads. Some of the best necklaces have red beads interspersed with old silver coins which are pierced near the edge and strung onto the necklace. Earrings are of silver. Sometimes earrings are made of coin. The women usually wear nothing underneath the blouse although occasionally several blouses may be worn one on top of the other. The head is usually covered with a shawl, or toalla. Sometimes a jaspe or resist-dyed shawl of the type known as reboza in the West is used as a head covering. But most often the materials are of white muslin or towel cloth. Indian women part their hair in the middle. Married women wear their hair in two braids interspersed with strips of woven cotton cloth either of red or of blue—the tecoyales previously mentioned. The braids are crossed behind the head at the base of the neck and the ends are pulled foward around the head from either side into a sort of crown which is then braided together in front, with the interbraided ends of the tecoyal tied into a sort of bow knot where the ends of the two braids come together. Unmarried women do not wear this crown effect but part their hair in the middle and wear it down the back in one single braid. In either case, however, the hair-do is hidden in public by the fall of head towel which both the married and unmarried women wear. The godmother, or madrina, who is chosen by the bride at the time of her wedding, fixes the bride's hair with the tecoyal for the first time. The groom is required to supply the colored cotton thread material which is used in the tecoyal. A woman's decorations include finger rings of gold and silver or of composition metal. Indian women never wear shoes, sandals, or other foot covering except under unusual circumstances.

When working about the house, when washing clothes at the riverside, and on practically all occasions when no Ladinos are expected the women are usually nude above the waist.

There is a measurable tendency on the part of Indian women to appear in one-piece cotton dresses of European pattern with the result that the "native" costume I have just described is not universal. The Indian woman wearing a gingham dress of European model never wears stockings or shoes, nor does she wear a European hat or other accessories of European or Ladino type. Usually she continues the use of the head towel whether she is wearing a vestido or a gingham dress. The advantage of the gingham dress from the Indian point of view is that it is cheaper, in fact it costs about one-tenth the price of a good, complete vestido outfit. Likewise it is more easily washed, and if torn or dirty may be discarded without great difficulty.

On three separate days during August and September of 1942 we made a series of observations covering a total of 2,541 Indian women and noted the costume that they were wearing. The results of this survey are shown in the accompanying table.

Table 1 Incidence of clothing types worn by Indian women and girls

Based on Random Observations for Three Separate Days During August and September, 1942

	No.	%
Total of subjects observed	2,541	100.0
Wearing Indian costume, total	1,592	62.7
Age 5—14	507	20.0
Age over 14	1,085	42.7
Wearing one-piece cotton dress, total	949	37.3
Age 5—14	617	23.8
Age over 14	332	13.5
Total of subjects 5—14	1,124	100.0
Wearing Indian costume	507	45.1
Wearing one-piece cotton dress	617	54.9
Total of subjects age over 14	1,417	100.0
Wearing Indian costume	1,085	76.5
Wearing one-piece cotton dress	332	23.5

Ladino law and regulations enforced by punishments have decreed that women be covered from neck to calf when appearing in public; thus an anxiety has been created which must be relieved by the practice of some custom of clothing. We have just seen that two alternatives are now present in the Indian culture: the one-piece cotton dress and the vestido. The cotton dress has the advantage that it costs only $1 or $2 in contrast to the $20 or so for the vestido. Either one of the costumes will lower the anxiety which is asociated with public nakedness, but only the vestido also tends to satisfy certain other anxieties associated with status and the attraction of the opposite sex. Indian swains regard with favor marriageable girls possessing vestidos, but do not like that a girl should have only cotton dresses. Married women without vestidos suffer from social discouragements or punishments of various kinds meted out by other Indian women and their husbands. Thus it is that the cotton dress is a mere utility garment adopted as an alternative on account of its lower cost. This also explains why pre-adolescent girls to whom marriage and full social status considerations do not fully apply are garbed in cotton dresses more frequently than adult women, as shown in the accompanying table. To sum up in behavioristic terms, the cotton dress for an Indian woman lowers her acquired anxiety with respect to punishment for exposure and also lowers her anxiety respecting money. On the other hand, only the vestido lowers the prestige or social status drive which must be satisfied if she is to receive the rewards of full integration into the female part of the Indian community.

When we turn to Indian men, we have two styles of clothing also. The "old" non-Ladino style of clothing may be described as follows. It consists first of a white shirt with a short tail which is left to hang out. The shirt has a soft collar band but a collar is never worn with it. The lower part of the body is covered by a pair of white cotton trousers hanging loosely to an inch or so below the knees and tied together in the back of the waist. In front there is a fly without buttons. This costume is almost universally worn by Indian men when at work in the milpa or about the house. Often the costume for heavy work consists of extremely ragged garments, but one does not lose his standing if his work clothes are in poor repair or nearly worn out. This type of costume, of course, is familiar to students of Indian culture in Spanish America from Mexico to southern Peru, and there is evidence to indicate that it was introduced during colonial times. It is doubtful that the costume has anything aboriginal about it.

The second style of clothing affected by Indian men is of European cut. It always consists of soft-collared shirt, and European type of pants supported by a belt. Occasionally the pants are supported by a native sash or girdle made of material similar to that worn by the women and woven in the western part of the country. With this Ladino style also goes a jacket. These garments are usually made of cotton drill or some other cheap material and cut according to European patterns. Usually they are rather tight around the waist and do not represent a very good tailoring job. However, they are regarded as valuable parts of the formal or festive costume by Indian men.

Shoes are practically never worn by Indian men and in the local definition of the situation the wearing of shoes is regarded more or less as a Ladino prerogative, although it is not always formally stated in these

Table 2 Incidence of footwear of Ladino and Indian males

Based on Random Observations for Three Separate Days During August and September, 1942

	Ladinos		Indians	
	No.	%	No.	%
Total subjects observed	268	100.0	907	100.0
Wearing shoes	82	30.5	5	0.5
Wearing sandals	156	58.3	738	81.4
Barefoot	30	11.2	164	18.1

terms. In Table 2 will be seen results of random observations made on three separate days during August and September, 1942. It will be seen that out of a total of 907 Indian men observed only five were wearing shoes. All of these individuals were recently discharged army conscripts who were wearing their army footwear. Seven hundred and thirty-eight, or 81.4%, of the total were wearing sandals called caites, and 164, or 18.1%, observed on these occasions were barefoot. It will be observed that the wearing of sandals and the custom of going barefoot are, however, not confined to the Indian caste. In our sample the overlapping of customs between the two groups with respect to footwear is shown by the fact that 156, or 58.3%, of the total number of Ladinos were wearing sandals, while 30, or 11.2%, of the total were going barefoot. Only 82, or 30.5%, were wearing shoes. The wearing of shoes is verbally stated to be a Ladino pattern only and Ladinos are ideally not supposed to wear sandals or go barefoot. It is obvious that according to this sample only a minority of Ladinos actually do wear shoes. Here again the matter of expense is involved and it is still true for practical purposes that the shoe wearing pattern is not a part of the Indian culture.

There is likewise a differential distribution of jackets as between Ladinos and Indians. On one Sunday in September, 1942, we observed a total of 511 Indian men with respect to the question of whether or not they were wearing jackets. This material together with observations on Ladinos appears in Table 3. It will be noted that only 24.4% of the Indian men were wearing jackets, whereas 41.1% of the Ladinos were so clad. The adoption of the jacket by Indian men and the cotton dress by Indian

Table 3   Incidence of jackets of Ladino and Indian men

Based on Random Observations on One Day (Sunday) in September, 1942

	Ladinos No.	Ladinos %	Indians No.	Indians %
Total subjects observed	264	100.0	511	100.0
Wearing jackets	106	40.1	125	24.4
Not wearing jackets	158	59.9	386	75.6

women represents the taking over of Ladino items into the Indian pattern. However, this difference should be noted; a jacket is a costume of high desirability which Indian men can not fully adopt because of the lack of funds. On the other hand, the cotton dress is a pattern of comparatively low desirability from the Indian woman's point of view which is grudgingly adopted again for the lack of funds.

Indian men usually wear straw hats. Hat making is a handicraft practiced by Indian men in San Carlos itself. The material is palm fiber imported from the coast. It is braided into strips about an inch wide. These strips in turn are sewed together in spiral fashion in order to form the hat. The hats are sold for cash by Indian men when they go on trading expeditions to other communities, and San Carlos has a considerable reputation in eastern Guatemala as the source of good, cheap headgear. The handmade hat is a relatively crude article with a wide, curled brim. It is useful as a sun shade but has little decorative appeal. Following the Second World War factory-made straw hats of fine weave and molded shape were introduced in the weekly markets and in the stores. Although the cost ranges from three to ten times that of a home-made straw hat, most of the younger Indians have acquired these articles to wear when dressed up. It is understood that the prestige factor in this change was introduced by younger men who had gone to Barrios to work for the fruit company there and who had observed the "elegant" factory-made straw hat among the higher employees at that center. Up to a few years ago the felt hat was considered a part of the symbolic apparatus of Ladino status. However, by 1948 a good share of Indian men were affecting factory-made felt hats on festive occasions and this old distinction between the castes may disappear.

Ladino women wear only clothing and accessories of European pattern, and they attempt to keep up with the current modes, although in a rather rustic fashion. Since I am not an expert on women's styles, I shall not attempt to describe them, but it should be stated that the following items of women's dress are exclusive to the Ladino caste and may in a sense be regarded as caste marks. The black lace head covering which is worn in church and on some other formal occasions is universal among Ladino women but is never worn by Indian women. Incidentally, whenever they are inside the church building the Ladino women always wear a lace covering on their heads based upon the Biblical injunction "but every woman that prayeth or prophesieth with head uncovered dishonoreth her head: for that is even all one as if she were shaven. For if the woman be not covered, let her also be shorn: but if it be a shame for a woman to be shorn or shaven, let her be covered. . . . Judge for yourselves: is it comely that a woman pray unto God uncovered?" (Romans I, Cor., 11:5, 6, 13.) On the other hand, Indian women remove their head coverings in the church. Although this difference of custom obviously serves as another symbol of difference between the castes, I have been unable to obtain an explanation as to why this transgression of the Biblical injunction is permitted either by the priest or by the Indian guardians of the Catholic religion.

All other European styles of headdress are exclusive to Ladino women whatever fashions may be involved. Instead of multiple strings of beads around the neck, the Ladino women wear single strand necklaces of beads, thin chains, and decorative pendants. Such European neck ornaments are never worn by Indian women. The only European dress pattern which is shared between Indian and Ladino women is the cotton one-piece dress already mentioned. Coats and top coats are exclusive to Ladino women. This is not to say that every Ladino woman owns or wears one of these garments but that no Indian woman wears a coat or top coat and no Indian woman possesses such articles. Shoes are worn exclusively by Ladino women. The use of brassieres, slips, and corsets, and other "foundation garments" is an exclusive Ladino female trait as are facial cosmetics. Both Indian and Ladino women wear shawls of cotton or wool. However, the Ladino woman uses this article only as protection around the shoulders. The Indian woman, on the other hand, uses the shawl only for carrying babies or for carrying loads. Among the Indians they are frequently blue or red and woven by Indian weavers in the western part of the country, whereas the Ladino shawls are always made of factory-manufactured material.

The Ladino men follow European patterns on the whole although in a somewhat rustic and countryfied style. The Ladino man often looks somewhat awkward when he is dressed up in collar, necktie, and suit of clothes. Ordinarily collar band shirts are worn without the collars and for everyday use neckties are seldom worn. Among the items of dress which are exclusive to Ladino men are the following. First, shoes and socks are practically never worn by Indian men. Many Ladinos, it is true, wear shoes without socks but on festive occasions socks are usually included. Neckties are exclusive to Ladinos as are pocket watches. A few Indians, on the other hand, have acquired wrist watches which are also worn by Ladinos. A few Ladino men wear special riding breeches, leather puttees, or short boots. This is not a general pattern among the Ladinos, but no Indian has such an outfit. Members of both castes usually ride in ordinary costume. Most Ladino men wear underwear, at least a pair of shorts. Underwear, per se, is not a part of Indian equipment, although Indian men occasionally wear the white work pants under European type pants for extra warmth. Ladinos who do heavy work, such as laborers, do not wear the Indian work costume of white cloth, but wear ordinary straight pants of European cut supported by a belt. Although Ladino men go barefoot on occasion, this is a sign of demoralization and low status within the caste. On the other hand, it is not considered particularly reprehensible for a Ladino man to wear sandals about his everyday tasks, although he should not wear them when dressed for ceremonial occasions. The highest class Ladinos never appear without shoes.

There are three barbers in town, all Indians. Each has a small shop set up in a room of his home. The equipment is crude but of European pattern and resembles that found in small town barbershops in most parts of Latin America. Conventional combs, scissors, and hand-operated clippers are used, as well as straight razors. The chair is an ordinary straight chair with arms. Two barbers charged five cents for a hair cut in 1948 and one charged ten cents. The latter provided a clean towel for each client. Tonsorial elegance is little valued by men of either caste for everyday appearances. A haircut and a barber's shave are usually obtained as part of the preparations for a party or a fiesta. Only younger men of both castes attempt to part their hair or to use pomades.

In summary certain differences in patterns of clothing between Indians and Ladinos may be observed in San Carlos. Some of these are of a caste nature and serve as symbols of membership in the respective castes, but at the same time it is obvious that there has been an interpenetration of the two cultures of a measurable degree.

So far as security feelings are concerned, there is no evidence that the clothing patterns of either Indians or Ladinos are inadequate to give protection against the elements. This is not so much on account of the great efficiency of the clothing patterns themselves as because of the relative mildness of the climate. In this connection it is worth noting that the Indians as a whole are better protected from rain than the Ladinos. The Indians use a rain cape made of strips of palm leaf sewn together in parallel fashion and tied around the neck. Although Ladinos do not disdain these capes in an emergency, the proper Ladino pattern is a sugger poncho which, however, relatively few men have acquired. So far as the men's clothing is concerned it would appear that the acculturation of the Indian man's costume has proceeded very nearly to completion at the present time. This means that clothing as a symbol of caste status is apparently losing its function so far as men are concerned, although it has not entirely passed out of the symbolic realm at present. On the other hand, the differences between women are much stronger, and the emotional effect seems to be more highly developed. A great deal of anxiety is felt if a family can not provide a proper vestido for a daughter who is of marriageable age. Helen Gillin had 16 interviews with housewives who expressed concern over their inability to provide their daughters with vestidos. In some cases they were planning nearly desperate measures to acquire the necessary funds. On the other hand, all vestidos are essentially of the same "style" so that no question of mode is involved. The anxieties of the Ladino women, on the other hand, are definitely concerned with style. There are no women, even among the so-called high society, who have large or elaborate wardrobes. Nevertheless, a good deal of alteration goes on and an upper class Ladino girl at least expects to have three to four new dresses each year, according to Helen Gillin's material obtained in interviews. New style ideas are apparently obtained in a rather desultory fashion from outside sources, mainly through the agency of women themselves who occasionally make trips to Guatemala City or to some other urban center. They may purchase a dress and they also bring back paper patterns and pictures in small quantity. No one in the community subscribes to a style magazine or a magazine that has a style department. The result of all of this is that the Ladino ladies' costumes even for dress occasions appear to be somewhat awkward and a trifle dowdy. However, modern influences are not lacking. For example, a number of young women in 1948 wore slacks for riding horseback, although they did not wear them about the streets or otherwise in public.

A special type of anxiety with respect to clothing exists among the Indians, at least. This is connected with the belief that one's soul is extended to his clothing. In other words, the clothing contains some emanations of the soul. Magical attack may be made upon the soul itself if witches are able to manipulate the clothing. For this reason, Indians do not like to sell their garments secondhand or to throw them away. When no more rags can be obtained for patching, when no more threads can be unraveled, the remains are buried secretly or burned. I have also seen Ladinos burying rags of their own clothing, although Ladinos claim that they do not believe in this "superstition." In line with their belief, the Indians are not averse to wearing the castoff clothing of individuals who appear to them to be rich or influential. In my own case at the close of each season I gave away several garments to what I believed to be deserving cases. At first I thought the great avidity with which they were begged for was based entirely upon utilitarian motives, but I discovered later that some of the recipients of these felt that they would keep with them a certain part of my essence by having my clothes. One man to whom I had given a pair of trousers in 1942 had a long story of his adventures to tell me in 1948 in which he attributed a large part of his good luck to my trousers. He kept them carefully in a box and wore them only on important occasions or times of crisis.

Part Five

Dress and the Individual

THE FACT THAT CLOTHING protects the individual physically as well as psychologically reminds us of the dual position of man within the biological and socio-cultural orders. The purpose of this section is to study adornment in relation to the individual as he functions as a biological organism and as a social self, normal or deviant.

A Biological Organism

Since the human being can function socially only because he is first a biological organism, the effects of clothing on this organism hold a certain primacy for consideration. The scientist, however, who relates the use or disuse of clothing to actual bodily processes recognizes that cultural patterns exert a great influence on these processes. Even eating, breathing, and sleeping are not left to raw biological impulse but are modified culturally.

In the scientific study of the effects of clothing on body physiology there has been consideration of metabolism, muscle tone, blood pressure, digestion, and breathing.[1] At various times there has been special interest in the impact of heavy or restrictive clothing on health and activity and in the effects of clean clothes on health.

The research study by Halverson represents a scientific examination of the effect of being clothed. He studied the degree to which a reflex, considered biological, seemed to be modified by clothing, one aspect of the culturally developed environment of the child. In the Meier study, thermal needs of human beings are discussed and the concept *clo* is introduced. Meier's precise evaluation of energy equivalents should inspire further economic comparisons of clothing versus fuel as a conserver of energy in different societies.

In some cases cultural equipment can compensate for biological weaknesses. Jaquith presents a therapeutic and clearly instrumental use of clothing in this way. She describes the use to which the pressurized suit has been put in the control of a malfunctioning circulatory system.

As man moves into space for which he is physically ill adapted, cultural adaptation through clothing seems the practical path to survival while maintaining spatial mobility. Space suits represent mankind's most elaborately contrived clothing; their construction is directed by a single-mindedness of purpose—survival. Expressive use of clothing to show status or as an outlet for the aesthetic are here at minimum. This is not to say that if life in space grew commonplace expressive elements might not creep into design. Just the same, the hazards of space may always keep the expressive minimal. The article from *Science News Letter* shows the great concentration on the protective function of space clothing in the present-day world.

A Social Self

Although in groups human beings can be categorized on sociological, anthropological, and biological grounds, each man and woman is also an *individual* within the socio-cultural and physical setting. The process

---

[1] G. V. N. Dearborn, "The Psychology of Clothing," *The Psychological Monographs*, Vol. 26 (1918), pp. 1–72.

whereby the biological entity is invested with socially and culturally acquired qualities is called "socialization."

Basic to socialization is person to person contact, or social interaction. During a lifetime each person participates in many social interaction situations. Some are fleeting encounters in which intimacy may develop. Others are of relatively long duration marked by the formation of multiple bonds reinforced by sentiments, common interests, and mutual dependency. In either case the individual does not behave in a random fashion. Instead he demonstrates that he has learned through precept, experience, or intellectual exercise how to interpret with a minimum of effort the social situation in which he finds himself and carry on necessary social exchange with ease.

Within the intimate, enduring systems of social relationships, such as the family or playgroup, the individual acquires the value and action patterns he will incorporate into his personal organization. For example, Pitcher points out that, consciously or unconsciously, parents stress personal appearance, including clothing, in training children for the basic male or female roles.

To test his understanding of the world, therefore, and to exert force on it the individual needs to rely on more than reflex actions to physical objects. He must refer to the significant persons within his socializing orbit in order to validate his concept of the world. He verifies what he sees and senses by communicating with others through symbols they mutually understand. Material objects can carry messages as cogently as verbal sounds, serving as symbols of the social setting which are susceptible to manipulation. Thus, dress and adornment become tangible means of gaining some control over the social situation.

As the individual learns that his attention to grooming and costume evokes certain responses from others, the appearance of others also comes to have meanings for him. Through his appearance, each person continually has on exhibition cues for the response of others. If these cues are ambiguous or inconsistent with the way that either participant defines the social situation, action may be thwarted or terminated. This might happen if an applicant for a white-collar job showed up for an interview in a blue shirt and overalls.[2]

---

[2] However, the reverse situation, an applicant for a blue-collar job appearing for an interview in white collar and business suit, might be acceptable since the business suit is a widely recognized symbol for the business interview.

Stone in his analytical scheme for the study of interaction does not overlook the part that total appearance plays in the identification of self and others. His article represents one of the most sophisticated theoretical attempts to incorporate dress as a significant symbol in social interaction. Goffman throws further light on the effect of appearance on self-identification as he points out the ego-supporting influences of cosmetics, clothing supplies, and related materials, and on the personal defacement that ensues when these props are taken away.

Ryan compared individuals' estimates of appearance with group perceptions of the same persons, testing the consistency with which definitions are formulated within the social situation and how accurately the individual responds to cues of interaction. Hoult explored a similar idea but noted how social distance affected the observer's dependence on clothing cues in making evaluations of others. Both of these researchers contributed to the study of dress by developing methodology and initiating investigations in an area subject to much conjecture.

Since with socialization comes inculcation of "correct" ways of presenting ourselves in various social situations, inability to "dress the part" may burden the individual with emotional stress and generate feelings of frustration and deprivation. In acculturative situations expressions of deprivation are quite complex. For example, individuals from a subordinate culture, such as that of the Sioux Indians described by Wax and Wax, can emulate clothing patterns fairly easily, given economic opportunity. But adjustments to the demands of the superordinate culture in more abstract areas, such as language patterns, manners, and morals are much harder to comprehend. As a result, deprivation of clothing may take on a symbolic significance far out of proportion to the value ordinarily placed on clothing.

A Deviant

"Deviance" is a term generally used to connote behavior that varies in considerable degree from society's norms. Cross-cultural studies indicate that definitions of deviance are not the same for all societies. What may be considered beyond reproach in one group may be highly suspect or even criminal in another.

Here we shall develop three aspects of deviance: personal deviance of the famous in which the individual is allowed to be different; personal deviance in which the individual is alienated in a general way from all social affiliations; and subcultural deviance in which the individual may reject the general norms of society at the same time that he identifies with marginal groups considered deviant by the general society.

A society's rewards and punishments exert powerful constraints on individuals to conform to its norms of behavior. Although some deviation from the norms is tolerated, and sometimes even encouraged in modern American society, there are limits beyond which idiosyncrasy will not be endured. A certain number of the peculiar, the eccentric, and the mentally deficient reside permanently in the limbo of marginality, but others who come to be considered a threat to themselves or to the society are forcibly removed from their social milieu. These people are ostracized, deported, or placed in mental or penal institutions.

According to the theory of social interaction, individuals react to themselves as social as well as physical objects. They are aware of social norms. They become conscious of their own appearance, behavior, and status, sensing that others may react to and evaluate these personal attributes on the basis of the norms. Cecil Beaton indicates how royalty, as examples of "famous" personalities, develop idiosyncratic styles which deviate from the norms of dress but are tolerated. Goffman and Miller, Carpenter, and Buckey on the other hand, are concerned with associations between general personal alienation from society and deviance in dress. Goffman first shows how the "normal" individual through his attention to dress, adornment, and personal grooming identifies himself and evinces his understanding of the rights and duties associated with a behavioral situation. He points out subsequently that the mentally disturbed person, through his lack of interest in the personal appearance he presents, indicates his loss of situational awareness and his rejection of society. Miller and associates describe a practical testing of the hypothesis that a change in appearance may result in self-acceptance which may render social situations more tolerable for the mentally alienated person.

Burma shows how body decorations may be used as symbols to mark affiliations with subcultural groupings whose behavior is held to be deviant by the general population. Such behavior may represent a solution to the need for identification with others when identification with society as a whole is unrealistic or unattainable.

Many social observers have commented on the use of clothing by teen-agers as a badge of identification. Recent gang wars in Britain, as reported in "The Clacton Giggle," provide examples of the use of dress by deviant teen-agers to demonstrate their social defiance and subgroup affiliations.

Supplementary Readings

Statements concerning the association between the individual's behavior and dress are included in the general works cited at the end of Part One. Other references are Barker and Adams (1939), Bates (1952), Cobliner (1950), Compton (1962, 1964), Coon (1962), Dearborn (1918), Douty (1963), Evans (1964), Flaccus (1906), Goffman (1963A, 1963B), Greenacre (1944), G. S. Hall (1898), Harnik (1932), M. Hart (1959), Irwin and Weiss (1934), Lonie (1948), Macaulay (1929), MacGuire (1964), Newman (1953), Physiology of Clothing (1964), Rich (1950), Ryan (1952, 1953A, 1953B), Silverman (1945, 1960), Thompson (1962), and Turner and Surace (1956).

A Biological Organism

The Differential Effects of Nudity and Clothing on Muscular Tonus in Infancy

H. M. HALVERSON

The present study was motivated by varying reports [1] of the strength of the grasping reflex in human infants. Although it is undoubtedly true that differences in gripping power between infants are due in great part to differences in native constitution, the marked variations in the strength of the reflex exhibited on different occasions by the same individual indicate the presence of factors other than native constitution whch affect the condition of muscular tonus. Among these factors, according to an earlier review of the literature,[2] are age, temperature, emotional excitement, waking state, and the state of hunger or satiation. Since tonus is essentially a proprioceptive reflex it may well vary with cutaneous factors, particularly in infancy. It therefore seemed profitable to investigate the differential effects of the presence and absence of clothing on tonus.

The effect of clothing upon the grasping response has received very little consideration. In fact, 6 of 13 investigators failed to state whether their subjects were nude or clothed. In the remaining seven studies the conditions under which the subjects were tested were as follows: clothed, 1; diapers and shirt, 2; diapers only, 2; entirely nude, 1. In one study it was stated that the subjects were undressed; however, the photographs indicate that the diapers were not removed. In any event the results obtained in these studies were not comparable, since the investigations varied with respect to apparatus and procedure.

---

[1] H. M. Halverson, Studies of the grasping responses in early infancy: I, II, III. *J. Genet. Psychol.*, 1937, 51, 371–449.

[2] *Ibid.*

Source: *Journal of Genetic Psychology*, Vol. 61 (September, 1942), pp. 55–67. Reprinted by permission of Mrs. H. M. Halverson and the publisher.

A. Method

1. GENERAL PROCEDURE

In general the procedure consisted in testing the strength of the gripping reflex (*a*) before undressing the infant, (*b*) after undressing him, and (*c*) after reclothing him. The subjects were divided into two groups, quiescent and activated. The subjects of the first group were kept as quiet as conditions permitted. The instructions were to handle each infant very carefully, to refrain from talking, and to avoid looking directly at his face. Despite these efforts to reduce disturbances to a minimum, the probability that carrying, undressing, and reclothing the subject may have influenced the results made it advisable to repeat the experiment on a second group of subjects who were kept physically active throughout by brisk handling, smiling, and playful talking.

2. SPECIFIC PROCEDURES

The infant of the quiescent group was carefully lifted from his crib by a nurse, carried in a horizontal position, and placed gently on a blanket-covered table at one end of the room where there was no draft. Both hands of the infant were then dried with a soft cloth and powdered, after which the nurse joined the experimenter and his assistant at a point well out of the infant's range of vision. After the infant had been left alone for two minutes, the experimenter and assistant approached the infant, tested his gripping strength, and then withdrew. The nurse now carefully undressed the infant without removing the clothes from beneath him, and then left him alone for two minutes before the second gripping test was given. Finally he was carefully reclothed, left to himself for two minutes, and tested for the third time.

In the second procedure the nurse, experimenter, and assistant remained close by the infant. The nurse throughout smiled and talked animatedly to the infant. She approached the crib, lifted the infant to a vertical position, and carried him to the table where he was placed supinely on the blanket. She then briskly dried and powdered the infant's hand, after which she took hold of his wrists and playfully manipulated his arms for two minutes. The gripping test was now given and the infant was undressed. After the nurse had manipulated the arms for two minutes, he was again tested. He was then reclothed and, after another two minutes of playful manipulation, tested for the third time.

Undressing and dressing caused little disturbance. The clothing consisted of a diaper, full-length loose stockings, undershirt, and loose-sleeved dress reaching to the feet. The undershirt and dress were equipped with buttons down the front. In undressing, the clothes were not removed from beneath the infant. The dress and undershirt were unbuttoned and spread out about him. The diapers were unpinned and similarly spread out, and the stockings pulled off. If the test caused a change in location, the infant was immediately restored to his original position so as not to interfere with the act of dressing.

Many infants cried during the course of the experiment. The records of those who cried during the 2-minute rest periods were discarded, whereas the records of infants who cried only momentarily during gripping were used. Infants whose diapers were damp were given dry diapers and left alone for at least 15 minutes before being tested.

The experiment was conducted in the nursery of the maternity hospital at the State Farm for Women at Niantic, Connecticut. The time selected for the experiment was 11 to 12:30 o'clock after the infant had awakened from an hour or more of sleep following the morning feeding. The temperature of the room on different days varied from 80° to 86° F. The distance from the crib to the table varied in individual cases from 9 to 15 feet.

The apparatus for testing the strength of the grip was a spring balance scale suspending a small stirrup with a grasping rod of wood.[3] The scale read to 25 lbs. in quarter-pound dimensions. The rod was 10 cm. in length and 1 cm. in diameter. A rider on the scale operated with the pointer and registered the maximum pull after the spring was released. The left hand only was tested and only one trial was made in each situation. The experimenter placed the rod against the palm and then drew the hand upward to full extension. The proximal interphalangeal joints of the three longest fingers were directly above the rod with the thumb opposed. The stirrup was then pulled steadily upward until the grip was broken or the infant's body was fully suspended. Infants who succeeded in supporting the full body weight were lowered as soon as it was evident that the feet were clear of the table.

[3] *Ibid.*

Table 1 Gripping strength in pounds and in per cent of body weight supported in the three situations: clothed, nude, and reclothed

	Quiescent group						Activated group					
	37 Boys		46 Girls		Boys and Girls		32 Boys		36 Girls		Boys and Girls	
Situation	Lbs.	% Wt. supported	Lbs.	% Wt. supported	Lbs.	% Wt. supported	Lbs.	% Wt. supported	Lbs.	% Wt. supported	Lbs.	% Wt. supported
Clothed												
Mean	4.4	42.6	4.5	50.3	4.5	46.8	4.6	41.5	5.0	52.9	4.8	47.6
Median	4.0	41.0	4.3	50.0	4.3	47.0	4.3	37.5	4.9	49.5	4.6	44.0
Sigma	2.1		1.4		1.8		2.0		1.7		1.8	
Nude												
Mean	6.5	64.4	6.0	66.3	6.2	65.4	6.3	58.6	6.5	67.6	6.4	63.4
Median	6.4	60.0	6.0	67.5	6.0	67.0	6.3	57.0	6.5	65.0	6.5	59.0
Sigma	3.0		1.7		2.4		1.9		2.0		2.0	
Reclothed												
Mean	4.8	47.7	4.5	50.0	4.6	49.0	5.2	47.7	5.1	54.2	5.2	51.2
Median	4.0	47.0	4.5	48.5	4.3	47.0	4.8	45.0	4.6	45.0	4.8	45.0
Sigma	2.1		1.4		1.8		2.2		1.9		2.0	

B. Subjects

Two hundred and thirty-four infants, viz., 121 boys and 113 girls, were tried on different days in both parts of the experiment. Of the total number of boys, 37 met the conditions of quiescence and 32 fulfilled the conditions of activation. Similarly 46 of the 113 girls were accepted as quiescent subjects and 36 as activated subjects. Inasmuch as 18 boys and 23 girls passed the requirements of both procedures, the total number of infants who served as subjects in the experiment was 110, of whom 51 were boys and 59 were girls. Thus there were more infants in the quiescent than in the activated group, and more girls than boys in each case.

In each group the boys were somewhat older and larger than were the girls. The mean age of the quiescent subjects was 9.7 weeks (boys 10.5 weeks, girls 9.1 weeks). The mean age of the activated subjects was 12.7 weeks (boys 14.2 weeks, girls 11.3 weeks). The age range was the same for both groups, viz., 1 to 22 weeks). The mean weight of the subjects was 9.8 lbs. (boys 10.2 lbs., girls 9.5 lbs.) for the quiescent group, and 10.6 lbs. (boys 11.3 lbs., girls 10.1 lbs.) for the activated group. The weight range was 5.3 to 14.7 lbs. for the former group and 6.9 to 14.7 for the latter group.

C. Results

Table 1 shows the mean and median measures, in pounds and in per cent of body weight supported, of the strength of the gripping response for both the quiescent and the activated groups. The measures for each sex are also given.

According to the data the response was considerably stronger in the nude situation than in either the clothed or reclothed situations for both boys and girls of both groups. The strongest response by the boys occurred in the quiescent nude situation; the strongest response by the girls occurred in the activated nude situation. Although gripping power was in general somewhat greater for the activated group than for the quiescent group, the mean difference in the strength of the reflex between the groups was relatively small in each situation for each sex and for the subjects as a whole. This was particularly true when the difference was expressed in terms of per cent of body weight supported.

The data on per cent of body weight supported further indicate that the girls were superior in gripping strength to the boys in all situations. It will be noted that in most cases variations in gripping power were greater for the boys than for the girls.

The mean and median measures show that the greatest difference in strength of the response between the nude and clothed situations, and between the nude and reclothed situations, occurred in the quiescent group of boys. Differences between the clothed and reclothed situations were generally slight, with the average gripping force slightly greater in the latter situation.

Although the gripping response was on the average considerably stronger in the nude than in the clothed or reclothed situation, analysis of the data disclosed individual trends inconsistent with those of the group. Table 2 shows the frequency with which the strength of the response increased, decreased, or remained unchanged from one situation to another. The mean and median amounts of the increases and decreases for the groups are expressed in pounds.

The data indicate that for both quiescent and activated groups a large majority (over 75 per cent) of the subjects revealed the group trends, viz., stronger gripping power when nude than when clothed or reclothed. For both groups the increase in strength from the clothed to the nude situation exceeded that from the reclothed to the nude situation. Only a relatively small number of subjects (10–17 per cent) of each group revealed reverse trends. A few infants of each group failed to show any change in the strength of the reflex with change one way or the other in the condition of dress. It is significant that despite the great variations from subject to subject, the mean difference in strength between the nude and clothed situations, and between the nude and reclothed situations, is greater for subjects who revealed the group trends than for subjects who revealed the reverse trends. There was no significant difference in gripping power between the clothed and reclothed situations. About one-half of the subjects gripped harder when clothed; the other half gripped harder when reclothed.

More than two-thirds of the subjects of each group, 58 quiescent and 46 activated infants, exhibited the strongest grip in the nude situation, and in 12 other instances the grip in this situation was stronger than in one of the

Table 2 *Frequency and amount of increase and decrease in gripping strength from one situation to another* (The mean and median measures of the amount of increase or decrease are in pounds)

	Clothed to nude					Reclothed to nude					Clothed to reclothed			
	No. cases	Mean	Median	Sigma	No. cases	Mean	Median	Sigma	No. cases	Mean	Median	Sigma
Quiescent group												
Increase	63	2.5	2.3	1.5	67	2.1	1.8	1.5	41	1.3	0.9	1.1
Decrease	14	1.0	0.9	0.5	11	0.9	0.7	0.9	34	1.1	0.8	0.8
No change	6				5				8			
Activated group												
Increase	53	2.2	1.9	1.5	54	1.7	1.7	1.2	33	1.6	1.4	1.2
Decrease	11	0.7	0.4	0.5	7	1.5	1.3	0.5	32	0.9	0.8	0.6
No change	4				7				3			

Table 3 *Clinging strength (in pounds) of crying and of non-crying subjects*

	Clothed					Nude					Reclothed			
	No. cases	Mean	Median	Sigma	No. cases	Mean	Median	Sigma	No. cases	Mean	Median	Sigma
Quiescent												
Crying	22	6.1	5.5	1.7	34	8.1	7.9	1.9	33	6.0	5.5	1.8
Non-crying	61	3.9	4.0	1.4	49	4.9	4.5	1.7	50	3.8	3.9	1.0
Activated												
Crying	11	6.3	6.5	1.3	25	7.4	7.5	1.8	19	6.4	6.8	2.0
Non-crying	57	4.5	4.3	1.8	43	5.8	6.0	1.8	49	4.7	4.5	1.8

other situations. About ⅛ of the subjects manifested their greatest strength when they were clothed, and less than ¹⁄₁₀ of them when they were reclothed.

It has been stated[4] that the grasping reflex functions more tenaciously in crying infants than in non-crying infants. In order to test the validity of this statement, the strength of grip was determined separately for subjects who cried during the tests and for subjects who did not cry. The results are presented in Table 3. It will be noted that the frequency of crying is highest in the nude situation and lowest in the clothed situation.

The data show that for both crying and non-crying subjects the power of grip was greater when infants were nude than when they were clothed or reclothed, and that in each of the three situations the grip was much stronger for the crying infants than for the non-crying infants. Comparison of Tables 1 and 3 indicates that in each situation the average gripping power of both quiescent and activated groups was substantially increased by the presence of infants who cried during the tests. The greater the frequency of crying, the greater the increase in the force of the grip.

Thirty-one subjects cried during each of the three tests. Their average gripping strength in each situation, viz., clothed 6.2 lbs., nude 7.8 lbs., and reclothed 6.1 lbs., differed very little from that of the entire crying group. Of these 31 infants, 16 supported the entire body weight when nude, three when clothed, and one when reclothed. One subject supported her full weight on all three occasions.

There were 39 instances, 20 in the quiescent group and 19 in the activated group, in which infants gripped with sufficient strength to support the body weight. The data show that in 33 of these instances the subjects were nude and that in 30 instances they were crying. The girls exhibited this superior gripping power on 26 occasions, and the boys on only 13 occasions. The 26 grips by the girls were achieved by 21 infants as follows: one girl in each of the three situations; three girls in each of two situations; 17 girls on only one occasion each. The 13 grips by the boys occurred only when the subjects were nude.

[4] M. Sherman, I. Sherman, & C. D. Flory, Infant behavior. *Comp. Psychol. Monog.*, 1936, 12, 1–107.

D. Discussion

1. EVIDENCE FROM THE LITERATURE

Results of other investigations lead one to expect a difference in the condition of tonus between the nude and the clothed situations. Irwin and Weiss[5] experimented with 50 infants by means of the stabilmeter-polygraph techniques and found that the group was twice as active when nude as when clothed. In addition, all but three of the infants "revealed trends consistent with the group findings."[6] Several studies[7,8,9,10] indicate that warmth had a quieting effect on infants, whereas cold appeared to stimulate them to action. In this connection it is generally accepted[11] that external cold tends to bring about an increase in bodily metabolism and an augmented muscular tone. Pratt[12] reports a greater amount of activity by infants when the diapers are wet than when they are dry and believes that the difference in activity between the two situations is probably due to changes in temperature rather than in humidity. In an earlier study wherein clothing was not a factor Irwin[13] found that variations in body temperature between 96° and 101.6° did not materially affect the motility of infants. Henderson and his associates[14] compared the effects of still air and of agitated air on adult male subjects

---

[5] O. C. Irwin & L. A. Weiss, The effect of clothing on the general and vocal activity of the newborn infant. In *Studies in Infant Behavior*, by O. C. Irwin, L. A. Weiss, & E. M. Stubbs, *Univ. Iowa Stud.*, 1934, 9, 151–162.

[6] *Ibid.*, p. 156.

[7] S. Canestrini, Über das Sinnesleben des Neugeborenen. Berlin: Springer, 1913. Pp. 104.

[8] A. Peiper, Die Hirntätigkeit des Säuglings. Berlin: Springer, 1928. Pp. 102.

[9] K. C. Pratt, Note on the relation of temperature and humidity to the activity of young infants. *J. Genet. Psychol.*, 1930, 38, 480–484.

[10] K. C. Pratt, A. K. Nelson, & K. H. Sun, The Behavior of the Newborn Infant. Columbus, Ohio: Ohio State Univ. Press, 1930. Pp. xiii + 237.

[11] W. H. Howell, A textbook of Physiology. (11th edit.) Philadelphia: Saunders, 1930 p. 52.

[12] Pratt, *loc. cit.*

[13] O. C. Irwin, Motility of young infants: I. Relation to body temperature, *Amer. I. Dis. Child.*, 1933, 45, 531–533.

[14] Y. Henderson, A. W. Oughterson, L. A. Greenberg, & C. P. Searle, Air movement as a stimulus to the skin, the reflex effects upon muscle tonus, and indirectly upon the circulation of the blood; also the effects of therapeutic baths. *Amer. J. Physiol.*, 1936, 114, 269–272.

naked to the waist and discovered in the latter case a marked increase in muscular tonus and intramuscular pressure. The subjects lay quietly in a room in which temperature and humidity were constant. Furthermore, according to these investigators [15], Barcroft (a reference we were unable to procure) "found that the fetus of a sheep delivered by Caesarean section in a warm bath has no tonus in its muscles until it is lifted out of the bath into the air; and that, if the cord is intact, the tonus disappears again when the fetus is replaced in the bath."

In view of the above findings and the results herein obtained, it is the opinion of the writer that in the present experiment the difference in strength of the clinging reflex between the nude and the clothed infants may best be accounted for by the differential physiological effects of changes in skin temperature. The evaporation of moisture from the skin has the effect of reducing its temperature and thereby reflexly exciting the muscles into a state of increased tonus.[16] Inasmuch as evaporation occurs faster when the skin is uncovered, other conditions being equal, the excitation would be greater under nude than under clothed conditions.

2. INCONSISTENT RESULTS

Reverse trends manifested by a relatively small number of subjects in each group are not easily explained. It can only be suggested that the procedure which was generally adequate to produce changes in the condition of tonus was also effective in producing changes in affective state which in some cases influenced the disposition to action. There is the probability that the stimulation from previous handling and testing was in some cases a more potent factor than clothing in determining the strength of the reflex in the reclothed situation.

3. AFFECTIVE RESPONSES AND THEIR RELATION TO GRIPPING POWER

The exclusion of crying and fretting infants made for greater uniformity in behavior during the pre-test periods and thus for more comparable results in the tests. Previous investigations [17] revealed that attempts to elicit

---

[15] *Ibid.*, p. 269.
[16] Irwin, *loc. cit.*
[17] H. M. Halverson, Infant sucking and tensional behavior. *J. Genet. Psychol.*, 1938, 53, 365–430.

the grasping reflex in emotionally disturbed subjects were frequently futile, and that even when such attempts were successful, great fluctuations in gripping power occurred unless a steady and forceful pull was maintained against the flexor tendons.

The tests evoked varying affective responses. Of the 453 tests, 3 per subject, 144 were attended by crying, 57 by smiling, and 252 by varying degrees of complacence or annoyance. The frequency of crying was higher for the quiescent group, whereas the frequency of smiling was higher for the activated group. However, it should be added that if the time limit for gripping had been extended, crying would probably have occurred in all cases in which subjects exhibited marked strength.

It has been noted that the mean gripping power of the crying subjects was considerably greater than that of the non-crying subjects. The simplest explanation of the marked strength exhibited by infants who cried during the tests is to ascribe the state of increased tonus to the energizing effects of emotional excitement. The explanation suffices for instances in which the strength of the reflex increased with crying which started before the body was fully supported, but may not apply to instances in which crying occurred only after the body was suspended. It seems highly probable that in the latter instances, and in the case of non-crying infants, strong gripping occurred as a result of a previously induced state of increased tonus and that the crying which ensued was occasioned by fear, postural discomfort, or severe muscular strain. Crying during the early stages of the pull appeared to be due to interference with the preferred supine posture.

4. REASONS FOR SEX DIFFERENCES

Three reasons may be advanced for the general superiority in gripping strength of the girls over the boys. In the first place, crying during the tests was relatively more frequent among the girls than among the boys. The difference between the sexes may be due to the greater age of the boys, inasmuch as it is generally accepted that the grasping reflex weakens with age. On the other hand, the difference may be due to strict observance of the conditions imposed by the procedure which resulted in the elimination of numerous prospective subjects, the majority of whom were boys. This is equivalent to saying that the girls as a whole experienced less difficulty than the boys in their adjustment to the experiment.

5. INDIVIDUAL DIFFERENCES

In any one of the three situations, both boys and girls exhibited marked individual differences in muscle tonus. Marked individual differences in tonus were exhibited also from one situation to another.

That the condition of muscle tonus varied greatly from subject to subject in each situation is indicated by the range of gripping strength. The range for the two groups in each of the three situations is given in Table 4. It was evident that some of the subjects could have supported more than the body weight. If the full strength of these infants had been ascertained, individual differences would have been even more marked.

Table 4

Quiescent group		Activated group
0.0– 9.3 lbs.	Clothed	1.0– 9.3 lbs.
2.3–11.8 lbs.	Nude	1.5–11.2 lbs.
1.0–10.8 lbs	Reclothed	1.8–11.0 lbs.

There was a relatively large number of subjects who consistently exhibited a strong grip, while an equally large number consistently exhibited a weak grip, in all three trials—an indication that factors other than the presence or absence of clothing were operative in determining the state of tonus. As a rule, a subject's performance in the clothed situation was predictive of his performance in the nude and reclothed situations.

It has been noted that the change in condition from clothed to nude produced a state of increased tonus in more than 75 per cent of the subjects in each group. However, the amount of the increase, measured in terms of pounds of gripping strength, varied greatly from infant to infant, viz., from 0.5 to 7.9 for the quiescent group and from 0.6 to 7.1 for the activated group. A small number of subjects of each group showed no change in gripping power, whereas a somewhat larger number showed a decrease. The amount of decrease in no case exceeded 2 lbs. Similar individual differences were shown in the change in muscle tonus from the nude to the reclothed situation.

E. Summary

The strength of the grasping reflex in infants under six months of age was tested successively in the clothed, nude, and reclothed situations for the purpose of determining the effect of clothing on muscular tonus. The subjects were divided into two groups, the quiescent and the activated. The investigation indicated:

1. For each group the change from the clothed to the nude situation resulted in a state of increased tonus and the change from the nude to the reclothed situation resulted in a condition of reduced tonus. This general trend was evidenced by more than two-thirds of the subjects of each group.

2. More than 75 per cent of the subjects of each group exhibited a stronger grip in the nude than in the clothed situation, and an equal number of each group gripped with greater force in the nude than in the reclothed situation.

3. There was no appreciable difference in tonus between the clothed and the reclothed situations for either group.

4. The reflex was in general manifested with somewhat greater strength by the activated group than by the quiescent group.

5. Crying brought about a generally increased tonic state. As a whole, subjects who cried during the tests exhibited greater gripping power than did the non-crying subjects.

6. The girls were generally superior to the boys in gripping strength. Three factors which may account for this difference between the sexes have been advanced.

7. Both groups revealed marked individual differences (*a*) in gripping strength in each of the three situations, and (*b*) in alterations in gripping strength with change in the condition of clothing.

8. The difference in the strength of the reflex between the nude and the clothed situations is due in part to changes in skin temperature.

Thermal Comfort

RICHARD L. MEIER

Now that it seems possible, even probable, that the world can be assured of a continuing supply of the familiar forms of energy at not unreasonable costs for tens of thousands, or even millions, of years into the future, an embarrassing question must be asked. Energy for what purposes? How much energy is really necessary? In order to find reasonable answers to such questions the basic human needs for comfort and convenience must be surveyed. The ways in which energy is employed in order to maintain an individual in equilibrium with his physical environment ought to be systematized. In addition, the ways in which energy can free humans from routine tasks and enable them to engage in an increasing range of activities should be considered. From such investigations it should be possible to establish how energy might best be used in the future, viewing the application of energy to human needs as a scientific problem rather than one of updating historical precedents. . . . This procedure requires a rather abrupt change in the mode of argument. We move from a description of very large-scale science-based technology to the individual human, the family unit, and the technics of everyday living where whatever science has been introduced is haphazard and far from systematic.

When conditions of comfort are barely adequate, the quantity of fuels consumed in the household is undoubtedly greater than that allocated to any other single category of use in the society. Much of this is used for space heating, a large amount for cooking, and only slightly less for heating water. A trifle goes for refrigeration, considerable amounts for lighting, and there are in addition a great number of miscellaneous applications.

Too often it is forgotten that food itself serves as a fuel. The 2,000 to 4,000 calories which are consumed by a person over a day are in turn emitted by the body. These calories can be conserved so as to keep human beings comfortable, but to do so efficiently requires a great deal of scientific knowledge about human comfort and about the properties of heat.

Source: *Science and Economic Development: New Patterns of Living,* Cambridge, Massachusetts: The M. I. T. Press, Massachusetts Institute of Technology (1956), pp. 97–102. Reprinted by permission of the publisher.

The latter subject was studied exhaustively in the nineteenth century, so that the last fifty years have brought only refinements in equipment and measurements. The research upon human comfort, however, has been quite recent and still affords many surprises as the subject is being advanced. The only comprehensive review of the recent studies upon thermal comfort is that edited by L. H. Newburgh (1949).[1]

The thermal needs of human beings stem principally from properties of their sensory nervous system. If, for instance, the average temperature of the skin should deviate more than 3°C from the standard figure of 33°C the nervous system would mildly, but definitely, protest. Another degree or two beyond that would result in real discomfort or illness. Within this range of surface temperatures a person has a capacity for adjusting his heat production by internal regulatory controls. The control mechanisms have apparently evolved in order to protect the brain and the internal organs from temperature variations, since they are now so elaborate and complex that a 1 to 2° deviation from the normal deep body temperature results in a noticeable loss of mental function.

There are primitive peoples, such as the Fuegian Indians at the tip of South America and the Australian aborigines, who manage to live virtually naked in freezing climates and have always constituted a challenge to this concept of comfort. However the work of Sir Stanton Hicks and colleagues (1934, 1938)[2] suggests that the cold is felt as keenly by them as it is by less well adapted persons but that the natives have developed an additional reflex for reducing the flow of blood in the skin and thereby are able to reduce the loss of body warmth. The skin is thus made to act more like a layer of insulation than a radiator.

In most cultures, sufficient clothing is worn outdoors to permit the release of just enough heat so that the skin temperature stays well within the comfort range. Inside a dwelling the air and walls can be heated so that fewer layers of clothing are required. In this system of thinking, clothing acts as a heat insulator, used for much the same purposes as the wrapping around a steam pipe, and can be measured accordingly. The unit of insulation value for clothing has quite appropriately been called a *clo* in North America. One *clo* is the amount of insulation necessary to maintain comfort in a normally ventilated room, with air movements less

---

[1] L. H. Newburgh, ed., *Physiology of Heat Regulation and the Science of Comfort*, Saunders, Philadelphia, 1949 (includes discussion of work of Sir Stanton Hicks, pp. 31-35).
[2] *Ibid.*

than 10 feet per minute, at a temperature of 70°F and a relative humidity less than 50%, while the subject is resting in a sitting position. (A *clo* = 0.648°C sec sq m/Cal; it allows the transfer of 5.55 Cal/sq m/hr at a temperature gradient of 1°C.) The amount of clothing ordinarily worn ranges from about 5 *clo* for bitterly cold weather to about 0.5 *clo* for midsummer.

The quantity of heat generated by the body increases with the degree of activity. Whereas a normal person in a sitting position generates about 100 Cal per hour, a slow walk will double the quantity, and a brisk hike with pack will quadruple it. The surrounding air in the latter instances must be relatively cool in order to permit comfort, even if minimal clothing is worn. The alternative is first, heavy perspiration and later, if cooling is not sufficiently rapid, heat prostration.

The role of perspiration is that of bringing a new cooling process into play—the evaporation of water at the skin surface. Since evaporation is carried out very close to the temperature-sensitive nerve endings in the skin, a large measure of relief may be afforded by perspiration. The rate of cooling however depends ultimately upon the relative humidity and air flow. Control of these two factors generally provides the most economical air-conditioning arrangement. Clothing can also be adapted so as not to hinder, but even slightly increase, the cooling qualities of perspiration.

Once it is seen how clothing can conserve energy it must also be admitted that it costs energy to manufacture. Does it really pay to wear clothing—speaking in purely energetic terms? This is an intriguing problem to which a convincing answer can be given.

In many environments it is possible to achieve thermal comfort by two alternative routes, (1) engaging in more physical activity and consuming enough food to make such effort possible, or (2) utilizing clothing as a means of heat insulation. The fiber in clothing requires soil resources which can otherwise be applied to the production of food, so a basis for comparison exists.

It appears, upon inspection of agricultural yields, that several tons of grain can be grown where one ton of cotton is now produced, making due allowances for cottonseed by-products. Similarly, a ton of wool can be obtained from grazing lands which would otherwise produce several tons of protein in the form of meat. Thus we can set up an equivalent:

1 kg cotton or wool = 2 to 3 kg carbohydrate or protein foodstuffs.

To convert the fiber into garments now requires about 1 kg of coal per kg of fiber. Knowledge of this fact permits establishing the cost of garments in terms of the caloric value of food and fuel (1.4 to 2.0 $\times$ 10^4 Cal/kg of garments).

In order to estimate per capita needs it is necessary to state what climate is assumed. A temperate climate, for instance, might have an annual average temperature around 15° C; it would normally require 5 to 6 kg of fiber. Thus the total energy cost of a person's clothing for a year comes to 7 to 12 $\times$ 10^4 Cal.

In the same climate, food requirements can also be estimated by using data available to physiologists. Food needs for a young man, clothed, 65 kg, doing moderate work, are 2880 Cal per day. For him unclothed, they can be calculated and come to 4100 Cal per man.

This is an increase in food consumption of 42%, due solely to absence of clothing. For a typical population, which includes both young and old persons, a 42% increase must be added to a basic 2500 to 2700 Cal per day per capita now considered to be barely adequate. Processing costs, transport, and allowance for waste should still be added.

In comparing the minimal annual food cost for thermal comfort (4 $\times$ 10^5 Cal) with the clothing cost (7 to 12 $\times$ 10^4 Cal) it will be seen that every calorie devoted to fibers is returned at least three- to six-fold in the saving of food. For colder climates the margin will be much greater, even if people develop heat-conserving reflexes like those of the Australian Bushmen, whereas for somewhat warmer climates more refined calculations are needed. For the tropics, clothing would need other justifications than energy economy. The newer synthetic fibers, in general, cost no more calories than the natural fibers, but they tend to wear longer, so that the saving in energy is still more marked if they are relied upon.

Clothing has uses and properties beyond those of thermal comfort. The design of suitable clothing for both a specified climate and a pattern of living may require many lifetimes of experience in order to achieve just the right compromise between:

Thermal comfort
Convenience (especially pockets)
Freedom from irritation
Launderability
Identification of social status and role
Cost.

If the world's styles were to be analyzed from the point of view of comfort, convenience, and efficiency (Rudofsky, 1947) [3] no culture would score well on its total array of creations, but each can contribute to an assortment that could appear to be most useful to meet the various combinations of world climate and human activity.

Of what garments would a minimum adequate wardrobe consist? By drawing upon the technical and cultural experience of both the East and the West it is possible to assemble an assortment that seems to be quite suitable.

First layers: ½ to 1½ *clo*
    tee shirts, shorts, blouses, Hindu sari, trousers of cotton or reinforced rayon, broad-rimmed hat, sandals

Second layer: 1½ to 2½ *clo*
    sweaters, trousers or kilts made of moisture-resistant warm fibers, shoes with fabric uppers, socks or stockings reinforced at points of wear, rain slicker

Third layer: 2½ to 3½ *clo*
    lined windbreaker, coveralls, overshoes or lined boots, helmet or hunter's cap, gloves

Fourth layer: 3½ to 4½ *clo*
    roughwoven greatcoat or parka, warm scarf, warmer knee-length boots, better-grade gloves

Because of the unwieldiness of any further layers, it is not convenient to wear more than 4 to 5 *clo*. Besides, Arctic peoples have found that sweaty damp underlayers can be disastrous to the insulation value and also the life of the garments. (Perspiration cannot be avoided whenever, for any reason, the level of activity must be increased.) Therefore, outdoor clothing should be designed so that the heat-retaining capacities can be readily altered. Recently, foamed-plastic garments have been developed which make possible much higher levels of insulation, but they do not yet solve the problem of varying the insulating capacity. Such garments do permit exposure to icy water or sleeping out-of-doors in the Arctic without important discomfort. In the long run, man may be able to improve upon the use of furs and textiles, but developments to date are still scanty.

The upper limit for convenient indoor clothing appears to be about 3 *clo*. Thus it is for meeting the requirements set by the weather immediately outside the shelter, which may be called the urban macroclimate,

[3] B. Rudofsky, *Are Clothes Modern?*, Paul Theobald, Chicago, 1947.

that the minimum adequate wardrobe must be designed. What this means for various parts of the world is indicated in Table 1.

Table 1 World requirements for thermal insulation in clothing

Area	Yearly Average for Comfort per Capita,* clo	Total,† clo
United States and Canada	2.9	4.8×10^8
Latin America and West Indies	1.8	3.5×10^8
Western Europe	3.1	9.5×10^8
Eastern Europe, Russia, Siberia	3.4	9.9×10^8
Near East (including Egypt)	1.9	1.8×10^8
Far East and East Indies	2.1	2.5×10^9
Australia and New Zealand	2.5	2.5×10^7
Africa (less Egypt)	1.9	3.4×10^8
World average	2.35 clo	5.7×10^9 clo

* Population-weighted averages compiled from the monthly maps of world climate zones, Climatology Unit, Research and Development Branch, Office of the Quartermaster General, 1943. They indicate the average amount of clothing to be worn with comfort in a shaded area outdoors, protected from the wind. For a suitable measure of annual needs this figure must be multiplied by a factor representing the rate at which clothing wears out—a difficult variable to ascertain.
† Based on 1950 population estimates, *U.N. Statistical Papers,* III, nos. 3–4, 1951.

Consulting the data on comfort collected by the physiologists reveals that it becomes very difficult to maintain thermal comfort at low levels of human activity when the temperature of the environment falls below 10°C (50°F). At the lower temperatures, comfort can be maintained only at considerable inconvenience—such as wearing gloves when sewing or reading. Thus, when fuel is very scarce, it seems likely that the most economical arrangement would be that of adding more clothing down to a temperature of 10°C, and then finding some suitable mode of space heating which would maintain the 10°C level no matter how far the exterior temperatures fell. Such an observation makes it possible to relate climate to thermal needs, taking clothing, climate, and space heating as a complementary ensemble.

⌘ Why She Lives in a Space Suit
PRISCILLA JAQUITH

Scattered around the U.S. today is a tiny group of persons—perhaps a dozen in all—who are walking around in space suits.

One is a farmer in Kanesville, Ill., who dons his when he plows his fields. Other space-suit wearers are a 62-year-old man in Santa Monica, Calif., another man in Redwood City, Calif.—and an attractive housewife here, Mrs. Sarah (Sandy) Waldrep, mother of two.

Mrs. Waldrep wears her space suit—the same used by jet pilots to keep them from blacking out in steep climbs and dives—while she cooks, shops, cleans. Each morning she climbs into the suit, pumps it full of air and begins her day. Her suit is an out-of-date 1959 model, but she cherishes it more than another woman would the latest Paris fashion.

The reason is that Mrs. Waldrep and the other "space men" are victims of a rare illness called orthostatic hypotension—which means blood pressure so low that when they attempt to rise from a lying-down position, their blood drains from the brain and they instantly faint. Only by means of a space suit can such people walk. By squeezing Mrs. Waldrep's legs, her suit forces blood upward into her upper body and head, maintaining circulation there and enabling her to function normally.

Perhaps the first civilian ever fitted with a space suit, Sandy Waldrep made medical history. Her experiment has been so successful that recently the Surgeon General of the U.S. issued a sheet of directions for doctors, instructing them how to modify pressure suits for other patients. As a result, today any doctor who feels a space suit might benefit his patient can learn how to adapt one.

Mrs. Waldrep found herself in need of a space suit because of an operation. A polio victim, she has been chronically ill since her teens, yet has managed to run her home and bring up a son and daughter. Between 1955 and 1960 she underwent 11 operations (she has had no less than 23 in her lifetime). After the last, in February 1960, she found herself flat on her back in bed, unable to rise without fainting. Remarked her doctor: "Well, I guess we'll have to get you a space suit."

Source: *Parade* (June 16, 1963), p. 8. Reprinted by permission of the publisher.

"I nearly laughed out loud," Mrs. Waldrep recalls. "But he meant it."

After a seven-month effort, they enlisted the aid of Lyndon Johnson, then a Texas senator, and arranged to obtain a space suit from near-by Carswell Air Force Base in Fort Worth. One morning there arrived at the Waldrep home two Air Force experts, Capt. Nicholas C. Nicholas and Tech. Sgt. Vernon O'Neill of the Physiological Training Branch, 824th Medical Group, at Carswell.

It was Capt. Nicholas and Sgt. O'Neill, working with Mrs. Waldrep, who really "invented" space suits as a practical medical tool. They based their efforts on studies made in 1956 by four doctors at Duke University School of Medicine on the effects of pressurized garments in low blood pressure cases.

Obsolete but Effective

Capt. Nicholas tried different types of space suits, finally settled on an obsolete S-2 partial pressure suit. He cut off the top of the suit at the waistline, added a low-pressure oxygen cylinder that could be filled with compressed air at any gas-station pump (Mrs. Waldrep's husband and son perform this chore about once a month).

After experimenting, a pressure of 1.5 pounds per square inch was found about right to keep Mrs. Waldrep's blood pressure equally distributed. On September 21, 1960, she got out of bed for the first time in 7 months, wearing the suit. That day she stayed up two hours.

"I would have stayed longer, but my ears were ringing, so I knew I'd better stop," she says. "Within a week, though, I got up some strength and was able to do a lot of things—cooking, sewing, almost everything but run the sweeper. I was alive again."

When she could leave the house, the first thing she did was go to a football game and watch her son play on the high school varsity team. Soon her life was back to normal.

"Of course, I get a lot of curious stares," Mrs. Waldrep grins. "Once at a supermarket a woman walked up to me and asked if she could touch me. 'I just wondered if you were real,' she said. People who see me usually do quite a double take. But all I can say is, bless the Air Force and Capt. Nicholas and Sgt. O'Neill. They're angels!"

Since Mrs. Waldrep's experience, space suits have been applied successfully in other cases, like that of the Kanesville farmer. The suits themselves are standard military surplus, easily obtained commercially from merchants who have been selling them for costume parties at prices ranging from $7.95 to $9.95. The Surgeon General's office emphasizes, however, that cases of low blood pressure serious enough to be helped by suits are extremely rare, caused usually by a stroke, a nerve operation or diabetes. Only a doctor is qualified to decide whether his patient has such a condition.

A few months after first donning her pressure suit, Mrs. Waldrep was able to discard it and walk by herself. This winter, however, she again became ill and underwent three more operations, remaining in the hospital six months. Once more the suit became necessary. Despite having spent such a long period on her back, Mrs. Waldrep was able to get up and walk around with the aid of the suit.

In fact, she walked right into the kitchen and baked herself and her husband a cake—to celebrate.

✤ Soft Suit Seen Safe For Lunar Surface Work

No radiation shielding in space suits will be necessary for astronauts working on the moon's surface, a scientist has reported.

Radiation on the moon's surface would not present a hazard to man unless a solar flare was in progress on the sun. These flares shoot flames and dangerous radiation millions of miles into space.

At the present time there is no way of predicting solar flares, but a warning-and-surveillance device kept on the alert for flares could tell moon voyagers of an oncoming flare so they might reach safety in a moon cave or spaceship in time.

Norman Belasco of General Electric's missile and space vehicle department, Philadelphia, told *Science Service* that a form-fitting suit similar to those now worn by astronauts, but adapted to the environment, would give sufficient radiation protection for man working on the moon.

Source: Science News Letter, Vol. 81 (March 10, 1962), p. 150. Reprinted by permission of the publisher.

Studies made by G.E. and Air Force scientists show that the rigid moon suits heavily padded with shielding to protect against radiation and meteoroids can be replaced by suits which are flexible and allow the astronaut to walk and work freely, he said.

Meteoroid hazards do not appear to be very great, he said, and problems of lunar dust can also be met. The greatest problem with such a suit is eliminating heat from the astronaut's body constantly so he does not become overheated. A thermobalance system to take care of this problem and to maintain an even internal temperature in spite of great changes in the outside temperatures is necessary, the G.E. supervising engineer for advanced life support systems said. His company is now busy developing such a suit.

He said the requirements are generally the same for an earth-orbit and moon suit. Astronauts could also wear this suit up to 500 miles above the earth. Satellite data have shown that up to this altitude no radiation danger exists. However, at 540 miles and above, going through the Van Allen radiation belts of trapped particles from the sun, radiation shielding is believed necessary.

A Social Self

✿ Male and Female
EVELYN GOODENOUGH PITCHER

How early do young children play a distinctive sex role, and how do parents accent sex differences in young children? Evidence from a recent study of mine suggests that by two and through ages three and four, boys and girls have strikingly different interests and attitudes, which their parents steadily influence and strengthen. . . . A closer scrutiny of the material comparing the father's interviews with those of the mother reveals a curious differential in parents' sex-typing.

Both fathers and mothers allow what appears to be tomboyishness in girls during the early years, while they try to discourage what might be feminine behavior in their sons. Their attitude seems to reflect the general pattern in America, where our culture tends to grant the female the privileges of two sexes: with impunity she can dress like a man; she can at will interchange the "little boy look" with cloying femininity. She can use any name—her own or her husband's—enter any job, any area of education, or she can make a career of motherhood. She can be independent or dependent, or both, as and when she pleases.

The male has no corresponding freedom. He is increasingly expected to help in the home, but this is largely because the woman without servants demands such help. Deviations in dress, appearance, or job that reflect the feminine are immediately suspect. If a man is actually feminine in his instincts, even homosexual, he must never appear to be so.

It was impressive to observe to what extent the father more than the mother was responsible for sharpening such differences. There were clear indications that fathers especially tended to emphasize what seemed to be an exclusive masculinity in their sons. "He gets mad if I tease him about his interest in anything girlish and therefore babyish," said one father

Source: The Atlantic, Vol. 211 (March, 1963), pp. 87, 90–91. Reprinted by permission of the author.

about his two-year-old son. "His father was furious when I painted his nails red," said a mother about her husband's reaction to fingernail polish on his son. And another mother remarked, "On Halloween a boy can't wear anything feminine. The idea of lipstick horrifies a father."

A direct question followed such observations as those I have just mentioned, and brought out the same contrast between father and mother. A father, when asked if he would be disturbed by aspects of femininity in his son, said, "Yes, I would be, very, very much. Terrifically disturbed—couldn't tell you the extent of my disturbance. I can't bear female characteristics in a man. I abhor them." But a mother said, "Jimmy is not as masculine. But he'll grow up to be considerate and kind. Gentlemanly, rather than masculine." Another father was distressed and scornful at signs of his son's femininity. "He's always interested in flexing his muscles. Perhaps he has to prove that he's masculine—that's why I call him feminine." The same boy's mother admitted that at one time she was very much concerned about her son's femininity, but reasoned thus, "I am aware these people make splendid contributions to the world. I'd try to help. I would turn all my energies to producing a good environment for him."

A father was also more likely to appreciate femininity in his daughter. One mother reported her husband's pleasure when she put their six-month-old daughter into a dress for the first time. "That's much nicer than these old pajamas," said the father. Another mother reported that her husband blanched when he found she had cut her daughter's long hair. "Promise me that you will never, never cut it again," he said.

. . . .

Only sparse examples could be gathered from the interviews to indicate that the mother was playing an active part in encouraging her son to a more masculine role insofar as interaction between the sexes, or the cultivation of manly custom, is concerned. Mothers are as likely to take their sons to a tea party as to visit a railroad yard, and are as likely to give their daughters overalls as dresses. The fathers appeared more likely to view the boy as a male trapped in a world of women and needing to guard his uncontaminated masculinity from association with the female sex.

Of course, the impact of this expectancy of the child appears in his everyday behavior. In children's drawings, we noticed that if a boy drew a person, he would almost invariably draw a boy, whereas girls would draw either girls or boys, almost indifferently.

Thus, it would appear that the father has much greater interest, and hence influence, than the mother in accentuating differences between boys and girls. He likes the little girl to be a little girl and enjoys her femininity, but expresses himself with intolerance about any show of femininity in his son. The mother, however, seems more like a mother animal, treating the babies in her litter with little distinction. Perhaps the mother can afford to be relaxed, since she knows that the worlds of both sexes are hers. She has no real need to promote the purity of either, except insofar as she wishes to please her husband and go along with general cultural mores.

It seems from the evidence I have here presented that boys and girls are from early age subjected to influences that would develop different characteristics. However, the parents interviewed were apparently unaware that they were doing or saying anything directly to foster in their children interest or lack of interest in people. They were probably influencing their children in two ways. First of all, by subtle rewards and punishments, if only those of tone of voice, they perhaps registered approval or disapproval as situations arose. Second, we assume that the girl tends to imitate the mother and the boy the father by reproducing their kinds and sources of interests.

The question arises whether parents really create such distinctions as I have described in otherwise undistinguished personalities. Or do parents —and all our cultural influences—just develop and accentuate tendencies that children are born with? Of course, it is impossible to come to any firm conclusions about whether or to what extent psychological sex differences are innate or learned or both. But however the differences arise, it is clear that they exist from a very early age in children in our society, and that we might do well to consider such differences in planning children's education.

88 Appearance and the Self
GREGORY P. STONE

A primary tenet of all symbolic interaction theory holds that the self is established, maintained, and altered in and through communication.

Source: A. M. Rose (ed.), *Human Behavior and Social Processes: An Interactionist Approach,* New York: Houghton Mifflin Co. (1962), pp. 86–118. Reprinted by permission of the author and publisher.

Seeking to probe this tenet, most investigations have emphasized discourse—or, somewhat inexactly, verbal communication—and have shown that language exerts a very great influence indeed upon the structure and process of the self. The present essay attempts to widen the perspective of symbolic interaction studies by isolating a dimension of communication that has received relatively little attention by sociologists and social psychologists—appearance. Except for psychoanalysts, some psychiatrists, and a few anthropologists, one finds almost no scholars willing to bend their efforts to the study of appearance.[1]

This paper seeks to demonstrate that the perspective of symbolic interaction, as it has been formulated by George H. Mead, requires (indeed, *demands*) a consideration of appearance for the adequate interpretation of social transactions as well as the careers of selves in such transactions. Mead's analysis of communication, it is suggested, suffers from what might be called a "discursive bias."[2] Consequently, there are crucial unanswered questions posed by his analysis of communication that can only be answered by extending and refining his perspective. This requires a demonstration that: (1) every social transaction must be broken down into at least two analytic components or processes—appearance and discourse; (2) appearance is at least as important for the establishment and maintenance of the self as is discourse; (3) the study of appearance provides a powerful lever for the formulation of a conception of self capable of embracing the contributions of Cooley and Sullivan as well as Mead; and (4) appearance is of major importance at every stage of the early development of the self. These assertions are all empirically grounded in the author's long-term study of dress as an apparent symbol (16).

[1] Erving Goffman (7) must be exempted from the indictment. Recently he has pushed sociological or social psychological analysis far beyond the conventional limits of a perspective that has restricted the study of social transactions to their linguistic characteristics, conditions, and consequences.

[2] Of course, the gesture is considered at length, and gestures may often be employed to establish appearances, as we shall see. However, Mead views the gesture as incipient discourse, more typical of communication in its rudimentary phases. The aptness of the vocal gesture for explaining the emergence of meaning in sub-social communication may be an important source of Mead's discursive bias. Even more than discourse, appearance presupposes an on-going social process for its meaning. Apparent symbols are often silent and are best intercepted by mirrors, while one's own ear always intercepts one's own vocal gesture about as it is intercepted by others. But mirrors are not always handy; so it happens that the silent appearance, even more than the vocal utterance, comes to require an audience which can serve as a mirror, reflecting one's appearance back upon himself.

Appearance, Discourse, and Meaning

According to Mead, meaning is established only when the response elicited by some symbol is the "same" for the one who produces the symbol as for the one who receives it.[3] "Same" appears here in quotation marks, because the responses are *really* never the "same." This is an integral feature of Mead's perspective and calls for some elaboration. The fundamental implication is that *meaning is always a variable*.

We can trace this variable nature of meaning to Mead's conception of the self as process and structure, subject and object, or "I" and "me." The "I" imbues the self with a certain tentativeness—a "certain uncertainty." As a consequence, any future line of action (for example, one's response to one's own symbolic productions) can never be fully anticipated. Mead put it this way:

So the "I" really appears experientially as a part of the "me." But on the basis of this experience we distinguish that individual who is doing something from the "me" who puts the problem up to him. The response enters into his experience only when it takes place. If he says he knows what he is going to do, even there he may be mistaken. He starts out to do something and something happens to interfere. The resulting action is always a little different from anything which he could anticipate. . . . The action of the "I" is something the nature of which we cannot tell in advance (14, p. 177).

But the meaning of a symbol, as we have said, is premised upon the notion that the response called out in the other is the *same* as the response called out in the one who produces the symbol—*always a little different from anything which he could anticipate*. Moreover, the other's response has the same characteristically unanticipatable quality.

Meaning, then, is always a variable, ranging between non-sense, on the one hand—the total absence of coincident responses—and what might be called boredom on the other—the total coincidence of such responses. Neither of these terminals can be approached very often in the duration

[3] "Response" is usually the production of other symbols. The term is distinguished from "symbol" merely to permit the observer to shift his view as he analyzes what is going on in the social transaction. Actually, all that distinguishes a "response" from any symbol in question is its occurrence later in time. I am indebted to my colleague, Keith Miller, for this clarification.

of a transaction, for either can mean its end. It is seldom that we continue to talk non-sense with others, and boredom encourages us to depart from their presence. Thus, meaning is present in communication when the responses that are symbolically mobilized only *more or less* coincide.

This raises the question of *guarantees* for the meaningfulness of social transactions. How can the transaction be prevented from spilling over into non-sense or atrophying into boredom? Because the self is in part an "I"—unpredictable—the risks of boredom are minimized; but, for Mead, the guarantee against non-sense in the transaction is "role-taking," or, more accurately, placing one's self in the attitude of the other. By placing one's self in the attitude or incipient action of the other and representing one's own symbolic production to oneself from that attitude, one guarantees that one's own response will be rather more than less coincident with the response of the other, since the other's incipient actions have become incorporated in the actions of the one producing the symbol. It is here, however, that a gap in Mead's analysis occurs, for a further question arises, and that question was not systematically considered by Mead: if role-taking is the guarantee of meaning, how then is role-taking possible? Obviously, one must apprehend the other's role, the other's attitude—indeed, the other's self—before one can take the other's role or incorporate the other's attitude.

At this point a shift in terminology is required to expedite the analysis of meaning and to provide initial answers to the questions that have been raised. Let us suggest that the guarantee against non-sense in the social transaction is heuristically better conceptualized as *identification,*[4] not role-taking or taking the other's attitude—at best a very partial explanation of how meaning is established in social transactions. The term "identification" subsumes at least two processes: *identification of* and *identification with*. Role-taking is but one variant of the latter process, which must also include sympathy,[5] and there may well be other variants.[6] Nevertheless, the point to be made is this: identification *with* one another, in whatever mode, cannot be made without identifications *of* one another. Above all, identifications of one another are ordinarily facilitated by appearance and are often accomplished silently or non-verbally. This can be made crystal

[4] The precedent has been incisively established by Nelson N. Foote (4).
[5] Mead himself distinguishes sympathy as a particular mode of "attitude-taking" in a seldom cited article (13); but for the empirical utility of the distinction, see Sheldon Stryker (17).
[6] An imposing taxonomy has been erected in Howard Becker (1).

clear by observing the necessity for and process of establishing gender in social transactions. Everywhere we find vocabularies sexually distinguished: there are languages for males only, languages for females only, and languages employed to communicate across the barriers of gender. Obviously, identifications of the other's gender must be established before the appropriate language can be selected for the upcoming discourse. Seldom, upon encountering another, do we inquire concerning the other's gender. Indeed, to do so would be to impugn the very gender that must be established. The knowing of the other's gender is known silently, established by appearances.

Appearance, then, is that phase of the social transaction which establishes identifications of the participants. As such, it may be distinguished from *discourse,* which we conceptualize as the text of the transaction—*what* the parties are discussing. Appearance and discourse are two distinct dimensions of the social transaction. The former seems the more basic. It sets the stage for, permits, sustains, and delimits the possibilities of discourse by underwriting the possibilities of meaningful discussion.

Ordinarily appearance is communicated by such non-verbal symbols as gestures, grooming, clothing, location, and the like; discourse, by verbal symbolism. Yet the relationship between the kinds of symbolism and the dimension of the transaction is not at all invariant. Gestures and other non-verbal symbols may be used to talk about things and events, and words may have purely apparent significance. In fact, appearances are often discussed, while discussions often "appear"—that is, serve only to establish the identities of the discussants. In the latter case, the person may seem to be talking about matters other than identifications of self or other, but may actually be speaking only about himself. "Name-dropping" serves as an example. In the former case, which we will term *apparent discourse,* whole transactions may be given over to the discussion of appearances, and this occurs most often when some new turn has been taken by the transaction requiring re-identifications of the parties. Indeed, apparent discourse is often *news* and vice versa.

Appearance and discourse are in fact dialectic processes going on whenever people converse or correspond. They work back and forth on one another, at times shifting, at other times maintaining the direction of the transaction. When the direction of the transaction shifts, appearance is likely to emerge into the discursive phases of the transaction; when the direction is maintained over a relatively long period of time and is uninterrupted, discourse is likely to be submerged in appearances. In all cases, however, discourse is impossible without appearance which permits the requisite identifications with one another by the discussants. One may, nevertheless, appear without entering the discourse. As Veblen suggested, we may escape our discursive obligations, but not our clothed appearances (19, p. 167).

Appearance and The Self

Appearance *means* identifications of one another,[7] but the question arises whether such identifications follow any ordered pattern. Mead's perspective insists that we look for the meaning of appearance in the responses that appearances mobilize, and we have examined more than 8,000 such responses supplied by interview materials to discern whether they are consistently patterned. Many responses are, of course, gestural in nature. One's appearance commands the gaze of the audience. An eyebrow is lifted. There is a smile or a frown, an approach or withdrawal. One blushes with shame for the shamelessness of the other's appearance or with embarrassment at one's own. The nature of our data precluded the study of such gestural responses unless they were recorded by the interviewer. Consequently, apparent discourse was examined for the most part—talk about appearance aroused, in particular, by clothing. Over 200 married men and women living in a Midwestern community of 10,000 population supplied the talk. Of the many statements these people made about dress, only statements referring to those who wore the clothing in question were scrutinized. These were construed as identifications of the wearer. Here we shall be concerned for simplicity's sake with only two modes of such responses: (1) responses made about the wearer of clothes by others who, we shall say, *review* his clothing; and (2) responses made about the wearer by the wearer—we shall call these responses *programs*. A third mode of response is relevant, but will not be considered here—the wearer's imagination of others' responses to his dress.

When programs and reviews tend to coincide, the self of the one who

[7] The question of how the meaning of appearance is guaranteed is germane and recognized, but will not be treated here. Aside from the "teamwork" analyzed so carefully by Goffman in his *Presentation of Self in Everyday Life* (7), other guarantees are suggested in his "Symbols of Class Status." (6)

appears (the one whose clothing has elicited such responses) is validated or established; when such responses tend toward disparity, the self of the one who appears is challenged, and conduct may be expected to move in the direction of some redefinition of the challenged self. Challenges and validations of the self, therefore, may be regarded as aroused by personal appearance. As a matter of fact, the dimensions of the self emphasized by Mead, Cooley, and Sullivan effectively embrace the content of the responses to clothing we examined in our quest for the meaning of appearance. In response to his clothes, the wearer was cast as a social object—a "me"—or, as we shall say, given some identity. A person's dress also imbued him with attitudes by arousing others' anticipations of his conduct as well as assisting the mobilization of his own activity. In Mead's terms, then, the self as object and attitude is established by appearance. However, the most frequent response to dress was the assignment of value-words to the wearer. One's clothes impart value to the wearer, both in the wearer's own eyes and in the eyes of others. Both Sullivan and Cooley underscore the relevance of value for any adequate conceptualization of the self; Sullivan, by referring to the self as comprised by the "reflected *appraisals* of others," Cooley, by emphasizing "imagined *judgments* of appearance." Finally, Cooley's emphasis upon self-*feeling* or the self as *sentiment* was provided with empirical support by this analysis. A person's clothing often served to establish a mood for himself capable of eliciting validation in the reviews aroused from others. The meaning of appearance, therefore, is the establishment of identity, value, mood, and attitude for the one who appears by the coincident programs and reviews awakened by his appearance. These terms require further discussion.

IDENTITY

It is almost enough to demonstrate the significance of the concept "identity" by referring to the rapidity with which it has caught on in social science. Recently re-introduced to the social sciences by Erik Erikson, the term has provided many new social-psychological insights. Specifically, fruitful inquiries into the sociological implications of the ego have been made possible by releasing the investigator from the commitment to argument and partisanship that alternative concepts such as "personality" demand. Identity, as a concept, is without any history of polemics. However, the impetus to discovery afforded by the term has been so great that its meaning threatens to spill over the bounds of analytic utility. Before its meaning becomes totally lost by awakening every conceivable response in every conceivable investigator (like the term "personality"), the concept must be salvaged.

Almost all writers using the term imply that identity establishes *what* and *where* the person is in social terms. It is not a substitute word for "self." Instead, when one has identity, he is *situated*—that is, cast in the shape of a social object by the acknowledgment of his participation or membership in social relations. One's identity is established when others *place* him as a social object by assigning him the same words of identity that he appropriates for himself or *announces*. It is in the coincidence of placements and announcements that identity becomes a meaning of the self, and often such placements and announcements are aroused by apparent symbols such as uniforms. The policeman's uniform, for example, is an announcement of his identity as policeman and validated by other's placements of him as policeman.

Such a conception of identity is, indeed, close to Mead's conception of the "me," the self as object related to and differentiated from others. To situate the person by establishing some identity for him is, in a sense, to give him position, and a pun permits further elucidation of the concept: identity is established as a consequence of two processes, apposition and opposition, a bringing together and setting apart. To situate the person as a social object is to bring him together with other objects so situated, and, at the same time to set him apart from still other objects. *Identity is intrinsically associated with all the joinings and departures of social life.* To have an identity is to join with some and depart from others, to enter and leave social relations at once.

In fact, the varieties of identity are isomorphic with the varieties of social relations. At least four different types of words were used to place and announce the identities communicated by clothing: (1) universal words designating one's humanity, such as age, gender, and community (we call these "universal" words because people everywhere make such distinctions); (2) names and nicknames; (3) titles, such as occupational and marital titles; (4) "relational categories," such as customer, movie-goer, jazz fan, and the like. Social relations, viewed as on-going transactions, can be classified according to the identities which must be placed and announced to permit entry into the transaction. Thus, *human relations* are those requiring both the placement and announcement of such universal identities as age, gender, or community membership. *Interpersonal relations* are those that may only be entered by an exchange of names or nicknames,[8] while *structural relations* are those that may only be entered by exchanging a name for a title. Finally, we may speak of *masses* as social relations that may be anonymously entered.

The distinction between interpersonal and structural relations seems, at this point, to have the greatest analytical utility. Since one's name ordinarily outlasts one's titles, interpersonal relations probably provide an important social basis for the continuity of identity. Structural relations, on the other hand, are more discontinuous and changing.

We can note how one's name is established by dress if we imagine Teddy Roosevelt without the pince-nez, F. D. R. without the cigarette holder, or Thomas Dewey without the moustache. One of our informants, a small-time real estate operator, was well aware of the significance of clothing in his attempts to personalize his occupational identity. Asked, "What do your fellow workers say and think when you wear something new for the first time on the job?" he replied:

> Well, I always have a new hat, and I suppose my clientele talks about it. But, you know, I always buy cheap ones and put my name in them. I leave them around in restaurants and places like that intentionally. It has advertising value.

The interviewer asked later, "Would you rather wear a greater variety or a smaller variety of clothes on the job?" and the informant replied:

> A smaller variety so you will look the same everyday. So people will identify you. They look for the same old landmark.

In response to the same question, a working man who had recently opened a small business said:

> A smaller variety for both sales and shop. I think if a person dresses about the same continually, people will get to know you. Even if they don't know your name, you're easier to describe. I knew an insurance man once who used a wheel chair. Everyone knew him because of that chair. It's the same with clothes.

---

[8] This characterization of interpersonal relations is not reversible. The exchange of names does not guarantee that an interpersonal relationship will always be established.

Distinctive, persistent dress may replace the name as well as establish it!

On the other hand, one's career within the structural relation is marked by changes of title, and the change of title demands a change of dress. All of the men in this study were presented with the following story:

> John had an excellent record as foreman in an automobile factory. Eventually, he and two other foremen were promoted to the position of division head. John was happy to get the job, because of the increase in pay. However, he continued to wear his old foreman's vest and work clothes to the office. This went on for several months until the division heads he had been promoted with began to avoid him at lunch and various social gatherings. They had dressed from the beginning in business suits and had mingled more and more with older managerial employees. John found himself without friends in the office.

When asked, "What finally happened to John?" about 80 per cent of the men interviewed predicted termination, demotion, or no further promotion (5, pp. 47–51). One informant, interviewed by the writer, quite seriously suggested that John was a potential suicide.

Appearances, then, are interrupted in social structures as identities are set apart; appearances, so to speak, endure in interpersonal relations where identities are brought into closer proximity. Yet we find that, in the context of structural relations, identities are given a somewhat different cast than in interpersonal relations. In the former, identities are qualified along the axis of value; in the latter, more usually along the axis of mood.

QUALIFICATIONS OF IDENTITY: VALUE AND MOOD

To engage meaningfully in some transactions it is enough to know merely "what" the parties are—to know their identities. This would seem often to be the case in the anonymous transactions of the masses. As Louis Wirth used to tell his students in his elaborations of the "massive" character of urban life, "You go to a bootblack to have your shoes shined; not to save your soul." The implication is, I think, that, when we become concerned with the bootblack's moods or his larger worth in terms of some scheme of value, our relations with him will lose their anonymous character. By so doing, we have, perhaps, disadvantaged ourselves of the freedom the city offers. Ordinarily, however, if transactions persistently engage the same persons or seem likely to continue into an ill-defined future, it is not enough merely to establish identities in the guarantee of meaningful discourse. Thus, when we are introduced to strangers who may become acquaintances or possibly friends, we *express* our pleasure with the introductions, and such expressions are ordinarily *appreciated* by those we have met. Or, meeting an acquaintance on the street, we inquire how he *feels* before the discourse is initiated. In a certain sense, interpersonal relations demand that the *moods* of the participants be established (as well as their names or nicknames) prior to the initiation of discursive phases in the transaction: that "Joe" or "Jane" is mad or sad will have definite consequences for the talk with "Jim" or "Joan."

Ordinarily, also, before a title is bestowed upon us or before we are invested with office, our identities must undergo qualifying scrutiny. In such cases, the qualification does not usually get accomplished in terms of our anger or sadness, but in terms of some assessment of our former careers and future prospects with reference to their *worth*. The tendency is to assess worth in terms of a relatively objective set of standards that can transcend the whim of the assessing one and the whimsy of the one assessed. Upon the initiation of what we have called structural relations, the *values* of the participating persons (as well as their titles) must be established.

Value and mood provide two fundamental axes along which the qualifications of identity are accomplished in *appraising* and *appreciative* responses to appearance. This seems obvious on the face of it: that a teacher is competent has different consequences for faculty-student transactions than that a teacher is a teacher; and that a teacher is temperamental or easy-going presents the possibility of a still different set of consequences for upcoming discussions. The differences between value and mood are suggested by the distinction that Park has made between interests and sentiments, that Helen Lynd has made between guilt and shame, or that Kenneth Burke has made between poetry and pathos (*poiema* and *pathema*). It is the difference between virtue and happiness, and, as we know full well, the virtuous man is not necessarily happy nor the happy man necessarily virtuous. The problem arises when we observe that happiness may be a virtue in some social circles or that one may be happy because he is virtuous (cynics might say "smug"). Value and mood, so patently distinguishable in discourse, merge together inextricably in experience. Can we conceive of feelings of pride without reference to a set of values? I think not, although it does seem possible to conceive of merit without feeling. Yet, in situations that are totally value-relevant, totally given over to matters of appraisal—the courtroom, the examination, the military review—the very constriction of feeling and mood, their suppression, may saturate the situation with a grim somberness that can transform dispassion into passion—as the austerity of the courtroom has provided a curiously fitting context for the impassioned plea; the silence of the examination room is interrupted by nervous laughter; the ordered rhythm of the march engenders song.

As Helen Lynd has written of guilt and shame, so we conceive value and mood:

> They are in no sense polar opposites. Both the guilt axis and the shame axis enter into the attitudes and behavior of most people, and often into the same situation. But there are for different persons different balances and stresses between the two, and it does matter whether one lives more in terms of one or the other (11, p. 208).

And we would add that one differentiating condition is the type of social relation that regularly mobilizes the time and attention of the person. Thus, we have found that value has a greater saliency for most men in their conceptions of self and others, while, for most women, mood has a greater saliency. This finding is ascribed in part to the American male's more frequent participation and absorption in the structure of work relations, in comparison with the American woman's more frequent preoccupation with the interpersonal relations she carries on with friends and acquaintances.

It is much more difficult to characterize value and mood than it has been to characterize identity. However, the responses to dress that were classified as words of value manifested the following references: (1) to *consensual goals,* such as wealth, prestige, or power; (2) to *achievement standards,* universalistic criteria applied to the assessment of one's proximity to or remoteness from such goals; (3) *norms* or rules regulating the pursuit of consensual goals; and (4) *moral precepts* stipulating valued behavior often employed in the assessment of character (e.g., cleanliness, politeness, thriftiness, and the like). Responses classified as mood-words were even more difficult to order, including references to ease and lack of ease in social transactions, liking, disliking, fearing, and dreading. Anxiety, monotony, rapture, and surprise also were included in the category, as were references to that ill-defined state which the informants called morale.

It may be helpful to borrow again from Helen Lynd, using her technique for contrasting guilt and shame to contrast value and mood. Table

Table 1 Value and mood as axes along which qualifications of identity are established

Phases	Value Axis	Mood Axis
Relational Basis	Structural relations	Interpersonal relations
Criteria	Universalistic Abstract Objective Detachment Poetic (Pious) Neutrality Scalar	Particularistic Concrete Subjective Attachment Pathetic Affectivity Absolute
Establishment	Rationalized Investment Conformity-deviation with respect to universal rules or a social code Future reference Legitimated by appeals to the appraisals of others	Spontaneously communicated Preoccupation or rapture Ease–dis-ease with respect to engagement in social transactions Present reference Legitimated by appeals to the expressions of the self
Relational Consequences	Stratification	Rapport

1 attempts to state the social relations for which value and mood *ordinarily* have the greatest saliency, the nature of the criteria which are applied in the establishment of value and mood, the processes by which these qualifications of identity are established, and finally the consequences for the social relationship when identities are qualified along one or the other axis. I wish to emphasize that the summary presentation in Table 1 is in no way meant to be definitive, and that the axes which are

characterized as value and mood, although they are set down in a contrasting manner, are not meant to be established as polar opposites. In particular, *sentiments* represent a convergence of the two axes in the qualification of identity. Sentiments are valued feelings or felt values, as for example in Cooley's "looking-glass self"—the sentiments of pride or mortification are *expressive* responses to the judgments or *appraisals* of others.

ACTIVATIONS OF IDENTITY: ATTITUDE

In a brilliant discussion, Kenneth Burke has established the essential ambiguity of the term "attitude": an attitude can be looked upon as a substitute for an act—the "truncated act" of John Dewey—or as in incipient act—a "beginning" from the standpoint of George H. Mead (2, pp. 235-247). The establishment of identity, value, and mood by appearances represents the person as *there, stratified* or assigned a particular distance, and *rapt* or engrossed. There remains the matter of his activation, the assessment of the path along which he has traveled, the path he is traveling, and where he is about to go. These aspects of the person—that he has acted, is acting, and will act further—are also established by appearance. We refer to them as *attitudes*.[9] Attitudes are *anticipated* by the reviewers of an appearance, *proposed* by the one who appears.

Appearance *substitutes* for past and present action and, at the same time, conveys an *incipience* permitting others to anticipate what is about to occur. Specifically, clothing represents our action, past, present, and future, as it is established by the proposals and anticipations that occur in every social transaction. Without further elaboration, I think that this can be clearly seen in the doffing of dress, signaling that an act is done (and another act about to begin), the donning of dress, signaling the initiation of a new act, and the wearing of dress, signaling that action is going on.

[9] Of course, the concept "attitude" is of central significance for the social psychology of George Herbert Mead, but, in some ways, it is the least satisfying of the terms we have characterized here. All the meanings of dress or appearance have an attitudinal or "activated" character. In particular, programs and reviews may be conceived as incipient, truncated, or on-going acts. It may be, in fact, that the concept "attitude" is of a different order from the concepts "identity," "value," and "mood," asking the observer to inquire not into the content or structure of the events under scrutiny, but rather to seize those events in their full-blown capacity as processes.

APPEARANCE AND THE SELF

The meaning of appearance, therefore, can be studied by examining the responses mobilized by clothes. Such responses take on at least four forms: identities are placed, values appraised, moods appreciated, and attitudes anticipated. Appearance provides the identities, values, moods, and attitudes of the person-in-communication, since it arouses in others the assignment of words embodying these dimensions to the one who appears. As we have noted earlier, this is only one part of the total picture.

Cooley, Mead, and Harry Stack Sullivan have reminded us often that such responses are reflexive in character, reverberating back upon the one who produces them and the one toward whom they are directed. In short, identifications of others are always complemented by identifications of the self, in this case, responses to one's own appearance. In a variety of ways, as a matter of fact, reviews of a person's appearances are intricately linked with the responses he makes to his own appearance. We have called the process of making identifications of the one who appears by that one a *program*. Programmatic responses parallel the responses that have been called reviews. One appears, reflects upon that appearance, and appropriates words of identity, value, mood, or attitude for himself in response to that appearance. By appearing, the person *announces* his identity, *shows* his value, *expresses* his mood, or *proposes* his attitude. If the meaning of appearance is "supplied" by the reviews others make of one's appearance, it is established or consensually validated, as Sullivan would have said, by the relative coincidence of such reviews with the program of the one who appears. In other words, when one's dress calls out in others the "same" identifications of the wearer as it calls out in the wearer, we may speak of the appearance as meaningful. It turns out, in fact, that this is the self, and this may be diagrammed as in Table 2.

In appearances, then, selves are established and mobilized. As the self is dressed, it is simultaneously addressed, for, whenever we clothe ourselves, we dress "toward" or address some audience whose validating responses are essential to the establishment of our self. Such responses may, of course, also be challenges, in which case a new program is aroused. This intimate linkage of the self and clothing was masterfully caricatured by a forty-year-old carpenter's wife who was herself working in a local factory.

Our guess is that a few bottles of beer were conducive to the spontaneous flow of words, but their import is none the less striking. The woman had interpreted a modified TAT scene as a religious depiction, and the interviewer asked her, after the completion of the stories, which card she liked best:

[*Interviewer:* Of those three, which did you like best? . . .] Oh, that is kinda hard for me to do. I like them all. This one here is good, and that one is good, and that one is good. I think, of course, religion should come first, but I still think this is first right here—of her trying to help this girl. [Note: the card depicts a well-dressed woman talking with another woman in rather drab masculine dress.] Looks to me like she is just telling her what she should do and how she should dress. Don't look very nice. I think that has a lot to do

Table 2 Schematic representation of the meaning of appearance, emphasizing the validation of personal appearance

Program of Appearance	Review of Appearance			
	Placement	Appraisal	Appreciation	Anticipation
Announcement	Identity			
Show		Value		
Expression			Mood	
Proposal				Attitude

with a person's life afterwards. If they can get straightened out on their personal appearance, they can get straightened out in their religion a lot quicker. You take personal appearance; goes with their minds. Their mind has to work to go with that. They get that straightened out; I think they can go back to religion and get that straightened out. I don't go to church now, but I used to be, and I am still, and always will be, regardless of what it is I ever do. I smoke a cigarette, drink a bottle of beer. I'm not Catholic. I'm Protestant. Church is my first thing. But this [informant hits the picture] comes first, before church. I don't care what anybody says. Clothes, our personal appearance, and getting our minds settled is how we should do. Some people don't believe that, but I do, 'cause you can go into a church and worship, but that ain't all that makes a go of this world. You have got to have something beside that. I don't care how much you worship. People can laugh at you. When you go into a church, they laugh at a girl dressed like this girl is or this woman is. They'll think she is not all there. But, if she gets herself fixed up, and looks nice, and goes to church like this picture here, they'll think she knows what she's talking about. I've seen too much of that. In other words, *clothes, personal appearance, can make one's life.* [Said slowly, deliberately, with much emphasis.] There is something about it that gives you courage. Some people would call it false courage, but I wouldn't. . . . I think anyone has to have a certain amount of clothes to give them courage. It ain't false courage either or false pride. It's just it. . . . Suppose it was just like it was when I went to that banquet tonight. Everybody told me how nice I looked, but I didn't think so. I had to feel right. . . . when I get the dress I feel right in, I feel like a million dollars. It makes an altogether different person out of me. That's an awful thing to say, but that's true for me.

Similar, but less dramatic, remarks abound in our interview materials. All point to the undeniable and intimate linkage of self and appearance. As a matter of fact, the analysis we have made permits a suggested modification of perhaps the best definition of the self in the social-psychological literature. Lindesmith and Strauss

. . . think of the self as: (1) a set of more or less consistent and stable responses on a conceptual level, which (2) exercise a regulatory function over other responses of the same organism at lower levels (10, p. 416).

Dispensing with the notion of levels of behavior, which seems unnecessarily misleading (surely the self exercises a regulatory function over discourse—a set of conceptual responses!), we suggest the following definition: *the self is any validated program which exercises a regulatory function over other responses of the same organism, including the formulation of other programs.* What this definition does is spell out the regulatory responses—that is, one's announcements, shows, expressions, or proposals—while linking their consistency to the consensual validations of others. Such selves are established in significant appearances which provide the foundations of significant discourse and which, of course, may be played back upon and altered as the discourse transpires.

Appearance and The Early Emergence of The Self

In explaining the emergence of the self, George H. Mead discusses at length the two stages of "play" and the "game." Prior to entering the stage of play, however, the child must have acquired a rudimentary language at least. We will call this early stage of rudimentary communication "pre-play." For Mead, the emergence of the self in society is inextricably linked to the expansion and consolidation of personal communication as the child participates in and successively generalizes an ever widening universe of discourse—that set of social relations that is mobilized by the symbols the child acquires. We may infer that the type of discourse changes in the different stages of the emergence of the self and shall suggest some possibilities. We shall demonstrate, however, the changing character of appearance in these stages. In particular, we will note how these changing appearances hinder or facilitate the establishment of sexual identity or gender for the child.

PRE-PLAY, INVESTITURE, AND THE UBIQUITOUS MOTHER

It is very difficult to establish in any verifiable way how the child acquires its earliest significant symbols, whether they be gestures or words, because the investigator cannot enter into the rudimentary "prototaxic" communication of the infant. At best, he can observe, make inferences, and check those inferences out against the inferences of family members.

It seems to be the case, however, that some "initiative" is required from the child in this early learning process. Cooley, for example, observed that parents imitate the noises and sounds of their very young children in greater degree than those children imitate the noises and sounds of parents (3, p. 25). These observations have since received further empirical support (12, p. 41). Apparently this phenomenon of "parental imitation" or, more accurately, parental re-presentation is usually linked with the infant's babbling. Through babbling, the child hits upon a word-like sound (often "ma-ma"). This sound is then represented to the child as a word, together with the appropriate behavior that is the meaning of the word. Through repetition, the child takes over the response pattern it calls out in the adult, and the sound consequently becomes a significant symbol within the domestic universe of discourse.[10]

Another hypothesis seeking to explain the infant's earliest entrance into

[10] There is further probative support for this hypothesis in the current research of Omar K. Moore at Yale University, where he is teaching two-and-a-half year old children to read and write. The child is first encouraged to "play" at an IBM typewriter—akin to babbling. An adult responds to the play by re-presenting the letter sound. Eventually the child takes over this response pattern of the adult and "learns" the letters of the keyboard.

communication has been proposed by I. Latif.[11] Initially, the presumed discomfort of the infant is "communicated" by a gross writhing and wriggling of the whole body, setting up a series of responses in the parental person—feeding, cuddling, diaper-changing, and so on. Over time these parental responses become differentiated out as the gross movement of the child is progressively curtailed. Ultimately, the mere beginning of movement can elicit the appropriate parental response. Significant gestures have been established.

The point in all of this is that the child enters discursive communication by, in a sense, "initiating" activity construed as symbolic by parental persons and established as meaningful by their persistent cooperative response. In contrast, the appearance of the infant is imposed. The diaper folded in front *invests* the child with masculinity; in back, with femininity. Or dressing the child in blue invests the child with masculinity; in pink, with femininity. In this way, the responses of the world toward the child are differentially mobilized. The world handles the pink-clad child and the blue-clad child differently. The pink-clad child is *identified* differently. It is "darling," "beautiful," "sweet," or "graceful"; the blue-clad child is "handsome," "strong," or "agile." At a very early age the investiture of the child provides the materials out of which the reflected sexual identity and its qualifications are formed. And in America the process of investiture is accomplished overwhelmingly by the mother.

One hundred and eighty-five of our informants were asked, "What is the earliest recollection you have of being made to wear particular clothes?" Then we asked, "Who made you wear them?" One hundred and twenty-six provided determinate answers to the question. Of these, 82 per cent named the mother as the "instrument of coercion"; 10 per cent named both parents. For more than 90 per cent of those recalling coercive investitures, the mother was recalled as the agent, usually the sole agent. There were no sex differences in these recollections. She was the sole agent for 83 per cent of the men and for 81 per cent of the women. She acted in conjunction with the father for 13 per cent of the men and for 8 per cent of the women.

It is sociologically significant, of course, that the prime agent of investiture for the men of this Midwestern community was a woman, and no matter how much we might be inclined to disparage Geoffrey Gorer's study of "the American people," these data do suggest that Gorer's "en-

[11] Discussed in Lindesmith and Strauss (10, p. 166).

capsulated mother hypothesis" has some basis in fact (8, pp. 55–68, 124–132).

Because of the ubiquity of the American mother as the prime agent of socialization for the child, it will be recalled, Gorer maintained that the "superego" of the American male was characterized by a significant feminine component manifested in extraordinary anxiety about and fear of homosexuality. We need not accept the entire line of analysis when we recognize, first, that the "significant other" for the male child in our sample has been almost unanimously recalled as the "significant mother," and, second, that the adequate early formulation of a sexual identity may have been impeded among men. Indeed, it may not be a "homosexual anxiety" that typifies American men as much as a generalized "sexual anxiety." If he is represented at all by the men of this Midwestern community, the American male may have found it difficult very early in life to establish who he was in sexual terms. Consequently, an adequate basis in which to "ground" subsequent announcements of maleness may not have been provided. As very young children, most of these men were invested with a program of appearance fashioned exclusively by women. This investiture process persisted beyond infancy, even, in some cases, into relatively late childhood. Their first reflected glimpse of themselves was provided by the eyes of a woman—a woman who, in fact, saw many of those men as girls. Some were dressed as little girls.

A fifty-three year old postal clerk provided a vivid recollection of the early stages in the life cycle as they were represented by dress:

I can remember back in the South, forty-five years ago, the children—boys—always wore dresses up to the time they were three or four years old. When I was about five, six, seven, or eight, they wore those little Fauntleroy suits. God damn! I hated those. Then knickers came. I wore those until I was about fifteen year old. I was fifteen and a half when I had my first long pants suit.

A sixty-three year old carpenter, born on a Midwestern farm, suggests that the earliest dress of little boys was not restricted to Southern regions:

Just one thing that always stood out in my mind. I wore dresses until I was six years old, and, as I remember, they were the Mother Hubbard type.

Knee pants, of course, were much more frequently recalled by the men in the sample as early garments in which they were forcibly dressed by the mother, and these were often interpreted as feminine representations. Asked to state his earliest memory of being forced to wear particular clothing, a twenty-seven year old oven-tender replied:

> Knee pants. [*Interviewer:* Who made you wear them?] Mother. [*Interviewer:* How did you feel about that?] I just felt like a girl in them. They reminded me so much of a dress.

The revulsion against being a "sissy," recalled by many of the male informants in the sample, was generally remembered in the context of investiture in short pants or "fussy" clothing. Again, the investiture was accomplished by the mother, whose decision they could not appeal.

Investiture takes on even greater significance for the interpretation of the meaning that clothing has for men in our society when we recall our earlier remarks about the establishment of identity. Identity, as it has been apprehended here, is only established in the collective or transactive process of announcement and placement. The knowing of gender is, as we have said, known silently. To appear in the dress of either sex is to announce one's gender, and the apparent announcement is seldom questioned. The gender is confirmed by ratifying placements. Dressed as someone he is not, by a ubiquitous mother, in clothing that is employed arbitrarily by his peers (and himself) to establish who he is, the American male may, indeed, have been disadvantaged very early with respect to the formulation of a sense of sexual identity. Advantages, rather, accrued to the female, who from the earliest age was dressed as she was by a mother from whose perspective she was provided with an adequate conception of herself in sexual terms.[12]

PLAY, COSTUME, AND DRESSING OUT

In his discussions of the development of the self (more exactly, the development of the "me"), George H. Mead does not concern himself so much with the establishment of the self *by* others—the phenomenon of investiture—as with the development of a self-conception *reflected* by the attitudes of others. Such attitudes or roles (Mead uses the terms interchangeably in his discussion of the self) are at first acted out. By acting out the role of the other, the child develops a conception of his own

---

[12] There may be a generational problem involved, but we cannot consider that problem in this place. We are speaking here of those who were adults by 1950, and whose childhoods occurred in the 1930's or earlier.

attitude or role as differentiated from and related to the adopted role. The acting out of the other's role is caricatured by the play of the child in which he amuses himself by acting out the role of the parents, the schoolteacher, the policeman, the cowboy, the Indian, the storekeeper, the customer, and various other roles that constitute the institutional fabric and legendary *personae* of the larger community or society. A mere consideration of these roles, incidentally, betrays the fact that at least two kinds of socialization go on in the stage of play. First, there is a genuine *anticipatory socialization* in which the child acts out roles that might quite realistically be expected to be adopted or encountered in later life, such as parental roles, common occupations, or customer. Second, there is a process of *fantastic socialization* in which the child acts out roles that can seldom, if ever, be expected to be adopted or encountered in later life—cowboy and Indian, for example. This is a point to which we will return.

Now this phase of play in the development of the self cannot be accomplished without costume. Acting out of role implies that one appear out of role. Play demands that the players leave themselves behind, so to speak. The players may do this symbolically by doffing their ordinary dress and donning extraordinary dress so that the play may proceed. Playing the role of the other requires that the player *dress out* of the role or roles that are acknowledged to be his own. Costume, therefore, is a kind of magical instrument. It includes all apparent misrepresentations of the wearer. As such its significance or meaning (the collective response that is mobilized—the coincidence of the wearer's program with the review of the other) is built upon the mutual trust of the one who appears and his audience. Collusion is required to carry off the misrepresentation: the parent, for example, cannot "really" insist that his child is, in fact, not a cowboy or a spaceman. Play is easily transformed into a vast conspiratorial secret, if it has not, in fact, begun secretly. As Huizinga has expressed it:

The exceptional and special position of play is most tellingly illustrated by the fact that it loves to surround itself with an air of secrecy. Even in early childhood, the charm of play is enhanced by making a "secret" out of it. This is for *us,* not for the "others." . . . The "differentness" and secrecy of play are most vividly expressed in "dressing up." Here the "extraordinary" nature of play reaches perfection. The disguised or masked individual "plays" another part, another being. He *is* another being. The terrors of childhood, openhearted gaiety, mystic fantasy and sacred awe are all inextricably entangled in this strange business of masks and disguises (9, pp. 12–13).

This element of secrecy would seem to imbue the play of children with sentiment—a nexus of value and mood—establishing for the child *involvements* with the identities that are appropriated in play in addition to the sheer objective *commitments* to such identities, emphasized by Mead. Making the point in another way, it may be that the consequence of childhood play, at least for some children, is not merely the formulation of the self as an object—an identity—differentiated from and related to the objects of play, but the establishment of the self as a sentiment—a base of "show" and expression—as Cooley insisted.

All respondents were asked, "When you were a child, did you ever dress up in anyone else's clothes?" Of the 180 replying to the question, 35 per cent disavowed dressing up in other people's clothing when they were children. The disavowal was predominately male. Fifty-nine per cent of the men replying to the question maintained that they had not dressed up in other people's clothing when they were children, and that figure compares to 14 per cent for the women responding to the question. Again, in a sense, the male child seems to have been "disadvantaged" in the phase of play. The clothing of the others in his earliest social world is not made available to him.

Indeed, one of the still striking features of childhood costume is the fact that boys' costumes are sold in considerably greater quantities than are girls' costumes.[13] Commercial costumes are generally more fantastic than the costumes available from the cast-off clothing of family members. The disavowals of the men do not mean, of course, that the men did not dress out when they were children, but that they did not dress out in clothing ordinarily worn by other people. Assuming that the "dressing out" of men, at least in the higher ranges of the status order, was facilitated by commercial costume and that the "dressing out" of women was facilitated by the ordinary dress of others, it may well be that the early conception of self established by men in the phase of play in this country and among the generations interviewed is, in fact, more fantastic than the early conception of self established by women, who can more often reflect upon their own appearance in the dress of and from the standpoint of others who are the *real* population of their social world. But this is a point for which we have no direct evidence.

Of course, the most striking difference between the sexes with respect to

[13] The assertion may be verified by telephoning the toy department in any large store. I have not yet found any exceptions to the rule.

the costume of play is, as we have said, found among those who dressed up in other people's clothing at all when they were children. More than half of the men did not, as Table 3 shows, and more than 85 per cent of the women did. Those who did recall dressing up in other people's clothing when they were children were asked whose clothing was worn, and

Table 3 The most intimate sources of costume mentioned by Midwestern men and women in their recollections of childhood play

Most Intimate Sources of Childhood Costume	Male Number	Male Per Cent	Female Number	Female Per Cent	Totals Number	Totals Per Cent
None	50	58.8	13	13.7	63	35.0
Parent, same sex	13	15.3	48	50.5	61	33.9
Parent, opposite sex	2	2.4	—	0.0	2	1.1
Sibling, same sex	6	7.1	10	10.5	16	8.9
Sibling, opposite sex	2	2.4	2	2.1	4	2.2
Extended kin	5	5.9	8	8.4	13	7.2
Unrelated adults and peers	7	8.2	14	14.7	21	11.7
Totals	85	100.1	95	99.9	180	100.0
$x^2 = 43.791$ *					$.05 > p < .001$	

* The last five rows were combined in the computation of the chi-square, which is for a sixfold table with two degrees of freedom. If the first row is eliminated from the analysis, and the chi-square computed for the second row and the combined remaining rows by sex, then $x^2 = 4.432$, and $.05 > p > .02$.

the responses were coded for the person standing in the most "objectively" intimate relationship to the informant. Table 3 shows that the parent of the same sex as the informant was the most frequently mentioned source of childhood costume in play.

Yet the male is again "disadvantaged." Even if we exclude from the analysis those informants who could not recall dressing in other's clothing during childhood, men are still significantly underrepresented among those who dressed in the clothing of the father, and women are significantly overrepresented among those who dressed in the clothing of the mother. Childhood play was accomplished by donning the costume of the relevant adult female model—the mother—among the women of the sample, while many men were denied the costume of the relevant adult male model. Among the men who could recall dressing in other's clothing, brothers and extended kin acted as sources of costume in somewhat greater than expected proportions (as did sisters and mothers!—but the numbers there are very small), while, among the women making such recollections, the mother was the sole source of childhood costume noticeably overrepresented. Small wonder that we are tempted to generalize that the men of our sample had a difficult time developing an adequate conception of their sexual identity. The adult models were often not available to them.

It may well be that discourse takes on a characteristic form during the stage of play. For one thing, the speech of the child may be what Piaget has called "egocentric." (15) At least, the child enters the stage of play before his egocentric language dwindles to less than 25 per cent of his discursive communication as recorded by Piaget and his associates. At this point the child is capable of socialized speech. Piaget hypothesizes that this occurs around the age of 7 or 8. On the other hand, the discourse of play is highly suggestive of "parataxic" communication. Sullivan, incidentally, did not restrict the concept to the depiction of psychotic behavior:

> Now let us notice a feature of all interpersonal relations. . . . This is the parataxic, as I call it, concomitant in life. By this I mean that not only are there quite tangible people involved . . . , but also somewhat fantastic constructs of those people are involved. . . . These psychotic elaborations of imaginary people and imaginary performances are spectacular and seem very strange. But the fact is that in a great many relationships of the most commonplace kind—with neighbors, enemies, acquaintances, and even such statistically determined people as the collector and the mailman—variants of such distortions often exist. The characteristics of a person that would be agreed to by a large number of competent observers may not appear to you to be the characteristics of the person toward whom you are making adjustive or maladjustive movements. The *real* characteristics of the other fellow at that time may be of negligible importance to the interpersonal situation. This we call *parataxic distortion* (18, pp. 25–26).

Consider a typical instance of play. The father returns home from work, is ambushed at the door, and "shot" by the young cowboy. The transaction has no "meaning" within the *real* father-son relationship—some psychoanalysts to the contrary notwithstanding! Instead, father and son are "of negligible importance to the interpersonal situation." The "fantastic constructs" of cowboy and Indian or "good guy" and "bad guy" are the relevant personifications or identifications with reference to which the discursive meaning is established. Of course, *as father,* the adult enables the young actor to carry off the performance, imbuing the play, as we have said, with a secrecy shared by *father and son,* charging the play with affect or mood.

THE GAME, THE UNIFORM, AND DRESSING IN

While the costume of play may be construed as any apparent misrepresentation of the self, permitting the wearer to become another, the uniform is precisely any apparent representation of the self, at once reminding the wearer and others of an *appropriate* identity, a *real* identity. The team-player is uniformed; the play-actor is costumed. When we asked our informants their earliest recollections of wanting to wear any particular item of clothing, they responded almost unanimously by recalling their earliest self-conscious appropriations of the dress of their peer groups. In a sense, the earliest items of clothing they wanted comprised the *uniforms* of the peer circle.

Among the men who experienced the wish for particular items of clothing in late childhood, most were concerned with escaping the investitures of the mother. The tenor of their remarks conveyed the undesirability of the clothing they were forced to wear as mother's sons. Thereafter, beginning in early adolescence, their comments focused more and more on the desirability and necessity of conforming to the dress established by their peers or demanded by the dating situation. The women, on the other hand, were concerned from the earliest ages with the desirability of conforming to the dress of peers. Rather than rejecting their early identities as mother's daughters, they began generally to enter the "game of life" at an earlier age than men, and this was represented in part by their self-conscious wishes to don the uniform of their peer circles at earlier ages.

I do not regard these findings as surprising. Indeed, they have been discussed widely by sociologists and social psychologists. It is recognized that women "come of age" more rapidly than men in our society. My only intention here is to frame these data in the perspective of socialization as it concerns the early development of a self-concept in the stages proposed

Table 4 *Tentative model for the investigation of processes of discourse and appearance in the early establishment of the self*

Stages of Early Socialization	Discursive Processes	Types of Discourse	Apparent Processes	Types of Appearance
Pre-play	1. Parental representation of infant babbling as verbal symbols (Cooley, Markey) 2. Progressive curtailment of whole body movement by parental intervention (Latif)	Conversation of gestures (Mead) Prototaxis (Sullivan) Signal communication, or designation, as in "ma-ma"	Investiture	Representation as infant, young child, and gender
Play	Identification with discrete differentiated others as in role-playing (Mead) 1. Anticipatory socialization 2. Fantastic socialization	Egocentric speech (Piaget) Parataxis (Sullivan)	Dressing out	Misrepresentation of the self Costume
Game	Generalization and consolidation of other roles Taking the role of the "generalized other" or "team"	Socialized speech (Piaget) Syntaxis (Sullivan)	Dressing in	Representation of peer-group affiliation Uniform

by Mead. Growing up is dressing in. It is signaled by the wish to dress like others who are, in turn, like one's self. The earlier representation of the self is formulated in play which is facilitated by costume. In play one does dress like others, but like others who are, in that case, unlike one's self.

In the stage of the "game," discourse undoubtedly takes on the character of developed speech—what Piaget called "socialized speech" or what Sullivan called "syntaxis." As the game is played, the person becomes an integral part of an on-going universe of discourse in every sense. The early socialization has been effected; a self has emerged. These stages and processes have been summarized in Table 4.

LATER SOCIALIZATIONS

It may well be the uneasiness attending the American's view of play and the game that inclines him to relegate such matters to the social world of children and disinclines him to acknowledge their central importance in adulthood. However, especially when we employ these processes to caricature socialization, we should not ignore the fact that they occur throughout life. Life must be viewed as a continuous socialization, a series of careers, in which old identities are sacrificed as new identities are appropriated, in which old relations are left behind as new relations are joined. Each critical turning point of life is marked by a change of dress, and, ordinarily, the new upcoming "game" is rehearsed prior to the entry upon the appropriate field of play.

Such rehearsals may be looked upon as the play of the adult. Momentarily the self is misrepresented as the adult plays at the roles he expects to enact in a near future. Particularly for American men, these rehearsals differ from the play of children by virtue of their rather more "realistic" appropriateness. They are much more frequently genuine *anticipatory socializations*. The child plays many more roles than he will enact in later life, while the roles playfully rehearsed by the adult are generally those he firmly expects to enact later on. But his *fantastic socializations* are also different. More often than is the case for the child, they occur in private. In the bathroom, behind closed doors and before a secret mirror, the man may become for an instant a boxer, an Adonis, an operatic virtuoso. The fantastic play of the child occurs in public, usually in areas set aside by the adult community precisely for such fantastic performances. The fact that the play of the adult is more realistic or appropriate, or, if not, more private, does not gainsay its significance. The rehearsal is often a dress rehearsal, and the more critical the turning point, the more likely the rehearsal is designed as a full dress affair—leaving school and entering the adult world of work, marriage, baptism, and the institutionalized recognition of death.

More realistic than adult play is the adult game. Indeed, we can conceive of life as a series of games—contests and engagements—that mark the progress of careers, culminating in losses and victories for the participants. Participation in the many "games" of life is, again, always represented by appropriate dress which assists the players in their identifications of one another and helps those on the sidelines—the spectators—to know, in fact, what game they are watching. However, these—the play and games of adults—are matters we must leave for a subsequent analysis in another place.

Summary

In this article, we have attempted to show the importance of appearance for any general theory of communication that is developed in the perspective of symbolic interaction. We have attempted to show also that the self is established, maintained, and altered in social transactions as much by the communication of appearances as by discourse. In this regard, by analyzing many statements evoked by clothed appearances, we have suggested a definition of the self that may have greater empirical utility than existing definitions. Finally, we have staked out the significance of appearance in the early socialization processes. In doing these things, our "real" goal will have been realized if we have encouraged one or two of our colleagues or future colleagues to look at the cloth on which, as Carlyle noted long ago, society may, in fact, be founded.

References Cited

1. Becker, Howard. "Empathy, Sympathy, and Scheler," *International Journal of Sociometry,* Vol. 1 (September 1956), pp. 15-22.

2. Burke, Kenneth. *A Grammar of Motives.* Englewood Cliffs, N.J.: Prentice-Hall, Inc., 1945.
3. Cooley, Charles H. *Human Nature and the Social Order.* New York: Charles Scribner's Sons, 1902.
4. Foote, Nelson N. "Identification as a Basis for a Theory of Motivation," *American Sociological Review,* Vol. 16 (February 1951), pp. 14–21.
5. Form, William H., and Gregory P. Stone. *The Social Significance of Clothing in Occupational Life.* East Lansing, Mich.: Michigan State University Agricultural Experiment Station Technical Bulletin 262 (November 1957).
6. Goffman, Erving. "Symbols of Class Status," *British Journal of Sociology,* Vol. 2 (December 1951), pp. 294–304.
7. Goffman, Erving. *The Presentation of Self in Everyday Life.* Edinburgh: University of Edinburgh Social Science Research Centre Monograph, No. 2, 1956.
8. Gorer, Geoffrey. *The American People.* New York: W. W. Norton & Company, Inc., 1948.
9. Huizinga, Jan. *Homo Ludens: A Study of the Play-Element in Culture.* London: Routledge & Kegan Paul, Ltd., 1949.
10. Lindesmith, Alfred R., and Anselm L. Strauss. *Social Psychology.* New York: The Dryden Press, 1956.
11. Lynd, Helen Merrell. *On Shame and the Search for Identity.* New York: Harcourt, Brace and Co., 1958.
12. Markey, John F. *The Symbolic Process and Its Integration in Children.* London: Kegan Paul, Trench, Trübner and Co., Ltd., 1928.
13. Mead, George H. "Philanthropy from the Point of View of Ethics," in Ellsworth Faris, Ferris Laune, and Arthur J. Todd (eds.), *Intelligent Philanthropy.* Chicago: The University of Chicago Press, 1930, pp. 133–148.
14. Mead, George H. *Mind, Self, and Society,* ed. by Charles W. Morris. Chicago: The University of Chicago Press, 1934.
15. Piaget, Jean. *The Language and Thought of the Child.* New York: Meridian Books, 1955.
16. Stone, Gregory P. "Clothing and Social Relations: A study of Appearance in the Context of Community Life." Unpublished Ph.D dissertation, Department of Sociology, University of Chicago, 1959.
17. Stryker, Sheldon. "Relationships of Married Offspring and Parent: A Test of Mead's Theory," *American Journal of Sociology,* Vol. 62 (November 1956), pp. 308–319.
18. Sullivan, Harry Stack. *The Psychiatric Interview.* New York: W. W. Norton & Company, Inc., 1954.
19. Veblen, Thorstein. *The Theory of the Leisure Class.* New York: Modern Library, Inc., 1934.

❀ Identity Kits

ERVING GOFFMAN

One set of the individual's possessions has a special relation to self. The individual ordinarily expects to exert some control over the guise in which he appears before others. For this he needs cosmetic and clothing supplies, tools for applying, arranging, and repairing them, and an accessible, secure place to store these supplies and tools—in short, the individual will need an "identity kit" for the management of his personal front. He will also need access to decoration specialists such as barbers and clothiers.

On admission to a total institution, however, the individual is likely to be stripped of his usual appearance and of the equipment and services by which he maintains it, thus suffering a personal defacement. Clothing, combs, needle and thread, cosmetics, towels, soap, shaving sets, bathing facilities—all these may be taken away or denied him, although some may be kept in inaccessible storage, to be returned if and when he leaves. In the words of St. Benedict's Holy Rule:

> Then forthwith he shall, there in the oratory, be divested of his own garments with which he is clothed and be clad in those of the monastery. Those garments of which he is divested shall be placed in the wardrobe, there to be kept, so that if, perchance, he should ever be persuaded by the devil to leave the monastery (which God forbid), he may be stripped of the monastic habit and cast forth.[1]

As suggested, the institutional issue provided as a substitute for what has been taken away is typically of a "coarse" variety, ill-suited, often old, and the same for large categories of inmates. The impact of this substitution is described in a report on imprisoned prostitutes:

> First, there is the shower officer who forces them to undress, takes their own clothes away, sees to it that they take showers and get their prison clothes—one pair of black oxfords with cuban heels, two pairs of much-mended ankle socks, three cotton dresses, two cotton slips, two pairs of panties, and a couple of bras. Practically all the bras are flat and useless. No corsets or girdles are issued.

---

[1] *The Holy Rule of Saint Benedict*, Ch. 58.
Source: *Asylums*, Garden City, New York: Doubleday and Co. (1961), pp. 20–21. Reprinted by permission of the author and publisher.

There is not a sadder sight than some of the obese prisoners who, if nothing else, have been managing to keep themselves looking decent on the outside, confronted by the first sight of themselves in prison issue.[2]

✂ Perception of Self in Relation to Clothing
MARY S. RYAN

To compare an individual's concept of her appearance with the concept of the group, girls rated themselves and the others of their group on a series of rating scales concerned with appearance. The five rating scales used applied to: extent of being well dressed, physical appearance of both face and figure, individuality in dress, and self-confidence. Subjects were also asked to estimate how they thought the group had rated them. Twenty-eight groups, each composed of eight Cornell University women students, were used as subjects.

Questions concerning background, social participation, and interest in clothing were asked, so that the relationship between these and the various ratings could be determined. Each girl also filled out the Bernreuter Personality Inventory, and the scores she achieved on self-sufficiency, dominance-submission, confidence, and sociability scales were compared with the rating scales and with differences in the rating scales. The general pattern of the relationships between self- and group-ratings and the estimation of the group ratings are shown in Table 1.

As the table shows, the most common pattern is that in which the self-rating is equal to the estimate of the group-rating and to the group-rating. The next two most common patterns are those in which the self-rating is equal to the estimate of the group-rating, and these are either higher or lower than the median group-rating.

There was a high correlation between the ratings on the various scales. That is, an individual who rated herself high, or whom the group rated

[2] John M. Murtagh and Sara Harris, *Cast the First Stone* (New York: Pocket Books, 1958), pp. 239–40. On mental hospitals see, for example, Kerkhoff, *op. cit.*, p. 10. Ward, *op. cit.*, p. 60, makes the reasonable suggestion that men in our society suffer less defacement in total institutions than do women.

Source: Psychological Effects of Clothing, Part IV: Perception of Self in Relation to Clothing, Cornell University Agricultural Experiment Station Bulletin No. 905 (1954), pp. 12–14. Reprinted by permission of the author and publisher.

high on one scale, tended to be rated high on all the scales. This high correlation may be wholly or partially accounted for by a "halo" effect,[1] —that is, the rating of any one trait is forced in the direction of the general impression of an individual, or it may be in part accounted for by a "logical error," which has an effect similar to that of the "halo." Traits that seem logically related are often rated similarly. High correlation may indicate, on the other hand, that the girls were rating not disparate characteristics but the same characteristic, or that these characteristics are related in some way.

Table 1 *Relationships between self-ratings and group-ratings and estimation of group-ratings*

Pattern *	Percentage of subjects
Self-rating = group-rating = estimate of group-rating	43.8
Self-rating = estimate > group-rating	11.2
Self-rating = estimate < group-rating	22.3
Self-rating = group-rating > estimate	8.5
Self-rating = group-rating < estimate	1.8
Self-rating > group-rating = estimate	6.7
Self-rating < group-rating = estimate	2.2
Self-rating ≠ group-rating ≠ estimate	3.6

* < Means "is less or lower than"; > means "is more or greater than"; ≠ means "is not equal to."

The degree to which the group was acquainted with the individual was one of the factors correlated with the ratings. The closer this acquaintance, the higher the group rating on w-d.[2] There was also a tendency, though a lesser one, for the girl to rate herself high if she was well known by the group. The girl well liked by the group also tended to rate herself higher, and the group tended to rate her higher, on all of the scales than the girl who was less well liked.

[1] Guilford, J. P. *Psychometric methods.* 566 pages. (Reference on p. 275 f.) 1936.
[2] Throughout the study "w-d" is used to indicate the scale which has "extremely well dressed" at one end and "very poorly dressed" at the opposite end. If high on the scale, it is either "above average" or extremely well dressed"; if low, it is "below average."

The girl from a large town and from a high economic level tended to be rated higher on w-d by herself and by the group than did the girl from a small town or a lower economic level. The size of the town and the economic level were not related to the ratings (either by self or group) for individuality or confidence. Since economic level was highly correlated with the size of the town, the results may be due to one of these factors and only incidentally due to the other.

On all the rating scales, there was a highly significant relationship between an individual's interest in clothes and both her self-rating and the median group-ratings.

There was no significant relationship between social participation, as measured in this study, and either the self-ratings or the median group-ratings on any of the scales.

Personality factors, as measured by the Bernreuter Personality Inventory, had almost no relationship to the median group-rating of the individual but were, in some instances, related to the self-ratings. The only relationship found between the median group-ratings and personality factors was that the individual who was scored as dominant was perhaps more often given a higher rating on w-d than a submissive individual. Both dominance-submission and self-confidence were related to the self-ratings, but self-sufficiency scores and scores on sociability were related to neither the self- nor the median group-ratings.

As pointed out, the personality measures used here are not completely satisfactory and can be taken only as scores for this test and not as actual measures of the trait named. No personality test has yet been devised that is completely satisfactory and accepted by all psychologists. In Part III of this study,[3] which involved a small sample, it was suggested that the Rorschach personality test showed promise for this type of investigation, but practical considerations made it impossible to use it with as many as 224 girls.

[3] M. S. Ryan, *Psychological effects of clothing*. Part III. Report of interviews with a selected sample of college women. Cornell Univ. Agricultural Experiment Station Bulletin No. 898, 1953.

⌘ Clothing and the Status Ratings of Men: An Experiment

THOMAS FORD HOULT

The experiments described in this paper were designed to demonstrate the extent to which types of clothing may affect the status ratings of men in certain social situations. From a theoretical point of view, such research is potentially important because, as Cooley pointed out long ago,[1] most human interaction is structured in terms of the judgments people make of one another. But upon what basis are these judgments made? What are the symbols by means of which group members recognize one another? In attempts to answer these crucial questions, a number of symbols which apparently function in the social rating process have been the subject of sociological investigation.

Dollard, for example, has pointed out that certain types of alcoholic drinks are important to some groups as symbols of their status.[2] Other status symbols which have been investigated include sex behavior,[3] burial practices,[4] family ritual,[5] and mate selection.[6] Expressions of each of these forms of behavior vary in importance to different status groups and may be signs indicating group membership. Thus, at funeral services, family position in the social hierarchy is indicated by the fact that among those low in status, burial services must be emotional, while those high in status eschew emotion at such a time.[7] Living on a certain street, or

[1] Charles Horton Cooley, *Human Nature and the Social Order,* New York: Charles Scribner's Sons, 1922, pp. 164 ff.
[2] John Dollard, "Drinking Mores of the Social Classes," in *Alcohol, Science and Society,* New Haven: Yale University Quarterly Journal of Studies on Alcohol, 1945, pp. 95–104.
[3] Alfred Kinsey, Wardell B. Pomeroy and Clyde E. Martin, *Sexual Behavior in the Human Male,* Philadelphia: W. B. Saunders Company, 1948, Chapter 10.
[4] William M. Kephart, "Status After Death," *American Sociological Review,* 15 (October, 1950), pp. 635–643.
[5] James H. S. Bossard and Eleanor S. Boll, "Ritual in Family Living," *American Sociological Review,* 14 (August, 1949), pp. 466–467.
[6] August B. Hollingshead, *Elmtown's Youth,* New York: John Wiley and Sons, 1949, pp. 432–434.
[7] Kephart, *op. cit.,* p. 641.

Source: "Experimental Measurement of Clothing as a Factor in Some Social Ratings of Selected American Men," *American Sociological Review,* Vol. 19 (June, 1954), pp. 324–328. Reprinted by permission of the author and publisher.

belonging to a closed group such as the First Families of Virginia, assume tremendous importance to some people while to others these patterns of living may be a joke.[8]

Although the forms of behavior mentioned have been subjected to scientific study, there has been little if any attention paid to clothing—male clothing in particular—as a symbol of status. The potential importance of clothing as such a symbol has been suggested by Young.[9] He points out that when there are no fixed symbols to mark the social elite in a stratified society, external features of life, such as clothes, are often used for this purpose. Popular acceptance of this belief is indicated by the cliche, "clothes make the man," and by the results of several government surveys. When a large sample of men were asked, "What are the most important things to look for when buying a summer sport shirt?" style was spontaneously mentioned most often by all three income groups delineated in the study.[10] Comfort and size were mentioned far less often than style. In a survey dealing with purchasers of sport coats, fifty-two per cent of the men queried said attractiveness and prestige were their reasons for buying such jackets; only twelve per cent mentioned economy.[11]

Thus, there is both popular and professional conviction that clothing can function as an important classificatory symbol in the social process of status rating. At the same time, this possible function of clothing is taken so much for granted that there is a scarcity of empirical data available to justify scientific generalization on the subject, especially where men are concerned. This situation was the motivating force behind the experiments described below.

Experiment I

PROCEDURE

After a suitable pre-test, the cooperation of thirteen men known to forty-six student judges was obtained.[12] The thirteen men were similar in age,

[8] Hans H. Gerth and C. Wright Mills, *From Max Weber: Essays in Sociology,* London: Kegan Paul, Trench, Trubner and Co., Ltd., 1947, p. 188.
[9] Kimball Young, *Social Psychology,* 2nd Edition, New York: F. S. Crofts and Company, 1947, pp. 419–420.
[10] *Men's Preferences Among Selected Clothing Items,* Miscellaneous Publication 706, Washington: U. S. Department of Agriculture, December, 1949, Table 16, p. 68.
[11] *Men's Preferences Among Wool Suits, Coats, and Jackets,* Preliminary Summary Report, Washington: U. S. Department of Agriculture, 1950, p. 5 and Table 19.
[12] All participants were members of a large principles of sociology class.

race and marital status.[13] Holding numbered identification cards, these men stood before the judges on two occasions. The first time, the men wore clothing chosen without forethought of the test in mind. On cards provided for the purpose, the men were rated by the judges in terms of the following factors: best looking, man I'd most like to date (or double date with), man I'd like to have as my class president, has the best personality, is the most likely to succeed after college, and is the most intelligent. These phrases were defined informally so that the judges were believed to be in substantial agreement on their meaning. The total ratings received by the men were then computed.[14] In confidential interviews, the four men rated lowest were asked to "dress up" for the second test, while the four rated highest were asked to wear inconspicuous old clothing for the second test. As a control group, the five men who received average ratings were asked to dress for the second test exactly as they had dressed for the first.

Two weeks after the first test, the men—dressed as planned—were again rated by the forty-six judges in terms of the same categories as before. In an effort to allay suspicion, the judges were told that a second rating was necessary because so many had misunderstood directions the first time.

FINDINGS

When the final ratings were computed, the men judged were divided into three basic groupings: Group I, the men who dressed up for the second test; Group II, those who "dressed down" for the second test; and Group III, the controls who dressed the same for both tests. Combining all categories in terms of which the men were rated, the raw scores obtained by the three groups on the two tests were as follows—First Test: Group I, 551; II, 1,249; III, 907. Second test: Group I, 570; II, 1,293; III, 890. Chi square analysis revealed that no real changes occurred

[13] All were 18–23 years old, Caucasian, and single.
[14] The judges were asked to list, in order from first to last choice, only the first four men they would choose for each of the categories; the pretest had revealed that it would be confusing to list more than four. The answers were scored arbitrarily by assigning a four to a first choice, three to a second, and so on. (See George A. Lundberg, *Social Research*, New York: Longmans, Green and Co., 1942, pp. 297–300, for evidence that arbitrary scoring of this nature is highly correlated with more technical methods of establishing equidistant intervals.)

in the ratings given the men on the second test when compared with the first. Thus, the clothing changes which were made were not associated with any changes in social ratings, as might be expected if clothing actually does "make the man."

It is possible that the negative results obtained in this experiment were due to recall on the part of the judges, but it is almost certain that the results were not due to the possibility that the clothing outfits did not change sufficiently for the second test. This latter possibility was ruled out after the clothing outfits were rated by an independent group of twenty-six judges. To save space, the results of the clothing ratings will not be given in detail. In essence, they indicated that the clothing changes, where made, were very noticeable. The clothing outfits of those who wore good clothes for the second test were rated significantly higher than were the outfits of the same men worn for the first test. The opposite occurred for the men who wore old clothing for the second test. The clothing of the control group of five men was judged about the same each time.

In a final attempt to ascertain why the first and second test ratings worked out as they did, the judges were asked to express their degree of social closeness with each of the thirteen men judged. This was done by having the judges indicate which one of five statements (arranged from most to least—for degree of social closeness expressed—as they were arranged by a panel of three independent judges) best expressed their degree of friendship with each of the thirteen men.[15] Again to save space, the detailed results of this procedure will not be discussed. The results indicated a fairly high degree of correlation ($+.67 \pm .11$)[16] between the rank of a man on his social ratings and his rank on social closeness with the raters.

Thus, to the degree that this experiment tested what it was meant to test, it indicated that the college student judges were not affected by clothing types when they judged college men they knew on items such as best looking, would like to date, and so on. If anything was associated with the ratings, it would appear to have been—as far as this test goes—the degree of social closeness of the men judged with those doing the judging.

[15] The statements, arranged from "most" to "least" were: 1. Is a very good friend of mine; 2. Is a good acquaintance of mine; 3. Know fairly well; 4. Know to speak to; 5. Know hardly at all. These were scored arbitrarily.
[16] All correlations calculated with Spearman's formula for establishing correlation of ranked data.

Experiment II

PROCEDURE

In this experiment, the pictures of men unknown to 254 student judges at two colleges [17] were rated during two tests in terms of categories chosen by fifty of the judges (categories chosen in a pre-test). Because the categories decided upon were very subjective, the results obtained for one only ("attractiveness") will be discussed here, although it should be noted that the results obtained for all were substantially the same. The category "attractiveness" is singled out because attractiveness can, to some extent, be judged from pictures. Further, as the Murphys have observed, it is concern with personal attractiveness which plays one of the most significant roles in intrapersonal psychological conflict; [18] this is true because it is commonly believed that social success is in large part a consequence of the judgments others make of one's personal appearance.

For the first test in the second experiment, on an appropriate questionnaire supplied for the purpose, all judges rated pictures of the heads of ten college-age men. Each judge had his own copy of the ten pictures, which were arranged as a single composite photograph. After the first test, the judges were divided randomly into two experimental and two control groups (one each at the two colleges). It was determined that the ratings made by the control and experimental groups at each college were substantially the same for the first test,[19] indicating that future comparisons between the control and experimental groups would be justifiable.

For the second test, one month after the first, the control groups were asked to rate the same pictures used for the first test. The pictures used by the experimental groups, however, were altered for the second test. The alterations were accomplished in the following manner: After the first test, the ratings made on attractiveness by members of the experimental groups were computed. The men rated were then ranked from first to last according to the scores accorded them. The head ranked first was then superimposed in the proper position on a body clothed in an outfit that

---

[17] Michigan State College and Indiana Central College.
[18] G. and L. B. Murphy, *Experimental Social Psychology*, New York: Harper and Brothers, 1937, Chap. 6.
[19] Correlation between the ratings of the experimental and control groups at Indiana Central College on this test was $+.93\pm.03$; at Michigan State, $+.95\pm.02$.

had been ranked last of ten outfits.[20] The head ranked second was combined with the clothing ranked next to the lowest, and so on. The resulting combinations were numbered and placed on a card in the same relative positions the heads had had on the picture used for the first test. The new arrangement was photographed and reproduced in sufficient numbers to give one copy to each member of the experimental groups for the second test. As controls, the same body in the same position was photographed to produce the various outfit pictures, and the pictures given to the control and experimental groups for the second test had heads of the same size. Thus, so far as is known, the only major variable introduced to the experimental groups was the different ranking clothing outfits.[21] Before the final results were computed, the control and experimental groups at each college were matched by frequency distribution on six items: sex, age, race, family income, type of area in which the respondent grew up, and father's occupation. This process reduced the experimental and control group at Indiana Central College to sixty-nine individuals each; at Michigan State, the final groups contained twenty-two cases each.

FINDINGS

Both control groups rated the pictures for the second test almost exactly as they had rated them for the first. At Indiana Central College, the correlation between the first and second ratings of the control group is expressed by the figure $+.98 \pm .01$; at Michigan State, the correlation was $+.94 \pm .03$. In contrast, both experimental groups (which had been matched—it should be recalled—with their respective control groups on six important variables; changed their ratings considerably on the second test as compared with the first. The change is illustrated by the fact that at Indiana Central College, the correlation between the first and second ratings of the experimental group was $-.14$; at Michigan State, the correlation between the two ratings made by the experimental groups was $-.08$. The change in ratings made by the experimental groups was associated positively with the ranking of the clothing outfits by the ten

[20] Outfits ranked on "appropriateness for college students" by ten independent judges.
[21] An expert photographer was employed to minimize variables due to the technicalities of making the composite photographs for the experimental groups.

independent judges. Thus, the higher ranked clothing was consistently associated with the men who rose in rank, and the lower ranked clothing was associated with the men who lost in rank. This is what would be expected if the adage that "clothes make the man" has any truth to it.

Discussion

It is believed that the above-described experiments are the first of their type to be reported; this fact may explain some of the methodological shortcomings which seem evident in retrospect. However, even considering their limitations, the experiments are empirical evidence of the varied conditions under which clothing may or may not be a factor in the status rating of men. Thus, the first experiment suggests that under certain social conditions, types of male clothing may be unimportant in status rating. At the same time, the second experiment lends weight to Hartmann's assertion that clothes ". . . involve extensive group reactions rich in meaning for the operation of many of our major community institutions. . . ."[22]

It would be convenient and meaningful if one could say categorically, as a result of the experiments, that college students, when judging their male peers, are affected by the clothing outfits of the men judged according to whether or not the men are known by the judges. But the experiments are too dissimilar and limited to permit such an easy generalization. Further, the reliability and validity of the experiments can only be estimated. The second experiment appears to have been reliable, since very similar results were obtained in two very different colleges; its validity is suggested by the fact that changes in ratings did not occur except in association with the major variable introduced for the second test of the experimental groups. The first experiment was not tested for reliability, but its validity is indicated to some extent by an analysis of the responses made by the judges. The results of this analysis are not given here; it is sufficient to state that the judges who would be most expected to be affected by type and style of clothing (those in higher status income-occupational groups) did make the greatest changes in their ratings on the second test as compared with the first.

[22] G. W. Hartmann, "Clothing: Personal Problem and Social Issue," *Journal of Home Economics*, 41 (June, 1949), p. 295.

Keeping all the limitations in mind, the following results were obtained with the two experiments:

(1) In a specified experimental situation, clothing did not appear to have been associated with important social ratings of some college men when they were rated by acquaintances; instead, the ratings made were associated with the degree of social closeness the judges expressed for the men judged.

(2) In another controlled situation, clothing appeared to be markedly associated with the attractiveness ratings of the pictures of some college-age men when the pictures were rated by college students unacquainted with the men pictured. The attractiveness ratings for men previously rated low went up when the men were pictured wearing clothing independently rated high in appropriateness; attractiveness ratings for men rated high went down when they were pictured wearing clothing rated low.

The two principal results outlined indicate that the data reported in this limited paper will support no more than very tentative conclusions, even for college students. But the data do have some significance in suggesting experimentally that clothing may play an important and measurable part in structuring the nature of interpersonal relationships under certain circumstances. It is true that "everyone knows" clothes play such a part in human society; however, the exact nature and extent to which clothing functions in an interacting world remain unknown, aside from the meager results obtained from the above-described type of experiments. Here, then, is a rich, untapped field for social research which cuts across the disciplines of home economics, psychology, sociology, and social psychology.

⅋ The Matter of Clothing

MURRAY WAX AND ROSALIE WAX

When a child complains about his clothing, this touches his parents on a vulnerable spot. Sioux parents, and especially grandparents, spend large

Source: Formal Education in an American Indian Community, Report of Cooperative Research Project No. 1361 conducted by Emory University and supported by the Cooperative Research Program of the United States Office of Education. This report has been published as a supplement to *Social Problems,* Vol. II, No. 4 (Spring, 1964). Reprinted by permission of the authors.

portions of their meager incomes giving their children the things that attract and please them. White observers sometimes criticize Indian parents as "indulgent," when they happen to observe an Indian shack in which a child is playing with a toy that must cost over ten dollars; however, Indian elders value the child's pleasure and do not perceive a moral virtue in denying the child those things for which they may have the money.

When a child complains about being picked on, his parents are stimulated to strike out against some external target, usually the family of the offender; but, when the child complains that he is being teased about his clothing, the parents usually blame themselves and do what they can to clothe him more suitably. Of course, the variations are great. If the child has no immediate kin and has been farmed out to distant relatives, his lack of clothing may be real and he may have no one to listen sympathetically to his plight. Or, if his family is unstable, the little money that comes into it may be spent on booze. To some extent, the children who are most affected by the sartorial standards of their peers are also most helpless about it, having no parents to aid them. It may be that children feel driven to wheedle better clothes off their parents in order to demonstrate to their peers (and themselves) that they do have elders who care intensely about their welfare. However this may be, in the present chapter our interest is in the parents, rather than in the dynamics of the peer group.

When a child is in the elementary grades, most parents tend to be as accommodating as their slender resources allow. If a child refuses to wear a new coat "because the other kids tease him," or "because all the other kids are wearing half-coats this year," many parents will buy him a new coat as soon as they can obtain the cash.

In the course of interviews, some parents remarked defensively that they told their children that "your clothes don't matter so long as they are clean." Yet, in each of these cases, we observed or learned that these particular parents do not dress their children in "neat but sturdy" clothes but instead do all they can to get them the apparel which is stylish among the school peers. Extremely poor parents (*e.g.,* those who send their children to boarding school so that they can eat) do not pay so much heed to the norms of peer clothing; usually, they have more elemental matters to worry about. Yet, one very poor mother explained that it was easier to care for boys because, if they did not grow too fast, they could wear the same jeans for three years, whereas girls unfortunately needed clothing more often.

Some teachers have told us that they praise children with clean clothing (which on the dusty Reservation usually means *new* clothing), and we are inclined to believe that many do this. The children seize upon this sanction to torment any schoolmate wearing worn, imperfect, or odd garments. We were surprised to learn how demanding were the sartorial standards of even the early grades:

My boy (Third Grade) doesn't want to wear his jeans. They kind of lost their color—they're kind of light blue like. He says, "That's faded; that's old; they'll laugh at me! I can't wear that." And even his socks, if just a little piece is tore off on the heel or someplace, he says, "Look what's happened. I'm not going to wear those."

I said, "My Goodness, nobody would notice." And he said, "Sure they will. They notice everything. They'll make fun of me. You're not going to school so you don't know how it is at school." Oh, he puts up a big fuss.

My girls (Fourth and Fifth Grade), they have to change anklets every day because when they go (to school) if they don't change anklets they'll say: "Gee, you're lazy, look at your anklets. Where did you get your gray anklets?" She says they really make fun like that. If I wash their anklets they say they want them clean, like new, really white. They say: "Can't you ever wash the anklets white?" And oh, I get mad at them. And they say: "Can't you iron better? Our dresses are wrinkled and we can't wear them." Oh they get me mad.

We (family) don't want them to dress in a faded dress or jeans because they really make fun of each other. So we have a hard time. We practically go broke. And they have to have new shoes every month. (April 25)

In many school districts it seems that some of the parental concern about clothes is translated into a kind of fanatical concern with cleanliness and whiteness like the stereotyped figures of washday soapland. Ideally, Sioux children change their clothes daily, and these are then subjected to an intensive treatment with the hottest water and strongest detergents by mothers who seem to spend a disproportionate share of their time either at the rental laundry or over a wash pail at home.

High School Clothing

When students leave the relatively countrified Day School and enter the high school in Pine Ridge town, they find themselves living in a community where the standards of dress are quite different from those of their local communities. In the country, even relatively affluent persons dress in work clothes day in and day out. Men and boys wear practical and sturdy wranglers' outfits. Married women, even those in their twenties, dress in the shapeless rummage clothes or homemade dresses which their mothers and mothers-in-law consider modest and decorous. In sharp contrast, most of the Bureau personnel (White and Indian) of the town of Pine Ridge dress with a middle class propriety of Western timbre.

Within the high school, the norms of dress are high: girls wear tailored blouses and skirts, or modest frocks and sweaters; boys wear conservative sports ensembles. The effect is startlingly proper, and the garments are expensive and not particularly practical to the climate and terrain of Pine Ridge, with its mud and dust and extremes of temperature (but then urbanized styles of dress always have a weird impracticality to them). To our knowledge, the school administration does not enforce these styles of clothing, rather confining itself to the usual genteelisms, such as banning slacks, the most sensible and modest garment for young ladies in cold or windy weather and therefore not to be tolerated. The administration does require a middle-class style of dress of its teachers, and the women, especially, do dress well and as if they devoted time and money to the task. However, it would be fallacious to regard the teachers' dress as providing more than a setting for the norms of proper apparel for these are defined and ruthlessly enforced by the peer culture.[1]

The purchase of these ready-made outfits puts a heavy and often unanticipated strain on the means of country families. Moreover, the strain is unrelenting, for even after a nice outfit has been purchased, the poor girl from the country finds that she is still being outdressed and outgroomed by her town rivals, and the ears of sympathetic parents are filled with complaints about those Mixedblood girls.

Inadequate clothing is the most common reason given by both parents

---

[1] Country Indians wear extravagant finery or dance regalia only on very special occasions. Their ordinary dress is drab and practical.

and daughters for the dropout of the latter from high school. Clearly, in some cases this is offered as a more presentable reason for dropping out than the more immediate and embarrassing ones of poor scholarship or "getting into trouble"; yet, there is no doubt that many parents believe that if their girls had modish new clothes they would remain in school and graduate. Our observations suggest, instead, that inadequate clothing is but the most obvious of a complex of difficulties suffered by the country girl of conservative family. She is handicapped both in the official side of the school and in the unofficial, informal side. Coming from a semiliterate family that speaks a lower status version of English, associating with peers of similar background, and attending an elementary school of meager scholastic impact, she enters high school at a marked disadvantage to the children from the families of Bureau employees. Even if these latter are not studious, they have a natural facility with "proper English" and are likely to be well grounded in reading and arithmetic. To the peer culture she is a hick, untutored in the "sophisticated" ways of Pine Ridge town. Accordingly, she finds herself baffled in her studies, lonely and snubbed out of class, and generally bewildered by the atmosphere of the high school. At this point she decides that had she only the proper clothes, everything would work itself right. Usually, she cannot obtain them and so she quits; for the rest of her life she will say that she might have finished high school and so gotten a good job if her parents had given her the clothes she needed:

A lot of the children of the government workers dressed better. The children who didn't have no clothes felt ashamed. My father and mother wanted me to go to school. But, I had only old clothing. I went, but I soon ran out of clothes. And, at school, they said I had to have certain clothing. I wrote my parents and told them what to order. Instead of sending the order off, they sent me dress goods and old shoes and stockings, and I didn't have no time to sew or anything in high school. (Respondent dropped out in 9th grade, Sept. 27.)

The next account by a sixteen-year-old girl tells us a great deal more about the complex situation of the girl who drops out of high school. It shows how a conservative girl may come gradually to realize that proper clothing "is not enough"; it also shows how the problem of clothing is often handled among the extended family of conservative Indians.

Anna Louise is a quiet and shy girl with a pretty face and figure; she looks like a Mixedblood, although she was raised by a conservative family. Her father and mother, now divorced, were both from country families, but his was quite conservative while hers was relatively progressive and comfortably prosperous; her mother's brother is a college graduate. Her story comes to us via her maternal aunt, partly from an interview, which the aunt tried to conduct in English but in which her niece would talk only Lakota, and partly by way of the recall of the aunt of incidents involving the maternal family of the girl. Anna Louise speaks:

When I went to high school, I just had the old clothes I had at the Day School, and the first day of school, when I went into the classroom, I looked at the other girls and then I looked at myself. My clothes were just faded and out of style, and I was embarrassed. Everybody was sizing me up, and I felt I was a freak. I sure didn't feel good.

I told my (paternal) grandmother, and she said, "Just White people wear White clothes, and you're an Indian." She didn't want me to wear a half-skirt and blouse. She wanted me to wear long dresses like an Indian.

So, I wrote to my Dad and asked for some money, so I could buy some clothes, but he didn't answer me. So, I got so mad I quit school (9th grade).

Then I went to Montana, where my sister was working. She's a nurse. She bought me new clothes, and I went to the (public) high school there. But I was way behind, because public school was too hard for me compared to government school. My report cards were really poor, so I quit, because I couldn't keep up with my grade.

Then I went to work baby-sitting [2] for my sister. I saved all my money, and I bought myself clothes, and I came back and started again here (high school in Pine Ridge).

Here the aunt continues the thread of the narrative:

Once my niece wanted to go to the formal dance given at the high school for the students. But they had to wear a formal, and she asked her father to give her the money. He never even answered. Then we [maternal relatives of the girl] thought we would all chip in and get her the formal. I thought it would cost maybe $4.75, but when I looked in the Ward's catalog, gee, I saw they cost $17.00!

Then my mother said, "Oh, those are not formals. Those are what you call

---

[2] "Babysitting" is a Pine Ridge euphemism for light housework (the family worked for will of course have small children).

bride gowns—what White girls wear when they get married. I will get her something."

So my mother went to Rapid City, and she bought a whole box of rummage clothes. We all looked through it, and we found an old, blue formal. We all thought it looked real nice and that Anna Louise would be happy to wear it. But she looked at it and said she didn't want to wear it.

Then Martin came home from college for vacation and we told him. He said, "Oh, you Indians are sure awful. She can't wear that kind of old-fashioned dress!" He was working then, and he gave us ten dollars, and we all chipped in some more, and we went to Chadron and we got her a formal for seventeen dollars. My mother said, "Be sure you don't get her a white one, because that's what they wear for weddings. So we got her a red one. Anna Louise thought it was real nice, and she said, "How did you know I wanted a red one!"

Anna Louise continues:

I was getting along good, until I started having trouble with civics and social studies.[3] No matter how hard I try to learn, it's too hard to catch on. When I have trouble with my problems, and I ask the teachers, they tell me to learn it from my book. What's the use of going to school when the teacher can't help you with your lessons?

Then, I can't get along with the Mixedbloods, especially the girls. One (Mixedblood) boy kept asking me to go to the show, but one of the Mixedblood girls didn't like that. She kept after me, called me names, like "big squaw" and things like that.

I complained and we were taken to the Principal's Office. Then the Mixedblood said I was just jealous of her because she was a cheerleader, and she said to the Principal, "She's just a dumb squaw." The Principal got after her (i.e., scolded her), but afterwards she and the other Mixedblood girls kept making fun and laughing at me. They even made fun of me in class. Every place I go, they'll be making fun of me and picking on me. So, I just quit.

Aunt:

Are you going back to Montana so you can get out of going to school?

Anna Louise:

[3] Many country-bred students complain of having trouble with high school social studies. The teacher responsible for these classes is notorious for her hostility to the ways of country Indians.

I'll still go to school there. It was the girls I didn't like.

Later, the aunt said to us, "I think she'll go back; she's only sixteen years old." We would tend to agree. The prognosis for Anna Louise is good as compared to the many other country girls who have been subjected to the torments of Reservation high school. Moreover, Anna Louise comes from an unusually stubborn family. Her sister (now residing in Montana) went back to high school and finished it when she was in her early twenties, married and with children.

This is our most detailed account of what parents (or, in most country families, elders) do about the problem of clothing. It is also the fullest statement by a dropout as to why high school girls from country families play truant or leave school. Clearly, clothes and lack of money to buy them are only part of the story. Giving a country girl a new and fashionable wardrobe would be like giving a poor flower girl an aristocratic English accent—both too much and too little.

A Deviant

❀ Fashions of Royalty

CECIL BEATON

Since royalty by its very definition is above the crowd, it stands to reason that the fashions of kings and queens should be individual and unique, abiding by their own rigid laws and prohibiting imitation by the lower classes. In the Middle Ages, for example, only the queens and princesses were allowed to wear veils of a length extending to their feet. There was a time, also, when the styles of royalty were extravagant to the point of fantasy: Richard II had elaborate coats costing upwards of twenty thousand dollars. Marie Antoinette, who delighted in being the leader of fashion, was responsible for seventeen fashion changes in women's hats between 1784 and 1786. It was the French Revolution that inhibited arbitrary and fickle behaviour, especially in masculine attire. By the time Queen Victoria had ascended to the throne, royalty was beginning to conform to conservative bourgeois patterns.

Queen Alexandra probably started the modern tradition that British royalty can wear anything. During her husband King Edward's reign she would wear spangled or jewelled and bead-embroidered coats in the daytime, an innovation which has now become an accepted royal habit. Or she might wear half-length jackets covered with purple or mauve sequins and garnished with a Toby Frill collar of tulle. These were clothes which most women would have worn at night, but the fact that she wore them during the day removed her from reality and only helped to increase the aura of distance that one associates with the court.

Though royalty is no longer the arbiter of fashion in the democratic countries, its influence is still felt today in certain European kingdoms,

Source: The Glass of Fashion, Garden City, New York: Doubleday and Co. 1954, pp. 274–278. Reprinted by permission of the author and publisher.

notably in Great Britain. British royalty generally has clothes that are best seen from a distance, and it has become virtually an established tradition that female members of the royal family shall wear pastel colours. It was not uncommon to catch a glimpse of the late Queen Mary wearing sweet-pea colours on an afternoon's outing to Earl's Court, or to see the Queen Mother Elizabeth wearing a pale blue outfit at a morning rally of the Victoria League.

Queen Mary wore almost the same style for the last forty years of her life: beaded evening dress, tailored coat and skirt, long-toed shoes, and rolled parasol, with a large toque perched high on the tall dressing of hair and taking the place of a crown. As Janet Flanner wrote, "She has resisted hints from dressmakers, worn her skirts long when skirts were rising, raised hers slightly when it was too late; her hats, during her super-sensitive sartorial twenties, caused them pain. Today, she satisfied everyone, even her family. She looks like herself, with the elegant eccentricities —the umbrella or parasol, the hydrangea-coloured town suits, the light lizard slippers, the tiptilted toque—of a wealthy, white-haired *grande dame* who has grown into the mature style she set herself too young." Queen Mary thus created an appearance for herself that served as an all-weather model, good for rain or shine. Wherever one saw her, everything about her neat silhouette was as compact and tidy as a ranunculus. You knew that you were in the presence of royalty; and, with true *noblesse oblige,* she was always reliable in her appearance, never letting you down, but turning up regularly with mechanical precision upon any occasion, however small.

❈ The Mentally Ill and Management of Personal Front

ERVING GOFFMAN

One of the most evident means by which the individual shows himself to be situationally present is through the disciplined management of personal appearance or "personal front," that is, the complex of clothing, make-up, hairdo, and other surface decorations he carries about on his

Source: *Behavior in Public Places,* New York: Free Press of Glencoe (1963), pp. 25–27. Reprinted by permission of the author and publisher.

person. In public places in Western society, the male of certain classes is expected to present himself in the situation neatly attired, shaven, his hair combed, hands and face clean; female adults have similar and further obligations. It should be noted that with these matters of personal appearance the obligation is not merely to possess the equipment but also to exert the kind of sustained control that will keep it properly arranged. (And yet, in spite of these rulings, we may expect to find, in such places as the New York subway during the evening rush hour, that some persons, between scenes, as it were, may let expression fall from their faces in a kind of temporary uncaring and righteous exhaustion, even while being clothed and made up to fit a much more disciplined stance.)

I have already suggested that a failure to present oneself to a gathering in situational harness is likely to be taken as a sign of some kind of disregard for the setting and its participants; gross cultural distance from the social world of those present may also be expressed. These expressive implications of well or badly ordered personal appearance are often discussed in etiquette books, sometimes quite aptly:

> But even in a casual encounter, and upon occasions when your habit can have no connexion with the feelings and sentiments which you have towards those whom you meet, neat and careful dressing will bring great advantage to you. A negligent guise shows a man to be satisfied with his own resources, engrossed with his own notions and schemes, indifferent to the opinion of others, and not looking abroad for entertainment: to such a man no one feels encouraged to make any advances. A finished dress indicates a man of the world, one who looks for and habitually finds, pleasure in society and conversation, and who is at all times ready to mingle in intercourse with those whom he meets with; it is a kind of general offer of acquaintance, and provides a willingness to be spoken to.[1]

An interesting expression of the kind of interaction tonus that lies behind the proper management of personal appearance is found in the constant care exerted by men in our society to see that their trousers are buttoned and that an erection bulge is not showing.[2] Before entering a

---

[1] Anon., *The Canons of Good Breeding* (Philadelphia: Lee and Blanchard, 1839), pp. 14–15.
[2] The difficulty of engaging in this kind of protective concealment is one of the contingencies apparently faced by men with leg paralysis. See E. Henrich and L. Kriegel, eds., *Experiments in Survival* (New York: Association for the Aid of Crippled Children, 1961), p. 192.

social situation, they often run through a quick visual inspection of the relevant parts of their personal front, and once in the situation they may take the extra precaution of employing a protective cover, by either crossing the legs or covering the crotch with a newspaper or book, especially if self-control is to be relaxed through comfortable sitting. A parallel to this concern is found in the care that women take to see that their legs are not apart, exposing their upper thighs and underclothing. The universality in our society of this kind of limb discipline can be deeply appreciated on a chronic female ward where, for whatever reason, women indulge in zestful scratching of their private parts and in sitting with legs quite spread, causing the student to become conscious of the vast amount of limb discipline that is ordinarily taken for granted. A similar reminder of one's expectations concerning limb discipline can be obtained from the limb movements required of elderly obese women in getting out of the front seat of a car. Just as a Balinese would seem ever to be concerned about the direction and height of his seat, so the individual in our society, while "in situation," is constantly oriented to keeping "physical" signs of sexual capacities concealed. And it is suggested here that these parts of the body when exposed are not a symbol of sexuality merely, but of a laxity of control over the self—evidence of an insufficient harnessing of the self for the gathering.

As has been suggested, the importance of a disciplined management of personal front is demonstrated in many ways by the mentally sick. A typical sign of an oncoming psychosis is the individual's "neglect" of his appearance and personal hygiene. The classic home for these improprieties is "regressed" wards in mental hospitals, where those with a tendency in this direction are collected, at the very same time that conditions remarkably facilitate this sort of disorientation. (Here, dropping of personal front will be tolerated, and sometimes even subtly approved, because it can reduce problems of ward management.) Similarly, when a mental patient starts "taking an interest in his appearance," and makes an effort at personal grooming, he is often credited with having somehow given up his fight against society and having begun his way back to "reality."

Therapy of Fashion

THEO K. MILLER, LEWIS G. CARPENTER, AND ROBERT B. BUCKEY

"Therapy of Fashion" was a pilot study recently completed at Napa State Hospital and was designed to recreate healthy feminine characteristics in a selected group of women patients. The study was sponsored by the San Francisco Association for Mental Health and carried out as a volunteer service project of The Fashion Group of San Francisco, Inc., the local branch of a national organization of key professionals in the fashion field. The project consisted of a series of three weekly classes attended by forty selected women patients in both the chronic and the acute categories.

The series began with a professional fashion show. Afterward, fashion experts advised individual patients about the type of clothes best suited to them. In subsequent sessions, the fashion experts gave demonstrations and instructions concerning correct facial make-up, hair styling, dress designing, proper foundation garments, and simple exercises to improve posture and develop poise. Leading San Francisco firms contributed cosmetic kits and dress fabrics for distribution among the participating patients.

With professional guidance, each patient was given the opportunity of designing a dress for herself and selecting the fabric and color combinations she liked best. Hospital personnel encouraged and assisted the patients to make their dresses. Two weeks after the classes were finished, twenty-six patients had completed their dresses. After a practice session in modeling they staged their own fashion show with the aid of the fashion experts before an audience of nearly 400 other women patients.

For some patients in the group, effects of the fashion project were dramatic and immediate. One woman in her early thirties had persistently refused to enter any socializing activities and had even been unwilling to use her privilege of going out on the grounds. She finally admitted that she was ashamed of her appearance and said that she never went to parties or dances because she "looked so terrible." After being fitted with

Source: Mental Hospitals, Vol. 11 (October, 1960), pp. 42–43. Reprinted by permission of the publisher.

proper foundation garments, she looked into a mirror and said, "My, I look so different." At the fashion show she went on stage clad in her new dress and looking confident and happy.

A patient from an acute ward felt the fashion project was the turning point of her illness. She reported enthusiastically that after one of the classes, "all at once the clouds rolled back, the sun was shining, and I felt like myself again." She left the hospital not long afterward.

To provide more systematic and comprehensive information on the results of the project, participating patients and staff members filled out evaluation forms. Patients were asked: (1) whether they thought the project had helped them look "very much better," a "little better," or "no better," and (2) whether attendance at the classes had made them feel "much better," a "little better," or "no better." The staff filled out similar evaluation forms except that the variable "acting" was substituted for "feeling." A second evaluation with the same questions was made a month later.

One conclusion was immediately apparent. In both first and second evaluations of both chronic and acute patients, a large majority of patients and staff indicated they noticed some improvement. However the patients tended to downgrade their improvement on the second evaluation, especially in the "looking better" and "feeling better" categories. The shift, however, was not great enough to present a basically different pattern.

It is the combined opinion of the authors that fashion as a therapy may well prove to be an additional tool in the reactivation of women patients, especially among those in the chronic group with long-term periods of hospitalization. Also noteworthy were the stimulating effect this project had on other patients, and the interest displayed by the ward staff. News of what was transpiring spread rapidly and resulted in many requests from other patients to be included in a subsequent series of classes. There was also a noted improvement in their personal appearance.

The close contact and individual attention the patients received from these well groomed and cultured professionals—even for so short a period—have been morale builders themselves. The fact that they took time out from their busy lives and occupations for preparation, in addition to devoting four full days at the hospital to be of service, is sufficient proof to the patients that there are people outside the hospital who are genuinely interested in their welfare.

⊗ Self-Tattooing Among Delinquents
A Research Note
JOHN H. BURMA

The culture trait of tattooing has a long history and is widespread throughout the world. The only scientific studies which have been reported are by anthropologists, who have concerned themselves with primitive societies. At least one generalization seems clear: generally tattooing appears to be a subcultural practice found in particular population categories (class, occupation, age, sex, etc.) rather than an established trait uniformly characteristic of a whole society. Little except of a popular nature has been written about tattooing among people of Western European extraction.

Nonstatistical, lay reports of the situation in America, commonly based on interviews with professional tattooers, suggest the following: (1) possibly one person in ten has a tattoo; (2) three to five times as many men are tattooed as women; (3) the basic motive is exhibitionistic; (4) the frequency rises in periods of crises, large-scale movements, the "holiday spirit"; (5) tattooing occurs most often when the client has been drinking; and (6) about one-third of the tattooer's work involves requests to erase, cover, or "clean up" existing tattoos.[1]

On a preliminary basis it seems reasonable to hypothesize that in our culture persons who have certain types of self-concepts will be more likely to tattoo themselves than persons with other self-concepts. Because of the increasing significance of self-concepts in the study of delinquency,[2] it becomes a matter of interest whether or not there may be a relationship

---

[1] H. Ebersten, *Pierced Hearts and True Love* (London: Verscholye, 1953); *Literary Digest*, March 27, 1937, pp. 22 ff; "Skins and Needles," *Time*, 41:65, March 1, 1943; "War Booms the Tattooing Art," *New York Times*, Section M, p. 38, September 19, 1943; "Old Tattooer Talks Shop," *Science Digest*, 17:21–23, March 1945; "Jap Gamblers Tattoo Selves," *Life*, 20: 12–14, March 11, 1946.

[2] For example, W. C. Reckless, S. Dinitz, B. Kay, "The Self Component in Potential Delinquency and Potential Non-Delinquency," *American Sociological Review*, 22:566–60, October 1957.

Source: Sociology and Social Research, Vol. 43 (May, 1959), pp. 341–345. Reprinted by permission of the author and publisher.

between the self-concepts related to delinquency and those related to self-tattooing. Although no analysis of this possible relationship has been made, Marshall Clinard and others have commented on it.

Before a major study of the possible relationship of various self-concepts to delinquency and to self-tattooing can be undertaken, it is first necessary to prove that a significant amount of tattooing does, in fact, occur among delinquents. The pilot study reported here attempts to do this, and in addition to learn something of the kinds of tattoos which exist; how, why, and under what circumstances the tattooing occurred; and something of the delinquent's attitude toward his tattoos. This study is neither definitive nor complete, yet it does present considerable data on the basis of which the hypotheses for a more conclusive study might be constructed.

Subjects for this report were inmates of the New Mexico Boys Training School, the Iowa Training School for Boys, and the Harwood School for delinquent girls at Albuquerque, New Mexico. In none of these institutions were all inmates or even all tattooed inmates interviewed. This might cast doubt upon the validity of some of the findings were it not that most of the data related not to persons, but to individual tattoos, of which well over 900 were observed and on 883 of which data were secured.[3]

The most overwhelming of the findings was that these were amateur "self-tattoos"; less than one-half of 1 per cent were applied by professionals. Over two-thirds were applied by the person himself, and the others by a boy or girl friend, sometimes on a "swapping" basis. Over 90 per cent were made by the use of ordinary sewing needle and India ink. Occasionally a razor blade or knife and fountain pen ink or graphite were used, usually because needle and India ink were temporarily unavailable.

Because not all inmates could be examined, no true statistical proportions of tattooed and nontattooed could be determined. The most accurate estimate the author can make is that at the New Mexico boys' school about 2 in 3 boys were tattooed, at the Iowa boys' school about 1 in 6 was tattooed, at the New Mexico girl's school possibly 1 in 3 was tattooed, and at the Iowa girls' training school, where only a cursory investigation was conducted, only about 1 in 25 was tattooed.

The data on number of tattoos per person were only exploratory, owing to less than 100 per cent coverage and the fact that a person with only 1

[3] Special thanks for their assistance is due Rupert Trujillo, Ted Fiebiger, Marie Aiken, Jean Fowler, Arthur Tenorio, Jack DeRyke, and Elvira Pacheco.

tattoo was more likely to be overlooked than a person with 10. However, the data are as follows: for the New Mexico boys (over 90 per cent coverage), the number of tattoos ranged from 1 to 25, and the median number was 5; for the Iowa boys (80 per cent coverage), the range was 1 to 14, and the median was 3; for the New Mexico girls (probably 60 per cent coverage), the range was 2 to 25, and the median was 10. These data show incontrovertibly that a large number of delinquents did have a significantly large number of tattoos.

The location of the 883 tattoos was determined with accuracy: about 32 per cent were between the wrist and the elbow, 23 per cent on the hands, about 17 per cent between elbow and shoulder, and the remainder on the fingers, face, and other parts of the body. The boys were considerably less likely to have tattoos where shirt sleeves could not cover their arms. The girls' samples showed them to have a higher proportion than the boys in visible spots like hands, fingers, and face, and also on their legs and thighs. Two-thirds of all tattoos were on the left side and 80 per cent on the outer parts of the arms. The single most common spot was between the thumb and forefinger on the left hand. None of the Iowa boys interviewed had face tattoos; 15 per cent of the New Mexico girls interviewed had 1 or more, and a full count of the New Mexico boys showed 12 per cent to have 1 or more such tattoos. Those who had only 1 or 2 tattoos usually had them where they could be covered up by shirt sleeves. Those with face tattoos usually had a considerable number of other tattoos, also.

By far the most common marks consisted of letters, most often the subject's own initials, but frequently the initials of a girl or boy, "Mom," or other words. Symbols were also frequent, with the most common being some variation of the "pachuco cross." Eight per cent of the tattoos studied had been left incomplete. Less than 1 per cent of the tattoos could be considered lewd in character. A number of tattoos had been marked out by new tattooing or by scars.

The interviewers attempted to learn the meaning of each tattoo, but with less than complete success. Frequently the answers were clear: "My initials," "my girl's initials," "all our gang had this," "pachuco cross." Often, however, the answers were vague, and, even discounting for evasiveness, it seems clear that many of the marks have little if any real significance and are in fact "just marks," much as ordinary 10- or 12-year-olds draw on their arms in schoolrooms throughout the nation—that is, except for the boys' initials on girls' arms, and vice versa, and for true gang symbols (which probably fail to exceed 10 per cent), the actual "content" of the tattoo seems of little use in analyzing self-concepts; certainly it seems less important than the fact of the tattooing itself. The chief exception seems to be the "pachuco cross" which, at least throughout the Southwest, has wide currency and is widely recognized by adults and by nondelinquents as well as by delinquents. It does serve as a gang sign for a few scattered groups, but it certainly does not indicate any nation-wide gang. That it does serve as a recognition sign for reference groups seems widely true. That is to say, a youngster in Albuquerque with a "pachuco cross" on his left hand may not belong to any gang at all, but if he moves to Los Angles, or even Chicago, this symbol will serve to make it easier for him to set up relationships with some peer groups and more difficult with others. As a generalization it may be said that the subjects usually were far more concerned with the neatness or artistry of their tattoos than with their symbolism.

For all three groups the age at first tattooing was early. The age range for the New Mexico boys and girls was from six to eighteen years, and for the Iowa boys eleven to seventeen. For each of the three groups the median age was fourteen and the modal age was fifteen. Exactly 100 of the 883 tattoos were acquired before their owners were in their teens.

As to the circumstances under which the tattoo was made, no information is available for the Iowa boys, but for the New Mexico boys and girls, over 40 per cent were applied in their own homes or the homes of friends, with about an equal number being acquired while in a training school or jail (despite rigid training school rules). None resulted from formal gang initiation.

The majority of tattoos, at least according to the informants, were applied "for fun," because of "wanting something to do," "just fooling around," "no particular reason." For those tattoos for which a clear reason could be elicited, the chief reason given by girls was because of a boy friend, with copying someone they saw, as the second reason. For boys, gang reasons and girl friends were the two chief motivations. Some informants indicated that when a boy or girl in tattooing used someone's initials, usually either sexual intimacy had occurred or "they want you to think it had."

About half of each group indicated all or most of their friends had tattoos, and about half had brothers who were tattooed. Nearly half of the girls and nearly one-fourth of the New Mexico boys said they had sisters who were tattooed, but only 4 per cent of the Iowa boys had tattooed sisters. About one-half of each group stated as their immediate reaction to their tattooing that they "felt good," were proud, or felt "tough." About one-fourth of the individuals of each group suffered remorse shortly after the tattooing. Questions were asked concerning the reaction of the subject's family to his tattooing, but the results could not be handled statistically because in a large number of cases the subject's parents still did not know, or the subject had no parents. In less than 5 per cent of the cases was the parent's reaction strongly unfavorable. In most cases where the subject's family knew about it, he was "fussed at" but not punished.

The subjects were also asked which tattoo they liked best, which least, whether they would like to have any tattoos removed and whether they expected to put on other tattoos later. The replies to these queries overlapped considerably, were conflicting in some cases, and frequently were hedged by "if." In each group the great majority judged the quality of tattooing and what the tattoo stands for as being paramount. Tattoos that were neat or artistic were liked; those that were of poor quality or incomplete were disliked. A considerable group of tattoos were disliked because they did not apply now—have a new girl or boy friend, moved from town, gang broke up.

Removal of all tattoos was desired by 75 per cent of the boys and 60 per cent of the girls. About 1 in 10 boys and 1 in 6 girls did not want any tattoos removed, and the remainder wanted some removed and some to remain. One in 3 girls said she "probably might" have more tattoos put on later, as compared to about 1 in 5 boys. The reasons given for wishing the removal of some or all tattoos were many, varied, and often vague. The two clearest and most common reasons were that they interfered with job possibilities, and that the particular tattoos were themselves unsightly and/or of poor quality. When asked why *other* boys had tattoos, the three most commonly given answers were: first, gang affiliation (although this varied from 45 per cent of the New Mexico boys to 5 per cent of the Iowa boys); second, that it made them feel "big" and "tough"; and third, copying others. In general, the boys seemed to show little insight into why girls were tattooed, but when urged to guess, their guesses matched the reasons actually given by the girls, namely, gang affiliation and boy friends.

Although this study is obviously an exploratory one, the author would like to conclude with the following general hypotheses: (1) Significantly more delinquents than nondelinquents tattoo themselves. (2) Significantly more boys than girls tattoo themselves, but when girls tattoo themselves they use at least as many tattoos as do boys. (3) The idea of tattooing oneself occurs to some people early, and is carried out at an early age, probably without much thought for the future. (4) Tattooing frequently, but not always, serves as a status symbol in certain peer groups, and it is only later that the subject realizes it is a negative status symbol in other groups. (5) Once tattooed, subsequent tattoos are put on with less compunction. (6) There is a close relationship between the kind of symbols most boys and girls *draw* on their arms and the symbols *tattooed* on by delinquents. (7) Self-tattooing is partial, but not certain, evidence of gang membership. (8) For some delinquents, tattooing is the result of certain self-concepts, and hence is a partial index of such concepts.

✂ The Clacton Giggle

Where to go for a giggle? In the teen joints of Soho, the word went out: make it Clacton. Like a flock of noisy starlings, more than 1,000 youths buzzed into the dismal North Sea resort for Britain's four-day Easter holiday. The weather was foul—and so, Clactonians decided, were their visitors. Most of the invaders "slept rough" on the beach, warmed only by their "birds" (girl friends) and quantities of "purple hearts" (goofballs). Inevitably, the giggling had to stop, for Clacton's invaders belonged to London's two hostile teen cults: the "Mods" (for Moderns), foppishly dressed youths who drive souped-up, chrome-plated scooters; and the "Rockers," who wear black boots, black leather jackets, drive powerful motorcycles, and scorn the Mods as "queer." The rumble erupted on the second day.

Roving mobs of cold, bored teen-agers swarmed over Clacton's pier, smashing windows, overturning cars, stealing liquor. Pistol in hand, one youth used a big storefront window for target practice. When a local type

Source: Time, Vol. 15 (April 10, 1964), pp. 32–33. Reprinted by permission of the publisher.

admonished the rioters, he was tossed over a 20-ft. bridge. Clacton police called for reinforcements from a neighboring town, fought pitched battles with the teen-agers, many of whom were armed with ax handles and furniture legs. Finally the bobbies restored order: over 60 youths were arrested on charges ranging from burglary to assault.

Wild Ones. The Clacton riot climaxed a longtime rivalry between the sartorially splendid Mods and the hot-rodding Rockers. One British sociologist claims that their hostility is based on class. The Mods are artisans and office workers, he claims, and look down on the Rockers, who tend to be scruffy worker types. As a London Mod explains the feud, "The Rockers are just interested in their cycles. This isolates them. Mods are more aware, fast moving, hip. With us, it's like a club. If you wear the right clothes, you're accepted."

The Rockers have no desire to be accepted. At truck stops outside London, they sit by the hour rolling cigarettes and jabbering intently about motorcycles. Only when a covey of new cyclists roars into the parking lot do they look up to see "who's got a new bike." Though they all look like Marlon Brando in *The Wild One,* they worry about their reputation as troublemakers, claim gravely: "That film did us a lot of harm." The Rockers do not conceal their disdain for the Mods. "The money we spend tripping around and going places, they spend on clothes," sniffs one. For a Rocker, clothes are strictly functional. "People don't seem to realize that a leather jacket is the warmest thing to wear when riding."

A Mod, by contrast, would rather go naked than don a leather jacket. Mod styles tend toward pastels and velvet, collarless polo shirts with horizontal stripes, and ankle-high "plimsoles" (sneakers) with thick white rubber soles. Mod girls wear no jewelry and no makeup save brown eye shadow and false eyelashes. Hairdos are short; flat shoes are In. Skirts vary from ankle-length to mid-calf.

The fashion Mecca for Mods is Soho's Carnaby Street, where a string of shops offers pink denim shirts, crimson leather vests and blazing red tartan pants for ultra-slicks. Most of the shops are owned by a young entrepreneur named John Stephen, who has whole-heartedly embraced Detroit's idea of planned obsolescence. Pants are pegged one month, bell-bottomed the next. "To the person who keeps up," says one of Stephen's clerks, "style can change every week. But some suits are in style for months."

Top Faces. London's top Mod hangout is an ill-lit, black walled club called The Scene, which boasts 7,000 members; at least 600 can be found dancing there to phonograph music every night. Mods change dances even faster than they change trouser-widths. The "Shake" and the "Bird" are both passé, and only the Rockers would be caught doing the Twist. The current dance craze is something called the "Face Twist," which has a tricky hand and heel movement that resembles a cross between a hula dance and a *High Noon* gun draw. While the Mods are still loyal to the Beatles, they have resurrected Bill Haley, one of the originators of rock 'n' roll, as their idol. "The pop papers said that Bill Haley would never come back," says one Mod. "It just proves they were wrong."

Modland's heroes are called "faces." Top faces right now are Patrick Kerr and Theresa Confrey, a young couple that demonstrates new dances on a popular TV record show, *Ready, Steady, Go*. When they got married last month, Patrick, ever aware of his sartorial responsibilities, wore a curly-brimmed grey bowler, velvet-collared thigh-length jacket and a grey velvet waistcoat. The bride wore a "skinny strapless evening gown." "We don't really like to fight," explained one Mod after the Clacton giggle. "Our clothes cost too much."

Part Six

Stability and Change in Patterns of Dress

THE SOCIAL ORDER exists through time. Changes occur in its cultural patterns and its social organization as individuals act as intermediaries. Although change seems inevitable, the degree and speed of change vary from society to society as does the social value placed on both the general idea of change and on specific changes. In the simple folk society stability instead of change is stressed, for tradition is characteristic in all phases of life. In a complex, industrial society, a strong faith in progress through change permeates all but the most sacred aspects of the society.

The emphasis on tradition or change is often reflected in the dress of the members of each society. In the folk society, patterns of dress may vary only slightly from year to year. In the industrial society, change in patterns of dress occurs swiftly and is often pursued. The general hypothesis concerning change suggested by Bush and London in Part Four is again relevant.

We shall examine tendencies toward stability or change seen in dress and adornment in the light of the following specific socio-cultural factors: custom, law, planned reform movements, culture contact, fashion, and fashion leadership.

Custom

We have chosen to use the term "custom" to describe the coercive socio-cultural force that encourages persistence in dress, whether in total costume or in elements of costume. Examples of persistency are found in traditional dress, survivals, and national dress.

Since stability is generally noticeable in the sacred parts of a culture, the anachronistic character of academic gowns, judicial robes, and church vestments is not surprising. These kinds of garb, derived from the ordinary dress of earlier eras, are symbolic of the value placed by a society on educational, legal, and religious institutions. Utility no longer matters, but symbolic references have been intensified. Stability in the outward appearance gives public notice of the stability of inner beliefs.

Convenient as it may be to label persistent design of dress and ornament as a survival, such a name is probably a misnomer if survival implies that the item in question has outlived its usefulness. In most cases change in function of dress or ornament has occurred. Usually at least some symbolic function remains. Buttons on men's suit cuffs are often cited as survivals, as are the cuffs of men's suits, and pocket flaps where there are no pockets. Conceivably, even in each of these cases a latent aesthetic function survives.

In the Flugel selection, we learn of garment features derived from earlier dress. They are survivals in the sense that they have lost practical utility; on the other hand, as retained, they may serve aesthetic or status functions.

National costumes worn by peasant groups may seem to be encysted for years without apparent change. When law or social coercion prevents copying the dress of the upper strata, national costume serves the psychological purpose of expression within the limits allowed. National costumes may be jealously preserved in order to maintain distinction from a superordinate group that threatens to destroy the way of life of the subordinate society. They visually reinforce group solidarity. National dress may also be an example of changing custom when it is revived by politicians as a symbol of national identity and independence, as is currently true in Nigeria.

Law

Pressures may be brought to bear to preserve existing patterns or to encourage change. Formal legal prescriptions and prohibitions for dress and personal decoration have been used to preserve status distinctions, to protect home industry, and, sometimes, to reinforce moral standards for modesty. Dress regulations have also been used to initiate change as pointed out in the selection on Japan by Nakagawa and Rosovsky in a later section.[1]

Hurlock illustrates how governments throughout the world have for different reasons, at various times, and with usually limited success tried to control consumption of clothing and related ornament by legal decree. Today sumptuary decree by governments is rare, occurring only in instances of extreme emergency such as wartime when textile resources are scarce, or in countries with planned economies and controlled resources.

Planned Reform Movements

The action of organized reform movements is usually directed toward changing patterns of dress or to revival of former ways of dress. Ideal dress for the reformer usually bears descriptions such as healthful, practical, hygienic, or comfortable. Aesthetic attributes may be included, too. Greek and Roman dress, for example, is often held as ideal in beauty as well as in comfort.

Planned reform movements that arise from other than legal sources exhibit strength and exert influence to the degree that their efforts can be organized and legitimized. In 1929 Jordan looked enviously at reform in women's dress as a *fait accompli* and called on men to join the Men's Dress Reform Party that would support men in a similar cause. As befitted the reformer, he recognized how both organization and the support of individuals of prestige would benefit his cause.

[1] See Culture Contact.

Culture Contact

We may examine change in situations of either isolation or culture contact. Change occurs more rapidly and to a greater extent in the latter case. Kingsley Davis stated the argument admirably in this manner: ". . . by the simple process of borrowing, a primitive society may become civilized within a century or so and thus jump across a cultural chasm that took thousands of years to bridge by independent invention." [2]

Because clothing and ornament are easily observable, their forms are readily transmissible to another culture. The techniques for their creation are also communicated rather easily. Symbolism, especially that requiring the help of language, is more difficult to transmit or borrow. Yet much of the symbolism of bodily covering and decoration is reasonably clear without the aid of verbal abstractions. Distinctions of age and sex, for instance, are quickly grasped by most people.

In the give and take of culture contact change generally occurs in both groups concerned, but the direction of flow is likely to be greatest from a superordinate to a subordinate group. The excerpt from Hughes's study of Gambell Eskimos illustrates flow of influence resulting from culture contact. These Eskimos have eagerly accepted ways of dressing from the technologically more advanced societies even if, from the standpoint of utility, their newly acquired ways of dress are inferior. Even when survival is at stake, humans are willing to compromise practical considerations for prestige. In a more extensive treatment of culture contact, Nakagawa and Rosovsky describe the outcome of the mixing of Oriental and Occidental clothing in Japan.

Fashion and Fashion Leadership

Within the general field of collective behavior fashion can be regarded as a special kind of social movement. Like all social movements it is rooted in change, and it functions as individuals and groups make adjustments to cope with the new developments around them. According to Blumer the fashion movement has a unique character:

[2] K. Davis, *Human Society,* New York: Macmillan Co. (1948), pp. 629–630.

The participants are not recruited through agitation or proselyting. No *esprit de corps* or morale is built up among them. Nor does the fashion movement have, or require, an ideology. Further, since it does not have a leadership imparting *conscious* direction to the movement, it does not build up a set of tactics. People participate in the fashion movement voluntarily and in response to the interesting and powerful kind of control which fashion imposes on them.[3]

Paradoxically, as people participate in fashion, they have opportunity to seek satisfaction from two antithetical kinds of expression simultaneously. On the one hand, the way is cleared for individual display of taste. On the other hand, identification with group standards for dress can also be demonstrated since fashion operates only within socially approved limits.

Fashion is observable in many realms other than dress and adornment. Manners, literature, architecture, industrial design, and even science and philosophy, succumb to the power of fashion. But it is fashion in clothing and personal ornament that intrude on the awareness of the public most insistently. Mass media constantly carry fashion's message to an ever growing audience. Television and the press become units in an intricate system of production and promotion of fashion items, and the kinds of mass-media promotion in turn become highly specialized. For example, not only are a number of periodicals specifically devoted to women's and even men's fashions, but these same publications are directed to a particular age or class level. These observations pertain not only to the Western world but to other areas as well. For example, both African and Western fashion coverage in Nigerian newspapers and popular periodicals is frequent and extensive.

Lang and Lang synthesize ideas on fashion from several classic writers. They examine the structural significance of fashion and define terms such as fad, fashion, and style. In addition, they cover the dynamics of fashion change, leadership patterns, and the social-psychological impact of fashion as a means of identification and differentiation within the social system.

Writers in the mass media often point to the influence of fashion leaders. In our modern and changing world, these prestige figures do not

[3] H. Blumer, "Social Movements," in R. E. Park (ed.), *An Outline of the Principles of Sociology*, New York: Barnes and Noble (1939), p. 217.

have dictatorial power, but exert their influence within the wider socio-cultural context. For socio-cultural controls exist which are supported in modern industrial society by a complex of economic relationships which bring together designer, manufacturer, wholesaler, retailer, customer, and producer of mass media in a highly interdependent system. A designer may provide an idea for a new costume and a manufacturer may execute it, but legitimizing of the new idea comes with its acceptance and use by prestige figures and its popularization through person-to-person contact and mass media. However if he is sensitive to trends, the designer may hold a key liaison position between fashion leaders and other customers, and the world of business.

As patterns of leadership exist, they are typically associated with an open-class system, for caste systems ordinarily do not encourage or allow change. It is not only a matter of who innovates, instigates, or introduces change but also of the position of the innovator within the class structure. Both rapid change and change that can be traced through several social levels ensue from social and economic conditions that enable people of the lower classes to emulate those in higher levels, who are in turn "forced" to change again and continue the cycle. Leadership often seems to lie with those who possess scarce and valued attributes or have control of scarce but valued commodities. Personality, appealing appearance, money, speech, family, occupation, political position can all be valued characteristics that in some combination may place an individual in a position of leadership. The leader must also be socially visible if he is to transmit influence. Leadership in fashion is frequently associated with members of the upper classes since those at the higher strata are likely to have access to the social characteristics associated with leadership. However, change in fashion can be stimulated by members of a lower stratum or a marginal group. For example, note the emulation of the worker's blue jeans or the beatnik's sandals by all classes.

Three types of leaders, traditional, legal, and charismatic, as classified by Max Weber,[4] can be found as influential on fashion and style. *Traditional* leaders still exist among members of royal families. *Legal* leadership is exercised by those occupying positions created by legal statute. Although their official leadership does not embrace sartorial realms, the

[4] M. Weber, *Essays in Sociology,* translated and edited by H. H. Gerth and C. W. Mills, New York: Oxford University Press (1946), pp. 78–79.

prestige of office may cast the role of fashion leadership on the legal official and members of his family, as in the case of the American president. *Charismatic* leaders, who draw attention to themselves on other than traditional or legal grounds, include a colorful group of individuals, ranging from the royal mistresses, demimondes, and dandies of yesteryear to stage, television, movie, and sports personalities of today.

Hurlock presents a description of fashion leaders which lends itself to analysis according to the Weberian categories outlined above. She gives examples of traditional leaders, by citing examples from royalty; of legal leaders, by citing the influence of American presidents and their families; and of charismatic leaders, by referring to the "uncrowned leaders of society." Each category can be updated by substituting current holders of these positions.

In the early nineteenth century Beau Brummel colorfully exemplified the charismatic leader. As he rejected the opulence and extravagance of the court costume of the pre-French revolution period and stressed restraint, conservatism, and exquisite concern for details of tailoring and grooming, he set a new picture for male fashions. Although Brummel himself did not find gainful employment compatible with the status of fashion leader he coveted, his costume symbolized the growing association of Western man with occupational roles.

American men, even the wealthy who can afford the life of the idle rich, have become increasingly drawn to occupational roles as an acceptable means of gaining prestige. With occupational roles central in their lives, men no longer have the leisure, even if they have the economic resources, to participate in fashion competition. The sober trends of nineteenth-century Western male fashions accompanied the transfer of fashion leadership to women. And women have continued to participate in fashion display and competition to the degree that they have retained the leisure necessary for such activity.

The trend toward increased employment of women in the twentieth-century leads to interesting speculation. As it becomes increasingly respectable and prestigious for a woman to be employed, she has less time to devote to dress and grooming. Simplicity and conservatism in dress along with greater concern for details in grooming seem to be growing trends in women's dress. Perhaps the dress of Mrs. Jacqueline Kennedy has been symbolic of woman's new role. "Understatement," as applied to

Mrs. Kennedy's dress may portend the same kind of change in women's clothing that perfection of dress portended for men a century ago.[5]

Supplementary Readings

Statements concerning stability and change in patterns of dress are included in the general works cited at the end of Part One. Other references are Allen (1931), Barber and Lobel (1952), Barr (1934), Bergler (1953), Blumer (1964), Bogardus (1924A), G. H. Darwin (1872), Flower (1892), Franzero (1958), Freudenberger (1963), S. O. Goodman (1964), Gorsline (1962), Gregory (1947A, 1948), Hurlock (1929A), Jack and Schiffer (1948), Janney (1941), Kandel (1962), Katz and Lazarsfeld (1955), Kroeber (1919), Lam (1938), Lerner (1957), Lynes (1951), Meyersohn and Katz (1957), Minnich (1963), Richardson and Kroeber (1940), Riegel (1963), Robinson (1958, 1959, 1961, 1963A, 1963B), Roshco (1963), Russell (1892), Sapir (1931), Simmel (1904), Sumner (1907), Veblen (1899), Vincent (1931), and Young (1937).

---

[5] After writing the above comments on fashion, we were pleased to read Professor Blumer's paper ("The Nature and Role of Fashion," 1964) which develops and considerably expands very similar ideas. Unfortunately the paper was not available for inclusion at this time. When published, it will be a "must" for students of fashion.

Custom

⚘ The Evolution of Garments

JOHN C. FLUGEL

The dress of modern men, though far from being entirely 'fixed', approximates, as we have seen, to this condition much more than does that of women. . . . We propose to use men's dress as a field for the investigation of one particular aspect of clothes evolution—an aspect to which Sir George Darwin drew special attention in his original contribution to the subject.

We know that natural selection, working upon the material provided by the spontaneous variation of living forms, moulds a race by allowing greater chances of survival to those who vary from the parent forms in a certain direction, the survivors then tending, in virtue of the laws of heredity, to hand on their peculiarity to their successors. In this process of evolution, variations in some directions help towards survival, while variations in other directions have no such value, and therefore do not tend to be perpetuated (except in so far as they may be biologically correlated with variations of the first kind). It thus comes about that evolution changes some parts of the bodily structure more than others; those parts which are not subject to essential or to correlated variations in the above sense tend to remain in their original condition. In this way, certain parts of the body may, so to speak, lag behind in the course of evolution, and may even persist when, through changes of other parts of the body, they have lost their original usefulness. They may thus become vestigial organs; and, as is well known, biologists can sometimes explain the nature and original function of a particular organ by reference to the past history of the race, even though this organ appears to have no present

Source: The Psychology of Clothes, London: Hogarth Press and The Institute of Psychoanalysis (1930), pp. 172–180. Reprinted by permission of Hogarth Press and Humanities Press.

use. So it is with clothes. The clothes we wear, especially the clothes of men, have many vestigial features, features which have no utility at present, but which can be shown to have been useful in the past. In some cases it is possible to trace, with a high degree of certainty, how these features originally came about and what purpose they originally served. In other cases their origin is still a matter of conjecture.

Let us consider a few examples, passing gradually from the easy to the more difficult.[1]

Men's tail-coats contain two buttons at the back. These buttons serve no purpose nowadays. They are survivals of a past when horses rather than motor-cars or railways were the principal means of conveyance. When a man was riding, it was often convenient to draw up the tails of his coat so that they did not come into too close contact with the flanks of the horse, and these two buttons are survivals from a time when buttons in this position were actually of use for this purpose. There are many other examples of this kind. Top-boots (other than 'Russian boots') usually have a part that is turned down at the top, this part often being made of different material from the rest of the boots and having a different colour. It is now a part that is purely ornamental, and has no useful function. But it is a survival from the time when the upper part of top-boots could actually be turned up to cover more of the leg when it was so desired. The tags by which top-boots were formerly pulled on still survive, but are again, for the most part, merely ornamental. They can often be seen at the side of the boots, but are now sometimes actually sewn down and are therefore completely useless; so useless, in fact, that in some boots new tags have been inserted in the side of the boot to take the place of the old ones which have lost their function. There exist several rather similar cases of the transition from the useful to the ornamental. The cuffs that ornament the sleeves of coats are now, for the most part, fixed and serve merely as decoration, but in former times coat-sleeves could often be turned back in order to display the highly ornamented sleeve of an inner garment.

In the case of trousers, we ourselves have in recent years had the opportunity to observe such a transition actually taking place. Men found that it was convenient to turn up the bottom of their trousers to prevent them getting muddy. To begin with, this was only regarded as a temporary measure, and the trousers were turned down again when the wearer came indoors from the muddy streets. But now, for a good many years, trousers

[1] Most of these examples are taken from the rich collection of Webb, 103.

have been made of which the ends are permanently turned up and cannot be turned down at all; so that the turned-up portion here has similarly become purely ornamental.

These examples illustrate a very general rule in the evolution of clothes, namely, that what was originally useful was later on retained for the sake of ornament.

Just one more example of this kind. The collars of men's coats usually have a small nick or cut-out portion at the point that divides the collar from the lapels. This obviously serves no present purpose, but it also can be shown to be a survival from the past when it had a function. At one time it was customary to turn up the back of the collar without turning up the lapel. Now the only way in which this could be done was by having a deep nick between the two. The present nicks are not deep enough to serve this function. They have, therefore, lost their usefulness, and are perhaps in process of disappearance, for they have already vanished from the dinner-jacket and have, for the most part, entirely vanished from waistcoats, though these formerly also had small collars with nicks in them.

This last fact, that the waistcoat had a collar and that this collar has a vestigial feature showing that the collar could be turned up, serves to remind us that the waistcoat itself is the relic of an outer garment, the upper part of which could be raised so as to protect the back of the neck. What was originally an outer garment has, in this case, become an inner garment; and this, in turn, illustrates an interesting feature to which historians of dress have drawn attention, namely, that when a new garment is adopted, there is a tendency for it to be put on over the old garment. This tendency has probably played an important part in the development of dress. Just as particular features of dress are slow to disappear, so also are individual garments themselves, which may persist even under circumstances that one would expect to lead to their disappearance. Sometimes, as here, an older garment is not displaced, but merely covered (a process analogous to that which psychoanalysis has shown to take place in the course of mental development). The significance of this tendency for the history of clothing as a whole lies largely in the fact that it leads to an increase in the number of layers, one above the other, of which a costume may consist.[2]

If in many instances of the development of dress the useful persists as

[2] Though of course it is very far from being true that all inner garments or underclothes were originally outer garments.

the merely ornamental, in some cases an ornamental feature may be developed in order to hide a utilitarian one. Thus it would appear that the clocks on socks and stockings represent a form of decoration that was originally designed to cover the seams with which stockings were then made, and which were regarded as unsightly. A particularly interesting example concerns the stripes that have in recent years been introduced down the sides of men's dress trousers. This seems to be in the nature of a reversion, such as is sometimes to be observed in the biological sphere also, when a particular individual will revert to characteristics that distinguished the race many generations ago. At one time trousers were made so tight that they had to be provided with buttons up the sides, which could be undone when the trousers were drawn on. These buttons later became hidden by a stripe. The stripe persisted after the buttons had disappeared (when no longer needed owing to the increased width of the trousers). In time the stripe itself vanished, but of late years, in an endeavour to make somewhat more ornamental the sombre black of evening trousers, tailors have resuscitated the stripe—thus harking back to a form of decoration which itself arose in the first place to hide a purely useful feature.

In some cases the gradual evolution of a garment may involve very great changes, so that its origin may only be detected in some small vestigial feature. This seems to be the case with that military equivalent of the tophat, the busby. The busby originally belonged to the Hussars, who were Hungarian soldiers and wore the peasant cap of Hungary. . . . It consisted of a cloth cap with a band of fur round the edge, itself originally, it would appear, part of a fur lining, the bottom end of which was turned up, thus showing the fur. Gradually the fur on the cap became wider and wider and the cloth part grew smaller and smaller. In many forms of the busby, the original shape of the hat . . . has completely disappeared. The only trace of its origin is to be found in the fact that the top of the busby is (or, at any rate, was) made of cloth instead of fur, but in one form of the busby—that worn by the Honourable Artillery Company—a vestige of the original shape is still to be detected in the small flap that hangs down at the side. . . .

Sometimes the retention of a vestigial feature may be due, or at least be attributed (such stories often contain legendary elements) to some particular event, which has given this feature a new value. A striking instance of this is the flash of the Royal Welch Fusiliers. Let Robert Graves, who served in that regiment, tell the story: 'The flash is a fan-like bunch of five black ribbons, each ribbon two inches wide and seven and a half inches long: the angle at which the fan is spread is exactly regulated by regimental convention. It is stitched to the back of the tunic collar. Only the Royal Welch are privileged to wear it. The story is that the Royal Welch were abroad on foreign service for several years in the 1830's and, by some chance, never received the army order abolishing the queue. When the regiment returned and paraded at Plymouth, the inspecting general rated the commanding officer because his men were still wearing their hair in the old fashion. The commanding officer, angry with the slight, immediately rode up to London and won from King William IV, through the intercession of some court official, the regimental privilege of continuing to wear the bunch of ribbons in which the end of the queue was tied—the 'flash.'[3] During the Great War there was a prolonged and obstinate struggle between the regiment and the Army Council, who saw in the flash a distinctive target for enemy marksmen. Nevertheless, the officers and warrant officers continued to wear it—with, it is said, the privately expressed approval of the King himself, who was Colonel-in-Chief of the regiment; and in 1919 the flash was officially sanctioned on service dress for all ranks, together with permission to retain another definite regimental peculiarity, the spelling of the word 'Welch' with a 'c'.

In all these cases the main outlines of development are fairly clear. But, as I said, there are other cases in which we can only surmise the course of evolution. The ornamental markings on boots and shoes, especially those markings which take the form of small perforations through a portion of the leather, have given rise to much conjecture. These markings are of great antiquity and can be traced to Roman times and even earlier. It has been suggested that the earliest shoemakers contented themselves with tying a piece of leather roughly round the foot. This would necessarily give rise to awkward puckers in the leather, puckers which could perhaps best be dealt with by the simple process of cutting them away. This would of course leave open slits in the shoe of a kind that are actually observable in some primitive examples to be found in museums; slits which probably became ornamental and gave rise to the vestigial features that still adorn so many of our own boots and shoes.

We saw in a previous chapter that ornaments loosely hung round the

[3] *Good-bye to All That*, p. 119.

body were probably worn earlier than actual clothes. When clothes were adopted they tended to cover these ornaments; and in some cases the ornaments themselves, so that they should not be unnoticed altogether, have come to be symbolically represented on the clothes. . . . This may possibly be the case with the stripes that ornament the sleeves of military and naval uniforms, stripes which perhaps originally represented bracelets such as were conferred on Roman soldiers as a reward for valour.

Interesting problems arise in certain cases as to why a given article of clothing or adornment should be worn on one side of the body rather than on the other. Plumes and feathers in hats are, I believe, nearly always worn upon the left side. This has been thought to be connected with the fact that plumes were often worn when fighting, and that a plume on the right side of the head would be likely to interfere with, or be damaged by, the free play of the sword.

A more difficult problem is presented by the fact that the buttons on men's garments are usually on the right-hand side, those of women's on the left. The true origin of this difference seems to be shrouded in obscurity. It has been suggested, however, that the practice may be connected with the desire to leave the right hand free in the case of the man, in order that he might hold his sword or implement, and the left hand free in the case of the woman. A woman, when buttoning up, would, it is supposed, grasp her attire with her right hand and push it over to the left, leaving her left arm free to carry a child. It is usual to carry children on the left arm (doubtless to leave the stronger right arm free for other purposes), and among many peoples children are, it is said, allowed to suck the left breast more than the right. The left side of a bodice could, if the right lapped over it, be pulled back without exposing so much of the person as would be necessary in the opposite case, and the garment could be afterwards replaced more easily with the right hand if this alone were free. These last explanations are, as I have said, little more than surmises. It is quite possible that the difference between the sexes in this matter of buttons has some other and more general meaning: for in folk-lore and superstition one very often finds that the right side has a masculine significance and the left side a feminine one, and it may very well be that the factors underlying these superstitions have played a part also in this particular instance of sex differentiation.

These examples of the detailed problems presented by the evolution of dress will suffice to show that, not only in its general lines is our costume determined by its past history, but that its smaller and more insignificant details also are, in many cases, in the nature of vestiges, comparable to the organs of similar nature that we carry in our body. To produce a new design or a new form of ornament is always a matter requiring thought and inspiration. It is easier and more comfortable to fall back upon conventional patterns, and tailors have no exemption from the laws of mental inertia. In sartorial evolution, as in the evolution of living forms, it often happens that only the more essential features are changed in the process of adaptation to fresh conditions; the others may remain unchanged, as witnesses to a state that is long past. The degree of antiquity may, as we have seen, vary very greatly. In some cases the ancestry of a sartorial detail is a relatively short one: in other cases our ornaments may still bear testimony to man's first fumbling efforts to encase his body; or, again, they may imitate decorations which, in their original form, were not strictly sartorial in type at all. Always, however, it is the fact that the products of such efforts have become conventionalised as ornaments that has allowed of their survival long after their utilitarian value had disappeared. Analogous cases of an organ acquiring a new function in the course of its vestigial history are not perhaps unknown to biological science. Certainly, they are common enough in anthropology, which teaches us that ancient rites and customs may be continued for new reasons when the old ones have been lost.

In other cases we see the exemplification of a further important general tendency, namely, that many ornamental details are, in their origin, not so much the successors as the accompaniments of utilitarian features. Here, as in other fields of applied art, human beings are seldom contented with the merely useful. Students of aesthetics may point out that the useful in itself tends also to be beautiful; but mankind as a whole, especially at the more primitive levels of development, has but little realisation or understanding of this principle. Men consequently seek to disguise the purely useful by ornamental features, and, as before, these features may persist long after the natural death of the originally useful features which they were designed to hide or mitigate.

We have seen also how conservatism may lead to the multiplication of actual garments; the old is not necessarily discarded or displaced, but may be merely covered. Finally, we have seen that the details of our clothes sometimes undergo reversions to a more primitive type. Even when we seek the new it is often easier to retrace old paths than to track out new ones. As in the sphere of biology (as cases of atavism show) or in that of psychology (as is shown by the phenomenon of regression, the importance of which has been so startlingly revealed by psycho-pathology), we seldom completely outgrow our own past, which is always ready to reassert itself if opportunity should offer.

Law

✾ Sumptuary Law

ELIZABETH B. HURLOCK

Class Distinctions

Where an aristocratic form of government prevailed, there seemed to be a strong tendency for fashions to remain stationary over long periods of time. The upper classes saw to it that there were "sumptuary laws" passed to prevent social inferiors from copying their clothing or manner of living. In a feudal society where the line of demarcation between classes was strictly drawn, the nobility displayed its superiority by abstaining from any form of productive labor. But as trade and commerce increased, and as the towns became the centers of wealth, the feudal lords found competition in the wealthy middle class, and, as a consequence were forced to set a new standard of differentiation. This took the form of conspicuous expenditure of money, rather than abstinence from work. Commercial aristocracies soon grew up in the different trading centers of Europe, and these set a new standard of luxury of living quite unknown in feudal days. The merchants who were princes in wealth, rather than by birth, were able, on account of their wealth, to outstrip the true nobility. Extravagance became so universal that the Church and Crown thought it necessary to put some check on the ostentatious display of the newly rich.

Sumptuary Laws

Accordingly, in the past, almost all nations used sumptuary laws to moderate the expenditure of private citizens of the lesser nobility or

Source: The Psychology of Dress, New York: Ronald Press Co. (1929), pp. 62–70. Reprinted by permission of the publisher.

bourgeoisie. While these were aimed primarily at extravagant expenditure on dress, they were not limited to it. They were often used to curb the so-called "ruinous extravagance" in connection with banquets, household decorations, and funerals. In ancient Greece and Rome, especially, they related more to the general mode of living than to dress. The Lex Orchia, for instance, was passed in Rome in the year 187 B.C. as a means of limiting the number of guests who might appear at a feast; the Lex Fannia, passed in 161 B.C., regulated the cost of entertainments.

During the reign of Edward III of England, a law prohibited more than two courses at dinner or supper, or more than two kinds of food at each course except on the principal festival days, when three courses were allowed. This applied to all people, regardless of rank or wealth. In France, by an edict of Charles VI, no one was permitted to have more than a soup and two dishes at dinner. Frederick the Great tried to suppress the use of coffee as a harmful luxury. From the seventeenth to the nineteenth centuries burial in woolen was prescribed by law, in England, as a means of lessening the importance of linen.

Purposes of Sumptuary Laws

Sumptuary laws were used primarily to preserve class distinctions. When members of the nobility found their position of supremacy encroached upon by the lower classes who had attained wealth, they passed laws to restore the respect for the inequality of ranks which had previously existed. How strong was this feeling of jealous propriety can well be illustrated by an historical incident connected with the wife of Philippe le Bel. When, as a bride, the queen made her triumphal entry into Bruges, in the year 1301, and when the whole population had turned out in festive attire to greet her, she is said to have exclaimed in indignation, "I thought I was the Queen, but I see there are hundreds."

Sumptuary laws were often used as a means of inducing people to save money. When nations were constantly engaged in wars, it was necessary to take precautions lest the mad extravagance of the people, and their senseless sacrifices on clothing and other luxuries, lead the country into bankruptcy. This was especially true in France and England during the seventeenth and eighteenth centuries, when people of small fortunes were ruining themselves in their attempt to copy the nobility.

From an economic point of view, sumptuary laws were very valuable as a means of encouraging domestic trade. The craze for foreign fashions has often led to the destruction of native industries and the unemployment of thousands of workers. An excellent example of this occurred during the sixteenth century when velvet caps, made from material coming from Italy and France, were the stylish headgear for men. To encourage home production, England passed a law compelling all persons over six years of age, except those of high position, to wear woolen caps, made in England, on Sundays and all holy days. This law remained in effect for twenty-six years and was very powerful in building up the English woolen industries.

Universality of Sumptuary Laws

How universal sumptuary laws were, is never fully appreciated until one begins to investigate the question. In almost every nation where any class distinctions were recognized, these laws appear at a time when the social structure has reached a stage of development where the national wealth is no longer in the hands of the nobility alone. Among primitive peoples, where the social development is rather slight, there are few instances of laws of this kind. The Chiochas forbade the common people to paint or decorate their bodies, while the Kaffirs punished severely any members of the lower classes who attempted to ornament themselves like their social superiors. In ancient Peru, the lower classes could not use gold or silver in any form except with the permission of the government.

In Greece and Rome. Ancient Greece and Rome had their sumptuary laws. According to the laws of Solon, Greek women might wear only three garments at one time, and the amount of money spent was regulated by the wealth of the family. In Rome, where the color and material of the clothing served to denote rank, laws were passed restricting the peasantry to one color, officers to two colors, commanders to three colors, and members of the royal household to seven colors. At the time of the Emperor Aurelian, men were not permitted to wear yellow, white, red or green shoes; these were reserved exclusively for women. Only ambassadors to foreign lands might wear gold rings, and men were strictly forbidden to wear silk garments of any sort.

From Rome, the custom of using sumptuary laws to curb extravagance was spread to northern Europe. In Ireland, before the Christian era, laws relating to the use of color by different ranks, were exactly the same as the Roman laws. One of the earliest French sumptuary laws related to the length of the toes of shoes, which stipulated that a Prince might wear points no longer than twenty-four inches while the poorer classes were limited to six inches. Under the rule of Philippe le Bel, only members of the royal household were permitted to wear miniver grey fur or ermine, while in the fifteenth century laws had to be passed to keep the clergy from wearing colored gloves.

In France. Charles IX was responsible for more sumptuary laws than any other French monarch. According to these, silks might be worn only by princesses and duchesses; ladies of high rank alone were permitted to carry muffs of fur or fine materials; the amount and quality of ornamentation of clothing was regulated according to the rank of the wearer; and the width of the farthingale was limited to one and one-half yards. These laws continued in effect until the Fall of the Bastille, when one of the first acts of the General Assembly was to abolish by solemn decree all laws relating to distinction in dress.

In England. In England, the first sumptuary laws came in the reign of Edward III. These decreed that ermine and pearls, except for headdresses, might be worn only by members of the royal family and those nobles whose income exceeded one thousand pounds. The tyrannical Henry VIII decreed that a countess must wear a train before and behind, fastened to her girdle, while a baroness and all below her in rank might not have this distinction. Men were compelled to wear their hair short, though their beards might be worn in any fashion they wished.

While Queen Elizabeth was an ardent devotee of fashion, she was very autocratic concerning the clothing of her people. One of her decrees was that "no great ruff should be worn, nor any white color, in doublet or hosen, nor any facing of velvet in gowns, but by such as were of the bench. That no gentlemen should walk in the streets in their cloaks, but in gowns. That no curled or long hair be worn, nor any gown but such as be made of sad color." She attempted to regulate the shape and length of men's beards, and to prohibit the students and faculty of Oxford from wearing ruffs around the neck and wrists of a width greater than that of one finger. James I, who followed Elizabeth, repealed all of these laws on the grounds that a high cost of living was advantageous to the commerce and trade of a nation.

In America. Americans have not always enjoyed the liberty in dress which they now insist upon. In the early Colonial days, America had her share of sumptuary laws, most of which were found in Puritan New England. Massachusetts prohibited the wearing of silver, gold and silk laces, slashed sleeves, ruffs, and beaver hats, on the ground that "excess of apparel among us is unbecoming to a wilderness condition and the professions of the gospel." While New Jersey was still a British colony, a law was passed which stated that "all women, of whatever age, rank, profession or degree, whether virgins, maids or widows, who shall after this act impose upon, seduce, or betray into matrimony any of his Majesty's subjects, by virtue of scents, cosmetics, washes, paints, artificial teeth, false hair, or high-heeled shoes, shall incur the penalty of the law now in force against witchcraft and like misdemeanors."

In Japan. Japan has produced the strictest sumptuary laws which the world has ever seen. These laws dictated how everyone should dress, work, speak, walk, sit, or even pray. Every class of Japanese society came under these laws and every provincial governor was required to enforce them. A farmer, for example, whose income was approximately $500 a year, could build a house sixty feet long, but no room of this house could contain an alcove, nor could tiles be used on the roof without special permission. No member of his family could wear garments of silk and even if his daughter should marry a man who was permitted to wear silk, the bridegroom was requested not to wear it at the wedding ceremony. If the farmer's income was only $100, the members of his family could not wear leather sandals, but had to content themselves with sandals of straw or wood with cotton straps. Sun-shades or paper umbrellas were prohibited to the lower classes, who had to protect themselves with straw raincoats or large straw hats.

While sumptuary laws may foster, in people whose lives are affected, a tendency to stand still and to be content with the position forced upon them, more often the desire for self-expression seeks an outlet in other fields.

Other Forms of Display

In the feudal days of the Middle Ages, when society was divided into two classes, the rulers and the ruled, and when the poorer classes were unable to imitate the leaders, the desire for display did not die out. Rather it took a different form in each case. The rulers turned their attention to lavish entertainment as a means of asserting their superiority. A Hungarian nobleman during the thirteenth century celebrated his son's wedding for an entire year, during which time he spent untold amounts of money in giving lavish entertainment. William of Orange, is said to have entertained, at one time, guests who brought with them 5,647 horses, while he himself already had a thousand mounted horsemen to provide for. During the visit the horses consumed 4,000 bushels of wheat, 8,000 of rye, 11,300 of oats, while the guests (in addition to the food eaten) drank 3,600 barrels of wine and 1,600 of beer.

Among the members of the lower classes, the desire for self-display was expressed through the development of a national costume, restricted in its use to them. Instead of attempting to imitate the clothing of the upper classes, gratification came from trying to outrival in beauty and elaborateness, the costumes of the other members of the same social class. In this way, the desire to be different was satisfied without in any way overstepping the line which divided one social class from another.

Evasion of Sumptuary Laws

However, this simple way of solving the problem did not last long. When wealth began to spread to the lower classes, means of evading the laws were soon devised. During the fourteenth century, for example, when costumes were elaborately decorated with hand work, the women of the lower classes learned to embroider so that they might increase the elegance of their costumes without at the same time infringing on the law which limited them in the amount of money which they might spend. When muffs were in fashion, the ladies of the French court chose ones made of sable and other costly furs. The ladies of the middle class, who were limited to muffs costing not more than twenty livres, soon discovered that catskin and dogskin looked so nearly like the good furs that, at a distance, few could tell the difference. They thus appeared on the streets carrying muffs that few could distinguish from those of the great ladies.

Discontent and Rebellion

Nor was discontent bordering on open rebellion an unheard of thing when sumptuary laws became too stringent. The Chinese people were aroused to great fury and open rebellion when ordered by their Tartar conquerors to cut off their hair as a sign of servitude. In many cases they preferred to lose their heads rather than lose their hair. When the Spanish prime minister, in the eighteenth century, attempted to abolish the sombrero, which had become a part of the national costume, a rebellion arose which resulted in the banishment of the prime minister. Queen Elizabeth's stern enforcement of her clothing edicts brought about a great deal of ill-feeling against the crown, and during the next reign all such laws were abolished to avoid open rebellion. The feeling, in France, against sumptuary laws was so bitter that after the Revolution it was unsafe to appear in clothing which might proclaim the wearer as belonging to the nobility.

During the last century, the Turks decreed that Greek and Armenian women might not wear skirts as long as they were accustomed to. Turkish officers, whose main duty was to trim off the skirts to the prescribed length, were stationed in each town. In addition to this, all Greek subjects were forced to wear dark caps as a sign of servitude; Armenian subjects, balloon-shaped headdresses; Jews, brimless caps like inverted flower pots, and the Turks, a red fez in place of the large turban, as a token of faithfulness to their Sultan. Resistance closely approximating civil war was the result. People set fire to the houses of those who were willing to accept the change and terrorized them if they appeared on the streets in the new costumes. For several years the discontent raged at a high pitch and it was only checked through military aid and brutal punishment.

Planned Reform Movements

Healthy Dress for Men
ALFRED C. JORDAN

Man, is, by nature, an unclothed animal; uncivilized man is naked today. When man was evolved from lower mammalian forms, he must have inhabited tropical regions. He lost his fur (or most of it), having no need for its warmth and protection.

When man's realms spread to temperate and cold regions, he sought warmth and comfort by wearing the skins of beasts—trophies of his skill as a huntsman—and he wrapped himself round with these. But warmth was not the first purpose of clothing; nor was "decency." The first purpose of clothing was adornment. Among wild peoples we find painting and tattooing even prior to clothes.

Some reformers in every country believe that man would be better off—both physically and morally—without clothes, allowing sun and air to play freely on his skin; placing absolute trust in the wonderful faculty of the skin for regulating temperature, and letting the skin carry out its important functions as an organ of excretion and a subsidiary organ of respiration—functions denied it by the masses of material under which men are in the habit of burying the skin. Point has been added to this argument by the recent discovery that the skin manufactures vitamin D—the antirachitic vitamin—when the sun's rays are allowed to act upon it.

The skin of an average overclothed civilized man is white, spotty and inelastic; the skin of a healthy man is brown, smooth and sleek.

Source: *American Medicine*, Vol. 35 (December, 1929), pp. 803–806.

Let us assume that in our climate, clothes are necessary; a necessary evil, if you will. Well, then, they should be as scanty as feasible. Thruout the Victorian era, men and women were grossly overclothed. What with Mrs. Grundy and Mrs. Gamp it became "indecent" to let any part of the human form be visible in public except the face and—on some occasions—the hands.

In "The Corner of Harley St.," Dr. H. H. Bashford says:

"If you cover up anything long enough, and refer to it slyly enough, you can be certain in the end of making its exposure indecent. If gloves became *'de rigueur'* for a couple of centuries, we should raise prurient titters at the mention of a knuckle. No, it's air and sunlight and the salt of a bracing sanity in these matters that is our crying need."

Women have abandoned that foolish attitude to their own immense gain. Men have only now begun to do so, and they have begun in a halfhearted way, and for sports only. For tennis, it is no longer "indecent" for a man to bare his arms—and his "Adam's apple," but he still fears to show his knees! I have played tennis in flannel "shorts" for several years, on public and private courts; nothing would persuade me to revert to trousers. Recently I played tennis wearing only a bathing slip; this in a mixed company of men, women and children. The question of "decency" did not arise; why should it? The absolute freedom of movement was most exhilarating and delightful; not least owing to the bare feet (on a grass court); it was a revelation to feel the toes doing their duty for once; the feet no longer lifeless props, but live and active members; each toe, well separated from its fellows, thrusting into the ground with every quick change of direction, aiding the speed and accuracy of each change.

An Englishman, recently returned from China, told me that the tennis club there had a rule making it compulsory for all players to wear shoes; I asked, in surprise, whether any player wished to wear boots, but he told me I had missed the point of the rule, which was to prevent Chinamen from playing barefoot, for they were so fleet that the Englishmen could not stay the pace, and found it necessary to handicap them in this way!

For bathing, too, a bathing slip is obviously the right and proper dress for a man. A "costume" which covers chest, abdomen and back is a chilling affair when wet, especially in a breeze; moreover, it prevents the sun's rays from reaching the skin, and thus deprives the bather of an essential part of the health value of his bath.

Holiday Wear

This year, many men have adopted a really healthy and sensible dress for their holiday. They have worn a tennis shirt and a pair of shorts and shoes. Some have added stockings, and on cool days a jacket or pull-over. Undoubtedly they have gained much in health and well-being thru dressing sensibly. But on their return to town—and to work—they have once more assumed their stuffy, ugly and unhealthy work-a-day clothes; reluctantly enough in most cases. The indictment against man's conventional dress has been told so often of late, that I need not enter into detail; no self-respecting man should continue to wear clothes that are dirty yet cannot be washed; clothes that compel profuse sweating, yet are so tightly applied round the neck and round the ankles that the heat and damp cannot escape. Man's evening dress is the perfect model of an unhealthy and unsuitable attire. Consider a man's plight at a dance, and contrast it with a woman's in her light and cool frock. He wears his coat and trousers for years and never has them washed; if they were white instead of black, he could not wear them two nights without having them washed. And then the "boiled shirt"! A horrible invention! And more horrible still, the starched collar, that grows limp after the first dance, and needs to be changed at frequent intervals during the evening.

The Unhygienic Doctor

Surgeons, in the operating theatre, set a fine example of hygienic perfection of cleanliness, yet they visit their patients in the conventional black that typifies "the doctor." They go from one patient to another without change of raiment. I wonder how much infectious disease they carry about with them!

The Remedy

As my friend, Dr. C. W. Saleeby puts it, "The dinner table, the drawing-room and the ball-room accept a standard of uncleanness which would never be tolerated on the tennis court or the cricket field."

To quote another friend and colleague, Dr. Leonard Williams:

Man still wears thick socks, woolen vest and long pants, and a shirt over which he places the ordinary coat, waistcoat and trousers which have been '*de rigueur*' for about a century. The weight of this assemblage of garments usually amounts to half a stone or more. The only men who are dressed in accordance with common sense are the athletes, but for ordinary purposes a man contents himself with a kit, inherited from his forbears, which is fantastic in its unsuitability. He wears a stupid costume as a matter of routine, and a sensible one on rare occasions only.

What, then, is the remedy? To wear sporting dress on all occasions? To report at the office in tennis or football kit, or in Scouts attire? Hygienically, nothing is wrong with the suggestion, but the esthetic side must be considered; an employer does not readily credit his clerks with a strong desire to "make good" and to further his interests if they come to work in sporting kit. Their thoughts must (he tells himself) be anywhere except on their jobs! And I think he is right! Slack and untidy dress does not conduce to keen and good work. But one can concede so much without admitting the need to perpetuate the objectionable clothes of convention. Far from it! Instead, let us take the sports models as our foundation, and build up, from these models, stylish and well-made garments of high-class materials and first-rate finish. Garments that will remove forever the reproach of drabness, dirtiness and unhealthiness from men's clothes.

My own plan (until something better is evolved) is to wear a suit consisting of lounge coat, shorts and stockings, all made to match, with shirt of rayon, suitably colored to tone with the suit. The shirt is open at the neck and needs no tie. Recently I have had other shirts made, so designed that they can be worn with or without a tie, and either over or under the coat collar. The shorts are tailored to "sit upon" the hips, so they need neither belt nor braces. Consequently, on a hot day, the coat can be removed, displaying the neat, silky shirt; no ugly waistcoat or braces. The lounge coat is not really a satisfactory garment; it is heavy and unshapely and needs padding and stiffening to keep it presentable. Some form of "jumper" would be far better.

The Men's Dress Reform Party

When women feel dissatisfied with their clothes, why, they try something different, and then go on changing from year to year without asking leave of their men-folks, altho, more often than not, it is they (the men) who "foot the bill."

Men, on the other hand, are timid creatures, fearful of defying convention and thus inviting chaff. Dissatisfied as they are with their clothes, few men have courage to change their style of dress.

Consequently, it is necessary to create a big organization to enable men to take united action. The manifesto in which the formation of the Men's Dress Reform Party was announced (in June) was signed by distinguished representatives of various professions and at once created worldwide interest. The letters that poured in to headquarters were full of enthusiasm and came from all parts of the world. Already visible results are forthcoming in the form of increasing popularity of the open-fronted shirt, and shorts for cycling, tennis and country wear. Lighter and brighter materials are beginning to be selected. In fact, an atmosphere favorable to reform has been created and will, inevitably culminate in a considerable amelioration in the plight of poor, overclothed and suffocated man. Hitherto, membership has been free to all; but it has now been decided to impose a subscription of 2/6 annually. Application should be made to the Hon. Secretary at 39 Bedford Square, London, W. C. 1.

It is often said that hygienic attire is suitable for summer, but too chilly for winter; that bare knees and open throats cause rheumatism and pneumonia. The fact is, however, that long-continued persistence in overclothing lowers resistance; so does overeating and especially *wrong* feeding. Most men who are engaged upon sedentary work eat far more than their digestive apparatus can deal with. And they feed wrongly; they eat far too much meat, sugar and starch and take not nearly enough "live" foods, such as fresh fruits and salads, whole-meal bread and milk, butter and cream. Chronic intestinal stasis is the great cause of rheumatic troubles, and it produces this unpleasant result by allowing putrefaction to go on in the intestines, with resulting toxemia and infection of the tissues. Live hygienically, and feed correctly, and you may defy the bogey of "colds" and "rheumatics." I have worn shorts and open shirt for the last three years and have been free from all complaints. I have never felt a desire to cover up my knees on account of cold, tho I have been glad to add a woolly cardigan and warm gloves in winter, and a wrap when the wind has blown chill.

All Must Join the Crusade

Let every man help on the good cause by joining the M.D.R.P. and planning concerted action with others in his district. In this way rapid progress is assured; such as will shortly render the continued existence of the "Party" unnecessary.

Culture Contact

❀ Changes in Eskimo Clothing
CHARLES CAMPBELL HUGHES

The desire for new, white man's style of clothing, especially for children, is a widespread culture pattern. On Christmas and the Fourth of July, holidays that are important to the Gambell people, many sport a new outfit. There is much money spent for clothing, especially through the large mail-order houses, but often a particular article is the wrong size, so that it soon wears out or is discarded. In addition, the cheapness of items is one of the most important factors considered in buying—but the cheaper clothing does not have the quality of long wear.

Other items purchased are radios, watches and clocks, toys (the store's order of expensive Christmas toys was very quickly sold out), toy pistol caps for the children at exorbitant prices, and rabbit and calf skins that have to be imported from the mainland United States. The rabbit skins are usually used only for the women's parka hood, but some of the younger girls now make entire jackets from them. Costing up to $2.50 each and requiring from ten to twelve for a parka, they are much less warm than any native skins available. The calf skins are used for decorating other skin sewing. Many of the women and young girls also have a great desire for cosmetics or "face powders" as they are called. Even young girls five or six years old are seen with lips reddened, following the example set by their older sisters.

. . . .

The same theme—that of recognizing the value of things now discarded but nonetheless being reluctant to use the old after the new has

Source: *An Eskimo Village in the Modern World*, Ithaca, New York: Cornell University Press (1960), pp. 211-212, 217-219. Reprinted by permission of the author and publisher.

been sampled—is seen also in the principal changes in clothing since 1940. The white man's style of clothing was used fifteen years ago, but it was most frequently worn only in the summer months and by the younger men. The majority of the old men still wore traditional skin pants and parkas even in the summer. The women were then, even as they are now, more conservative in matters of dress, although the young girls were wearing woolen stockings, dresses, and other mainland items.

Native clothing before the coming of the white man had always been of skin. Sealskins predominated, although reindeer hides traded from the Siberian shore were very valuable, especially for the winter trapping costume. Following the introduction of Gambell's own reindeer herd, fawn-skin and doeskin clothing became very common. One of the warmest winter-hunting outfits for men comprised reindeer and sealskin socks worn inside sealskin boots (or reindeer boots for trapping); inner pants of reindeer and outer pants of sealskin; a fawn-skin parka covered by a waterproof intestine parka . . . in turn covered by a canvas garment of similar construction. The women's costume generally resembled the men's, with a "jumper" taking the place of the pants. (Some variations occurred in terms of season, decoration, and special clothing for ceremonials.)

There are several important changes since 1940. First, intestine parkas (made from either mukluk or walrus intestine) have practically disappeared from the hunting wardrobe. These were exceedingly effective in blocking the wind and keeping out the rain, and in 1940 they were quite common. Another change is the decline in use of bird-skin parkas, which were extremely warm. The parka, pants, and socks of reindeer mentioned in the previous paragraph have disappeared, and they have been replaced with white man's materials such as alpaca or sheepskin. . . . This clothing is decidedly inferior, even for Eskimos having a measure of inurement to cold. The only sealskin parkas worn for hunting during the research year were worn by white men. Sealskin boots have given way to rubber boots much of the time, although the sealskins are still used for the winter hunting and trapping.

There is, in summary, a great increase in the use of white man's clothing on all age levels, but particularly among the younger generation. As noted previously, army-style clothing is especially popular with the young men. . . .

Many Sivokakmeit themselves recognize that their contemporary clothing is not as warm as what they used to wear. One young man, rubbing his hands together in the canvas gloves he was wearing and trying to warm them after having pulled a seal out of the icy March ocean, said: "We don't wear the right kind of clothes." A woman agrees in these terms: "The blanket parkas that women wear now don't keep them as warm as the older skin parkas." And a young hunter, speaking of the change in clothing that the younger generation has made, says:

And they don't dress right anymore. . . . A lot of them don't wear any more reindeer parkas. Course a lot of them would still wear a reindeer parkie but they think it's clumsy. And they freeze in these alpaca parkies. They try to use these alpaca parkies for substitute for reindeer parkie, or sealskin. And they're just like cloth—wind just goes through them. But some of them wears this intestine parkie between the snowshirt and the parkie—to keep the wind out. A lot of them don't have it now. A lot of them will say it smells; some of them will say it tears easy and they try to use these water repellent and windbreaker cloth for parkie, which never come close to this intestine parkie. This nylon stuff, windbreaker cloth, never comes close.

A comment by one of the older generation is a good summary:

Yeah, people buying more clothes, especially for the school children. Those that have some money to buy. All winter now they're using rubber boots and shoe packs [a type of boot]—even 18–25 year old boys and girls, they don't use Eskimo boots now. And pretty soon, we, too, won't use them—if we buy big enough boots for winter. But traveling from here to Savoonga and trapping, Eskimo boots better for any kind weather, hot or cold. And our alpaca coats —we used to have deerskin and bird parkas; now no more, except Duncan, Rudolph, Clinton, and Jonathan. We're using all alpaca-lined parkas; not very warm. We should use either walrus or mukluk intestine, bleached, between our alpaca and snow-parka—to keep out the wind.

In many diverse and subtle ways the utilitarian aspect of clothing has given way to its prestigeful qualities. This is especially true for most of the clothing worn by girls. Light jackets and slacks, rubber boots, head scarves, and wool gloves form their costume for much of the year (along with other ways of adorning the body acquired from the mainland, such as using cosmetics and cutting their long black hair in order to use home permanents). Costume jewelry from the white world is popular, even among very young girls, and the ancient Eskimo women's decoration of beads laced throughout the long strands of braided hair is disappearing.

One further aspect of the change in clothing patterns since 1940 was briefly noted before: many of the girls are not learning to sew the skins from which the only feasible winter-hunting clothing can be made. One man sees the latter development in these terms:

No—now the girls don't want to sew. You watch now in town. [Do they make boots?] No, no. Now is changed. Just wear overshoes. Before, make skin boots, mittens, raincoat, skin pants. Not now. I see just curly hair; just walking around in town.

❈ The Case of the Dying Kimono
KEIICHIRŌ NAKAGAWA AND HENRY ROSOVSKY

Introduction

The current Japanese street scene presents a colorful and confused picture to the Western observer. He is constantly made aware of a mixture or co-existence of Occidental and Oriental influences. Sometimes the spectacle is highly pleasing, as in the case of some modern Japanese architecture. At other times, these mixtures achieve the effect of an unkind caricature, combining the worst characteristics of East and West, as in the case of Japanese popular music blaring through thousands of loudspeakers. This mixture in styles of life is particularly noticeable in fashions. A casual stroll through Tokyo reveals a wider spectrum of types of clothing than perhaps anywhere else in the world. One would see ladies gracefully attired in the beautiful kimono and ladies wearing Paris fashions; gentlemen in Western suits, and also sometimes wearing kimono or a cutaway; workmen in the traditional *happi* coats with the crests of their employers emblazoned on the back; girl students in middy-blouse uniforms and boy students in black stiff-collared quasi-military uniforms; young toughs sporting the local version of the long-forgotten zoot-suit—all this, and more. This profusion of fashions would, of course, decrease in the smaller cities and especially in the rural areas. But it never disappears entirely,

Source: "The Case of the Dying Kimono: The Influence of Changing Fashions on the Development of the Japanese Woolen Industry," *Business History Review*, Vol. 37 (Spring–Summer, 1963), pp. 59–68. Reprinted by permission of the publisher.

and therefore is a fundamental characteristic of Japanese modernization.

In this essay we will attempt to analyze the relations between changes in fashions, one aspect of the changing consumption pattern, and the development of the woolen and worsted industries. Usually the cotton industry has been regarded as the best representative of Japanese modernization, but this is not so if we want to investigate the effect of changing tastes on the structure of the domestic economy. Modern Japanese fashion history—and by modern we mean following the Meiji Restoration of 1868—might be conceived as the very gradual Westernization of Japanese clothes. In this process, cotton textiles were less important than wool. Cotton fabrics were never widely used for Western clothes, except as undergarments and shirts, and summer dresses for women; woolens and worsteds dominated this field. Furthermore, cotton fabrics, as we shall see, had been rather well known before Japan's opening to the West, and the industry had prospered in several parts of the country in the first half of the nineteenth century.[1] On the other hand, the woolen and worsted industries were completely a product of Japan's re-established contact with the West in the 1850's and 1860's. Wool was hardly in use before the Restoration, and the industry developed parallel to the gradual Westernization of clothes. In contrast to Europe, woolens and worsteds developed later than cottons, and the establishment of this industry is a good illustration of the industrial revolution in a non-Western setting.

The Westernization of Japanese Fashions

Japanese clothes before the 1860's were almost entirely confined to indigenous fashions. Basically these consisted of a great variety of kimono, a loosely fitted robe worn with a broad belt, made either of silk, mixed silk and cotton, cotton, or linen.[2] Warmth was achieved by additional layers of clothes, and also by padding the garments with raw cotton

---

[1] On the cotton industry during the Tokugawa period, see Sanpei Takako, *Nihon kigyō-shi* (History of Textile Manufactures in Japan) (Tokyo, 1961), Part II, Chap. V, and particularly pp. 150–58.

[2] For the history of Japanese fashions, a most useful source is Ema Tsutomu, *Nihon fukushoku shiyō* (Outline of the History of Japanese Fashions) (Kyoto, 1944). The kimono itself is an outgrowth of a kind of undergarment called *kosode* and worn by the upper classes between the eighth and twelfth centuries. This gradually became an outergarment, and the basic style was fairly well set by the fourteenth century.

or silk. Until the end of the fifteenth century, linen had been the most popular fiber, but from that point on the growing cotton industry increasingly restricted the use of linen. The silk industry developed from the end of the sixteenth century, yet silk always remained a luxury of the rich, and sumptuary regulations—abolished only after the Restoration—restricted its use to the samurai and noble classes, well under 10 per cent of the population. (Other classes, notably the merchants and rich farmers, frequently violated these regulations.)[3] There does not exist reliable quantitative information for this period, but it is generally agreed that just before the Restoration, the average Japanese would have worn some form of cotton or linen kimono, while a rich person might have been clad in silk.[4]

At this time woolens were virtually not manufactured in Japan—indeed, they were almost unknown.[5] Some woolen and worsted fabrics (such as Raxa and Grofgren) had been introduced at the end of the sixteenth century by Spanish, Portuguese, and Dutch merchants, but the closing of the country by Tokugawa Iemitsu[6] in 1639 to anything but very limited Dutch and Chinese commerce prevented this trade from developing. Until the Restoration wool remained a luxurious commodity, used only by the richest nobles as accessories—much the way furs are used today.[7]

Among the first Japanese to adopt Western clothing were the officers and men of some units of the shogunal army and navy.[8] Sometime in the

[3] Sanpei, *Nihon kigyō-shi*, pp. 107, 115, 124, 143–46, 150, 197–201.
[4] Chihō-shi Kenkyū Kyōgikai (Local History Society), *Nihon sangyō-shi taikei* (History of Manufactures in Japan) (Tokyo, 1961), vol. I, p. 271.
[5] Thomas Carlyle Smith says that in the Bunka era (1804–18) some sheep were imported from China to provide wool for the Tokugawa family. See *Political Change and Industrial Development in Japan: Government Enterprise, 1868–1880* (Stanford, 1955), p. 63. In terms of output, this could not have amounted to much.
[6] Japanese proper names are throughout cited in the Japanese manner, with the surname preceding the given name.
[7] Nihon Orimono Shimbunsha (Japan Textile News Co.), *Dai Nihon orimono 2600-nen shi* (A 2,600-Year History of Textiles in Greater Japan) (Tokyo, 1940), vol. I, pp. 220–23, vol. II, p. 266. Some wool was imported as early as the Ashikaga period (1392–1568). See Smith, *Political Change*, p. 63.
[8] Osaka Yōfuku-shō Dōgyō Kumiai (Osaka Association of Merchants and Tailors of Western Suits), *Nihon yōfuku enkaku-shi* (The History of Western Suits in Japan) (Osaka, 1930), pp. 26–28. The Tokugawa shogun was the effective ruler of Japan until 1868. In that year, during the Meiji Restoration, power was ostensibly returned to the Emperor.

1850's these men adopted woolen uniforms patterned after the style of those worn by English marines stationed at Yokohama. To produce these uniforms could not have been an easy matter. The cloth had to be imported,[9] and tailors had to be trained in the comparatively difficult art of fitting Western-style suits.[10] Perhaps the most significant aspect of this early adoption of Western styles was its public origin. For quite a while, the public sector remained as major champion of the new garb.

The Meiji Restoration of 1868 may well have been the most important date in Japanese history. It gave Japan a strong central government, committed to abolishing "feudalism," and eager for Westernization and economic development. These policies were reflected in the clothes in which the new government chose to be seen. When the Duke of Edinburgh visited Japan in 1869, the Imperial Court decided to receive him in formal Western dress. In 1870, naval academy cadets were ordered to wear British-style uniforms, while army cadets followed the French model. The turn of policemen and mailmen came in 1871, and that of workers on the sole national railway line, running between Tokyo and Yokohama, in 1872.[11]

During 1871 there also occurred an interesting debate involving ministers of the central government and members of the court. The issue was whether senior officials of the central and local government should wear Japanese or Western dress. The Westernizers won, and an Imperial Re-

[9] Between 1859 and 1868, imports of woolen fabrics for the army and navy amounted to between 20 and 40 per cent of total imports.

[10] The kimono, being a loose garment, presented no special problems of cutting and fitting. Until recently, most Japanese women were capable of putting these garments together entirely by hand. Western garments require a much closer individual fit, and the Japanese needed special training in order to become Western-style tailors. In the late 1850's and 1860's there were a few foreign tailors catering to the small foreign settlements in Yokohama and Kobe. Some of these establishments took Japanese apprentices, and they in turn became the first native entrepreneurs in this trade. In 1886 the Association of Merchants and Manufacturers of Western Suits was founded in Tokyo with 123 members. See *Tōkyō yōfuku shokogyō dōgyō kumiai enkaku-shi* (The History of the Tokyo Association of Merchants and Manufacturers of Western Suits) (Tokyo, 1940), pp. 53–72. In 1890 there was issued the first style book (*fukusō zasshi*) designed to introduce the newest fashions of Europe to the tailors and the public. See *Nihon yōfuku enkaku-shi*, p. 134. Some sewing machines had been in use since the 1860's, and in 1887, a special sewing-machine school was founded in Tokyo mainly for the benefit of apprentice tailors. The Singer Co. established a school, also in Tokyo, in 1907, and here the students were largely housewives and young girls.

[11] *Nihon yōfuku enkaku-shi*, pp. 65–88.

script of that year reflected the official view: the court was ordered to abandon its Sinicized costumes—they were considered effeminate and un-Japanese—and courtiers and bureaucrats were urged to adopt Western clothing which was thought to be much more practical.[12] And when, in 1877, the new conscript armies of the central government faced the last internal challenge to the new regime during the Satsuma Rebellion, they were dressed in woolen uniforms while the insurgents wore the traditional cottons and silks of the samurai. The symbolic aspects of the battle were probably clear to victor and vanquished.[13]

In this way, by the 1880's, European fashions had conquered a small but symbolically important corner of the market, and their influence was spreading slowly—always from the top down. The higher echelons of society in Tokyo started to frequent European-style entertainments—social dances, garden parties, musicales—and they would often appear in tuxedo or other forms of evening dress.[14] The Empress and ladies of the court began to be seen in dresses. During this decade the Ministry of Education ordered that Western-style student uniforms be worn in public colleges and universities; private universities followed only at a much

---

[12] The government had the Emperor say the following things: "The national polity (*kokutai*) is indomitable, but manners and customs should be adaptable. We greatly regret that the uniform of our court has been established following the Chinese custom, and it has become exceedingly effeminate in style and character. . . . The Emperor Jimmu [660–585 B.C.] who founded Japan, and the Empress Jingu [201–269] who conquered Korea were not attired in the present style. We should no longer appear before the people in these effeminate styles, and we have therefore decided to reform dress regulations entirely." *Ibid.*, pp. 80–81. What Emperor Jimmu's reaction would have been to the cutaway must remain an open question.
[13] The Satsuma Rebellion was an uprising on the part of former Kagoshima samurai led by Saigō Takamori. The differences in dress during the rebellion can be seen in the contemporary paintings contained in *Gaho kindai 100-nenshi* (A Hundred-Year Pictorial History of Modern Japan) (Tokyo, 1951), vol. IV, pp. 316–19.
[14] At that time foreigners had extra-territorial rights in Japan, and the government thought that the rapid spread of Western manners and dress would enable it to get rid of the unequal treaties at an earlier date. In line with this policy the government sponsored, beginning in 1883, a variety of nightly social affairs at the *Rokumeikan*, a Western-style building in Tokyo. These affairs were attended by foreigners and high-class Japanese, all in Western dress. See Tōkyō Fujin-Kodomo Fuku Seizō Oroshi Kyōdō Kumiai (The Cooperative Society of the Manufacturers and Wholesalers of Ladies' and Children's Suits in Tokyo), *Tōkyō fujin-kodomo fuku gyōkai 30-nenshi* (A Thirty-Year History of the Ladies' and Children's Suits Traders of Tokyo) (Tokyo, 1960), pp. 9–12. Some of the department stores also opened Western-dress sections at this time. See Shirokiya Co., *Shirokiya 300-nenshi* (A Three-Hundred-Year History of the Shirokiya) (Tokyo, 1957), p. 252.

later date.[15] Businessmen, teachers, doctors, bankers, and other leaders of the new society made use of Western suits by the end of the nineteenth century, mainly at work or at large social functions, and in 1898, the total consumption of woolen fabrics reached about 3,000,000 yards, almost all imported from England and Germany.[16]

Thus, by the opening of the twentieth century—about thirty years after the Restoration—Western dress was a symbol of social dignity and progressiveness. In addition, it was usually a pretty good indication of public employment. The victory in the Russo-Japanese War (1904-1905) and the economic boom associated with it, turned the eyes of Japan even more toward Europe, and widened somewhat the narrow circle of people using wool and Western suits. It is, however, necessary to underline how limited the use of this type of dress was at that time. The vast majority of Japanese stuck to their own fashions, and even those few who, voluntarily or involuntarily, changed to "modern" dress, discarded it as soon as they returned home in favor of the more comfortable kimono. Indeed, Western dress for streetwear and Japanese dress at home remained the general rule for a very long time.[17]

At the beginning of the twentieth century a development of much greater long-range consequence was taking place within indigenous Japanese styles. Western clothing was confined to a small elite, but the nature of Japanese clothes was also affected by the new times. From the turn of the century, woolens and worsteds showed their real gains not in the narrow demand for Western suits, but in the adoption of these materials for kimono. This process deserves some attention, because it was the demand for wool and worsteds for kimono which really established this branch of manufacturing in Japan.

[15] *Nihon yōfuku enkaku-shi,* pp. 113–14. Obviously these transformations took quite some time. In Reischauer's charming essay on the great Japanologist Serge Elisséeff, we read that after Elisséeff was admitted to Tokyo imperial University in 1908, he "soon shifted from the student uniform to a kimono and *hakama,* the formal double skirt, then worn by the more old-fashioned students and men of education." Edwin O. Reischauer, "Serge Elisséeff," *Harvard Journal of Asiatic Studies,* vol. XX (June, 1957), p. 11.

[16] Tōyō Keizai Shimpō-sha (The Oriental Economist), *Nihon bōeki seiran* (Foreign Trade of Japan: A Statistical Survey) (Tokyo, 1935), p. 243.

[17] For example, see S. Uenoda, *Japan and Jazz* (Tokyo, 1930), p. 133: "Upon arrival at his home, the first thing [the Japanese] does is to change from his foreign clothes to a kimono. It is unutterably relieving and refreshing to be thus released from the *yoke of foreign clothing*" (italics supplied). Since one generally sits on the floor in a Japanese house, rather tight Western suits or dresses are not particularly suitable.

When contact was re-established between Japan and the rest of the world—in the 1850's and 1860's—it became possible to import woolen cloth on a greatly expanded basis. And from that time on, woolens were in extensive demand especially as winter accessories for kimono. A variety of overcoats specifically designed to be worn over kimono became popular, and these types—*tombi, nijūmawashi, azumakōto*—were generally made of wool.[18] Even the ordinary blanket was used as a shawl by women, and at the end of the 1880's especially the red blanket was in vogue for winter wear. Much more important, however, was the adoption of worsted goods for the kimono proper, and this became a popular practice in the 1900's. Already at the end of the Tokugawa period considerable quantities of light, worsted "muslins" (*muslin de laine*), preferably in red or violet, were imported for use at ladies' *haori* and *obi*.[19] In 1881, a Japanese artisan, Okajima Chiyozo, developed a technique of printing designs especially pleasing to local taste on the plain imported muslins. These printed muslins—called *Yūzen* muslins—[20] became extremely popular, and as a result, in 1896, muslins amounted to 40 per cent of total imports of woolens and worsteds.[21] *Yūzen* muslins were the first worsteds in extensive daily use by the Japanese. When the technique of printing became mechanized in 1907 at the dyeworks of Inahata Katsutarō in Osaka, the use of these materials spread even further, and eventually led to the establishment of many big worsted mills—first weaving works and then also spinning establishments.[22]

Together with the muslin boom, there existed also a slow but steady increase in the demand for serges intended as materials for kimono. The light, soft, and beautifully patterned muslins were especially suited for

---

[18] *Tombi* and *nijūmawashi* were the Japanese versions of the "inverness" (the coat worn by Sherlock Holmes). It became especially popular in the 1890's. *Azumakōto* was a ladies' coat with wide sleeves and collarless, and therefore comfortable over a kimono. See *Nihon yōfuku enkaku-shi*, pp. 97–98, and *Tōkyō fujin-kodomo fuku gyōkai*, pp. 44–46.

[19] Ikegami Shōichi, *Mosurin to sono torihiki* (The Muslin Trade) (Osaka, 1926), p. 8. *Haori* is a kind of short or three-quarter length cape, and the *obi* is the broad belt worn with a kimono.

[20] *Ibid.*, pp. 15–17. The name *Yūzen* comes from a technique of dyeing silks, developed at the end of the sixteenth century by a Kyoto painter named Myazaki Yūzen. See *Dai Nihon orimono 2600-nen shi*, vol. I, pp. 182–83.

[21] *Nihon bōeki seiran*, pp. 246, 249.

[22] *Inahata Katsutarō kun den* (The Biography of Inahata Katsutarō) (Osaka, 1938), pp. 317–325.

women and children. The serges, mostly imported from Germany, had plain designs and a harder finish, and were favored by men. Although serges were not particularly fitted for mass production and never commanded as wide a market as muslins, their quality was quite similar to Western suitings. In fact, the demand for serges as kimono materials was most responsible for the eventual establishment, at a much later date, of the industry specializing in worsteds for Western suiting.[23]

This brings us to the time of World War I. As has been shown, until this time, from the point of view of the masses, there was no general Westernization of clothes but rather a gradual adoption of the new fiber wool together with the continued use of silk and cotton. The people had become acquainted with wool but there were still two enormous obstacles to the more widespread use of Western fashions: the Japanese continued to prefer their own styles, and wool remained comparatively expensive. There were always cheaper substitutes among the traditional clothes.[24]

The Japanese economy underwent extremely rapid development during World War I, and this was a great stimulus for the Westernization of national life. Among what might be called the "smart-set," the slogan *bunka seikatsu*—literally cultured or civilized life, actually meaning a Western style of life—began to be heard. These people craved for *bunka-jūtaku* (cultured houses), *bunka shoku* (cultured food), and *bunka fuku* (cultured clothes), and all this meant the same thing: Western ways were preferred.[25] These tendencies continued in the 1920's, and spread considerably through the Great Earthquake of 1923. This disaster almost completely destroyed Tokyo and Yokohama, the largest metropolitan complex in the country, and this sad event became something of a turning point in Japanese fashion history. Over 700,000 dwellings were leveled, and millions lost all their possessions—including their clothes. Many of the victims replaced their clothing with a larger proportion of Western things, in part because the pattern of demand had slowly shifted to greater emphasis on this type of fashion, and also because it was said that the kimono had proved dangerous during the quake since its long

---

[23] Dai Nihon Orimono Kyōkai (Textile Society of Greater Japan), *Senshoku 50-nen shi* (A Fifty-Year History of Dyeing) (Tokyo, 1935), pp. 202–203, and Daidō Keori K. K. (Daidō Worsted Mills, Ltd.), *Ito hitosuji* (Spinning and Weaving for Eighty Years) (Tokyo, 1960), vol. I, pp. 157–59.

[24] Among other things, kimono have the advantage of lasting much longer than Western clothes. Styles change less frequently, and since the garment is loose it can fit successive generations of wearers.

[25] *Nihon yōfuku enkaku-shi*, pp. 190–91.

sleeves and train prevented rapid movement.[26] Even though the latter was not a very plausible reason—after all, the Japanese had long experience with both earthquakes and kimono—it may well have affected popular tastes. Also in the 1920's, primary and secondary school students contributed to increased Westernization. After the Great Earthquake, many of the schools adopted plain blue-serge Western-style uniforms. The popularity of social dancing and gymnastics intensified these tendencies.[27]

And yet, until the 1930's, the majority of Japanese continued to wear kimono, and Western clothes were still pretty much restricted to out-of-home use by certain classes. Since most Japanese women were still quite confined to the home, a large potential market was eliminated. Even when Japanese women began to appear more frequently as members of the labor force, either in industry or in service occupations, they usually remained in kimono. It is true that the conductresses of Tokyo's municipal busses went into Western wool uniforms in 1924, but that was an exception. Wherever Japanese women worked—in department stores, offices, bars, as telephone operators, or factory workers—they usually performed their tasks in kimono, if necessary covered with aprons and dusters.[28]

The 1930's was a decade of rapid stylistic changes, generally favoring the increased use of Western clothes. In 1932 a bad fire broke out at the Shirokiya Department Store in Tokyo. Fourteen people died, including eight salesgirls, and twenty-one others were badly injured. The kimono was once again blamed for many of the casualties. It allegedly prevented the salesgirls and female customers from making a rapid exit.[29] Certain witnesses also claimed that some of the victims refused to jump from the upper stories of the store into the waiting fire nets because panties are not normally worn with kimono and the leap might have compromised their modesty. No doubt much of this is legend, but like the Great Earthquake it illustrates the popular frame of mind.

The real trend towards Western dress in the 1930's is explainable in more rational terms. By this time most of the people had worn Western-

---

[26] *Tōkyō fujin-kodomo fuku gyōkai*, pp. 70–72.
[27] *Ibid.*, pp. 66–67. In the big cities primary and secondary school boys were already dressed in Western uniforms in the 1900's.
[28] *Ibid.*, pp. 89–90. See also *Gaho fuzoku-shi: nihonjin no seikatsu to bunka* (A Pictorial History of Japanese Life) (Tokyo, 1958), vol. XV, pp. 1022, 1023, 1040–41, and vol. XVI, pp. 1062–63.
[29] *Shirokiya 300-nenshi*, pp. 488–89, 494–95.

style school or army uniforms, and presumably had acquired a kind of taste or habit for these types of clothes. In addition, the stature of young Japanese men and women had also changed. They had grown taller, their legs were longer, the busts of the women were a little larger, and this made the new styles more flattering.[30] Furthermore, Western fashions themselves—especially women's fashions—had changed. The skirts were shorter and the sleeves narrower, increasing the comparative advantage of dresses vis-à-vis the kimono if one wanted to lead a more active life. Meanwhile, as we shall see in the following section, the woolen and worsted industries had experienced considerable growth. They were now more productive and the real price of woolen textiles had declined. As a result of all of these factors, by the outbreak of World War II most working women and quite a few housewives wore Western dress. The same was true of the men working in offices or factories. Already in the 1920's the Western suit had reached the upper classes of the provincial cities and in the 1930's it was ubiquitous in general business circles. Male work clothes also reflected the Westernizing influences. Cotton, woolen, or worsted work clothes, following Western patterns, were used in most factories and the use of bicycles for delivery and message purposes contributed in no small measure to the use of pants. The group least affected by all of these changes must have been the farmers, and they still made up over 40 per cent of the gainfully occupied population in the late 1930's. More important, however, at home, in the cities and the country, most Japanese continued to relax, eat, and sleep, in their indigenous clothes.

The post World War II period does not reveal any startling new developments. Westernization of fashions has continued at an even more rapid pace, and the street scene, as we have described it, remains confused. The kimono is dying—there can be no doubt of that—but it will remain part of the Japanese way of life for a good many years to come.

This admittedly superficial survey of fashion history has, we hope, provided some idea of the changing nature of demand for wool textiles and Western clothing since the Restoration. Specifically, we have attempted to identify three phases: (1) from the end of the 1860's to the end of the nineteenth century, the period of first contact, when there

[30] For example, in 1900 the average twenty-year-old male was 160.0 cm. tall and the average female measured 147.9 cm. By 1940, these measurements were 164.5 cm. and 152.7 cm. respectively. See Japan, Mombushō (Ministry of Education), *Gakko hoken tōkeisho* (School Health Statistics), 1960, pp. 158–60, 170–71. Also Tokyo University, *Taiikugaku-kiyo* (Review of Physical Education) (June, 1960), vol. I.

occurred the spotty adoption of Western clothing mainly in official circles, and when the government was the main source of demand; (2) from the beginning of the twentieth century until the 1920's, the period when Western fabrics—muslin and serge—were adapted as kimono cloth; and (3) from roughly the Great Earthquake until the present, the years during which Western fashions have come into more general use.

Fashion and Fashion Leadership

Fashion: Identification and Differentiation in the Mass Society

KURT LANG AND GLADYS LANG

Within modern society there is a segment of behavior and belief generally recognized as being under the sway of fashion. There are fashions in science and education no less than in styles of living; in art no less than in clothes and furnishings. But a definition of what fashion entails is more difficult than such denotative identification. To illustrate particular fashions or fashionable beliefs does not identify the basic nature of fashion per se.

When we call something a fashion, the judgment usually involves a bit of debunking. Pinning the fashion label on a cultural commodity is an effective, if roundabout, way of demoting it. The label suggests, first, that the commodity is *transitory*, not lasting or permanent. Second, its *novelty*—not any intrinsic rationality—governs its acceptance; the value of what is fashionable is independent of its rational utility. Third, the label suggests the *trivial*. Fashion is allowed free sway because it is assumed to move only within the limits of what is culturally approved. Traditional ways of doing things, institutionally accepted attitudes, ideas that matter are not affected, and thus individuals are free to indulge themselves in the marginal, and sometimes bizarre, vagaries that the world of fashion opens to them.

Fashion, then, connotes the transitory, the novel, the trivial. But the

Source: *Collective Dynamics*, New York: Thomas Y. Crowell Co. (1961), pp. 465–487. Reprinted by permission of the publisher.

label also implies a force beyond individual control. Fashion is a collective creation. It is determined by what *they* say. The world of fashion is not so much available to people as imposed on them. In one way or another it dictates to everyone. It is contagious. Any individual or group may resist a particular fashion, but fashion, as such, cannot be resisted.

There is [according to Sumner] no arguing with fashion. . . . The authority of fashion is imperative as to everything which it touches. The sanctions are ridicule and powerlessness. The dissenter hurts himself; he never affects the fashion.[1]

The Power of Fashion

Fashion is here treated as an elementary form of collective behavior, whose compelling power lies in the implicit judgment of an anonymous multitude. This view is questioned by persons who point to a well-organized industry which, through its advertising campaigns, foists on a gullible public what one critic called "the overwhelming flood of cultural sewage that is manufactured especially for the taste of the low-brow and middle-brow."[2] There are, of course, fashion industries and formal communication systems which promote the products of these industries. In view of this, can one call the sway of fashion spontaneous?

It is a basic question whether public taste is first manufactured and then disseminated through organized channels and foisted upon the mass *or* whether changes in the moods and life conditions lead to irrational and widespread changes of taste even without promotion. To what extent the tastemakers merely cater to the changing whims of the great public and to what extent they manipulate changes which are thereafter legitimated by mass acceptance will be illustrated by reference to the "New Look."

THE NEW LOOK: AN EXAMPLE

The collective resistance to the New Look in 1947 is often cited as an example of the limits beyond which women will not be dictated to by fashion. Actually the natural history of the New Look provides a first-rate illustration of the compelling nature of fashion innovation.

[1] William Graham Sumner, *Folkways* (Boston: Ginn & Company, 1906), p. 194.
[2] Winthrop Sargeant, *Life,* XXVI (April 11, 1949), p. 102.

THE FASHION IS PLANTED

The New Look involved two major changes in women's dress: the shape was to be radically altered, and the skirt noticeably lengthened. According to fashion publicists, after two decades of the "American Look," marked by slim hips, casual appearance, reasonably short skirts, etc., the female was to cloak herself in hourglass fashion: round shoulders (no more exaggerated padding), sucked-in wasp waist, and, most important, very long skirt.

This new round-shouldered, hourglass fashion, like other major style innovations, was planted. "Months ago," wrote *The New York Times* on September 7, 1947, "the Western world learned that skirts this autumn would be full and longer, hips padded, waists waspishly thin, shoulders daintily rounded. . . ." Among the style planners or norm creators responsible were "a bunch of Paris and New York designers," the custom designers, like Christian Dior, Sophie Gimbel, and Hardy Amies. The first to adopt the New Look were the chic clientele of these designers. Thereafter the fashion received public legitimation by those who customarily are named best-dressed women by the style planners and the style communicators. It was legitimated also by royalty and Hollywood movie stars, who traditionally have acted as style leaders and thereby give something in the nature of official status to projected fashion innovations. For instance, Princess Elizabeth of England was reported to be ordering her wedding trousseau in calf-length skirts.

The New Look also had to be disseminated to a wider audience. A full-scale, well-organized publicity campaign aimed at familiarizing people everywhere with the New Look well ahead of the time dresses in the style were available for sale in stores catering to the general trade. First, there had to be pictures. Women not only had to hear about the New Look; they had also to see it. The first to wear a new fashion are not necessarily the members of the smart international set who order from the top couturiers. Mass fashions are "tested" by professional *modistes* who appear at racetracks, theaters, parties, and other public gatherings to display newly created apparel. *Vogue* and *Harper's Bazaar* featured the New Look, and by the time it reached other magazines of the fashion press—*Mademoiselle, Seventeen, etc.*—the New Look seemed familiar indeed.

Publicity and production must go hand in hand. Through their advance publicity, volume manufacturers, who had secured models from Paris, assured themselves of a demand for the new models. Newspaper ads for the smarter stores began to feature the change. *Women's Wear Daily,* the garment trade paper, began to talk of the new styling, and style consultants for the small shops and large department stores everywhere catering to mass taste began to order the new dresses.

In other words, the New Look was promoted and sold to the public through certain tested and well-organized channels. These networks of communication existed long before the New Look and would long survive it. Through them, the New Look was planted. The change in styling was the initial result of an idea germinated in the fashion industry and nourished by publicity and organization.

THE NEW LOOK MEETS RESISTANCE

How strong was collective opposition to the proposed change? Newspapers and magazines publicized the advent of the change, but it was dramatized even more by the isolated instances of organized resistance reported concurrently. College students protested to the New York Dress Institute. A rumor had it that the J. Arthur Rank Organization in England would continue to dress its film stars in short skirts. *Time* (September, 1947) said: "The furor over the new fashions rose to a fine, shrill pitch. Across the land, women by the *hundreds* (sic)—and city editors too—flocked to the banners of resistance." Most publicized was the resistance of a group of women in Dallas, Texas, who demonstrated against the new style. According to one report (*Collier's,* October 11, 1947), thirteen hundred women in that city "formed the 'Little Below the Knee Club,' sworn to hold the hemline at that elevation. . . ." Meanwhile a legislator in Georgia announced that he would soon introduce a bill banning long skirts. That summer of 1947 the polls showed that a majority of American women disliked the new styles—but would wear them anyway.

The most singular, and certainly the most drastic, effort to halt the New Look occurred in England. In September, 1947, the Labour government was reportedly considering a decree governing the length of women's skirts. The postwar period found Britain continuing some of its rationing restrictions to regulate the use of scarce materials and to fight the black market and inflation. Moreover, England was hoping to promote its export market and achieve a more favorable balance of trade. Behind the opposition to the fashion innovation was the legal force of government.

Here is a puzzle. Can Sir Stafford Cripps (or anyone else) prevent women's skirts being longer if Fashion decrees that they shall be? That the ruling [Fashion's ruling for the New Look] is idiotic and anti-social at a time when we need to save every yard of material is obvious. Nor does anyone, outside the trade, want skirts longer. Men find short skirts more comely than the half-length style that flops around the woman's calf. Women find the short skirt much more comfortable and women's organizations in America and Paris are protesting against the dictatorship of Paris. . . . Anyway, whatever the reason, I find no one bets on Sir Stafford winning this battle if he engages in it. You may plan peace and war, but women's clothes are like the weather—beyond the control of government.[3]

What resistance developed outside official government undoubtedly was not a matter of dwindling national dollar reserves. Nor was it a matter of taste or a deliberate effort to resist the crowd. An English girl summed up the dilemma common to women everywhere:

. . . I know from daily contact with working girls who take a pride in their clothes, that they are thrown into a quandary. I heard one of them saying, "I don't know whether to try to scrounge a lot of coupons [rationing] and sell off my clothes or just appear dowdy." [4]

She went on to cite George Orwell's observation that fashions, by making working girls almost indistinguishable from the wealthy, were helping to break down class barriers. Might not the New Look, she asked, in this period of scarcity and hardship, again widen the gulf between the classes?

While there was some annoyance and concern over the command to change wardrobes and isolated, if well-publicized, instances of deliberate opposition, the New Look caught on and had a lasting effect on women's dress styles. If by the season of 1948, one year after the New Look was "sweeping the country," most skirts did not quite reach the decreed ten or eleven inches from the floor, they were nevertheless considerably nearer

[3] Critic (pseudonym), *New Statesman and Nation*, XXXIV (September 20, 1947), p. 225.
[4] Letter to the Editor, *New Statesman and Nation*, XXXIV (October 4, 1947), p. 270.

the floor than they had been for decades. Also gone were the huge padded, mannish shoulders which had so long seemed natural to women.

We have, then, to account for the success of the New Look by considering two aspects of fashion change: first, why women everywhere conform to a change and, second, why there is any change at all. Consideration of both may clarify what is meant by the "compelling nature of fashion."

THE COMPELLING NATURE OF FASHION

The fashion world plans and makes available clothes, and, where the major source of supply is ready-made, women must for practical reasons go along. Yet to follow a major change in fashion means for most women a complete turnover in wardrobe. Had women everywhere in 1947 simply replenished their current wardrobes, bought one new dress or one new suit, this would not have constituted a major turnover in fashion. If fashion were a mere caprice in what is available, the styles of yesteryear would not be altogether inappropriate after the change. For instance, when the sack dress, the trapeze, and the chemise were promoted in 1957, many women bought one of the new creations, but the older, more closely fitted dresses did not thereby seem inappropriate. It is unlikely that any, save the most modish, felt compelled to discard or alter entire wardrobes. Fashion induces a change in mass taste. The short skirt, which one season seems esthetic and appropriate, comes to look ugly and out of place—somehow improper.

In this context, we are using taste to designate the subjective preference for which there are no objective standards. We are not concerned here with esthetic judgment—that is, with the cultivation in the individual of a standard of beauty and truth which secures the gentleman, the scholar, and the esthete from the influences of the vulgar. Fashion is a collective phenomenon and has an objective existence apart from any individual. It makes attractive what often seems outrageous and bizarre to the preceding generation as well as the next. The standard set by fashion is, according to Sapir, "accepted by average people with little demur and is not so much reconciled with taste as substituted for it."[5] In the mass, most are

[5] Edward Sapir, "Fashion," *Encyclopedia of the Social Sciences* (New York: The Macmillan Co., 1931), VI, pp. 139–44.

"average," and taste becomes what fashion is all about. Taste implies a purely subjective judgment with which there is no arguing, but esthetic judgment requires a certain consistency with esthetic principles as well as an evaluation of the functional relevance of an object.

How the fashion process operates to produce a simultaneous change in the personal taste of individuals all over is well illustrated in this letter by an American returning in 1947 to the United States after a year abroad:

> At every airport where we stopped on the way back from China I started watching the women coming the other way. At Calcutta the first long skirt and unpadded shoulders looked like something out of a masquerade party. At the American installations in Frankfort (also in Vienna) a lot of the newer arrivals were converted and were catching everyone's attention. At the airport in Shannon I had a long wait; I got into a conversation with a lady en route to Europe. She was from San Francisco, and told me that there they still hadn't been completely won over—just as many were wearing the long skirts as not. But as she flew East, she found that just about everybody in New York had gone in for the new styles and she was happy she wasn't staying or her wardrobe would have been dated. By the time I took the train from New York for home, my short skirts felt conspicuous and my shoulders seemed awfully wide! Two weeks now and I am letting down hems, trying to figure out which of all my China-made clothes can be salvaged, and going on a buying spree!

The operations of the bandwagon and the way in which it snowballs are well illustrated. When the first few fashion leaders adopt a new style, they identify themselves as members of an elite apart from the rest of the world. In this age of rapid communication, the news of their adoptions soon spreads and helps to make the new mode familiar. The first few to dress in it are objects of interest and excitement; they are different, strange. A few more follow, impelled to be *à la mode* by the need to assert their difference from those less fashionable. The bandwagon is gradually on and soon it begins to roll. In the end no one can afford to be different. The final blow comes when the woman standing aside appears ridiculous even to herself. "They" are no longer odd; she herself is. Popular taste, even one's own, has changed. But in the meantime the fashion innovators may already be striking out in new directions.

Thus, the collective change in taste—an objective trend—is dictated not by an organized fashion industry but by the nature of fashion itself. The essence of fashion lies in its caprice: the transitory shift in some trivial area toward novelty for the sake of novelty. Fashion, then, is a process by which the taste of a mass of people is collectively redefined.

Fashion, Custom, Style

Not only have the times to suit a change, but the particular change has to meet the demands of the times. Hence, life conditions are not entirely unrelated to fashion changes. In connection with the New Look, it is relevant to note that uniforms and uniformity had been a way of life during the war. In England there had been mass production of one-style utility dresses, utility shoes, and other garments, to be had only in exchange for rationing coupons. This meant that people wore uniforms even as civilians. After the war ended, matériel shortages necessitated continuation of rationing in clothing. There had also been a need to "pull together" during the war. For a brief time after the armistice, the camaraderie gained in air raid shelters, the spirit of mutual effort, the impelling breakdowns in class barriers, and other unifying forces, carried over from the wartime period, continued to exert their influence. But as the sense of danger passed, the spirit of competition and individual aggrandizement began once more to dominate the economy. The New Look, with its accent on "the illusion of being different," fitted the changing temper of the times.

Whenever a fashion has met the mood of the public and fitted its way of life, neither religious or legal decrees against it have succeeded. Indeed, some "fashion" changes are cues that major social changes are occurring. A major fashion change no longer concerns merely the trivial. Its appeal is more lasting and does not rest on novelty alone.

It is the visible sign that a transformation is taking place in the intellect, customs, and business of people. . . . Taine wrote this profound sally: "My decided opinion is that the greatest change in history was the advent of trousers. . . . It marked the passage of Greek and Roman civilization to the modern. . . . Nothing is more difficult to alter than a universal and daily custom. In order to take away man's clothes and dress him up again you must demolish and remodel him.[6]

[6] Pierre Clerget, "The Economic and Social Role of Fashion," *The Annual Report of the Smithsonian Institution*, Washington, D.C., 1914, p. 763.

There is something to fashion besides the subjective judgments of individuals. The movement of fashion marks a trend in the collective definitions of taste, which can be objectively charted, like the ups and downs of hemlines or the use of certain layouts in homes. But certain other objective patterns that are clearly not fashion also affect the design of apparel and homes. It is necessary to distinguish the influence of custom and style from that of fashion.

FASHION AND CUSTOM

What identifies fashion is its novelty value, its seeming departure from custom. Fashion, Sapir tells us, is "the legitimate caprice of custom"; it is custom in the guise of departure from custom.[7] In going along with fashion, we deny the oldfashioned; what counts against the latter is its age. But custom completely lacks novelty value. It is age that legitimates custom. Custom is time-honored rather than fashionable and is passed down from generation to generation.

The word custom is used to apply to the totality of behavior patterns which are carried by tradition and lodged in the group. . . . Custom is often used interchangeably with convention, tradition and mores, but the connotations are not quite the same. . . . Such terms as custom, institution, convention, tradition and mores are, however, hardly capable of a precise scientific definition. All of them are reducible to *social habit* or, if one prefers the anthropological to the psychological point of view, to *cultural pattern*.[8]

Custom is universal to the group. Everybody conforms to custom, and custom is necessary if a group is to function as a group. It constitutes the body of common understandings that survive the individual members and sets off one group from another in the larger society. Members of any collectivity reassert their in-groupness, or solidarity, each day as they adhere to the ways of doing things that are traditional to their way of life. But in fashion people exercise their personal option in areas that do not fundamentally matter to set themselves apart. However compelling a fashion change appears, it is in the last analysis a matter of taste.

Consider the matter of men's clothing. An officer of the Federal Reserve Bank, asked what was adequate compensation for wearing his wife's hat

---

[7] Sapir, *op. cit.*, p. 140.
[8] Edward Sapir, "Custom," *Encyclopedia of the Social Sciences*, IV, p. 658.

to the office some morning, first answered, "Fifty thousand dollars." Then, after thinking it over for a moment, he said, "it would have to be as much as he could expect to earn the rest of his life, since afterward he could never expect to hold a position of financial responsibility again; and in the end he concluded that no price would be enough for the loss of prestige entailed."[9] That a man should wear a man's hat rather than a woman's is not a matter of fashion; it is a matter of custom. It is part of the social heritage, and for society at large it is not a trivial or laughing matter. We can be quite certain that the banker never once entertained the thought that he might choose to wear his wife's hat anywhere (save a masquerade party), let alone to his place of work. Were some men to start wearing women's hats, the group would somehow feel threatened. The established order of things would have been questioned; the individual deviant would be punished or quickly diverted.

Fashion operates without disrupting group unity so long as capricious deviation from customary norms occurs *within* the frame-work of the larger body of mores and does not offend. Through adherence to fashion, individuals legitimate and indulge their need for personal deviation without either risking ostracism or threatening group solidarity. It provides them with the illusion of being different. But fashion differs from custom in that it affects only those areas of life that are both trivial and peripheral. Fashion is not so much significant to our day-to-day experience as functionally irrelevant. Mass deviations from custom are permissible as long as they leave untouched the central ethos of the culture. Sapir tells us that there is a "reconciliation of individual freedom with social conformity which is implicit in the very fact of fashion."[10] We are not fundamentally in revolt from custom but we have a yen to break away just a bit. In fashion there can be found certain accepted ways of revolt.

Many speak of fashions in thought, art, habits of living and morals. It is superficial to dismiss such locutions as metaphorical and unimportant. The usage shows a true intuition of the meaning of fashion, which while it is primarily applied to dress and the exhibition of the human body *is not essentially concerned with the fact of dress or ornament but with its symbolism.* There is nothing to prevent a thought, a type of morality or an art form from being the psychological equivalent of a costuming of the ego. Certainly one

---

[9] Agnes B. Young, *Recurring Cycles of Fashion* (New York: Harper & Brothers, 1937), p. 187 f.
[10] Sapir, "Fashion," *op. cit.,* p. 140.

may allow oneself to be converted to Catholicism or Christian Science in exactly the same spirit in which one invests in pewter or follows the latest Parisian models in dress. Beliefs and attitudes are not fashions in their character of mores but neither are dress and ornament. In contemporary society it is not a fashion that men wear trousers; it is the custom. Fashion merely dictates such variations as whether trousers are to be so or so long, what colors they are to have and whether they are to have cuffs or not. In the same way, while adherence to a religious faith is not in itself a fashion, as soon as the individual feels that he can pass easily, out of personal choice, from one belief to another, not because he is led to his choice by necessity but because of a desire to accrete to himself symbols of status, it becomes legitimate to speak of his change of attitude as a change of fashion. *Functional irrelevance* as contrasted with symbolic significance for the expressiveness of the ego is implicit in all fashion.[11]

FASHION AND STYLE

Style, like fashion, refers to matters of taste, except that "style doesn't change every month or every year. It only changes as often as there is a real change in the point of view and the lives of the people for whom it is produced."[12] Style is the characteristic or distinctive mode of expression, the prevailing taste in some field of art or in artifacts, that reflects the outlook either of some person or group of persons. One can define style as the *permanent element in fashion*. Although the actual changes seem to occur rapidly, suddenly, and dramatically, the style of life changes only over longer periods. It reflects a secular change.

Hence, fashions are not really innovations but recurrent deviations. They are not so much born as rediscovered.[13] The cyclical nature of fashion, the tendency of many fashions to repeat themselves at intervals, has been documented in a number of studies of women's apparel, music, and even hog "styles."[14] Among the most careful documentations of the long-term cyclical nature of fashion is Kroeber's work (some of it in

---

[11] Sapir, "Fashion," *op. cit.*
[12] Elizabeth Hawes, *Fashion Is Spinach* (New York: Grosset & Dunlap, Inc., 1940), p. 5.
[13] Rolf Meyersohn and Elihu Katz, "Notes on a Natural History of Fads," *American Journal of Sociology*, LXII (May, 1957), p. 597.
[14] *Ibid.*, p. 598. See, in addition to Kroeber cited below, particularly Young, *op. cit.*

collaboration with Richardson).[15] He used the change in the length and width of skirts in full-dress toilette from 1844 to 1919. The duration of any one phase in a cycle was found too long to be attributed to the influence of any one designer. Major changes occurred as social conditions changed and generations succeeded one another. Some fashions (or fads) follow shorter cycles; for example, the reblossoming of fake flowers seems to follow a seven-year cycle.[16] Popular tunes seem to be revived after approximately twenty years. In 1957 many of the "new" popular songs were revivals of popular tunes from the 1930's and some from the 1920's. They were old enough to have a nostalgic, not deadening, effect on the older members of the population and to be really new for young people. When fashions are old enough to be new, they may be born again.

Finally, fashion involves fairly minor changes in taste. Its cyclical movement is confined by the prevailing style. But the concrete relationship between style changes and fashion changes needs study. One may suddenly discover that an accretion of apparently minor alterations has produced a major change in style. For instance, women's dress in the Western world today expresses a style basically different from that fifty years ago, a change that can be traced directly to the "Roaring Twenties." American couturier Norman Norell wrote:

Women are still wearing, and throughout this century will continue to wear changes that came about in the Twenties: short hair; interesting make-up; red, red lips; the basic black dress (before the Twenties black was worn only for mourning); the color beige; fake jewelry; short skirts; plain pumps for daytime; nude stockings, and gloves that pull on easily. These are just a few of the things that were launched in the Twenties.

Clothes also became easy and comfortable for the first time. They were loose and sexy and a woman could relax, untrammeled by rigid bones, stays and long skirts. What's more, she could go from morning to dinner without changing.[17]

[15] The classic work by Alfred L. Kroeber is "On the Principle of Order in Civilization as Exemplified by Changes in Fashion," *American Anthropologist,* XXI (1919), pp. 235–63. Also Jane Richardson and Alfred L. Kroeber, *Three Centuries of Women's Dress Fashions: A Quantitative Analysis,* University of California, Anthropological Records, V, No. 2, 1940.
[16] *The New York Times,* March 29, 1957, fashions page.
[17] "Four Inside Views of Fashion," *The New York Times Magazine,* June 19, 1960, p. 20.

Since the middle and upper as well as the lower classes now go into the world and work, the styling of woman's clothes has to emphasize not only esthetic but practical needs. The style limits the fashions that may be reborn; corsets that inhibit breathing, skirts that sweep the floor, hair that requires hours of arranging, etc., can return only when the prevailing style of life changes.[18] At the same time, the prevailing taste for practical clothes, in which women may live from morning through evening, can be attributed to the many small fashion changes that have come through the years—including quick drying, little-iron fabrics, a lack of frou-frou, etc.

THE REALM OF FASHION

The fashion process is the manner in which new fashions are born (or revived) and spread in mass society. What kinds of ideas, what ways of doing things, what among the objects we buy, what activities are subject to the whims of fashion? What are the areas in which custom leaves an area of tolerance, and when does this tolerance evolve into a compulsion to conform to a new pattern?

The fashion process operates in many areas where the choices made are not functionally relevant to some goal or purpose to be achieved. Nystrom, discussing the economics of fashion in women's clothes, has talked about *taste* as the "ability to discern and appreciate what is *beautiful* and *appropriate*."[19] But what is beautiful and what is appropriate are always matters of judgment and subject to qualification. One can judge what is beautiful and appropriate at a given time and place only from certain standards. Absolute standards of beauty and fitness, however, are seldom attainable; there can be no objective test for them.

This applies to many areas other than feminine dress. It applies equally, for example, to the feminine face and feminine contours. Over the years the average contestant in the Atlantic City beauty pageant has changed in height, hair style, weight, general facial features, and body contours. Was the standard of 1924 right and is the present one misguided? In international contests does one judge among Miss China, Miss Sweden, and Miss Togoland by Caucasion standards of good looks? Or, to take another

---

[18] In 1960 elaborate hair styles taking little time were made possible through the popularization of wigs and hairpieces. Women could change their hair style as quickly as they could change from one wig to another.
[19] Paul Henry Nystrom, *Economics of Fashion* (New York: The Ronald Press Company, 1928), p. 3.

example, it may be appropriate to wear a tie when teaching a college class, but how can we demonstrate the wearing of a tie to be really "proper"? As William Graham Sumner pointed out long ago, fashion operates where there can be no proof of validity. Because of this, one can only deprecate but not argue with legitimate fashion.

. . . they [certain rules of conduct] are fashions because they are arbitrary, have no rational grounds, cannot be put to any test, and have no sanction except that everybody submits to them.[20]

Nor do fashion changes depend on manipulation. The fact that wearing apparel, particularly women's, is used so often to illustrate the fashion process has focused attention on the network of communication through which fashions are produced and promoted. Where these networks exist, they do of course permit, within certain limits, manipulation of the mass by organized interests. But control over what is made available on the market and use of the mass media to stimulate consumer demand are not indispensable to the fashion process. Fashion often is in evidence even where there is no organization of this kind, though it probably diffuses more slowly.

We have found no evidence, for example, that fashions in given names are deliberately promoted. Among the names most common to girls born in Boston in the seventeenth century were Hannah, Abigail, Mehitabel, Bethiah, and Dorcas. Also fairly common were the "meaningful" names of abstract qualities: Mercy, Thankful, Desire, and the like.[21] How many Mehitabels and Mercys do we find now? Certainly very few. Names given babies change even from year to year, and one can sometimes mark a man's age by his given name. Nor is this simply a matter of infants bearing names like Franklin D. Roosevelt Jones, as in the popular song.

The suggestion is often made that just as in an earlier period names were strongly influenced by patriotic figures, so they now are influenced by the celebrities of screen, radio, and athletics. Undoubtedly there is some such influence but it is not so strong as to be easily demonstrated statistically. *Gone With the Wind* was the most read book of the nineteen-thirties, and its two chief feminine characters bore the curious names Scarlett and Melanie. One can now find a few girls bearing these names, but they have certainly not seriously affected our name pattern. Since actors and actresses often take stage

[20] Sumner, *op. cit.*, p. 195.
[21] George Stewart, *American Ways of Life* (Garden City, N.Y.: Doubleday & Company, Inc., 1954), pp. 210–11.

names, the reasoning, in fact, often has to be reversed. An actress' name may rise to sudden popularity, not because babies are named after her, but because she herself took the name that was becoming fashionable. The same may be said for heroes and heroines of novels and plays.[22]

What makes names in general—not any particular name—subject to fashion? In the matter of names, as in all fashion, one can be different but not too different. Stewart points to a tendency for the total number of given names in circulation to increase. New names are manufactured, while old ones are revived along with the new.

. . . the commonest way of manufacturing a name is to take elements of established names. Thus there are a number of suffixes that indicate or suggest a feminine ending. Here we have -ie, -etta, -ene, -illa, -elle. Then the name manufacturer may select the first part of some standard name, and thus produce Kathetta, Marilla, or Elizene.[23]

Not all social circles participate equally in this game of invention. At one time it was thought to be a peculiarity among Negroes. By now it has been fairly well established that the practice is most typical of those sometimes called "poor whites" and those slightly above them on the social and economic scale. At the other extreme, the Blue Book circles of New York City also make use of it. Fashion innovation in its most extreme and bizarre forms is usually found among those who can afford to be different and those who have something to gain by it. A fashion, once established, is followed by those in-between, the middle classes, whose sensitivity to the mode makes them the mainstay of most fashion movements.

Even science is not altogether exempt from fashion. Medical practice has its fads. Within the last few decades, science writers have successively hailed as keys to the cure of mental disease electro-shock therapy, brain operations (lobotomies), and tranquilizing drugs. Tranquilizers can become fashionable among noninstitutionalized persons as well as in therapy. Yet, the hold of fashion in science is shaky, for the appropriateness of drugs, operations, or shock treatments is subject to empirical test. Fashion holds sway only in those circles where, instead of relying on evidence, the general taste is followed. Once an objectively validated answer is widely available, a standard set by fashion will no longer be acceptable.

[22] George Stewart, *American Ways of Life* (Garden City, N.Y.: Doubleday & Company, Inc., 1954), pp. 210–11.
[23] *Ibid.*

The area subject to fashion, though limited, includes all those market decisions in which individual preferences are reflected and those of others affirmed or rejected. That there are fashions of saving or spending has been shown in a study of war bonds.[24] The injunction to honor thy mother may become unfashionable in some circles as too much honoring induces suspicions of mother-fixation. Modes of expression, even the modulation of one's voice and certainly the whole code of manners, can enter into fashion. Individual preferences may be conscious efforts to satisfy one's own esthetic, intellectual, creative, social, or medical needs; that is, an individual may be deliberately pursuing the taste he has developed. But the choices are not derived from esthetic or scientific principles. They express a need for individuation without the risk of group disapproval. By adopting what is fashionable, one identifies with a group. By being ahead of others in one's adoption, it is possible to succeed in standing out in a group and yet be reaffirming its collective preferences.

Fashion and Social Structure

The motives of those who innovate a fashion are quite different from the motives of those who follow. "The essence of fashion consists in that it is practised by only a part of the group, but that the totality should just be on the way to it."[25] Because the appeal of fashion depends primarily on novelty, it must always, as the novelty fades, fasten on new patterns.

A classic picture of the diffusion of a fashion is set forth in the writings of Thorstein Veblen. A fashion, he held, usually begins with the adoption of innovations by members of the leisure class who have money. Some fashions are attractive for no other reason than their great expense. The dresses custom-made in the great fashion houses command exorbitant

---

[24] George Katona, *Psychological Analysis of Economic Behavior* (New York: McGraw-Hill Book Co., 1951), p. 79. ". . . during the war most people knew that other people—their neighbors, friends, and colleagues—were buying war bonds, were saving part of their income, or were abstaining from spending in one or the other respect. There was hardly any such verbal expression as 'spending a lot of money is out of place during the war,' but it appeared that the accepted pattern of behavior, the one which represented climbing on the band wagon, was represented by buying war bonds or putting money in the bank. This was, for most people, not frugality . . . as spending reached record levels."

[25] Georg Simmel, "Die Mode," *Philosophische Kultur. Gesammelte Essais* (Leipzig: Kroner, 1919), p. 41.

prices not only because they are in great demand and thus scarce; their fantastic price itself contributes to the demand. The style itself is less important than the need to consume what is dear and therefore a mark of prestige. Only a fresh supply of "Veblenish" models can keep pace with the demand.

This "Veblen" effect [26] is effective only among the fashion leaders, who are then emulated by the socially ambitious middle classes. After being taken up by the latter, the fashion trickles down to the broad masses until cheap imitations bring it within the range of everyone. The diffusion of the fashion immediately means its depreciation as a symbol for invidious comparison. A copy indistinguishable from the original is still not an original. Once machine-made replicas of the latest mode are offered to the mass at reasonable prices, the patterns themselves lose in value. The upper classes also abandon any area as a means of displaying their status when the status symbols become too popular and too widely available.

Just as soon as the lower classes begin to copy their style, thereby crossing the line of demarcation the upper classes have drawn and destroying the uniformity of their coherence, the upper classes turn away from this style and adopt a new one, which in its turn differentiates them from the masses: and thus the game goes merrily on.[27]

A "snob" effect works against universal adoption of a fashion and thus counteracts the bandwagon effect which induces women to follow along. Among some groups, demand for a fashion decreases precisely because others share in it. The first to accept a new fashion are therefore also the first to abandon it as soon as too many others have accepted it. An extreme example of this is the deliberate effort on the part of some to be indifferent to fashion.

IDENTIFICATION AND DIFFERENTIATION

Whatever the diverse private motives that induce conformity to fashion, *social* valuations are essential. The movement of fashion exemplifies the basic collective process of definition. Each individual seeks the security that comes from conforming and knowing where he belongs as well as

[26] H. Leibenstein, "Bandwagon, Snob, and Veblen Effects in the Theory of Consumers' Demand," *Quarterly Journal of Economics*, LXIV (1950), pp. 183–207.
[27] Georg Simmel, "Fashion," *The American Journal of Sociology*, LXII (May, 1957), p. 545.

distinction from among his fellow men. Fashion satisfies both. Simmel wrote:

Two social tendencies are essental to the establishment of fashion, namely the need for union on the one hand, the need for isolation on the other. Should one of these be absent, fashion will not be formed—its sway will abruptly end.[28]

Fashion becomes more significant as a means of identification and differentiation when social contacts are secondary, fleeting, and relatively anonymous, and when individuals are only partially integrated in specific associations but react as part of a larger mass. Hence, individuals are more concerned with the appropriateness of their behavior and, at the same time, less certain of what is appropriate. The styles that become fashions—in dress, in housing, in consumption pattern, in art—are short cuts through which one's place in a large and diffuse status system is easily recognized, even on casual contact.

Where custom rules and the society is clearly stratified, people learn how to dress, express themselves, behave, and think as befits their station. A highly regimented society might institutionalize dress (and other areas in which fashion reigns) and freeze class divisions. In such a society, uniforms serve important functions. For some, they are means of binding anxiety as well as testimonials of status. They show that a person belongs and differentiate him from those who do not. The wearing of uniforms is one way of ruling out fashion. Yet where masses of people are forced to wear the same uniform and still seek distinction, fashion has a way of reasserting itself. American soldiers in World War II took to wearing a variety of colored scarves, while members of the British Desert Army adopted corduroy pants, suede shoes, scarves, and fly-switches as their distinguishing apparel.

The individual choices through which individuals seek to identify themselves result in some patterning of public preferences. The fashion movements describe long-run definitions and redefinitions about what is proper and right, whether it be a product, a given name, a magazine, an educational theory, etc. To the individual this choice is a very personal thing. It is a symbol of the ego, the core of the self, his social personality. Even an unimportant individual, by his fashion, becomes the representative of a joint spirit. Hence, broad fashion movements depend on the

[28] *Ibid.*, p. 546.

existence of social democracy in some form. On the other hand, it is sometimes suggested that the increasing emphasis on social conformity and standardization of products will immunize the mass society to fashion. The next section, in particular, takes up the relation of the mass market to fashion.

THE MARKET AND FASHION MOVEMENTS

According to a theory now abandoned, fashion movements were believed to be closely connected with the business cycle. Especially during periods of depression, it was said, lively fashions served to compensate for the drabness of human existence generally. Women's fashions, if nothing else, would at least reintroduce gaiety. Young's study, however, found no consistent relationship between women's dress and the ups and downs of the business cycle,[29] and what the theory claimed for the feminine mode cannot even be claimed for other areas of fashion.

Fashion movements are much better understood in relation to broad changes in the market than to simple fluctuations in business activity. There has been a major change in the American market over the last few decades. Marketing men in the 1920's, according to the editors of *Fortune,*

> divided all consumers into two groups, the "class" and the "mass" market. The "class" market consisted of the very wealthy and somewhat less wealthy, who could buy almost offhandedly all the comforts and luxuries of life, including the time of numerous menials; the "mass" market consisted of the remainder, some of whom were just beginning to buy the durables that are now commonplace.[30]

Today, they continue, the great "mass" has been converted into a new moneyed middle class which seems destined, sooner or later, to become *the* American market. The graduated income tax and excess profits taxes limit "class," while social security, social services, and lack of immigration delimit "mass." Where fashion once served above all to conserve the preeminence of class over mass, the various consumption patterns now in fashion help primarily to bring into being and to sort out new groupings who share, not a similar socioeconomic status, but similar taste. The

[29] Young, *op. cit.*
[30] Editors of *Fortune, The Changing American Market* (Garden City, N.Y.: Hanover House, 1955), p. 15.

differentiation is not so much in terms of class but from a mass that has been leveled in certain respects.

This growth of the middle-class market in many areas has not altogether negated the "trickle-down" theory of fashion change. Although now differentiated less clearly by their fabulous wealth from the bulk of the middle classes, there are still upper-class fashion leaders. What has changed is the rate at which a new fashion diffuses and this, in turn, has affected the way the fashion game is played. The middle class has always been the true carrier of fashion.[31] Emulation of the upper classes is imperative if the middle classes are to maintain their separateness from the lower classes, out of which many have risen. But the advance of so many into the middle class has put more purchasing power where it can be effectively used to follow fashion by a class ordinarily most susceptible to it. The increase in demand brings about keener competition and hence more rapid dissemination and quicker succession of fashions. To keep up with changing fashion entails great expense.

Still, the increasing cost of fashion has not led to its abandonment, the claims of the popular press notwithstanding. It does mean, however, that differences in class and, to some degree, in income now express themselves somewhat less in novelty than in unique and individual styling, in the quality of workmanship, in the appropriateness of dress for a variety of occasions. The upper classes still differentiate themselves from those below them in many subtle ways. Visitors to the United States comment publicly on how well dressed even the ordinary working girl *appears*.[32] The development of cheap synthetic fibers has further contributed to this trend. Fine materials and workmanship, rather than novelty, have become the true marks of the "fashionable."

The stepped-up pace of communication and the quick adaptation of the clothing industry to any shift have also made fashion more important in other areas of life. To the extent that one cannot readily distinguish the

---

[31] Simmel, *op. cit.* See also Nancy K. Jack and Betty Schiffer, "Limits of Fashion Control," *American Sociological Review*, XIII (December, 1948), pp. 730–38. In this attempt (inspired by the advent of the New Look) to investigate the limits within which fashion designers must remain if they are to be followed, the authors point out that at the "middle level" skirt lengths were more extreme (longer or shorter) than at the "top level" or among "average women." This seems to be empirical corroboration that the middle classes are least resistant to the demands of fashion.

[32] "There goes an American . . . The classless way they dress. Filing clerk and company president's wife. The same nylons, little hats, tweed suits, navy-blue dress." *Vogue* (February 1, 1950), p. 125.

fashion worn by Mrs. Astor from that worn by the girl in the typing pool, novelty in dress has been de-emphasized. But fashions in hair styles, furnishings, music and art, houses, recreation and resorts, have become more important. Some of these are beyond the means of even the new middle-class market. Therefore, the realm in which an individual feels subject to the dictates of fashion now seems a more meaningful hallmark of class in the mass society than do the externals of dress.

CLASS, STATUS, AND TASTE

Stratification—that is, the ranking of individuals in a hierarchical order—may be based on a number of criteria. Following Max Weber, one usually speaks of "class stratification" if the ranking is based on the person's relation to production and determines his potential for acquiring material wealth. One speaks of a "status system" when a society is "stratified according to the principles of their consumption of goods as represented by special 'styles of life.' "[33] Every system of social stratification is related to consumption patterns, but it is possible that either production orientations (class) or consumption orientations (status) predominate. Very little can be said as to the general economic conditions that make for a predominance of stratification by "status."

When the bases of the acquisition and distribution of goods are relatively stable, stratification by status is favored. Every technological repercussion and economic transformation threatens stratification by status and pushes class situation into the foreground. Epochs and countries in which the naked class situation is of predominant significance are regularly the periods of technical and economic transformations. And every slowing down of the shifting of economic stratification leads, in due course, to the growth of status structures and makes for a resuscitation of the important role of social honor. . . .[34]

Thus, in prosperous and economically stable periods, status predominates. A number of well-known writers see a major change in the underlying principle of stratification.[35] A system of valuation based on what a man produces is being replaced with one that is based on what a man chooses to do with his money and time. What is relevant in this thesis is

[33] H. H. Gerth and C. Wright Mills (eds.), *From Max Weber: Essays in Sociology* (New York: Oxford University Press, Inc., 1946), p. 194.
[34] *Ibid*.
[35] Among them, David Riesman, Russell Lynes, and Vance Packard.

the assumption that where once occupation identified class, and class, through the style of life that grew up around it, dictated taste, we have come to a point where taste alone is sufficient to endow a person with high status. Hence, competition revolves around the symbols of status, which rather than expressing status, now come to determine it. Fashion leadership supposedly guarantees a position of prestige, whereas once it was only position already acquired that enabled a person to act as a fashion leader.

Whether the middle masses of the affluent society have really acquired life "styles" is a very real question, though the consumption orientation—especially where there is a high degree of residential mobility and fleeting contact—is beyond dispute. To illustrate this consumption orientation, McLuhan cites an advertisement for Lord Calvert whisky, showing the "Man of Distinction" holding a glass of whisky in his hand.

What really emerges from this item is the notion of distinction and culture as being a matter of consumption rather than the possession of discriminating perception and judgment. . . . This whiskey ad bristles with techniques of persuasion. It is a blatant proclamation on culture as understood today. Consumers of expensive and refined clothes and whiskey, as pictured here, are cultured. They are distinct from the herd.[36]

Here is another ad typifying the same trend, titled "Without a Word Being Spoken":

. . . a new Cadillac car states the case for its owner with remarkable clarity and eloquence. For people everywhere have come to know and accept the "car of cars" as the dwelling place of America's front-rank citizens—and wherever highways lead, the man who sits at its wheel is accorded the courtesy that goes with respect.

But whereas fashions and other symbols of economic achievement can be bought, style of life cannot. Russell Lynes has depicted with some insight how one can discern from a person's choice of clothes, furniture, salads, games, reading, entertainment, and even the "causes" he endorses whether he is highbrow, middlebrow, or lowbrow.[37] Whatever the tastes by which people may be distinguished, one critic reasons that:

---

[36] Marshall McLuhan, *The Mechanical Bride* (New York: Vanguard Press, 1951), pp. 57–8.
[37] Russell Lynes, *Life,* XXVI (April 11, 1949), pp. 99–102. See also Lynes, *The Tastemakers* (New York: Harper & Brothers, 1954).

What culture and civilized living we have today is provided by the interaction of two groups—the esthetically radical highbrows and the somewhat more conservative and stable upper-middlebrows. Beneath the upper-middlebrows there yawns an awful chasm peopled by masses whose cultural life is so close to that of backward children that the difference is not worth arguing about. Lower-middlebrows and lowbrows may be bank presidents, pillars of the church, nice fellows, good providers or otherwise decent citizens, but, culturally speaking they are oafs. . . .[38]

FADS AND FASHION

From one point of view a fad is only a special variation of fashion. Nystrom, for example, calls a fad "a miniature fashion in some unimportant matter or detail"; anything more important and far-reaching is fashion.[39] Accordingly, since any difference in effect is only a matter of degree, it can safely be disregarded. Some patterns, like men's wristwatches, bobbed hair, lawn tennis, and crossword puzzles, which are now accepted as part of culture have indeed arisen as fads. But on the whole, fads are the highly transitory and somewhat bizarre behavior in which people, from time to time, seem to indulge themselves when on something of a rampage. Most fads last less than a year. In many instances, to make a hard and fast distinction is difficult, and in the preceding pages no attention was paid to whether something was fashionable or faddish.

It is nevertheless possible, and often productive, to distinguish between the two. Faddish behavior involves fewer people, is more personal, shorter in duration, and tends to be socially disapproved. There is "something unexpected, irresponsible or bizarre" about many fads (or crazes).[40] Among the more widely publicized have been the swallowing of goldfish, sitting on flagpoles, wearing one earring at a time, shaving the top of one's head, crowding into telephone booths, etc. The persons who engage in wild fads are not neccessarily under great personal stress or abnormally isolated from the main current of society.[41]

Fads and fashions serve somewhat different societal functions. In following fads, people set themselves apart, so that faddish behavior is a

[38] Sargeant, *op. cit.*, pp. 102 ff.
[39] Nystrom, *op. cit.*, p. 3.
[40] Sapir, *op. cit.*
[41] Ralph Turner and Lewis Killian, *Collective Behavior* (Englewood Cliffs, N.J.: Prentice-Hall, Inc., 1957), p. 208.

countervailing fashion movement that, within very restricted limits, challenges the *status quo*. Moreover, fads disseminate very rapidly and thus cut across class lines, whereas fashion reinforces the prevailing class structure. Fads afford an opportunity for quick recognition and momentary notoriety. By following fads, dissatisfied and restless individuals manage to express in a mild and harmless way their protest against the boredom they experience in their normal way of life.

Both fashion and fad are alike, however, in that they involve the dual attempt at "identification with" and "differentiation from" others in the mass society. The persons whom one copies are often one's intimate associates, but the collectivity from which one sets himself apart is vaguely conceived and abstract, sometimes designated as "square." In empirical research, some distinction in terms of duration, numbers involved, triviality, etc., may be useful. But limiting the term "fad" to definitions that are less important and universal but nevertheless rapidly and widely adopted raises a number of interesting questions: What makes some innovations of the fad type, even though they diffuse widely, less compelling? How does one account for the occasional fad that becomes fashion? Do fads flourish when the dominant stratification is by class or by status? The difference in the societal functions of fad and fashion especially needs clarification and development. For example, the scion of an upper-class family *may* wear leather patches on the elbows of his suit jacket, pepper his speech with ain'ts and mispronunciations, and belch at the table. Is this faddish behavior and, if so, does it help to obliterate the *status quo?* Is faddish behavior most typical of those who feel alienated from the society, or of the unqualified mass, or of those, like this upper-class youth, so assured of their status that they can afford to adopt the mannerisms and inventions of lower classes—such as jazz—and so give impetus to new fads?

The most significant aspects of fashion and faddish behavior are those that relate them to social structure. What does fashion mean for the group, and how important is the group for fashion? If fashion is the caprice of custom, how capricious can different individuals, groups, and societies be? What areas of deviation from custom are permissible at various times? Under what circumstances is it fashionable to be in fashion? And in what groups is it most fashionable not to follow fashion? Above all, is fashion inevitable in any mass society, and under what conditions may its influence be minimized and maximized?

Fashion also needs to be related to social change. While fashion changes often appear irrelevant or trivial, they are generally related to more significant behavior. Both fashions and fads serve as weathervanes indicating changes in the social structure and in the style of life.

The Arbiters of Fashion
ELIZABETH B. HURLOCK

Fashion rules the world but who rules fashion? At every age there have been a few men and women who have stood out as the dictators in matters of fashion, but in many cases these were not the most outstanding leaders in other phases of life. And yet they ruled as autocratically as the most despotic monarch and their word was law in all matters pertaining to dress. At one time it was a foregone conclusion that fashions should originate within the court circles. Today there is no definite place of origin and fashions spring up everywhere, outside of the court as well as within it. Many hold that the demi-mondaines are at the present time the most powerful of all of our fashion dictators and they are held to blame for the extremes and immodesties of fashion which now exist.

Not every one who can design an attractive new style can hope to be accepted as a fashion dictator. He or she must first gain recognition in some field of activity and must stand out from the rest of the social group. In every age fashions have been set by persons of great prestige. This prestige may have come from skill in warfare, from position as a member of a royal family, or from success in some profession or some form of athletics. Among primitive peoples it was the successful warrior who determined how feathers, paint, and other forms of ornamentation should be worn. If there was an hereditary aristocracy it was always the king and his family who set the fashions for the other members of the tribe. Among civilized peoples the same principle holds true. It is always the leaders in social or political affairs who are looked upon as the real leaders of fashion. In monarchies, the royal family and royal favorites, by virtue of their position and power, reflect their personal preferences in matters of dress in the clothing of the people of the nation. Stylists play

Source: The Psychology of Dress, New York: Ronald Press Co. (1929), pp. 102–108, 111–117. Reprinted by permission of the publisher.

into the hands of the fashion leaders and what they design is done to please the monarchs to whom they cater.

In Former Times—Supremacy of the Court

In order to understand how supreme was the power of the court in all matters relating to dress, one must realize the status of the king in past generations. Perhaps the best illustration of this may be taken from the daily program of Louis XIV of France. In those days when the king was looked upon as a divine ruler, there accompanied this exalted status a desire for pomp and show which would seem almost unbelievable at the present. The royal family was expected to live up to a standard which would mark them off as superior to the rest of the nation and this meant a constant pageant of ceremonious display. It is said that King Louis took his position very seriously and worked hard to live up to his ideal of what a king should be.

His daily program was arranged so as to keep him in the center of the stage in the life of the nation. His arising in the morning was an occasion of great ceremony. When he got out of bed, he first put on his wig, then his breeches and stockings. Each article of clothing was handed to him by a great lord only after it had passed through the hands of several lesser lords. During this ceremony his courtiers were admitted in stated order according to their rank. His simple breakfast came to him only after passing through the hands of many nobles of different degrees. His dinners and suppers were served at small tables while the court looked on in reverential silence. At work or at play he was constantly surrounded by people of high rank whose main duty seemed to be to admire his every action. When one considers how supreme his position was and how it typified the position of the monarchs of the past, one can readily understand why it was that the nation as a whole followed the fashions of the court.

Physical Defects and Fashions

Royal fashions were often originated to cover up some physical defect of a member of the royal household or to increase the illusion of regality.

A king was supposed to look and act his part. If nature did not endow him with a regal appearance, he felt that he had to make up for this deficiency by dressing for the part he was supposed to play. Any physical defect would detract from an imposing appearance and court dressmakers vied with each other in devising clever means of covering nature's deficiencies.

Shoes with long points came into favor during the reign of William Rufus because one of his court favorites, Count Fulk of Anjou had feet misshapen with bunions which he was very anxious to cover up. The King was so pleased with this novel method of concealment that he eagerly accepted the style and a fashion was thus established which lasted for nearly three centuries. Long skirts were brought into favor because the daughters of Louis XI of France had misshapen legs and feet. Charles VII adopted long coats to cover ill-shaped legs, and Louis XIII, who was prematurely bald, used a peruke made in imitation of long curls. Hoop skirts were said to have originated with Madame de Montespan to conceal defects produced as a result of an accident.

Queen Elizabeth, in spite of the homely appearance which historians accord her, was exceedingly vain and ordered the court dressmakers to produce fashions which would cover up her defects and make the most of the good features she possessed. One of her naturally good features was her small waist and in order to enhance it she used a corset to constrict the flesh to thirteen inches. Cloth proved to be too weak, so whalebone was used to reinforce it. The high neck ruff which is so characteristic of that period, was adopted by the Queen to cover up a long, thin and unshapely neck. The late Queen Alexandra adopted a jeweled collar to hide a disfiguring birthmark on her neck. When she decided to dress her hair low, she was followed not only by the women of England but also by the women throughout the world.

Royal Whims

Often fashions have arisen from styles which have appealed to a royal personage and have been accepted on their merits alone with no particular attention to the covering up of a personal defect. Isabella of Bavaria, Queen of Charles VI of France, introduced a headdress which took the form of enormous protruding horns. The hennin, which was the name given to this monstrosity, was quickly adopted by the women of the court and each vied with the other to see which could wear the largest, handsomest, or most grotesque. Queen Claude, wife of Francis I, introduced into France, from Spain, the "vertugadine" and the high-heeled slipper, both of which were harmful and troublesome to the extent of causing many edicts against their use. To Catherine de' Medici may be traced the fashion of wearing corsets, ruffs, and paint which prevailed so extensively in the sixteenth and seventeenth centuries. She maintained that all women of good birth and breeding should have a waist thirteen inches in diameter and ordered all women of the court to produce a waistline of this sort by the use of corsets.

French Royal Fashions

Mary Stuart, the Scottish queen of Francis II, afterwards Mary Queen of Scotts, was responsible for several important fashions which she brought out during her brief reign of one year at the French Court. The small gold cap which bore her name was the fashionable headdress of the women of that period. To her also is due the honor of having established the French tri-color as a livery for the Swiss guard. The red represented Switzerland, the home of the men composing the guard; the white, the royal house of France, while blue was for Scotland, the birthplace of the queen. Henry II set the pace for the most extreme and effeminate masculine styles. The clothing of men closely resembled that of women and rings, necklaces, earrings, corsets, ruffs, and rolls of artificial hair were a part of every costume. The King's love for paint, powder, and perfume led to the fashion of using these even for everyday attire. Marie Antoinette, the youthful queen of Louis XVI, was a powerful fashion dictator during her time. New styles in headdress were her special contributions to the fashions of the day. The "hedge-hog" style, the "half-hedge-hog," the "milk-sop," and the "mad dog" are a few of the grotesque names which were given to the eccentric styles which followed each other in rapid succession. These were so elaborate that it was often necessary to have them "built up" for several weeks at a time. Louis XVI, though a less powerful dictator than his queen, established several fashions which have had a very lasting influence. Before his time, handkerchiefs had been oblong in form. The King, however, preferred the square form to the long, scarf-like one and issued a decree that only square handkerchiefs should be made or used in France.

NAPOLEON

When Napoleon made himself Emperor of France, he left no stone unturned in his effort to make the French court the most beautiful of the world. In matters of fashion, as in matters of state, he was the sole dictator. He not only decided what the men and women of the court should wear, but he gave them materials with specific instructions as to how to make them up. In addition to this, he decreed that no one should appear twice in his presence in the same costume. He was successful in re-establishing the elaborate dress of women which had been characteristic of the pre-Revolutionary days, but only the dandies of the court circles were willing to go back to the effeminate costumes which were worn by the men of those times.

English Fashion Arbiters

The English royal arbiters have been fewer and less influential than those in France. Henry VIII was in his way as tyrannical a dictator of fashions as was Napoleon. When he grew tired of seeing his men wear long hair, he ordered them to cut it off. Because he liked to see women's hair, he ordered women to abandon the headgear which they had formerly worn and to wear their hair in two long braids. Queen Elizabeth, who displayed a similar tendency toward tyrannical dictatorship, decided not only what the people of the land should wear but what they should not wear. Silk stockings, in place of woolen ones, were a part of her contribution to the world of fashion. One of her ladies-in-waiting, Mistress Montague, presented her "for a new yeare's gift, a paire of black, knit, silk stockings," according to the new Spanish style. The Queen was so pleased with the gift that she never again wore woolen stockings. Soon the fashion spread to the court circles and hence to the women of the wealthy middle class. The piercing of ears for earrings and the use of mirrors in public as well as the excessive use of powder and paint, were fashions set by the Queen and were accepted by the men as well as the women of the day.

James I was a coward and lived in fear of being stabbed by a dagger. As a protection against this, he wore clothing well padded and stuffed which led to a fashion which lasted many years after his death. The wearing of roses over the ear, and the arrangement of the hair in a "lovelock" over the forehead, were fashions introduced by the frivolous Charles I. Beards were cut off and faces clean shaven to fit in with this effeminate attire.

QUEEN VICTORIA

In more recent times, Queen Victoria stood out as an important arbiter of fashions for the nations of the civilized world. Because of the improved methods of transportation and manufacture, her influence was more widespread than that of many former monarchs. On a visit to Balmoral, the Queen adopted the Highland suit of Scotch tartan for the English princes. Soon boys of from five to ten years of age throughout the world appeared in modified forms of the Highland costume. When the Queen grew stout and assumed a style that helped to hide the lines of her body, puffs and paddings appeared on the dress of other women. Extreme modesty also led her to revive the crinoline so that the ladies of her court might not be forced to abandon their social duties on account of approaching maternity.

. . . .

Royal Favorites

Next in power and prestige to the royal family in the determination of fashions have been the court favorites. In earlier times the kings' mistresses had unlimited power in matters of fashion arbitration. Many of the most outstanding fashions of the past may be traced to a whim of a royal favorite, as readily accepted as if they had been determined by a beloved queen. To Agnes Sorel, famous beauty and favorite of Charles VII of France, is due the credit of introducing the fashion of wearing gowns which left the bosom uncovered to the waist. False hair and wigs were also popularized through her influence and this led to the establishment of one of France's greatest industries. Madame de Pompadour and Madame du Barry, both of whom were mistresses of Louis XV and of very humble origin, were responsible for fashions so extreme that they verged on immorality even in that day of lax morals. The pannier dress, whose circumference soon reached eighteen feet, tiny shoes, parasols, enormously high headdresses, paint, powder, and patches were a few of the contributions of these two favorites to the dress of fashionable women of the day.

Masculine Favorites

The courts of the past have had their masculine favorites also. The two best known examples in history are Sir Walter Raleigh, one of Queen Elizabeth's devoted admirers, and Beau Brummell, the boon companion of George IV at the time when he was Prince Regent. In the absence of a king, Sir Walter Raleigh was the uncrowned dictator of the masculine fashions of his day. To him is due the credit for introducing the whalebone corset, the fashion of piercing the ears for enormous jeweled earrings, and the wearing of necklaces, bracelets, perfume, paint, and powder.

BEAU BRUMMELL

Beau Brummell is accredited with the revival of elegant attire for men in the latter part of the eighteenth century. He introduced tasteful, artistic designs in masculine dress in place of the gaudy ones which prevailed before his day. His position as unquestioned arbiter of fashion was due to his status as close personal friend of the Prince and what he wore was copied by the men throughout the kingdom. His favorite costume, and the one which was most frequently imitated, consisted of a blue coat with velvet collar, black trousers and shoes, a white neckcloth, opera hat, and white gloves which he always carried. Black evening dress with a white waistcoat was introduced by him in place of the brilliantly colored one which had previously been worn. Even today many of his innovations are accepted as the standard of correct attire for men.

Some Rulers Not Interested in Dress

There have been times in the history of every nation when the rulers were not interested in any matters pertaining to dress. This lack of interest was sometimes due to a personal whim and sometimes to religious or economic pressure which caused aversion to extravagant expenditure on clothing. As a result, fashion was temporarily pushed into the background and had to play a very subservient rôle in the life of the nation. It would have been impossible in the days of a strict monarchy for courtiers to outdress their rulers and out of deference to them they had to follow whatever styles these rulers might choose to set. During a period of this kind fashions were consequently very dull and showed a tendency to stand still over a long interval of time.

In Florence, during the Renaissance, there was no attempt on the part of the court to set definite fashions for all to follow. Instead, each lady of culture created her own fashions to suit her personality. James I of England was far more interested in a life of ease and comfort than in personal adornment. During his entire reign of twenty-two years, he did not introduce a single new fashion, though his fear of assassination caused him to carry certain existing fashions to ridiculous extremes. Again under the Georges, English fashions were very dull. Society within the court circles reflected the personality of the rulers and it is, therefore, not surprising that the fashions of the day offered little in the way of beauty or interest.

Decline of Royal Prestige

With the decline in the power of the crown there came a decline in the prestige of the court as a center for fashion. Almost a century before the French Revolution actually took place, a spirit of insubordination and hatred toward royalty had grown up among the masses. The consequence was that they no longer were so eager to derive their fashions from the usual source, the court, and turned to a new source of inspiration. The court, however, still retained its influence on fashions for the nobility and for foreign nations. In later years in England, the court, while still maintaining the respect and love of the people, has lost some of its prestige in determining what the fashions for the nation will be. The fact that strong royal opposition to short skirts and bobbed hair has in no way retarded the growth of these styles would certainly suggest that royal opinion in connection with matters of fashion is not what it used to be.

In America

The rise of democratic forms of government throughout the Western world has necessitated the formation of new centers of fashion. In America, the most logical center is the White House. And, if the old order of events still held, the President and his wife would be looked upon as the national dictators of fashion. But this is not the case. With the exception of President Buchanan and President Arthur, the executives of the American people have paid little attention to fashionable attire. Perhaps if they were younger when they came into office, and if they had fewer affairs of state to attend to they would be able to devote more time to setting fashions for the nation to follow. As a rule, the President is too serious-minded to be a true "dandy" and his wife is too dignified to be interested in fashions which would appeal to the more frivolous women of the country.

The American "Royal Family"

Occasionally if the American "royal family" is very much beloved by the people, the personal preferences of color and styles of clothing of its different members are used by the commercial interests for the establishment of new fashions which have a purely patriotic flavor. While there has been in no sense an attempt to dictate what others shall wear, they are copied because of their popularity with the people of the country. During the last few administrations, there have been a number of cases of this sort. While President Roosevelt was in office, his daughter Alice was affectionately looked upon as "Princess Alice." Her popularity was so great that her personal preferences were copied throughout the country. Light blue was her favorite color and it soon became the fashionable color for the women of the nation under the name "Alice blue." In the spring of

1921, Mrs. Warren Harding chose as the predominant color of her wardrobe a darker shade of blue. At once the manufacturers proclaimed "Florence Harding blue" as the new color. When Mrs. Coolidge showed a fancy for red, the press throughout the nation proclaimed that red was to be the newest and most outstanding color of the feminine wardrobe. And for a season that prophecy came true to such an extent that there were few women throughout the country who did not possess a red garment of some sort.

Uncrowned Leaders of Society

When there is no predestined fashion center from which fashions are sure to radiate, the "uncrowned leaders of society" are in many cases the real fashion dictators. These individuals whose ability in some particular field has won them a popularity and recognition which places them before the public gaze, soon find that what they wear is copied by their fellow-countrymen much as if they belonged to the royalty of the old days. They are not, however, permanent dictators of fashion as were the members of the nobility. They are popular idols who rise and fall. Often the public will adopt a style no matter how hideous, exaggerated, or eccentric it may be, simply because it has been worn by a celebrity. Let that person disappear from the limelight, however, and the fashion which he was responsible for dies out at once.

The Stage and Fashions

The stage has offered excellent opportunities for the attainment of widespread popularity and prestige. When a man or woman has reached "stardom," the world opens its doors to them in much the same way it would have to high-ranking nobility. Even since the days when the actresses of the royal theatres in France were among the favorites of the King, every eccentricity of a popular actress has been copied, and what she wears is worn everywhere.

At the end of the last century, women in America took up the fashion of wearing a Jersey and kilted skirt. This originated in England where it was devised to show off the beautiful figure of Lily Langtry, the "Jersey

Lily," as she was fondly called. The thin and fat, the tall and short and the young and old, accepted it with equal delight. When Die Walküre was first presented, white wings like those on Brunhilde's helmet appeared everywhere on the hats of women. The Chanticleer headdress of pheasant feathers which was so popular some twenty years ago came from the play "Chanticleer." When Irene Castle was at the height of her dancing career, her clothing was used as the model for fashionable women's clothing of the day. At the time when Raquel Meller took the New York public by storm with her Spanish songs, fashions enjoyed a Spanish element that lasted as long as did her popularity.

The Cinema and Fashions

In recent years the popularity of the cinema and its far-reaching effect have made screen stars more powerful in the determination of present-day fashions than the actors and actresses of the legitimate stage. The nation-wide publicity which is given to them, has made them the popular heroes and heroines of the day. What they do, say, think, eat, or wear serves as a model for their devoted followers.

The rage for Mary Pickford's curls only gave way to the bob when the War made truly feminine fashions take a back seat. Gloria Swanson was responsible for the "boyish bob" style of haircut and for the robe de style type of evening dress. The "Spanish spike" heel made its first appearance in Hollywood and soon replaced the low flat heel which the modern flappers had previously sponsored. The fashionable thin figure which all women are striving to attain had its origin among the screen stars. All screen heroines are slender and each woman, as she watched them, decided that she must be slender, too. As a result, dieting, massage, exercise, and medicine were soon employed to reduce the women of the country to the proportions which the screen stars possessed. Even in Europe, where in the past the buxom type was the national ideal of feminine beauty, the slender figure has surpassed it in popularity to such an extent that restaurant owners and candy manufacturers report they are on the verge of bankruptcy.

Sports and Fashions

In the last few years sports have attained such widespread popularity that the successful sportsman, or sportswoman, is ranked among the outstanding figures of the day. Nation-wide publicity is given to their every action and they stand before the public gaze as much as do the cinema stars. Dressmakers and manufacturers have wasted no time in capitalizing their prestige as an asset to fashion-making. Helen Wills, the American tennis champion, established a style in eyeshades which replaced the conventional hat for sportswear. So great was its popularity that for one summer it greatly affected the millinery business. Mlle. Lenglen, the French tennis marvel, inaugurated the style of short, full-skirted, sleeveless sports frocks which the women of the athletic world have copied to such an extent that the old type of sports clothing has completely disappeared. To her also is due the credit for originating the fashion of bright head coverings and bandeaux which are today a necessary accessory to the sleeveless sport costume.

The masculine sports stars are not without power in the sartorial world. Golf champions are the models for masculine golfing costumes just as the clothes of tennis champions are copied by all tennis-players. Manufacturers of ready-made sports clothing for men eagerly watch what the star players wear and capitalize this in the establishment of fashions for the rest of the sports world.

Annotated Bibliography

JOANNE BUBOLZ-EICHER, ELEANOR KELLEY,
AND MARY ELLEN ROACH

COMPILERS' NOTE: The following annotated bibliography is arranged alphabetically by author. An author's publications are arranged chronologically if he is cited more than once. All references in the supplementary readings appended to each section may be located by matching author and date of the reference with author and date in the bibliography.

Formal compilation of the bibliography began at Michigan State University in 1961 at the time Joanne Eicher assumed her position in the Department of Textiles, Clothing, and Related Arts. Informally, the compilation began years before as scholars in numerous places, as well as Michigan State University, became intrigued by the idea of the socio-cultural aspects of dress. Eleanor Kelley was involved from the beginning with compiling categories for searching, format, and processing. The bibliographical process began with the compilation of a list of approximately 100 key reference terms related to dress and adornment. It continued with the systematic use of them in (1) searching four major indexes (Poole's Index to Periodical Literature, International Index to Periodical Literature, Readers' Guide to Periodical Literature, and Cumulative Book Index) and the Michigan State University card catalogue, and (2) scanning available course syllabi from several universities, and bibliographies from books, theses, and articles.

We attemped to locate references which related to socio-cultural factors associated with clothing and appearance. As the topic is not neatly or systematically catalogued or indexed, we were challenged to use ingenuity in the search for materials.

When Joanne Eicher and Mary Ellen Roach were encouraged to assemble a book of readings, the latter brought new resources to the bibliographic process. The book progressed, and the number of citations grew. At least two thousand were annotated and considered for inclusion; finally, the selections were narrowed to those published materials which seem most related to our framework for analysis.

As every scholar knows, bibliographic searching is never-ending, for each reference leads to another tantalizing citation. No doubt many similar readings exist awaiting inclusion in another publication.

Acoca, M. (1963), "Luck With Your Locks, Young John," *Life*, Vol. 54 (May 24, 1963), p. 16.

Social pressure exerted against young boy who does not wear the haircut considered appropriate for his age and sex in the United States.

Allen, D. (1925), "Personal Decoration—Some Aspects of the Evolution of Adornment," *The World Tomorrow*, Vol. 8 (March, 1925), pp. 76–79.
Popular treatment of contemporary attitudes toward adornment. Includes comments on hygiene and moralizing.

Allen, F. L. (1931), *Only Yesterday*, New York: Harper and Bros., pp. 89–93.
Discussion of dress reform in 1920's. Emphasis on moral aspects, i.e., modesty.

Allen, F. L. (1952), *The Big Change*, New York: Harper and Bros., pp. 8–9, 119–120, 192–193, 201–203. [Also in: Bantam Books (1961).]
Twentieth-century trends in dress mentioned include change to informality, change in sex-role symbolism of dress, and decreasing salience of clothing as a stratification symbol.

Allport, F. H. (1924), *Social Psychology*, Boston: Houghton Mifflin Co., pp. 392–394.
Fashions originate with manufacturers and are quickly worn by those wishing to assert individuality. The latter give the impression that all are adopting style and so the follower follows. Author feels that fashon is kept moving by pursuit and differentiation. Fad is fashion reaching the pitch of crowd behavior. People feel compelled to conform.

Allport, F. H. (1939), "Rule and Custom As Individual Variations of Behavior Distributed Upon a Continuum of Conformity," *American Journal of Sociology*, Vol. 44 (May, 1939), pp. 897–921.
A discussion of the development of a continuum of conformity to American folkways, mores, and fashions. The author has used several aspects of clothing to illustrate the continuum.

Altekar, A. S. (1962), *The Position of Women in Hindu Civilization*, 3rd ed. Delhi: Motilal Banarsidass, pp. 279–304.
A historical treatment of dress and ornament of Indian women. The introduction of stitched clothes is discussed as well as the economic "insurance" of ornaments.

Anderson, R. (1964), "The Shape Makers," *Chicago Tribune Magazine*, (May 31, 1964), pp. 6–9.
A popular article on the American industry specializing in providing foundation garments for molding the figure of the American woman to the current ideals. Some comments on the reasons for using corsets and brassieres are made.

Andreen, J. H., Gibson, J. W., and Wetmore, O. C. (1953), "Fabric Evaluations Based on Physiological Measurements of Comfort," *Textile Research Journal*, Vol. 23 (January, 1953), pp. 11–22.
Experiments indicate that comfort depends largely on the geometry of fabric construction and the manner in which it is worn on the body. Skin temperature, skin wetness, heart rate, and rate of sweating were studied to determine the individual's comfort.

Angelino, H., Barnes, L. A., and Shedd, C. L. (1956), "Attitudes of Mothers and

Adolescent Daughters Concerning Clothing and Grooming," *Journal of Home Economics,* Vol. 48 (December, 1956), pp. 779-782.

Study to determine what, if any, differences were present between mothers' and daughters' opinions concerning clothing and grooming.

Anspach, K. (1958), "Style in Dresses," *Journal of Home Economics,* Vol. 50 (March, 1958), p. 229.

Abstract of a study of differences in choice of dress style by women of different characteristics, to ascertain the extent and nature of choice stability in design and to compare market offerings with consumers' preferences.

Anspach, K. (1959), "Clothing Research in Home Economics," *Journal of Home Economics,* Vol. 51 (November, 1959), pp. 767-770.

Summary of clothing research by home economists as reported through the *Journal of Home Economics* and U.S.D.A. from 1925-1958. Includes all areas of clothing research.

Aria, E. (1915), "Fashion, Its Survivals and Revivals," *Fortnightly Review,* Vol. 98 (November, 1915), pp. 930-937.

Discussion of what was fashionable in 1915 and the sources of inspiration for the fashions.

"Art and the Well-Dressed Woman," *Practical Home Economics,* Vol. 27 (May, 1949), pp. 263-265.

A study of the relationship of art to the portraiture of well-dressed women suggests that modern taste denies to well-dressed women the sumptuous effect and so artists no longer portray them.

"'Astings Hain't 'Ad It So Bad Since 1066," *Life,* Vol. 57 (September 18, 1964), pp. 61-63.

Report of activities of British teen-age groups called the Mods and Rockers. Prominent in their habits are their distinctive dress and grooming practices.

Bach, M. (1953), "The Douks Are At It Again," *Christian Century,* Vol. 70 (December 16, 1953), pp. 1452-1454.

Discussion of tactics used by the Doukhobors in resisting authority. They maintain that by parading nude they are showing the world how they must meet God. They came into the world naked, and thus they must leave it.

Bader, I. M. (1963), "An Exploratory Study of Clothing Problems and Attitudes of a Group of Older Women in Iowa City," *Adding Life to Years,* Institute of Gerontology, State University of Iowa, Vol. 10 (October, 1963), pp. 3-6.

This study indicates that older women are interested in their clothing, take pride in their appearance, and tend to retain clothing attitudes and behavior from their middle-aged years.

Balch, E. S. (1904), "Savage and Civilized Dress," *Journal of the Franklin Institute,* Vol. 157 (May, 1904), pp. 321-332.

Discussion of variety in clothing and ornament worn by different people. Author finds customs of dress for savages no more "queer or irrational" than those for civilized people.

Baldwin, F. E. (1926), *Sumptuary Legislation and Personal Regulation in England,*

Baltimore: Johns Hopkins Press, *Johns Hopkins University Studies in History and Political Science,* Vol. 44, pp. 1-282.

A study of English laws which regulated the intimate personal conduct of men. These laws were almost entirely concerned with food and clothing; however, regulation of clothing was more prevalent.

Ballin, A. S. (1885), *The Science of Dress,* London: Sampson Low, Marston, Searle, and Rivington.

A book on "healthy" dress written for women by a woman. It strives to promote "healthy" dress which is nevertheless somewhat fashionable and deals with children's clothes as well as women's.

Bane, L. (1935), "Overtones of Clothing," *Journal of Home Economics,* Vol. 27 (October, 1935), pp. 513-514.

Discussion of why we wear what we wear. Includes modesty and protection as reasons.

Barber, B. (1957), *Social Stratification,* New York: Harcourt, Brace and Co., pp. 146-151.

An analysis of the status symbolism of clothing.

Barber, B. and Lobel, L. S. (1952), " 'Fashion' in Women's Clothes and the American Social System," *Social Forces,* Vol. 31 (December, 1952), pp. 124-131. [Also in: Bendix, R. and Lipset, M. (ed.) (1953), *Class, Status and Power,* Glencoe, Illinois: Free Press, and Bobbs-Merrill Reprint No. S-335.]

"Fashion" has many meanings. It may have both latent and manifest functions in American social system, e.g., in the economic system, in the age-sex role structure, and in the class system.

Barker, G. H. and Adams, W. T. (1959), "The Social Structure of a Correctional Institution," *Journal of Criminal Law, Criminology and Police Science,* Vol. 49, pp. 417-422. [Also in: Young, K. and Mack, R. W. (ed.) (1960), *Principles of Sociology,* New York: American Book Co., pp. 40-46.]

The author mentions the tendency of boys in a correctional institution to strengthen the negative aspects of a boy's self concept by giving negative nicknames which refer to bodily defects, such as "pimples." Thus a boy's already poor concept is further weakened. It is believed this is done to build up the self concept of the namer.

Barnett, H. G. (1953), *Innovation: The Basis of Cultural Change,* New York: McGraw-Hill Book Co., pp. 139-140, 314.

Topics include deviant means of reaching goals, such as zoot suits or other fads in clothing.

Barr, E. de Y. (1934), "A Psychological Analysis of Fashion Motivation," *Archives of Psychology,* Vol. 26 (June, 1934), pp. 1-100.

Investigation of the practical problems of choice in the selection of women's clothes. Concerned with the motives underlying choice of fashion—confined in this study to daytime dress.

Bartley, L. and Warden, J. (1962), "Clothing Preferences of Women 65 and Older," *Journal of Home Economics,* Vol. 54 (October, 1962), pp. 716-717.

Researchers concluded that the 65-year or older women who were studied were relatively satisfied with outer clothing available in today's markets. They wanted clothing which was becoming in color, line, and style; comfortable; easy to care for and put on.

Basett, H. C., Burton, A. C., and Gagge, A. P. (1941), "A Practical System of Units for the Description of the Heat Exchange of Man with His Environment," *Science,* Vol. 94 (November 7, 1941), pp. 428–430.

The authors present a set of units for measuring thermal activity and insulation. Using these units of measurement, a researcher can systematically study the relationship of man's comfort to clothing, temperature, and bodily exercise.

Bates, M. (1952), *Where Winter Never Comes,* New York: Charles Scribner's Sons, pp. 100–117.

Writer considers adaptation of clothes to the tropics in physiological terms. He also includes a preliminary discussion of the functions of clothing.

Battista, O. A. (1959), "Why We Dress the Way We Do," *Science Digest,* Vol. 46 (October, 1959), pp. 27–31.

Discussion of aspects of today's clothing that are survivals of man's attempts at protection in previous times.

Baumgartner, C. W. (1963), "Factors Associated with Clothing Consumption Among College Freshmen," *Journal of Home Economics,* Vol. 55 (March, 1963), p. 218.

Abstract of dissertation designed to examine relationships among economic, social-psychological, and personal factors influencing clothing consumption.

Bayha, A. E. (1932), "Children's Clothing," *Practical Home Economics,* Vol. 10 (September–October, 1932), pp. 275–276, 313, 331.

Presentation of criteria to be used as guides in selecting appropriate clothing for children. Some psychological-sociological implications.

Beals, R. and Hoijer, H. (1959), *An Introduction to Anthropology,* New York: Macmillan Co.

See index for references to clothing and ornament.

Beaton, C. (1954), *The Glass of Fashion,* Garden City, New York: Doubleday and Co.

A book on fashion leaders, including actresses, the demi-monde, royalty, socialites, designers. Emphasis is on women's dress.

Beauvoir, S. de (1952), *The Second Sex,* translated and edited by H. M. Parshley, New York: Alfred A. Knopf.

See index for references to dress and costume.

Bell, Q. (1947), *On Human Finery,* London: Hogarth Press.

Theoretical treatment using Veblen's concepts as a basis for organization. Contains material on moral standards, fashion, fashion change, sexual differentiation in dress, archaistic dress.

Benedict, R. (1931), "Dress," *Encyclopedia of Social Science,* Vol. 5, New York: Macmillan Co., pp. 235–237.

Discussion of origins and evolution of dress. Reference to various theories, including modesty and protection.

Benson, E. J. (1934), "Personality in Dress," *Practical Home Economics,* Vol. 12 (November, 1934), p. 328.
Author observes that we pass judgment on people we meet and that clothing is one means of conveying personality to others. Special note made of the dress of teachers.

Bergler, E. (1953), *Fashion and the Unconscious,* New York: Brunner.
Author seeks to prove that clothes are a masculine invention thrust upon women, that they are man's reassurance against his own repressed fears of woman's body, and the repressed fantasies connected with it. He feels that the unconscious (a homosexual hatred of women by fashion creators) may be a force which sets the fashion.

Berkeley-Hill, O. (1942), "The Psychology of Clothes," *Indian Journal of Psychology,* Vol. 17 (September–December, 1942), pp. 141–145.
Discussion slanted to Flugel's three reasons for wearing clothing: modesty, protection, decoration. Concludes with remarks on the future of clothes.

Bernard, L. (1926), *Introduction to Social Psychology,* New York: Henry Holt and Co., pp. 541–563.
Fashion viewed as collective behavior. Fads and fashion are a means of advertising the self. Author believes the two strong elements of fashion are imitation and competition within conformity.

Bettelheim, B. (1950), *Love Is Not Enough: The Treatment of Emotionally Disturbed Children,* Glencoe, Illinois: Free Press.
See index for references to clothing, dressing, modesty, and undressing.

Bettelheim, B. (1954), *Symbolic Wounds, Puberty Rites and the Envious Male,* Glencoe, Illinois: Free Press, pp. 211–214.
A consideration of transvestitism in initiation rites.

Bierstedt, R. (1957), *The Social Order,* New York: McGraw-Hill Book Co., pp. 203–205.
Fashion reconciles simultaneous desire for expressions of conformity and individuality. Discussion of the function of fashion, the sanctions applied to dressing improperly, and the reluctance of people to be "out of style."

Biester, C. (1952), "Academic Costume Tells a Story," *Practical Home Economics,* Vol. 30 (June, 1952), pp. 251, 270.
Article concerned with the origin of and usage of academic costume. Both descriptive and historical.

Binder, P. (1954), *Muffs and Morals,* New York: William Morrow Co.
Treatment of dress handled in a popular style. Emphasis on moral attitudes toward clothing and adornment. Also comments on occupational dress, clothing and age-sex roles, sumptuary law, accessories, hairdressing, cosmetics, fashion leadership, and influence of the East.

Binder, P. (1958), *The Peacock's Tail,* London: George G. Harrap and Co.

Writer discusses men's dress and seeks to discover why man has given up the art of dress. She deals with the history of men's dress and the influences on it. Also examines the whole purpose and meaning of it.

Blackmore, B. (1927), *Clothing Purchased by Farm Families in Tompkins County,* Cornell University Agricultural Experiment Station Bulletin No. 615.
Results of study showed higher income and capital were expressed more clearly in women's than in men's clothing and in the clothing for older daughters more clearly than in that for other members of the family. Financial ability made little difference in the buying of work clothing; however, more of the financially able families were buying dress clothing.

Blair, M. H. (1953), "Changes in Appearance of Women 45 to 65 Years of Age Which Affect Use of Ready-to-Wear Garments and Commerical Patterns," *Journal of Home Economics,* Vol. 45 (April, 1953), pp. 248–250.
Study initiated to determine clothing problems faced by older women. Concerned with relation of cut and style to comfort and satisfaction. Found that women who maintained weight of age thirty-five had no more problems than younger women.

Blaker, M. (1943), "Fashions in 1943," *Journal of Home Economics,* Vol. 35 (February, 1943), pp. 73–76.
General fashions in dress of 1943 described as quite feminine and different from the slacks worn on the job. Ingenuity was shown in designs which were in keeping with the L85 order for slim trends. Author noted that the L85 order did not cause the trend to slim lines and short skirts. It merely hastened the evolution of a trend which had already begun.

Blanc, C. (1877), *Art in Ornament and Dress,* London: Chapman and Hall.
Analysis of design principles plus instruction in their application in personal adornment for men and women.

Blanchard, F. S. (1953), "Revolution in Clothes," *Harper's Magazine,* Vol. 206 (March, 1953), pp. 59–64.
Discussion of significant trends in men's and women's clothing in an age of informal living.

Bliss, S. H. (1916), "The Significance of Clothes," *American Journal of Psychology,* Vol. 27 (April, 1916), pp. 217–226.
Discussion of why man wears clothes. Author states that clothing originated because man felt incomplete and dissatisfied with himself. This dissatisfaction led to a strong impulse to supplement the body with clothes.

Block, V. L. (1937), "Conflicts of Adolescents with Their Mothers," *Journal of Abnormal and Social Psychology,* Vol. 32 (July–September, 1937), pp. 193–206.
Study of junior high boys and girls. Several of the conflicts cited by adolescents in the study deal with clothing use or purchase.

Blumer, H. (1939), "Collective Behavior," in Park, R. E. (ed.) *An Outline of the Principles of Sociology,* New York: Barnes and Noble, pp. 275–277, 279–280.
A classic statement on fashion as a social movement.

Blumer, H. (1964), "The Nature and Role of Fashion," paper presented at the 1964 meeting of the American Sociological Association, to be published in one of the American sociological journals.
A critical appraisal of previous comments on the role of fashion and a cogent analysis of the social nature of fashion.

Boehn, M. von (1929), *Modes and Manners: Ornaments,* London: J. M. Dents and Sons.
This book tells the story of the highly important "trifles" called ornaments, which have accompanied the progress of fashion as characteristic attributes.

Boehn, M. von (1932), *Modes and Manners,* translated by Joshua, J., 4 Vols., Philadelphia: J. B. Lippincott Co.
A description of fashion from the middle ages to the eighteenth-century. Relates fashion to the life of the times.

Boehn, M. von and Fischel, O. (1909), *Modes and Manners of the 19th Century,* 3 Vols., New York: Dutton and Co.
A historical work which includes a descriptive account of the intellectual, political, and artistic life of the time.

Bogardus, E. S. (1923), *Essentials of Social Psychology,* Los Angeles: J. R. Miller Press, pp. 120–137.
Detailed discussion of elements of fashion, including the imitation process through which fashion becomes current, invention as a necessary fashion antecedent, and the thriving of fashion on novelty. Also comments on the psychology and purposes of dress. Fashion cited as a contributor to progress.

Bogardus, E. S. (1924A), "Social Psychology of Fads," *Journal of Applied Sociology,* Vol. 8 (March–April, 1924), pp. 239–243.
Longitudinal study made over a ten-year period. Each year individuals were asked to name what they considered the five leading fads of the time. The 735 tabulated fads fell into eight major categories. Of these, the two categories associated with men's and women's dress included 83.5 per cent of total fads recorded.

Bogardus, E. S. (1924B), *Fundamentals of Social Psychology,* New York: Century Co., pp. 151–167, 178–186.
Discussion of elements of fashion, the fashion process, the craze, the fad, the psychology of dress. Seven principles of fashion given.

Bonner, H. (1953), *Social Psychology,* New York: American Book Co., p. 391.
Comments on fads and fashion.

Boulton, C. R. (1898), "The Power of Frills," *Canadian Magazine,* Vol. 12 (November, 1898), pp. 19–24, Toronto: The Ontario Publishing Co.
Includes statements on functions of dress, such as, instrumental use and symbolism.

Bousfield, P. (1925), *Sex and Civilization,* London: Kegan Paul, Trench, Trubner, and Co., pp. 67–75.
Brief reference to the limiting effect certain kinds of clothing have on normal muscular growth and general activity of women.

Bowie, A. and Dickens, D. (1942), *Clothing Supplies of Socially Participating White Farm Families of Mississippi,* Mississippi Agricultural Experiment Station Technical Bulletin No. 30.
Analysis of clothing owned by members of socially participating white farm families. Families in study with smallest amount of clothing did not have adequate wardrobes for social participation. More social participation took place in families with more adequate clothing.

Boyle, F. (1905), "Savages and Clothes," *Monthly Review,* (September, 1905), pp. 124–138.
Generalizations on the superior health position attributed to "savages" who wear no clothes.

Brannigan, E. (1932), "A Century of Fashion," *Practical Home Economics,* Vol. 10 (December, 1932), pp. 379–380.
Relates the fashion changes from 1750 to 1850 to the cultural changes (mainly political) of three periods during this time span. General ideas posed within a rather loose framework.

Brasie, M., Brew, M. L., Fitzsimmons, C., Rankin, M., and Smart, R. C. (1947), "Research Areas on Textiles and Clothing," *Journal of Home Economics,* Vol. 39 (December, 1947), pp. 620–624.
Discussion of the application of economic, psychological, and sociological concepts and frames of reference to research problem areas in clothing and textiles.

Bredemeier, H. C. and Toby, J. (1960), *Social Problems in America,* New York: John Wiley and Sons, pp. 17–18.
Comments on socio-cultural standards for physical beauty or attractiveness.

Brew, M. (1948), *American Clothing Consumption,* 1879–1909, Chicago: University of Chicago Press.
This volume contrasts the clothing habits of women in two different years, 1879 and 1909. In the study kinds of clothing worn are considered, also the weights or amounts on the body at one time. The author maintains that clothing customs are culturally determined.

Brew, M. (1954), "Development of Clothing Budgets," *Journal of Home Economics,* Vol. 46 (October, 1954), pp. 578–582.
Discussion of criteria which should be included in development of clothing budgets, especially those for low-income families. Author points out that standards need to be realistically applicable to low-income families.

Brown, I. C. (1963), *Understanding Other Cultures,* Englewood Cliffs, New Jersey: Prentice-Hall, pp. 25–27, 70–74, 129.
A book for the general reader with little background in anthropology. Material on clothing's functions and aesthetic aspects.

Brown, R. W. (1954), "Mass Phenomena," in Lindsey, G. (ed.), *Handbook of Social Psychology,* 2 Vols., Cambridge, Massachusetts: L. Addison-Wesley Publishing Co., pp. 867–870.
Discussion of fashion, fads, and crazes.

Bunzel, R. (1931), "Ornament," *Encyclopedia of Social Science*, Vol. 11, New York: Macmillan Co., pp. 496–497.
Discussion of various aspects of ornament: kinds, reasons for use, and methods of study. Study of ornament considered an easy way to study tribal patterns as expressed by individual members.

Burke, K. (1950), *A Rhetoric of Motives*, New York: Prentice-Hall, pp. 119–122, 215.
A discussion of Carlyle's doctrine of clothes. Develops idea of clothes as symbols.

Burma, J. H. (1959), "Self-Tattooing Among Delinquents," *Sociology and Social Research*, Vol. 43 (May, 1959), pp. 341–345.
Exploratory study which concludes with the hypothesis that in our culture persons who have certain types of self-concepts will be more likely to tattoo themselves than persons with other self-concepts. Institutionalized delinquents in two different states used as subjects.

Bush, G. and London, P. (1960), "On the Disappearance of Knickers," *Journal of Social Psychology*, Vol. 51 (May, 1960), pp. 359–366.
Authors present a rationale for the formulation of three hypotheses that they propose be used in analysis of the differentiation function of clothing. The relation of clothing to social roles and self concepts of wearers of particular articles is considered.

Cadden, V. (1957), "Do Clothes Make the Boy or Girl?" *Parents' Magazine*, Vol. 32 (December, 1957), pp. 40–42, 90.
An account of high schools' adopting dress codes on the assumption that better dress makes for more appropriate behavior.

Cannon, K. L., Staples, R., and Carlson, I. (1952), "Personal Appearance as a Factor of Social Acceptance," *Journal of Home Economics*, Vol. 44 (November, 1952), pp. 710–713.
Study of several groups of elementary and high school students to determine to what extent personal appearance is a factor in social acceptability. Individuals were first rated for personal appearance, then given sociometric tests. Appearance was significantly associated with acceptability among high school students only.

Carlyle, T. (1921), *Sartor Resartus*, New York: Charles Scribner's Sons.
Essay on humanity; clothes used as symbols for changing forms of conventions, creeds, laws, customs, and fashions of society.

"Catholic Crusade for Modesty," *Literary Digest*, Vol. 82 (August 30, 1924), pp. 25–26.
Report of a world-wide campaign for modesty in clothing which followed the stand taken by Pope Pius XI regarding immodest clothing.

Catt, C. (1927), "Short Skirts and French Dictators," *Forum*, Vol. 77 (April, 1927), pp. 575–585.
Discussion of how the French control what people wear. In discussing a "shock-

ing" article about women in trousers, the author poses the question whether the reverse may also be tried, i.e., will men be put into skirts. Predicts a revolt against fashion's dictates.

Chamber's Encyclopedia (1959), London: George Newnes.
See index for references to costume and adornment.

"Changes 1960, Quick Look at the Life and Times Beginning," *Vogue*, Vol. 135, (January 1, 1960), pp. 90–103.
Prediction of fashion changes for the 1960's.

Chase, E. W. and Chase, I. (1954), *Always in Vogue*, Garden City, New York: Doubleday and Co.
Popular style autobiography of a longtime editor of *Vogue*. Includes detail on the history of the fashion magazine, *Vogue*. Also comment on fashion itself.

Chopra, P. N. (1963), *Some Aspects of Society and Culture during the Mughal Age (1526-1707)*, Agra: Shiva Lal Agarwala and Co., pp. 1–31.
A comprehensive treatment of Indian dress during the sixteenth and seventeenth centuries. Detailed information on variety in dress and grooming customs. Caste-class differences are indicated.

"Church Decrees in Women's Dress," *Literary Digest*, Vol. 87 (November 21, 1925), p. 32.
When skirts were getting shorter, Pope Pius XI reissued a previous decree on modesty in dress. It stood in opposition to publicity about women's emancipation from garments that "trail, envelope and clog."

"The Clacton Giggle," *Time*, Vol. 15 (April 10, 1964), pp. 32–33.
News report of riot of British teen-age groups, the Mods and Rockers. Differences between groups are underscored by their considerable attention to distinctive dress.

Clawson, A. H. (1942), "Safety Clothing for Women in War Production," *Journal of Home Economics*, Vol. 34 (December, 1942), pp. 727–729.
A discussion in which a psychological implication of the use of safety clothing for women in war work is proffered. According to the author, men do not feel that women should be in manual-type industrial occupations; therefore, women need to dress like workers, not like women, in order to foster a desirable impression of competence in work.

Clerget, P. (1913), "The Economic and Social Role of Fashion," *Smithsonian Institution Report*, Washington, D. C., pp. 755–765.
Author asserts that the appearance of a new style of garment is the visible sign that a transformation is taking place in the intellect, customs, and business of a people. Article documented with historical examples.

Cobliner, W. G. (1950), "Feminine Fashion as an Aspect of Group Psychology: Analysis of Written Replies Received by Means of a Questionnaire," *Journal of Social Psychology*, Vol. 31 (May, 1950), pp. 283–289.
Study of eighteen Hunter College students to determine why they dressed as they did.

370   Annotated Bibliography

Cohn, D. L. (1940), *The Good Old Days,* New York: Simon and Schuster.
Study of change as revealed through pages of Sears Roebuck catalogue. Changes in clothing and other items listed for sale reflects social, economic, technological, and aesthetic change.

Colas, R. (1933), *Bibliographie générale du Costume et de la Mode,* Paris: Librairie René Colas 8, Rue de l'Odéon.
Classic bibliography on history of costume (in French).

Coleman, J. S. (1961), *The Adolescent Society,* Glencoe, Illinois: Free Press, pp. 30, 37, 43–57, 72, 90–91, 164–172, 231, 293.
A study which indicates that dress and physical attractiveness are important criteria considered in evaluating popularity and status in schools in both small rural towns and large urban centers.

Collier's Encyclopedia (1962), Crowell-Collier Publishing Co.
See Index volume for references to clothing and fashion.

Columbia Encyclopedia (1956), Vol. 1, New York: Columbia University Press.
See *Clothing* p. 411 and *Costume* p. 466.

Compton, N. H. (1962), "Personal Attributes of Color and Design Preferences In Clothing Fabrics," *The Journal of Psychology,* Vol. 54 (July, 1962), pp. 191–195. [Also in: "Dissertation Abstracts," *Journal of Home Economics,* Vol. 55 (March, 1963), p. 218.]
Study of freshmen women at University of Maryland. Relationships found between color and design preferences and personality scores. Findings support concept that clothing items play a role in helping individual conform to ideal self.

Compton, N. H. (1964), "Body-Image Boundaries in Relation to Clothing Fabric and Design Preferences of a Group of Hospitalized Psychotic Women," *Journal of Home Economics,* Vol. 56 (January, 1964), pp. 40–45.
A study of hospitalized psychotic women to determine if relationships exist between perceived body-image boundaries and clothing fabric and design preferences. Results showed that subjects whose body boundaries were weak tended to reinforce them through clothing choices and that women of large body size were more secure than those of smaller proportions.

Compton's Pictured Encyclopedia (1956), Chicago: F. E. Compton and Co.
See *Dress,* Vol. 4, pp. 106–113 and *Clothing,* Vol. 3, pp. 273–276.

Cooley, C. H. (1909), *Social Organization,* New York: Charles Scribner's Sons, pp. 305, 336.
Clothing of medieval times used to illustrate points made in a discussion of Tarde's terms "custom imitation" and "fashion imitation."

Cooley, C. H. (1925), *Social Process,* New York: Charles Scribner's Sons, pp. 12, 299.
Discussion of Paris fashion. Mention of change in fashion and the fact that an individual lives within the market and takes his ideas from it.

Coon, C. (1962), *The Origin of Races,* New York: Alfred A. Knopf, pp. 62–68.
Comparison of physiological adaption of the races to cold.

Cooper, L. F. (1951), "Blue Jean Age vs. Panty-Waist." *Good Housekeeping,* Vol. 133 (July, 1951), p. 51.
Humorous account of clothing restrictions of a generation ago. Author writes that these restrictions account for her generation being "twitchy."

Crawford, M. D. C. (1940), *Philosophy in Clothing,* New York: Brooklyn Museum.
Discussion of variations in human apparel beginning with technical differences among tailored, draped, and composite garments, and continuing with their evolution. Archaeological approach to discussion of use of pigments for adornment and use of needle for sewing tailored garments.

Crawford, M. D. C. (1941), *The Ways of Fashion,* New York: G. P. Putnam's Sons.
An analysis of the fashion industry. Both American and international aspects are considered.

Crawley, E. (1912), "Dress," *Encyclopedia of Religion and Ethics,* edited by Hastings, Vol. 5, New York: Charles Scribner's Sons, pp. 40–72.
Original essay reprinted in *Dress, Drinks, and Drums* (see following entry).

Crawley, E. (1931), *Dress, Drinks, and Drums,* edited by Theodore Besterman, London: Methuen and Co., pp. 1–175.
The portion of the book on dress covers such topics as origins, functions, types of dress, dress for various portions of the body, the social-psychology of dress, dress for special personages or deities, and social control exercised over dress.

Cressey, P. (1932), *The Taxi-Dance Hall: A Sociological Study in Commercialized Recreation and City Life,* Chicago: University of Chicago Press, pp. 5, 7, 98.
Comment on similarity in dress of girls in taxi-dance hall. Also discussion of how cosmetics and dress help girls attract customers and how change in dress aids girls in assuming roles.

Crook, W. N. H. (1932), "Clothes and the Man," *Journal of Home Economics,* Vol. 24 (June, 1932), pp. 507–510.
Discussion of clothes for men throughout the ages. Includes comment on symbolic implications of certain types of clothing.

Crooke, W. (1906), *Things Indian,* London: John Murray.
A brief encyclopedia. Contains information on armor, dress, embroidery, jewelry, pearls, shawls, symbolism, tatooing, silk, and weaving. Descriptions of caste differences.

Cunnington, C. W. (1936), *Feminine Attitudes in the 19th Century,* New York: Macmillan Co.
Description of social conditions during nineteenth century. Extensive comment on dress.

Cunnington, C. W. (1941), *Why Women Wear Clothes,* London: Faber and Faber.
Author considers psychological factors in accounting for why women wear clothes. Purpose of sexual attraction emphasized.

372   Annotated Bibliography

Cunnington, C. W. (1948), *The Art of English Costume,* London: Collins.
Analytical comments as well as historical detail concerning costume design. Symbolism, aesthetic standards, and sex-attractiveness of dress among topics covered.

Cutolo, S. R. (1956), *Bellevue Is My Home,* Garden City, New York: Doubleday and Co., pp. 135, 184, 196, 221, 255, 273.
Autobiography of physician at Bellevue Hospital. Occasional references to significance of clothing and appearance to patients and staff.

Darwin, C. (1958), *The Voyage of the Beagle,* New York: Bantam Books, pp. 176–198.
Account of Darwin's observations concerning the Fuegians. Detail on their adornment, physical appearance, and ability to withstand cold without clothing.

Darwin, G. H. (1872), "Development in Dress," *Macmillan's Magazine,* Vol. 26 (September, 1872), pp. 410–416. [Also in: *Popular Science Monthly,* Vol. 2 (November, 1872), pp. 40–50.]
Application of evolutionary theory to study of survivals in dress.

Dauncery, E. C. (1911), "The Functions of Fashion," *Living Age,* Vol. 269 (June 24, 1911), pp. 790–794.
Author says we cannot completely isolate ourselves from the dictates of fashion at a given time without appearing to be "odd." Therefore, fashion dictates our mode of dress to us.

Davidson, D. S. (1947), "Footwear of the Australian Aborigines: Environmental vs. Cultural Determination," *Southwestern Journal of Anthropology,* Vol. 3 (Summer, 1947), pp. 114–123.
Discussion of the development of footwear for the Australian Aborigines, possible reasons for it, and purposes of it. Conclusion reached that development of footwear may not be a result of environment.

Davis, A., Gardner, B., and Gardner, M. R. (1941), *Deep South,* Chicago: University of Chicago Press.
See index for references to hair, clothing, and skin color.

Davis, E. C. (1939), "Bride Wore White," *Science Newsletter,* Vol. 35 (June 3, 1939), pp. 346–348.
Data from archaeological studies used to support discussion of Roman dress customs.

Davis, K. (1948), *Human Society,* New York: Macmillan Co. pp. 75–79, 372–373.
Discussion of fashion and fad in dress, songs, and dances. Priestly dress considered in relation to position of religious leader in society.

Dearborn, G. V. N. (1918), "The Psychology of Clothing," *The Psychological Monographs,* Vol. 26, (1918), pp. 1–72.
A lengthy discussion of effects of clothing on physiological processes, an individual's social movements among fellows, and individual attitudes and behavior. Its ambitious effort to include biological as well as social and psychological reactions is unique.

Dewey, J. (1925), *Experience and Nature,* Chicago: Open Court Publishing Co., pp. 137-139, 304.
Significance of appearance is examined.

Dickins, D. (1944), "Social Participation As A Criterion For Determining Scientific Minimum Standards in Clothing," *Rural Sociology,* Vol. 9 (December, 1944), pp. 341-349.
Social-psychological welfare used as a basis for interpreting inventories of clothing wardrobes. Writer believes that social participation determines in a large measure what we have in wardrobes.

Dickins, D. and Bowie, A. (1942), *A Guide to Planning Clothes for the Mississippi Farm Family,* Mississippi State College Agricultural Experiment Station Bulletin No. 372.
Authors determined what clothing members of socially participating farm families owned and the frequency of its replacement.

Dingwall, E. J. (1957), *The American Woman,* New York: Rinehart and Co., pp. 189-199.
Discussion of the clothing of the 1940's with particular emphasis on sexual and erotic connotations.

Doob, L. W. (1952), *Social Psychology,* New York: Henry Holt and Co.
See index for references to fads, fashions, and clothing.

Dooley, W. H. (1930), *Clothing and Style,* New York: D. C. Heath and Co., pp. 81-88, 220, 251-273.
Contains sections dealing with emotional influences of fabrics used in costume, relationship of clothing to health, reasons for changes in fashions, and factors influencing dress. Mention made of modesty, political influence, custom, religion, commercial interests.

Dooley, W. H. (1934), *Economics of Clothing and Textiles,* New York: D. C. Heath and Co., pp. 22-102.
Discussion of psychological reasons for wearing clothing and for clothing choices. Also comment on socio-economic influences on clothing use.

Doran, J. (1855), *Habits and Men,* New York: Redfield.
A comment on costume in which writer is interested in "raiment and manners as links in the chain of social life," that harmonize and beautify the whole. A potpourri of subject matter is covered, including queens, hats, wigs, modes, tailors, beaux, and "odd" fashions. Much literary allusion and historical illustration.

Douty, H. I. (1963), "Influence of Clothing on Perception of Persons," *Journal of Home Economics,* Vol. 55 (March, 1963), pp. 197-202.
A study of the part clothing plays in structuring perceptions of persons. Projected colored photographs of persons were used as stimuli for judges of personal traits. Findings indicated that clothing affected judges ratings of the persons whose pictures they saw.

"Dress and Its Eccentricities," *London Society,* Vol. 12 (1862-1881), p. 283. [Also in: *Every Saturday,* Vol. 4 (September 21, 1867), pp. 369-372.]

Interesting discussion of how "slavish" we are to fashion, even to the point of sacrificing modesty. What is considered fashionable in one period is odd in appearance in another because of social conditioning. False hair, false color, false stomachs, false ears, for example, can be used without compunction where they are considered needed.

"Dress Codes, Cool or Square?" *Senior Scholastic,* Vol. 73 (November 21, 1958), pp. 10–11.
Pros and cons of "better dress" codes for schools are discussed.

"Dress Regulations of Lancaster Conference Mennonites," *The Pennsylvania Dutchman,* Vol. 4 (March 1, 1953), p. 7.
List of dress regulations adopted by Mennonites in October 7, 1881, revised and approved September 16, 1943.

Driver, H. E. (1961), "Clothing," *Indians of North America,* Chicago: University of Chicago Press, pp. 133–156.
Discussion of the relation of the clothing of North American Indians to other aspects of their lives. Descriptions of the major styles of clothing worn, clothing materials used, and the relation of clothing to environment and economy.

Dunlay, K. (1928), "The Development and Function of Clothing," *Journal of General Psychology,* Vol. 1 (1928), pp. 64–78.
Discussion of four theories for origin of clothing: modesty, immodesty, adornment, and protection.

Ebeling, M. and Rosencranz, M. L. (1961), "Social and Personal Aspects of Clothing for Older Women," *Journal of Home Economics,* Vol. 53 (June, 1961), pp. 464–465.
A study of older women's clothing practices. Rural-urban differences are evaluated.

Ecob, H. G. (1900), "A New Philosophy of Fashion," *Chautauquan,* Vol. 31, (September, 1900), pp. 604–608.
General thesis of the "new philosophy" is that there is a need for rational, intelligent fashions which can come about only through educating women. Author especially concerned with clothing evolution which can bring women's fashions up to date with their emancipated station in life.

Eichler, L. (1924), *The Customs of Mankind,* Garden City, New York: Nelson Doubleday, pp. 500–558.
A discussion of origins of dress in which the protection motive is emphasized. Also comment on primitive dress and ornamentation and the relationship of the development of dress to the times.

Ellis, A. (1962), *The American Sexual Tragedy,* New York: Grove Press, pp. 15–65.
Author suggests that in our society women must dress "romantically, fashionably, distinctively, extensively, sex-enticingly, and properly." Dress becomes an extension of, or actually the woman's whole personality. Clothes used to camouflage defects become an integral part of the woman's total image and serve not

only as a means of attracting male attention but also of achieving status with other females.

Ellis, H. (1936), *Studies in the Psychology of Sex,* 4 Vols., New York: Random House.
Author discusses modesty, ideals of beauty, and grooming practices in this early, classic study. Cross-cultural references are included. See index for specific pages.

Elwin, V. (1951), *The Tribal Art of Middle India,* London: Oxford University Press.
Study of declining tribal art in middle India. Writer comments on decoration of the body, tribal dress, use of cowrie shells, combs, head dresses, tattoos, castes, wedding customs, and masks.

Encyclopedia Americana (1963), New York, Chicago, Washington, D. C.: Americana Corporation.
See dress and costume.

Encyclopedia Britannica (1960), Chicago, London, Toronto: Encyclopedia Britannica.
See dress; also see yearly supplements for section on fashions for the year.

"Environments," *New Yorker,* Vol. 36 (December 24, 1960), pp. 20–21.
Discussion of the creation and use of suits designed to be worn in "hostile environments." Outer suit designed to protect from environment, inner apparatus to create a suitable environment.

Evans, S. E. (1964), "Motivations Underlying Clothing Selection and Wearing," *Journal of Home Economics,* Vol. 56, (December, 1964), pp. 739–743.
Researcher found that adolescents' primary motives for wearing clothing involved dependence upon others, while their primary motives for purchasing involved independence. Age and popularity were significantly related to clothing behavior while age, intelligence, sex, and parental occupation and education were not.

Evelyn, J. (1951), *Tyrannus: or, The Mode,* Oxford: B. Blackwell.
A discourse on sumptuary laws concerned with modes of dress in England. Introduction contains comments on actual modes of dress of the period.

Family Economics Review, Consumer and Food Economics Research Division, Agricultural Research Service, United States Department of Agriculture.
The annual December issue of this quarterly carries a summary of economic trends in clothing and textiles. Related social trends are noted.

Fenichel, O. (1930), "The Psychology of Transvestitism," *International Journal of Psycho-Analysis,* Vol. 11 (April, 1930), pp. 211–227.
Case study of male subject with homosexual tendencies. Clothing used as means of expressing desires of being a woman.

"Fetish of Clothes," *Current Literature,* Vol. 26 (October, 1899), p. 336.
Brief account of the "tangible and mystic influence" of clothes.

Finestone, H. (1957), "Cats, Kicks, and Color," *Social Problems,* Vol. 5 (July, 1957), pp. 3–13. (Also in: Bobbs-Merrill Reprint No. S-84.)
   Statement concerning sartorial role distance of young drug users.

Flaccus, L. W. (1906), "Remarks on the Psychology of Clothes," *Pedagogical Seminary,* Vol. 13 (March, 1906), pp. 61–83.
   Research study using G. Stanley Hall's questionnaire concerning: effects clothing has on self-feelings, attitudes toward clothing expenditures, relation of clothing to perception of others, care of clothes, grooming, and reform in dress.

Flower, B. O. (1892), "The Next Forward Step For Women: Or Thoughts on the Movement for Rational Dress," *Arena,* Vol. 6 (October, 1892), pp. 635–644.
   Article relates movement for rational dress to general movement for women's rights. Cites importance of reform clothing to health and its practicality for activities of women. Supports arguments by adding names of prestigeful women who support movement.

Flugel, J. C. (1929A), "Clothes Symbolism and Clothes Ambivalence," *International Journal of Psycho-Analysis,* Vol. 10 (April–July, 1929), pp. 205–217.
   Discussion of the phallic symbolism of various objects of clothing, also vaginal and uterine symbolism. Author says this symbolism relates to modesty and protection theories. Clothing creates conflicts, i.e., free clothing symbolizes independence while restrictive clothing symbolizes confinement.

Flugel, J. C. (1929B), "On the Mental Attitude to Present-Day Clothes," *British Journal of Medical Psychology,* Vol. 9 (1929), pp. 97–149.
   Report of 132 replies out of 10,000 distributed questionnaires on clothing. Includes discussion of answers to questions on the effect of clothing on behavior and health and on attitudes and opinions related to clothing.

Flugel, J. C. (1930A), "A Dress Reform Dream," *International Journal of Psycho-Analysis,* Vol. 11 (October, 1930), pp. 497–499.
   The clothing dream analyzed on basis of sexual implications.

Flugel, J. C. (1930B), *The Psychology of Clothes,* London: Hogarth Press.
   Classic book on clothing, written from a psychoanalytic point of view. Discussion of functions of clothing, i.e., satisfaction of motives of modesty, protection, and decoration. Analysis of other factors related to clothing such as individual differences, fashion forces.

Flugel, J. C. (1945), *Man, Morals and Society,* New York: International University Press, pp. 135, 138–139, 294.
   Topics covered include taboos of women attending religious services without "proper" dress, taboos on clothes in contemporary society, conventions of dress which are purely arbitrary, and revolt of the "leftish" to unorthodox dress.

Foley, C. A. (1893), "Fashion," *Economic Journal,* Vol. 3 (September, 1893), pp. 458–474.
   Discussion of relation of fashion to consumption. Author feels that in order to view fashion as a coefficient in demand, we must investigate both the history and present manifestations of fashion.

"For 280 Degrees Above," *Newsweek,* Vol. 55 (January 25, 1960), pp. 80–81.

Discussion of the characteristics of space suits. Author feels clothes will make or break the space man. Since space is not fit for man, man must be fitted for space.

Form, W. H. and Stone, G. P. (1955), *The Social Significance of Clothing in Occupational Life,* Michigan State University Agricultural Experiment Station Technical Bulletin No. 247.
An appraisal of the relevance of clothing in a man's most crucial role, his occupation. Comparisons drawn between two groups, blue collar and white collar workers.

France, A. (1933), *Penguin Island,* New York: The Modern Library, pp. 37–42.
Satire on human history, in which clothes are used to illustrate expansion of custom and law.

Frank, S. (1959), "She Knows What Women Will Wear," *Saturday Evening Post,* Vol. 231 (June 27, 1959), pp. 34–35, 102, 105–106.
Report of an interview with the late Tobe. This well-known expert, in predicting fashions, said that women dress as they do because clothes are one of their few symbols of success, because of the status value of the clothes, and out of vanity.

Franzero, C. M. (1958), *Beau Brummell: His Life and Times,* New York: John Day Co.
A biography of the early nineteenth-century arbiter of men's fashion who set a pattern for elegance in men's dress based on simplicity and impeccable grooming.

Freudenberger, H. (1963), "Fashion, Sumptuary Laws, and Business," *Business History Review,* Vol. 37 (Spring–Summer, 1963), pp. 37–48.
A review of seventeenth- and eighteenth-century sumptuary laws in Europe. Writer attempts to account for such laws and relate them to business.

Frost, E. M. (1948), "Fashion—A Reflection of a Way of Life," *Journal of Home Economics,* Vol. 40 (May, 1948), 245–246.
Author states that psychologists have become increasingly interested in the fact that man has experimented with his appearance since prehistoric times. She believes that fashions down through the ages have reflected man's way of life.

Fuchs, S. (1951), *The Children of Hari,* New York: Frederick A. Praeger, pp. 330–342.
Descriptive treatment of clothing and adornment of castes belonging to lowest stratum of Indian society. Age and sex differences are noted.

Funk, W. (1937), *So You Think It's New,* New York: Funk and Wagnalls, pp. 13–444.
Comments on nudity and a humorous comparison of our cosmetics with those of ancient times.

Furniss, L. E. (1873), "The Bondage of Furbelows," *Appletons' Journal,* Vol. 9 (January, 1873), pp. 75–78.
Discussion of reasons why women cannot afford to go against the dictates of

fashion despite the fact there are many nonpractical aspects of fashions. Article also summarizes fashions current at the time the article was written.

Galletti, R., Baldwin, K. D. S., and Dina, I. O. (1956), *Nigerian Cocoa Farmers,* Oxford: Oxford University Press, pp. 246–252.
A well-organized study of patterns of clothing consumption among Yoruba families.

Garland, M. (1962), *Fashion,* Baltimore: Penguin Books.
Comprehensive study of international fashion. Introductory chapter on body exposure.

Garma, A. (1949), "The Origin of Clothes," *Psychoanalytic Quarterly,* Vol. 18 (April, 1949), pp. 173–190.
Discussion of the symbolism of clothes in dreams of pregnancy. Clothes are unconsciously perceived as maternal protection.

Ghurye, G. S. (1951), *Indian Costume,* Bombay: The Popular Book Depot.
In his introduction, writer carefully traces Western literary and philosophical thought concerning social significance of dress. He compares Indian thought with that in the West. He also develops a classification system to be used in analyzing dress and gives for additional background a brief sketch of costume in Ancient Persia, Mesopotamia, Egypt, and Greece. The rest of the book is devoted to Indian costume as seen in its historical setting. He states that costume functions to reveal caste only in a very broad manner.

Gill, E. (1931), *Clothes,* London: Johnathan Cape.
A series of essays in which the qualities of clothes are analyzed in relation to usefulness, decency, dignity, and adornment. Both utilitarian and symbolic aspects of clothing are discussed.

Gill, E. (1944), *It All Goes Together,* New York: Devin Adair Co., pp. 34–44.
Writer says clothes are natural and proper to man. They are not primarily for warmth, convenience, or even for modesty, but for dignity and adornment. He suggests that man, when he chooses nakedness, does so for reasons of humility, convenience, and pleasure.

Gillin, J. P. (1948), *The Ways of Men,* New York: D. Appleton–Century Co., pp. 209–220.
In a description of the culture of the Old Order Amish of Lancaster County, Pennsylvania, writer points out that dress and adornment stimulate maintenance of group customs and symbolize the religious "peculiarity" of the culture as based on Scriptures.

Gillin, J. P. (1951), *The Culture of Security in San Carlos,* New Orleans: Middle American Research Institute, The Tulane University of Louisiana, pp. 34–39.
Study of clothing and ornament in same Guatamalan pueblo studied by Tumin (1952). Author interested in acculturation, i.e., intertwining of Indian and European culture. He studied Ladinos and Indians who shared some cutural elements in their ways of life, even though each group had a distinct mode of life.

Gilman, C. P. (1905A), "Why These Clothes?" *Independent,* Vol. 58 (March 2, 1905), pp. 466–469.
Humorous account of the impractical and nonrational nature of clothes. Moralizing on detrimental effect of heavy and restricting clothing.

Gilman, C. P. (1905B), "Symbolism in Dress," *Independent,* Vol. 58 (June 8, 1905), pp. 1294–1297.
Author discusses how various articles of clothing express ideas their owners wish to reveal. Examples are mourning dress and the "gentleman's" white shirt. He thinks clothes of men were originally more symbolic than those of women.

Gladwin, T. (1947), "Climate and Anthropology," *American Anthropologist,* Vol. 49 (October, 1947), pp. 601–611.
Discussion of man's adaptations to changes in geographical areas or climactic conditions. Clothing mentioned quite frequently in relation to adaptation to climate.

Godkin, E. L. (1867), "The Rationale of the Fashions," *Nation,* Vol. 5 (November 21, 1867), pp. 418–419.
Discussion of the relation of conformity and nonconformity to the adoption of new fashions. Comments on copying of upper class fashions by those of low status. Author believes following fashions does not mean improvement but simply change.

Goffman, E. (1959), *The Presentation of Self in Everyday Life,* Garden City, New York: Doubleday and Co.
Author approaches study of behavior from the standpoint of a stage and actors. Within this framework he discusses everyday life in American society. Many implications for understanding of clothing usage.

Goffman, E. (1961A), *Asylums,* Garden City, New York: Doubleday and Co., pp. 20–21.
Author refers to the total of equipment used by an individual in grooming and dress as his "identity kit" which is needed in establishing the self.

Goffman, E. (1961B), *Encounters,* Indianapolis: Bobbs-Merrill, pp. 145–147.
Illustration of use of clothing to express role distance, i.e., to disavow complete affiliation with a status role, such as that implied by occupation, age-sex, race, or wealth.

Goffman, E. (1963A), *Behavior in Public Places,* New York: Free Press of Glencoe, pp. 25–28, 33–35, 64–69, 108–109, 198, 203–205, 211–213.
Many references to clothing and appearance as factors to be reckoned with in face-to-face interaction.

Goffman, E. (1963B), *Stigma,* Englewood Cliffs: Prentice-Hall.
In a discussion of many kinds of stigma, writer makes a number of references to the effect on the individual of the inability to conform to standards for what society would call "normal" appearance.

Goodhart, C. B. (1964), "A Biological View of Toplessness," *New Scientist,* Vol. 23, (September, 1964), pp. 558–560.

Writer attributes hesitancy of females to bare breasts to biological reasons. The breasts serve as "releasers" of courtship behavior because of coloration.

Goldman, M. I. (1963), " 'From Sputnik to Panties:' Is Economic Development Really that Easy?" *Business History Review,* Vol. 37 (Spring–Summer, 1963), pp. 81–93.
Effect of Communist revolution on fashion in Russia. Country's problems now involve transition from an economy of scarcity, in which heavy industry has been emphasized, to one of greater abundance in which more fashions and other consumer products are available.

Goodman, N., Dornbusch, S. M., Richardson, S. A., and Hastorf, A. H. (1963), "Variant Reactions to Physical Disabilities," *American Sociological Review,* Vol. 28 (June, 1963), pp. 429–435.
A study of cultural evaluation of various types of physical disabilities that modify appearance. It was found that Jewish and Italian children held different preference patterns, and that mentally retarded and emotionally disturbed children held preference patterns that differed from the normative.

Goodman, S. O. (1964), "We're Setting Pace in Men's Fashions," *The Washington Post* (March 21, 1964), p. A16.
Good illustration of legal leadership in fashion. Influence of American congressmen and presidents on men's fashions noted.

Gordon, L. (1953), *Economics for Consumers,* New York: American Book Co., pp. 112–146.
Analysis of fashion written from an economist's point of view. Author disregards fundamental psychological motives of dress. He defines fashion as acceptance.

Gorsline, D. (1962), "What the Presidents Wore," *Gentleman's Quarterly,* Vol. 32 (March, 1962), pp. 100–101, 167–173.
Comment on the sartorial leadership of American presidents.

Gray, L. H. (ed.) (1932), *Mythology of All Races,* 13 Vols., Boston: Marshall Jones Co. (for Archaeological Institute of America).
See index for references to clothing, costume, and dress.

Greenacre, P. (1944), "Infant Reactions to Restraint," *American Journal of Orthopsychiatry,* Vol. 14 (1944), pp. 204–218. [Also in: Kluckhohn, C., Murray, H. A., and Schneider, D. M. (eds.) (1953), *Personality in Nature, Society and Culture,* New York: Alfred A. Knopf, pp. 498–514.]
A series of reports in one paper. Part one is a case study of a twenty-year-old who was physically and psychologically restrained. Part two is a review of experimental work in restraint. Part three is a summary of folk customs for swaddling, a form of physical restraint.

Gregory, P. M. (1947A), "An Economic Interpretation of Women's Fashions," *Southern Economic Journal,* Vol. 14 (October, 1947), pp. 148–162.
A discussion which relates fashion change to the economy, especially to economic fluctuations.

Gregory, P. M. (1947B), "A Theory of Purposeful Obsolescence," *Southern Economic Journal*, Vol. 14 (July, 1947), pp. 24–45.

Discussion of two main techniques of purposeful obsolescence, limitation of durability, and artificial style change. The author cites women's clothing as a classic example of artificial style change.

Gregory, P. M. (1948), "Fashion and Monopolistic Competiton," *Journal of Political Economy*, Vol. 56 (February, 1948), pp. 69–75.

Discussion of the problems growing out of competition in the fashion industry. Author holds that fashion controls the industry and also what women wear.

Grosse, E. (1898), *The Beginnings of Art*, New York: D. Appleton and Co., pp. 53–114.

A study of primitive art from a sociological approach. Personal decoration, ornamentation, representative art, the dance, poetry, and music are considered.

Gummere, A. M. (1901), *The Quaker*, Philadelphia: Ferris and Leach.

An attempt to trace the development of Quaker costume and its eventual decline in use. The dress of the Quaker man changed little after the time of Charles II while the dress of women underwent observable evolutionary changes.

Hall, C. (1938), *From Hoopskirts to Nudity*, Caldwell, Idaho: Caxton Printers.

A review of the fashions of the past seventy years that attempts to show that clothes react upon those who wear them, for good or ill, and that even the most absurd fashion may be a vital part of life.

Hall, G. S. (1898), "Some Aspects of the Early Sense of Self," *American Journal of Psychology*, Vol. 9 (April, 1898), pp. 351–395.

Author believes that dress and adornment early become important factors in a child's consciousness of self. Psychological use of clothing can aid in a child's ego development.

Hall, K. B. (1956), "A Study of Some of the Factors that Contribute to Satisfactions and Dissatisfactions in the Clothing of 92 Urban Low-Income Families," *Journal of Home Economics*, Vol. 48 (March, 1956), pp. 214–215.

A study in which the following factors were found related to the amount of clothing owned, and the satisfaction of the husband and wife: age, education, number of children, social activities, whether wife worked, and kind of work wife did.

Halverson, H. M. (1942), "The Differential Effect of Nudity and Clothing on Muscular Tonus in Infancy," *Journal of Genetic Psychology*, Vol. 61 (September, 1942), pp. 55–67.

Discussion of factors affecting conditions of muscular tonus. An experiment performed in which gripping reflex of infants was tested before undressing, after undressing, and after reclothing. It was found that the reflex response was consistently stronger in the nude situation.

Hampton, F. A. (1925), "The Psychology of Fashion," *Discovery*, Vol. 6 (March, 1925), pp. 111–113.

The adoption of a new fashion or the modified revival of an old one may represent a change of taste or opinion in a majority and an attempt to stabilize new views.

Harberton, F. W. (1882), "Rational Dress Reform," *Macmillan's Magazine*, Vol. 45 (April, 1882), pp. 456–461.

A discussion of the fact that clothing is not rational in its styling. Author says we have forgotten what our form is really like, that clothing has ceased fulfilling its original purpose of being a useful servant and has become a species of tyrant subjecting the human form to inconvenient, unsightly, and tormenting control.

Harding, M. E. (1933), *The Way of All Women*, New York: Longmans, Green, and Co., pp. 32–33.

A psychological analysis of women in which there is a brief discussion of a woman's use of clothing and make-up to create an image and to express personality.

Harms, E. (1938), "The Psychology of Clothes," *American Journal of Sociology*, Vol. 44 (September, 1938), pp. 239–250.

Motives for dress arise from natural environment, sociological and cultural phenomena, and metaphysical, supersensory, religious experience. Modesty, adornment, and protection are directed toward these environmental factors.

Harnik, E. J. (1932), "Pleasure in Disguise, the Need for Decoration and the Sense of Beauty," *The Psychoanalytic Quarterly*, Vol. 1 (April, 1932), pp. 216–264.

Psychoanalytic orientation to analysis of dress. Discussion of sexual symbolism of clothes.

Harrington, M. (1962), *The Other America*, New York: Macmillan Co., p. 5.

Brief statement on leveling effect of mass-produced clothing on appearance of socio-economic groups in America. Even the hungry appear well dressed.

Hart, H. (1927), *The Science of Social Relations*, New York: Henry Holt Co., pp. 126 127.

Expansion of thesis that modesty, as related to clothing, is culturally oriented.

Hart, M. (1959), *Act One*, New York: Random House, pp. 175–178, 199–201.

Excellent example of personal reaction to clothing deprivation.

Hartmann, G. W. (1949), "Clothing: Personal Problem and Social Issue," *Journal of Home Economics*, Vol. 41 (June, 1949), pp. 295–298.

Discussion of the psychological implications of clothing. Clothing regarded as both a stimulus and a response.

Hawes, E. (1938), *Fashion is Spinach*, New York: Random House.

Author discusses many aspects of the world of fashion. In contrasting fashion and style she considers fashion frivolous and evil, style gentle and sensible.

Hawes, E. (1939A), *Men Can Take It*, Boston: Little Brown Co., pp. 46–82.

Discussion of conformity in dress of college men and businessmen.

Hawes, E. (1939B), "Men Can Take it," *Reader's Digest*, Vol. 35 (August, 1939), pp. 52–54.

Condensed version of above book.

Hawes, E. (1942), *Why is a Dress?* New York: Viking Press.

A résumé of what is involved in dress designing, slanted toward interests of perspective designers. Comments on the various functions of clothes.

Hawes, E. (1943), *Why Women Cry,* New York: Reynal and Hitchcock, pp. 87–93.
Discussion of the effects of uniforms or other clothes worn at work on the wearers and others around. Author reports attempts at individuality even in uniforms, also double mores. An example of the latter was that women could not wear slacks to work, but had to wear them in the plant.

Hawes, E. (1954), *It's Still Spinach,* Boston: Little, Brown Co.
Evaluative statement on contemporary dress. Dress that distorts the shape and motion of the body is criticized. Interesting critical comments on nightgowns, hats, shoes, make-up, foundation garments, and why people dress. Dressing is defined as everything that is done to the body to "prepare for display."

Hawthorne, H. B. (ed.) (1955), *The Doukhobors of British Columbia,* Vancouver: University of British Columbia, pp. 145–146.
Author describes the Doukhobors' use of nudism as a weapon against the government. He also discusses the reasons for its use and its effectiveness.

Hays, H. R. (1958), *From Ape to Angel,* New York: Alfred A. Knopf, pp. 165–166.
Sexual attraction mentioned as a motive for the origin of dress and adornment. Modesty disregarded as a motive since many naked people have no sense of shame.

Hazlitt, W. (1933A), "On Fashion," in Howe, P. P. (ed.), *The Complete Works of William Hazlitt,* Vol. 17, London: J. M. Dent and Sons, pp. 51–56. [Also in: *The Edinburgh Magazine* (September, 1818).]
Author discusses fashion which he attacks as being frivolous and vain. He also comments on how the bringing of fashion to the common people has affected them.

Hazlitt, W. (1933B), "Thoughts on Taste," in Howe P. P. (ed.), *The Complete Works of William Hazlitt,* Vol. 17, London: J. M. Dent and Sons, pp. 57–66. [Also in: *The Edinburgh Magazine* (July–October, 1818).]
Taste defined as sensibility to the different degrees and kinds of excellence in the works of art or nature. Author discusses this excellence and the people who disdain it, as well as those who search for excellence in areas where it does not exist.

Heard, G. (1924), *Narcissus: An Anatomy of Clothes,* London: Kegan Paul, Trench, Trubner, and Co.
Author applies evolutionary theory to clothing and relates clothing form to architectural form.

Herskovits, M. (1956), *Man and His Works,* New York: Alfred A. Knopf, pp. 24, 255–256.
Author refers to Kroeber's study of dress as "evidence of culture as a superorganic phenomenon." He discusses relationship of technology to clothing development.

Hertzler, A. E. (1940), "Problems of the Normal Adolescent Girl," *California*

Journal of Secondary Education, Vol. 15 (February, 1940), pp. 114–119.

Study of girls' presentations of their problems. For some girls the pressure for clothing was noted as an acute problem. Twenty-one per cent felt they did not have enough clothes for their needs and 11 per cent had feelings of inferiority because of their deprivation.

Hiler, H. (1929), *From Nudity to Raiment,* London: W. and G. Foyle.

Author's purpose was to contribute "to the history of mankind in its first steps in the long journey towards civilization, and help to place costume in its proper position amongst the conventional arts."

Hiler, H. and Hiler, M. (1939), *Bibliography of Costume,* New York: N. W. Wilson Co.

Extensive index of costume references. Introductory chapter, "Costumes and Ideologies," is a résumé of various approaches to the study of clothing.

Hill, D. (1930), "A Short Wave Length on Colonial and Modern Dress," *Practical Home Economics,* Vol. 8 (April, 1930), pp. 109, 116.

Comparison of individual articles of apparel of colonial times and the 1930's.

Hirn, Y. (1900), *The Origins of Art,* London: Macmillan Co. pp. 204–206, 215–227.

Author discusses clothes as a means for attracting the opposite sex. He points out that clothes may have been invented, not to conceal nudity, but to set it off. He proposes that wearing of clothes originated for superstitious reasons connected with sexual characteristics. He also discusses clothing and decoration as a means of showing status and commanding fear and respect.

Hirning, L. C. (1961), "Clothing and Nudism," in Ellis, A. and Abarbanel, A. (eds.), *The Encyclopedia of Sexual Behavior,* New York: Hawthorn Books, pp. 268–283.

Writer traces the origin of clothes, suggesting that primary functions were decoration and symbolic magical practice. He discusses adoption of distinctive dress for the sexes, and suggests that both modesty and protection are secondary motives for clothes. According to his point of view, there has been a development of sexual arousal through concealment as a function of clothes. He discusses also transvestitism and the development of social nudism.

Hobson, W. (1948), "The Business Suit," *Fortune,* Vol. 38 (July, 1948), pp. 102–105, 120–122, 126.

Although there was considerable regional variety in appropriate dress for the American businessman in 1948, the double-breasted suit was the only acceptable garb in all areas.

Hoebel, E. A. (1958), *Man in the Primitive World,* New York: McGraw-Hill Book Co., pp. 239–251.

Description of the clothing and ornament primitive man devises as he strives to effect what he believes are improvements upon his body.

Hoffman, A. M. (1957), "Clothing Behavioral Factors for a Specific Group of Women Related to Aesthetic Sensitivity and Certain Socio-Economic and Psychological Background Factors," *Journal of Home Economics,* Vol. 49 (March, 1957), p. 233.

A study of the relationships of aesthetic sensitivity, and certain socio-economic and psychological background factors to differences in choice of, use of, and attitudes toward clothing.

Hoffman, A. M. (1962), "Gerontology in Iowa Clothing Problems and Clothing Behavior of Older Women," *Adding Life to Years,* Institute of Gerontology, State University of Iowa, Vol. 9 (September, 1962), pp. 3–6.

Discussion of the limited emphasis placed on research concerning clothing for older people and the implications of psychological and sociological aspects of clothing for older women.

Hoffman, A. M. and Bader, I. M. (1964), *Social Science Aspects of Clothing for Older Women,* Department of Home Economics and Institute of Gerontology, State University of Iowa (September, 1964).

An annotated bibliography of readings related to clothing for older people.

Hollander, S. C. (1963), "A Note on Fashion Leadership," *Business History Review,* Vol. 37 (Winter, 1963), pp. 448–451.

Stimulated by the Robinson (1963A) discussion of fashion, the writer challenges the validity of a "trickle-down" model of fashion behavior which implies a dominant position for the designer. He feels no one individual or group can order changes in what the public wants in fashions. See Robinson (1963B) for reply.

Holley, B. (1919), "Psychology in Woman's Dress," *Forum,* Vol. 61 (June, 1919), pp. 749–751.

Writer believes expressing individuality through dress is a means of creating a more interesting and distinctive person.

Hollingworth, L. S. (1935), "The Comparative Beauty of the Faces of Highly Intelligent Adolescents," *Journal of Genetic Psychology,* Vol. 47 (December, 1935), pp. 268–281.

A study in which the facial attractiveness of highly intelligent adolescents was compared with that of adolescents of ordinary intelligence. Results showed that the highly intelligent group was as a whole more attractive.

Holmberg, A. R. (1950), *Nomads of the Long Bow: The Siriono of Eastern Bolivia,* Smithsonian Institution, Institute of Social Anthropology Publication No. 10, Washington: U.S. Government Printing Office, pp. 19–21.

Description of a people who use clothing to adorn themselves and to protect themselves from insects, but who, for the most part, do not wear clothes. They do use other adornment abundantly. Author describes the relationship of specific ornaments and adornments to age, sex, and status.

Holtzclaw, K. (1956), "Costume and Culture," *Journal of Home Economics,* Vol. 48 (June, 1956), pp. 401–404.

Discussion of how costume reveals the traits of a culture at any given period of history.

Hood, M. P. (1959), "Modern Pakistani Dress with Traditional Influence," *Journal of Home Economics*, Vol. 51 (May, 1959), pp. 336-339.
Discussion of Pakistani dress, its origin, its variations. Special description of the dress of the working women.

Hoper, L. H. (1874), "Fig Leaves and French Dresses," *Galaxy*, Vol. 18 (October, 1874), pp. 504-510.
Discussion of why women wear certain fashions. According to author, "Sin led to the invention of dress, and now dress lures the souls of the weak and vain among women into sin." Elias Howe and the sewing machine blamed for the fact that women must now be conspicuous to be considered well dressed.

Hostetler, J. A. (1963), *Amish Society*, Baltimore: Johns Hopkins Press, pp. 131-147, 184, 198, 230, 311.
Amish ways of dressing are emblems of the group and are rooted in religious concepts. They express social unity in a material form and as emblems of the society are indispensable for integration of the society. Garb not only admits the individual into full membership but also clarifies his role and status within his society.

Hoult, T. F. (1954), "Experimental Measurement of Clothing as a Factor in Some Social Ratings of Selected American Men," *American Sociological Review*, Vol. 19 (June, 1954), pp. 324-328.
A study designed to show the extent to which clothing affects status ratings of men in certain social situations. Findings indicated that, if the subjects were known to the judges, clothing did not seem to be associated with social ratings. On the other hand, if subjects were unknown, ratings were higher when men wore clothing previously rated high in appropriateness.

"How Long Will the Chemise Last?" *Consumer Reports*, Vol. 23 (August, 1958), pp. 434-437.
In analyzing the style change that brought in the chemise, writer agrees it is time for change, but questions whether this new style is desirable. He observes that consumers buy modifications which are not too extreme and carefully store their old clothes.

Howells, W. W. (1948), *The Heathens*, Garden City, New York: Doubleday and Co., pp. 122, 132, 165, 166, 237-238.
Discussion of mourning dress, dress of religious participants, costume of the Navaho witch, dress of the Siberian shaman or medicine men.

Howells, W. W. (1954), *Back of History*, Garden City, New York: Doubleday and Co.
Archaeological tracing of history, including description of dress of different peoples. See index for specific references.

Hoyt, E. E., Reid, M. G., McConnell, J. L., and Hook, J. M. (1954), *American Income and Its Use*, New York: Harper and Bros., pp. 33-37.
Although authors recognize it is practically impossible to arrive at physiological

and psychic standards for clothing, they present some tentative minimums for Americans.

Hughes, C. C. (1960), *An Eskimo Village in the Modern World*, Ithaca, New York: Cornell University Press, pp. 211–219.
Discussion of spending patterns of Gambell Eskimos for clothing and the effect of culture contact on their patterns of dress.

Huizinga, J. (1949), *Homo-Ludens: A Study of the Play Element in Culture*, London: Routledge and Kegan Paul, pp. 13, 183, 192–194.
Theme advanced is that dressing up in play allows the person to become another being. Author sees an element of play in the evolution of men's and women's dress. He suggests, for example, that by the eighteenth century women's fashions began to "play." Today, however, he detects a return to simplicity and naturalness.

Hurlock, E. B. (1929A), "Motivation in Fashion," *Archives of Psychology*, Vol. 17, No. 111, pp. 5–71.
An investigation of the motives that lead people to follow fashion. The researcher attempts to test some of the current fashion theories to see if there is any relationship between them and fact.

Hurlock, E. B. (1929B), *The Psychology of Dress*, New York: Ronald Press Co.
The author studies the causes and characteristics of the fashion impulse in a realm where fashion is especially powerful, that of clothing and personal adornment. She brings together and coordinates varying theories and opinions concerned with dress.

Hurlock, E. B. (1955), *Adolescent Development*, New York: McGraw-Hill Book Co., pp. 198, 246–259, 423, 469–470.
Author considers that style of dressing is a powerful factor in attracting the opposite sex and that fashion is more important to individuals than becomingness. She discusses adolescent interest in clothes and decoration, the development of standards of good taste, and the importance of being in style. In addition she comments on the appearance characteristics of adolescent leaders, the use of clothing to hide defects, and how clothing leads to relaxation in social roles.

Hurlock, E. B. (1956), *Child Development*, New York: McGraw-Hill Book Co., pp. 477–479, 551–552.
Discussion of the development of a child's interest in clothing and appearance, the effect of clothing on behavior and self-confidence, the change from interest in ornamentation to becomingness with age, and the influence of clothes on personality and an individual's concept of self.

"The Ideal Wife is Shiny," *The Daily News*, Salisbury, Southern Rhodesia (July 8, 1963). [Also in: *Atlas*, Vol. 6 (November, 1963), p. 310.]
African ideals for female physical beauty.

Ilfeld, F. and Lauer, R. (1964), *Social Nudism in America*, New Haven, Connecticut: College and University Press.

Using interviews, questionnaires, and their own observations, the writers gathered data in several American nudist camps. Their data throw light on the nature of nudism as a social movement.

Ingalls, I. (1956), "Clothing Problems of the Grade School Girl," *Journal of Home Economics,* Vol. 48 (June, 1956), pp. 422–425.

Study to determine if merchandise available on the market is meeting the needs of 9- to 12-year-old girls. Researcher points out that psychological adjustment and emotional problems as well as growth development are related to clothing needs.

Irwin, O. C. and Weiss, L. A. (1934), "The Effect of Clothing on the General and Vocal Activity of the New Born Infant," *Studies in Infant Behavior,* University of Iowa Studies in Child Welfare, Vol. 9, No. 4, pp. 151–162.

Researchers, interested in whether clothing becomes a mechanical restraint and in turn detrimental to muscular development of an infant, found that activity and crying decreased when infants were clothed.

Jack, N. K. and Shiffer, B. (1948), "The Limits of Fashion Control," *American Sociological Review,* Vol. 13 (December, 1948), pp. 730–738.

Dress length used as one measurable aspect of mass behavior in a study of the reciprocal roles of leader and follower, i.e., of norm creator and conformist. Illustrations from three levels of magazines were selected to represent the top level of fashion design, a middle level, and the average woman. Measurements were made for the period 1929–1947. Researchers concluded there are decided and clear-cut limits within which fashion controls may operate in a given population in a given period of time.

Jackson, M. (1935), "The Function of Clothes," *Spectator,* Vol. 155 (November 8, 1935), p. 772.

Writer says the original purpose of dress was warmth, but morality and ornament were also involved. Women derived the use of dress as ornament from men, but now men are doomed to a graceless and disagreeable uniform.

Jackson, M. (1936), *What They Wore: A History of Children's Dress,* Woking, Great Britain: George Allen and Unwin.

Historical account of children's dress from time of caveman. Final chapter is a history of the shoe.

Jacobi, J. E. and Walters, S. G. (1958A), "Social Status and Consumer Choice," *Social Forces,* Vol. 36 (March 1958), pp. 209–214.

Discussion of the impact of social forces on consumer choice. Report includes a critique of Barber and Lobel (1952) study followed by an exploratory study of decision making in the purchase of women's dresses.

Jacobi, J. E. and Walters, S. G. (1958B), "Time Sequence and the Response Error," *Sociological Review,* Vol. 6 (December, 1958), pp. 229–239.

Discussion of common causes for response errors. Study of dress-buying habits used by researchers to test their hypotheses.

Janney, J. E. (1941), "Fad and Fashion Leadership Among Undergraduate

Women," *Journal of Abnormal and Social Psychology,* Vol. 36 (April, 1941), pp. 275–278.

Report of observation of undergraduate women in a small college to determine fad and fashion adaptation. A definite pattern in initiation and use of fads was found. Academic status and income failed to correlate with fad acceptance.

Jaquith, P. (1963), "Why She Lives in a Space Suit," *Parade* (June 16, 1963), p. 8.

Description of therapeutic use of an obsolete space suit as a pressure suit in treatment of low blood pressure.

"Japan's Patriotic Coiffure," *Living Age,* Vol. 334 (February, 1928), pp. 368–369.

Description of a coiffure called the "aviator's twist" created in honor of an attempt by Japanese airmen to cross the Pacific.

Jenny, J. J. (1944), "Clothing and Hygiene," *Ciba Symposia,* Vol. 6 (December, 1944).

A review of the purposes of clothing, the development of European clothing, unhygienic fashions, and scientific research concerned with hygiene of clothing.

Johnson, D. (1959), *The Nudists,* New York: Duell, Sloan and Pearce.

A report on nudism in America with references to similar movements in Europe. Rationale of nudist movement presented, also discussion of public and legal responses to nudist groups.

Jordan, A. C. (1929), "Healthy Dress for Men," *American Medicine,* Vol. 35 (December, 1929), pp. 803–806. [Also in: *Franco-British Medical Review,* Vol. 6 (November, 1929), pp. 42–46.]

A spirited call for an organized effort to reform men's dress. The writer says men's dress should be reduced in amount and coverage, made light in weight, washable, and loose fitting.

Jourard, S. M. and Secord, P. F. (1955), Body-Cathexis and the Ideal Female Figure," *Journal of Abnormal and Social Psychology,* Vol. 50 (March, 1955), pp. 243–246.

A study measuring the relationship between women's satisfaction with parts of their bodies and the size of these parts. It was found that the ideal size of body parts was significantly smaller than actual size with the exception of the bust where the ideal size was larger.

Journeyman (1930), "Miscellany," *The New Freeman,* Vol. 1 (March 15, 1964), p. 7.

Short article on the "Pope's recent ukase against short skirts," and the publication of his twelve rules for "dressing with Christian modesty." References to similar attempts of Puritans in Massachusetts to control modesty and simplicity in dress.

Kandel, M. (1962), Presidential Fashions have Impact on Men's Clothing Style," *New York Times* (February 25, 1962), p. Fl.

A brief comment on sensitivity of men's clothiers (retailers and manufacturers) to the part that presidential prestige can play in fashion change for men.

Included are historical references as well as speculation on the influence of President Kennedy.

Kardiner, A. (1945), *The Psychological Frontiers of Society,* New York: Columbia University Press.
See index for references on adornment, appearance, cleanliness, and clothing.

Katz, E. and Lazarsfeld, P. F. (1955), *Personal Influence,* Glencoe, Illinois: Free Press, pp. 247–270.
Study of how face-to-face contacts influence the fashion behavior of women. Fashion leadership in the local community is examined in relation to life-cycle position, fashion interest, gregariousness, and social status.

Keane, H. (1961), Why We Dress As We Do: The Story of Fashion," *Forecast for Home Economists* (February, 1961), pp. 34–39.
A combination of perceptive comments concerning motivations for dress and traditional kinds of prescriptions for what to wear.

Keesing, F. M. (1958), *Cultural Anthropology,* New York: Rinehart and Co., pp. 202–204.
An anthropological analysis of the symbolic and other functions of dress and adornment.

Kelley, J. (1949), *College Life and the Mores,* New York: Teachers College, Columbia University, pp. 16–18.
Discussion of origins of dress fads and mores on campus and the relationship of fad adoption to other social situations.

King, E. M. (1882), "Rational Dress," *Knowledge,* Vol. 2 (July 21, 1882), pp. 132–133.
Writer makes a plea for dress that will not impair women's health and yet will be beautiful because it is in harmony with the form of the moving, working body.

Kirkpatrick, E. L. (1929), *The Farmer's Standard of Living,* New York: Century, pp. 100–121.
A study concerned with how much the farm family spends on clothing and with kinds of items purchased. Conclusions are that farm families must continue to give more consideration to clothing because of its social significance.

Klapp, O. E. (1962), *Heroes, Villains, and Fools,* Englewood Cliffs, New Jersey: Prentice-Hall, pp. 1–3.
Analysis of American ideals of beauty. The democracy is no more free of typing than the traditional society, but there is more choice in type. Fashion is seen as a kind of self typing in which certain social types currently have prestige.

Klein, A. I. (1963), "Fashion: Its Sense of History—Its Selling Power," *Business History Review,* Vol. 37 (Spring–Summer, 1963), pp. 1–2.
Brief comment on historical parallels in fashion.

Klitzke, D. M. (1953), *Clothing Inventories of Outerwear: 103 New York Farm Families,* Cornell University Agricultural Experiment Station Bulletin No. 892.
In a study of New York farm families it was found that important factors

affecting clothing accumulation were age, occupation, and size and composition of the family.

Kluckhohn, C. Leighton, D. (1946), *The Navajo*, Cambridge: Harvard University Press, pp. 5, 28–29, 44.

Clothing references include information on the influence of the Spanish, other white men, and Pueblo Indians on Navajo dress.

Kroeber, A. L. (1919), "On the Principle of Order in Civilization As Exemplified by Changes of Fashion," *American Anthropologist*, Vol. 21 (July, 1919), pp. 235–263. (Also in Bobbs-Merrill Reprint: No. A-137.)

An analysis of fashion change in which pictures found in magazines were the source of data. Researcher set up definite criteria for studying selected design details, such as width of skirt and length of point of shoe, and noted changes in measurements through time. He maintains that cultural factors affect style change.

Kroeber, A. L. (1948), *Anthropology*, 2nd ed., New York: Harcourt, Brace and Co., pp. 331–336.

A discussion of style change based on writer's earlier studies of style variability in women's dress.

Kroeber, A. L. (1957), "Kinds and Properties of Styles," *Style and Civilizations*, Ithaca, New York: Cornell University Press, pp. 1–27. [Also in: paperback, University of California Press (1963) and Bobbs-Merrill Reprint No. S-153.]

Author applies findings concerning change in styles of dress to the understanding of civilization in general. Style is considered a generic concept applicable not only to dress but also to many other kinds of behavior. Author illustrates how judgments of what is beautiful vary both from society to society and through time.

Kyrk, H. (1923), *A Theory of Consumption*, New York: Houghton Mifflin Co., pp. 266–270.

Writer discusses changes in fashion, cyclical patterns in fashion, and the cause of changes. She suggests that, "as wealth increases, and as methods of production cheapen, our consumption to a greater extent must conform to the dictates of fashion." The pattern of cycles is caused by the imitation of fashion change which causes rapid spread. When a fashion reaches the bottom income level, it collapses and a new one arises.

Lagniappe (1963), "A Thirteenth-Century Castilian Sumptuary Law," *Business History Review*, Vol. 37 (Spring–Summer, 1963), pp. 98–100.

Annotated translation of a representative sumptuary ordinance of thirteenth-century Castile.

Lam, M. M. (1938), "Fashion: Its Role in Hawaii," *Sociology and Social Research*, Vol. 23 (September, 1938), pp. 55–61.

Fashion viewed as an agent of acculturation in a situation of culture contact and conflict in Hawaii. Fashion facilitates the cultural assimilation of the second and third generation of Hawaii.

Lang, K. and Lang, G. E. (1961), *Collective Dynamics*, New York: Thomas Y. Crowell Co., pp. 465–487.
Authors note that fashion is difficult to define. They discuss the concept as it relates to custom, style, social structure, identification and differentiation, the market, class, status, taste, and fads.

Langdon-Davies, J. (1928), *Lady Godiva: The Future of Nakedness*, London: Harper and Bros.
A satirical projection to a time when there will be a utopia in which nakedness is the practice.

Langner, L. (1959), *The Importance of Wearing Clothes*, New York: Hastings House.
An analysis of dress based on Adler's concepts of inferiority and superiority. Writer relates clothes to sex, civilization, social conduct, and the arts.

LaPiere, R. T. (1938), *Collective Behavior*, New York: McGraw-Hill Book Co., pp. 186, 195–196, 205.
Author says women's dress more susceptible than men's or children's to fads. He discusses cycles in dress fashion and offers a rationalization for irrational practices in the field of style leadership. A main thesis is that there are only so many possible changes in fashion, therefore repetition must occur.

LaVarge, P. (1960), "Putting the Charm in Order," *Vogue*, Vol. 136 (October 15, 1960), p. 108.
Discussion of how dress can develop personality. Author uses her own life experiences as narrative background for the article.

Laver, J. (1937), *Tastes and Fashion: From the French Revolution Until Today*, London: G. G. Harrap.
Writer relates fashion historically to the culture of the time.

Laver, J. (1952), *Clothes*, London: Burke Publishing Co.
Author points out the relationship of fashion to architecture. He discusses the hierarchical, seduction, and utilitarian motives in dress as well as many other topics.

Laver, J. (1959), "Fashion: A Detective Story," *Vogue*, Vol. 133 (January, 1959), p. 76.
Fashion designs likened to the architecture of a given period. They do not just evolve from designers' brains but reflect other signs of the times. Three motives for dress are: to show class, to attract the opposite sex, and to serve utilitarian purposes. Interesting chart of how a garment will appear to people ten, twenty, or more years after time of introduction.

Laver, J. (1963), "Chic-ness Crosses the Channel," *New York Times Magazine* (November 24, 1963), pp. 86–87.
Discussion of the increasing acceptance and spread of French fashion in Great Britain. Covers the origin of the national reputation English women have for dowdiness and reasons for a change to greater chic-ness.

Laver, J. (1964A), *Museum Piece*, Boston: Houghton Mifflin Co., pp. 234–251.

Annotated Bibliography 393

An autobiographical account of the author's first tangential association with the field of fashion and his subsequent growing interest in the history and psychology of clothes.

Laver, J. (1964B), "A Short Short History of the Female Form," *This Week Magazine, The Milwaukee Journal* (May 31, 1964), pp. 12–13.
A brief historical summary of changing ideals for the female form from Egyptian times until the present.

Lee, D. (1959), *Freedom and Culture,* Englewood Cliffs, New Jersey: Prentice-Hall, pp. 31, 143–147.
Clothing mentioned as a means of keeping physical entities strictly separate in our society. Author points out that the Greeks regarded body image as a part of image of self.

Lerner, M. (1957), *America As a Civilization,* New York: Simon and Schuster, pp. 600–603, 639–650.
Comment on American ideals for beauty and appearance of the woman. General discussion of patterns in manners and taste in America and how they have changed, plus specific comment on women's and men's fashions. Author says fashions not set by leisure class but by upper middle class, including college girls and young matrons of the professional and small-business class, who are the carriers of fashion change.

Lewis, H. (1955), *Blackways of Kent,* Chapel Hill: The University of North Carolina Press, pp. 53–64.
Analysis of dress and adornment of the Negro in a typical southern community in the Piedmont area. Relationship between dress of the Negro and the American regional pattern is noted.

Linton, E. L. (1887), "The Tyranny of Fashion," *Forum,* Vol. 3 (March, 1887), pp. 59–68.
Discussion of the imitative instinct of men and some of the ludicrous fashions of savages and Western society. Writer notes that fashion is changing rapidly today (1887) as opposed to earlier time's slow changes. Also notes that women are always complaining of the tyranny of fashion, but they do not revolt.

Linton, R. (1936), *The Study of Man,* New York: Appleton-Century-Crofts, pp. 301, 302, 345, 415–417.
Discussion of the variation of ornaments which give satisfaction in different cultures and the social and psychological functions they may perform. Mention made of the diffusion of ideas or objects through fads. Clothing provides responses to many needs in our culture, i.e., offers protection, regulates sexual behavior, indicates status.

Linton, R. (1955), *The Tree of Culture,* New York: Alfred A. Knopf.
See index for multiple entries under topic clothing.

Lips, J. E. (1947), *The Origin of Things,* New York: A. A. Wyn, pp. 46–75. [Also in: paperback, Premier Book (1964).]
Discussion of the varying standards of attractiveness among primitive peoples.

Lones, L. L. (1953), "Clothing and First Impressions," *Journal of Home Economics,* Vol. 45 (December, 1953), pp. 740–742.

Writer experimented with her college class to determine what influence, if any, the mode of dress of the instructor had on their first impression of her as a person. Since she was new in the community, the students had no previous value judgment on which to base their reply.

Lonie, M. (1948), "Anthropometry and Apparel," *American Journal of Physical Anthropology,* Vol. 6 (September, 1948), pp. 353–361.

Report concerned with sizing of clothing based on anthropometric data. Standardization of patterns and garments in terms of actual persons' sizes, not ideals, the ultimate aim.

Loomis, C. P. (1936), "The Study of the Life Cycle of Families," *Rural Sociology,* Vol. 1 (June, 1936), pp. 180–199.

Evidence presented to validate observation that family expenditures for clothing vary with life cycle of the family. For example, expenditures increase naturally when children are eligible for marriage.

Loomis, C. P. (1960), *Social Systems: Essays on Their Persistence and Change,* Princeton, New Jersey: D. Van Nostrand Co., pp. 212–248.

Note clothing references in section entitled "The Old Order Amish as a Social System."

Loos, A. (1958), "The New Vamp," *Vogue,* Vol. 131 (March 1, 1958), pp. 128–133.

Comparison of the chemise dress of 1958 with the garments of the vamps of the twenties.

Lowie, R. (1940), *An Introduction to Cultural Anthropology,* New York: Rinehart and Co., pp. 68–85, 120–128.

Author describes the development of means of making cloth, motives for wearing clothing, and cultural variety in clothing and ornament. In discussing motives, he supports most strongly an ornamentation theory.

Lundberg, G. A., Schrag, C. C., and Larsen, O. N. (1958), *Sociology,* revised ed., New York: Harper and Bros.

See index for references to fashion.

Lynd, R. S. and Lynd, H. M. (1929), *Middletown,* New York: Harcourt, Brace and Co.

See index for references to clothing, fashion, and related topics.

Lynd, R. S. and Lynd, H. M. (1937), *Middletown in Transition,* New York: Harcourt, Brace and Co.

See index for references to clothing, fashion, and cosmetics.

Lynes, R. (1950), *Snobs,* New York: Harper and Bros., pp. 43–45.

There are many varieties of snobs. Among the types discussed are the taste snobs with a sub-category of male and female clothes snobs.

Lynes, R. (1951), "Gaudy to Drab to Gaudy," *Harper's Magazine,* Vol. 202 (April, 1951), pp. 43–48.

Author traces the theme of gaudiness in men's dress since the French Revolution. He sees a trend in the direction of gaudiness once more in the 1950's.

Lynes, R. (1954), *The Tastemakers,* New York: Harper and Bros.
A lively account of the people and pressures that have shaped American taste for the last dozen decades. See index for fashion.

Lynes, R. (1957), *A Surfeit of Honey,* New York: Harper and Bros., pp. 65–85, 101, 102.
Writer describes the part clothing plays in a teenager's concept of a lady. He discusses the clothing of men and the different images that clothing promotes. He says clothing reflects a man's personality and place in life.

Macaulay, E. (1929), "Some Notes on the Attitude of Children to Dress," *British Journal of Medical Psychology,* Vol. 9 (1929), pp. 150–158.
Attitudes toward clothing were derived from essays written by elementary school girls and boys. Dominant concern of subjects was with decorative, modesty, and comfort aspects of clothing.

MacGuire, A. (1964), "Britain's New Super-Gangs: A Teenage Phenomenon," *Atlas,* Vol. 8 (September, 1964), pp. 79–82.
A consideration of the social-psychological components of the adolescent Mod-Rocker phenomenon. Author indicates that more than status-seeking is involved, that differences in role definition, especially of masculinity and femininity, separate the two groups.

MacIver, R. M. (1937), *Society,* New York: Farrar and Rinehart, pp. 181, 370, 377, 585.
Writer defines fashion as "the socially approved sequence of variation on a customary theme." He discusses fashion in relation to custom, etiquette, social role, and mentions periodicity of fashions. Fashionable goods, he points out, function as a base for social ranking.

Manch, J. (1956), "The Dress-Right Program in the Buffalo Public Schools," *The Bulletin of the National Association of Secondary School Principals,* Vol. 40 (November, 1956), pp. 81–84.
Since it was felt that poor dress habits helped foster juvenile delinquency, a dress program was set up through the Inter-High School Student Council of Buffalo. Response of students found encouraging after five months.

Marcus, H. S. (1948), "Fashion is My Business," *Atlantic Monthly,* Vol. 182 (December, 1948), pp. 43–47.
This article is written by one of the owners of Neiman-Marcus. He discusses how fashion is related to culture and relates fashion to "taste" of customers.

"The Masculine Mode," *Time,* Vol. 83 (February 28, 1964), p. 83.
Writer's theme is that men, too, are subject to fashion, for they can buy only what is available to them. They are thus often subject to the dictates of industry. Men's fashions are often, but not always, started by presidents.

Mason, O. (1920), *Woman's Share in Primitive Culture,* New York: D. Appleton Co., pp. 41–90, 161–187.

Topics discussed include: the art of weaving as performed by women in different cultures, the dress of Eskimo women, and the variety of ways used by women of different cultures to adorn themselves.

McCleary, G. (1959), "Clothing—The Fabric of Family Relations," *What's New in Home Economics,* Vol. 23 (September, 1959), p. 210.

Author says that family members speak about themselves through their clothes. Children as well as teenagers and adults express their needs, desires, and demands for self-determination through the clothing they wear.

McDonnell, E. K. (1935), "Fashion and the Hollywood Handicap," *Saturday Evening Post,* Vol. 207 (May 18, 1935), pp. 10–11, 42, 46.

Writer sees Hollywood fashions beginning to take some of the prestige away from Paris gowns in the 1930's.

McHale, K. (1926), *Comparative Psychology and Hygiene of the Overweight Child,* Contributions to Education, No. 221, New York: Bureau of Publications, Teachers College, Columbia University.

An experimental analysis of differences between the psychology and hygiene of the overweight child and that of the normal-weight and underweight child. Three weight groups of children were compared for the purpose of confirming, modifying, or destroying prevailing attitudes toward overweight people in physical, mental, emotional, educational, and social areas.

Mead, M. (1939A), *Coming of Age in Samoa,* New York: William Morrow and Co.

Anthropological study of adolescents in Samoa. Clothing references scattered throughout the book. Appendix III contains a description of the Samoan dress after it was influenced by Western cultures.

Mead, M. (1939B), *From the South Seas,* New York: William Morrow and Co.
See index for references to clothing.

Mead, M. (1956), *New Lives for Old, Cultural Transformation—Manus, 1928–1953,* New York: William Morrow and Co.
See index for references to clothing.

Meier, R. L. (1956), *Science and Economic Development: New Patterns of Living,* New York: John Wiley and Sons and Massachusetts Institute of Technology, Technology Press, pp. 97–102.

Researcher compares economy of using clothing to retain body heat versus using food to supply calories necessary to maintain body heat. He works out per capita needs in a unit called clo. With this unit as a basis of estimate he develops a minimum adequate wardrobe and a chart of world requirements.

Merriam, E. (1960), *Figleaf,* Philadelphia: J. B. Lippincott Co.

Satire on the business of being in fashion. Writer especially notes the extreme ends to which women are willing to go in order to be in fashion. Attention also given to men's fashions.

Meyersohn, R. and Katz, E. (1957), "Notes on a Natural History of Fads," *American Journal of Sociology,* Vol. 62 (May, 1957), pp. 594–601.

A natural history of fads or fashions, a particular type of social change, is told as a succession of chronological stages, each characterized by interaction among producers, distributors, and consumers. No specific references to clothing but many implications.

Miller, S. (1928), "Old English Laws Regulating Dress," *Journal of Home Economics,* Vol. 20 (February, 1928), pp. 89–94.
Discussion of how old English laws tried to enforce dress conformity. Writer relates old laws to present day attempts at legislation.

Miller, T. K., Carpenter, L. G., and Buckey, R. B. (1960), "Therapy of Fashion," *Mental Hospitals,* Vol. 11 (October, 1960), pp. 42–43.
Report of therapeutic effect of attention to dress on mental illness.

Miner, H. (1956), "Body Ritual Among the Nacirema," *American Anthropologist,* Vol. 58 (June, 1956), pp. 503–507. [Also in: Young, K. and Mack, R. W. (eds.) (1960), *Principles of Sociology,* New York: American Book Co., pp. 59–62, and Bobbs-Merrill Reprint No. S-185.]
A satiric treatment of body care and ritual in America.

Minnich, H. B. (1963), *Japanese Costume,* Rutland, Vermont: Charles E. Tuttle Co.
A history of Japanese costume. Chapter 12 includes description of the effects of culture contact in nineteenth and twentieth centuries, i.e., contact with Occidental fashions.

"The Mods vs. The Rockers," *Life (International),* Vol. 37 (July 27, 1964), pp. 14–21.
Picture report of behavior of British adolescent groups called the Mods and Rockers. An individual's attention to dress and grooming symbolize his identification with one or the other of the groups.

Mohyeddin, S. and Battelle, P. (1962), "Pakistani Women," *Cosmopolitan,* Vol. 153 (September, 1962), pp. 38–51.
Changes in the roles as well as the clothing of Pakistani women are discussed. Mention made of the psychological effects that either discarding or assuming the veil may have on these women.

Monro, I. S. and Cook, D. E. (1937), *Costume Index,* New York: H. W. Wilson Co.
Classic bibliography of references to clothing.

Monro, I. S. and Monro, K. M. (1957), *Costume Index and Supplement,* New York: H. W. Wilson Co.
Supplement to Munro and Cook (1937). See above.

Moore, H. T. (1922), "Further Data Concerning Sex Differences," *Journal of Abnormal and Social Psychology,* Vol. 17 (July–September, 1922), pp. 210–214.
Writer states that mental tests are inadequate for establishing mental differences between the sexes. In a sample of conversations on Broadway he found considerable difference in the conversational interests of men and women. Men tended to discuss money, business, and amusement. Women talked about men, home, and clothes.

Moore, W. E. (1951), *Industrialization and Labor: Social Aspects of Economic Development,* Ithaca, New York: Cornell University Press, p. 216.

In discussing the difficulties of deciding ethnic origin of persons of mixed racial background, writer cites the present-day Mexico custom of deciding the percentage of Indianness on the basis of clothing worn and language spoken.

"Morality and Good Taste in Apparel," *America,* Vol. 93 (July 2, 1955), p. 342.

Comment concerning appearance on the market of dresses which fit the requirements of a papal decree on modesty in clothing.

Morita, T. (1959), "The Secret Art of Wearing Kimono," *This Is Japan,* Vol. 7 (September, 1959), pp. 162–163.

An article explaining customs involved in wearing the kimono. A kimono must be not only a work of art but also seasonally correct. Author mentions that Japanese men have often displayed their wealth in their wives' clothes.

Moss, M. (1904), "Machine Made Human Beings," *Atlantic Monthly,* Vol. 94 (August, 1904), pp. 264–268.

Main theme is conformity of man in all areas of life. Clothing and fashion discussed in this light.

Mumford, L. (1938), *The Culture of Cities,* New York: Harcourt, Brace and Co., pp. 98–105.

Observations on the growth of fashion as an ordering element in the Baroque city.

Murchison, C. (ed.) (1935), *A Handbook of Social Psychology,* Worcester, Massachusetts: Clark University Press, pp. 798–844.

Discussion of functions of clothing including protection, adornment, modesty, and status identification. Deals briefly with footwear.

Murdock, G. P. (1934), *Our Primitive Contemporaries,* New York: Macmillan Co.

See index for clothing and related word entries.

Murtagh, J. M. and Harris, S. (1957), *Cast the First Stone,* New York: McGraw-Hill Book Co., pp. 281–282.

Description of personal defacement that comes to women forced to wear prison-issue clothes.

Myrdal, G. (1944), *An American Dilemma,* New York: Harper and Bros., pp. 761–763.

Analysis of trait of emotionalism as attributed to Negroes and as supposedly shown in love of the gaudy, the bizarre, the ostentatious. Writer points out that Negroes do not have enough money to be terribly ostentatious and that they generally imitate common American dress. This dress may look bizarre because of skin coloring or the fact that cast off clothing may not always harmonize in the "approved way."

Nakagawa, K. and Rosovsky, H. (1963), "The Case of the Dying Kimono: The Influence of Changing Fashions on the Development of the Japanese Woolen Industry," *Business History Review,* Vol. 37 (Spring–Summer, 1963), pp. 59–80.

Effects on dress of co-existence of Occidental and Oriental influences in Japan. Historical treatment with implications for wool industry.

"'Naked' Revolution," *Newsweek*, Vol. 53 (April 27, 1959), p. 63.
Discussion of the control assumed by women members of the Sons of Freedom as they protest education of their children in Canadian schools. Nudism often used to reinforce protest.

National Council of Women of the United States (1892), "Symposium on Women's Dress," Parts 1 and 2, *Arena*, Vol. 6 (September and October), pp. 488–507, 621–634.
Interesting nineteenth-century discussion of suitable dress for women in different walks of life. Suggestions were an outgrowth of a proposed study of suitable business women's dress to meet demands of health, comfort, and good taste. A journalistic reflection of women's movement for emancipation in dress.

deNegri, E. (1962A), "Yoruba Women's Costume," *Nigeria Magazine*, No. 72 (March, 1962), pp. 4–12.
The author considers that Yoruba women's costume reflects attitudes of the men at the time such garments are in fashion and that fashion is an indication of the attitudes and thinking, socially and economically, of the people.

deNegri, E. (1962B), "Yoruba Men's Costume," *Nigeria Magazine*, No. 73 (June, 1962), pp. 4-12.
Garments now popularly called national costume throughout southern Nigeria were once known as "Yoruba Costume." Author discusses the general characteristics of this costume as well as recent innovations which have helped adapt it to the rapidly changing society of Nigeria.

Newcomb, A. P. (1902), "Hats and Habitations," *English Mechanic and World of Science*, Vol. 75 (April 18, 1902), pp. 198–199.
Lecturer presents theory that there are structural similarities between architecture and hats in many cultures at various times in their history.

The New International Encyclopedia (1930), New York: Dodd Mead Co.
See dress, dress reform, and costume.

Newman, R. W. (1953), "Applied Anthropometry," in *Anthropology Today*, International Symposium on Anthropology, Chicago: The University of Chicago Press, pp. 741–749.
Information on anthropometric study of American boys and girls carried on between 1937 and 1939 under direction of U.S.D.A. Data are incorporated into "Commercial Standards," and are subject to voluntary acceptance by the clothing trade. Author says main concern not with the active living organism but with helping the trade in mass producing "clothing shells" for forms of specified measurements.

Nystrom, P. (1928), *Economics of Fashion*, New York: Ronald Press.
Author defines fashion, style, mode, fad. He discusses the nature of the fashion cycle, the psychology of fashion, and the relationship of such things as custom, modesty, utility, and art to fashion. In addition, he traces the origin and development of fashion and new advances in the fashion world.

Ogburn, W. and Nimkoff, M. (1955), *Technology and the Changing Family,* Boston: Houghton Mifflin Co., pp. 125–128.

Discussion of the increase in production of family members' clothing outside the home.

Orwell, G. (1933), *Down and Out in Paris and London,* New York: Harcourt, Brace and Co., pp. 127–129.

Author discusses the effect his pawning of his clothes for rags and a little money has on people's attitude toward him and treatment of him.

Owst, G. R. (1933), *Literature and Pulpit in Medieval England,* Cambridge: The University Press, pp. 390–411.

Medieval preachings against finery and excess in clothing.

Packard, V. (1959), *The Status Seekers,* New York: D. McKay Co., pp. 128–138.

In focusing on the class structure of our society, especially the symbols of status-rank, the author refers to men's and women's clothing and fashion.

Palmer, B. M. (1937), "Clothing for Older Women," *Journal of Home Economics,* Vol. 29 (December, 1937), pp. 692–693.

Study to determine why older women select the clothing they wear. Practical reasons such as quality and wearability, were often put ahead of psychological reasons.

Park, R. E. and Burgess, E. W. (1924), *Introduction to the Science of Sociology,* Chicago: University of Chicago Press, pp. 933–934.

Discussion of the ideas of Sombart and Sumner on fashion. Fashion considered related to reform but distinguished by being irrational.

Parsons, F. A. (1920), *The Psychology of Dress,* Garden City, New York: Doubleday, Page and Co.

In tracing the history of dress from medieval to present times the author relates patterns of dress to the times. He says "a man's clothes, like other reactions to his needs, are his material response to a demand for them, and by the results he must stand or fall, whether judged commercially, socially, artistically, ethically, or by a simple standard of common sense."

Parton, J. (1869), "Clothes Mania," *Atlantic Monthly,* Vol. 23 (May, 1869), pp. 531–548. [Also in: *Victoria Magazine,* Vol. 25, p. 876.]

Discussion of the rise and fall of a fashion. Author feels we respond to fashion because of shame which we have for a physical defect that we think we have.

Patten, S. N. (1913), "The Standardization of Family Life," *The Annals of the American Academy of Political and Social Science,* Vol. 48, Part 2 (July, 1913), pp. 81–90.

With the change from rural to urban living in the United States, old family standards are replaced by new. Author uses data on clothing expenditures to illustrate the passing of the family from an emotional basis to an economic basis, the changing of women's activities from a sensory to a motor basis.

Pear, T. H. (1957), *Personality, Appearance, and Speech,* London: Allen and Unwin, p. 66.

Discussion of the relationship of appearance (including dress) to speech and personality and the habit of attaching stereotyped personality characteristics to persons with specific appearance features. Also comment on certain appearance features which distinguish classes.

Pendleton, W. N. (1856), "The Philosophy of Dress," *Southern Literary Messenger,* Vol. 22 (March, 1856), pp. 199–211. [Also in: *Blackwood's Magazine,* Vol. 53 (February, 1843), p. 230–234.]
Discussion of men's fashions. Observations include evaluative terms such as vain, modest, snob, graceful indifference, affects airs, affectation.

Perrin, F. A. C. (1921), "Physical Attractiveness and Repulsiveness," *Journal of Experimental Psychology,* Vol. 4 (June, 1921), pp. 203–217.
Study to determine to what degree physical attractiveness affects acceptance among college students.

Philip, B. R. (1945), "A Method for Investigating Color Preferences in Fashions," *Journal of Applied Psychology,* Vol. 29 (April, 1945), pp. 108–114.
A study of men's and women's color preferences for afternoon dresses. Color found a more significant variable for women than for men.

Phillips, J. W. and Staley, H. K. (1961), "Sumptuary Legislation in Four Centuries," *Journal of Home Economics,* Vol. 53 (October, 1961), pp. 673–677.
A study of sumptuary legislation from 1700–1900. It was noted that sumptuary laws increased as fashion changes increased in frequency and that sumptuary laws were short lived in the English colonies of North America.

"The Physiology of Clothing," (1964), *Ciba Review,* No. 4.
A comprehensive survey of scientific study of the relation of clothing to physiology. Psychological, cultural, and historical data are included as background.

Pitcher, E. G. (1963), "Male and Female," *The Atlantic,* Vol. 211 (March, 1963), pp. 87–91.
A study of how early in life a child plays a distinctive sex role and how parents accent sex differences. Includes references to clothing and appearance in relation to femininity and masculinity.

Plant, J. S. (1950), *The Envelope,* New York: The Commonwealth Fund.
A psychological analysis of behavior in which the term "envelope" is used to describe the complex of adjustments that the child develops as a result of social pressures. See index for references to ways clothing is used in the adjustment.

Poll, S. (1962), *The Hasidic Community of Williamsburg,* New York: Free Press of Glencoe, pp. 59–69, 103–107, 212–220.
A study of the Hasidim, a conservative religious community that has succeeded in resisting assimilation in New York City where secular forces are at their peak. The use of clothing is closely integrated with religious practice.

Quigley, D. (1897), *What Dress Makes of Us,* New York: E. P. Dutton and Co.
Late nineteenth-century prescriptions for dressing hair and for selection of hats, and other clothing. Discussion of line, figure types, dress for the elderly.

In preface author uses ridicule to encourage conformity to her aesthetic standards for clothing and appearance.

Radcliffe-Brown, A. R. (1933), *The Andaman Islanders*, Cambridge: The University Press, pp. 121–127, 281–289, 312–323.

Writer discusses functions of three kinds of personal ornament: scarification, painting, putting on ornaments. Scarification marks status passage from child to adult and bestows power or social value. Painting impresses social value on individual and others. Ornaments serve display or protective functions.

Rainwater, L., Coleman, R. P., and Handel, G. (1958), *The Workingman's Wife*, New York: Oceana Publications, pp. 197–198.

Discussion of clothing choices of working men's wives. The group of women who responded selected simple clothes and agreed that a party dress should be dressy, but not too much so.

Raushenbush, W. (1930A), "Fifteen Million Women Can't Go Nude," *The New Freeman*, Vol. 1 (May 24, 1930), pp. 250–251.

Commentary on inadequacy of both sizing and styling of ready-made clothes for women.

Raushenbush, W. (1930B), "Nine Out of Ten Take a Bath," *The New Freeman*, Vol. 1 (June 18, 1930), pp. 323–325.

Author notes that even if the bulk of fashion business is with the lower—middle-class woman, industry does not pay attention to her. Instead, production is for the climbing middle class.

Raushenbush, W. (1930C), "The Woman Nobody Knows," *The New Freeman*, Vol. 1 (March 15, 1930), pp. 10–12.

Comment on the unpredictability of fashion in 1930, a year when hemlines were going down, and on the problem that uncertainty was for manufacturers and retailers.

Rea, L. (1950), "Clothing and Child Development," *Journal of Home Economics*, Vol. 42 (November, 1950), pp. 717–718.

Consideration of the relationship of clothing to a child's comfort and to his development of personality. Also discussion of how to obtain clothes that meet the requirements of personality and physical comfort.

Read, K. H. (1950), "Clothes Help Build the Personality," *Journal of Home Economics*, Vol. 42 (May, 1950), pp. 348–350.

Author gives insights into how children feel about criticism and into how they are influenced by clothing.

Redfield, R. (1941), *The Folk Culture of Yucatan*, Chicago: The University of Chicago Press.

Author mentions: differences in costume associated with differences in status, wearing of folk costume and city clothes, and class symbolism in folk costume. See index for references to fashion and costume.

Redlich, F. (1963), "A Needed Distinction in Fashion Study," *Business History Review*, Vol. 37 (Spring–Summer, 1963), pp. 3–4.

Writer suggests German word "Tracht" for use in the field of fashion to identify short-term changes.

Reik, T. (1953), "Men, Women, and Dresses," *Psychoanalysis,* Vol. 1 (Winter, 1953), pp. 3–16.

An attempt to relate a woman's statement "I have nothing to wear" to little girl's complaint about her lack of male sex organs.

Reiss, A. J. and Rhodes, A. L. (1963), "Status Deprivation and Delinquent Behavior," *The Sociological Quarterly,* Vol. 4 (Spring, 1963), pp. 135–149.

Study testing hypothesis that adolescents suffer feelings of status deprivation and frustration, in invidious comparisons of their own style of life symbols with peers in higher classes, that generate delinquent behavior. To get data researchers used a question concerning adolescents' feelings about their clothes and houses as compared to other students in their school.

Rich, W. E. (1950), "The Correlation of the Super-Ego with Clothes," *Psychoanalytic Review,* Vol. 37 (October, 1950), pp. 358–362.

A study of nudity among women mental patients. Writer feels that the harshness of the unconscious and the rigidity of the superego may cause unnecessary restrictions and a loss of enjoyment and efficiency. Case studies illustrate rebellious and regressive types of nudity.

Richardson, J. and Kroeber, A. L. (1940), "Three Centuries of Women's Dress Fashions," *Anthropological Records,* Vol. 5 (1940). [Also in: Kroeber, A. L. (1952), *The Nature of Culture,* Chicago: University of Chicago Press, pp. 358–378.]

Research project in which dimensions of designs on fashion plates were measured quantitatively in order to evaluate change. Researchers plotted changes in fashions, including skirt width and length and other dimensions, in formal clothing for women. Many hypotheses as to what causes fashion changes are set forth.

Rickert, E. (1948), *Chaucer's World,* New York: Columbia University Press, pp. 333–346.

Passages on male and female fashions and shopping in fourteenth century London. Stress is placed on the folly of fashion extremes.

Riegel, R. E. (1963), "Women's Clothes and Women's Rights," *American Quarterly,* Vol. 15 (Fall, 1963), pp. 390–401.

Writer discusses the push for dress reform for women in the middle and late nineteenth century. The advocates of this movement felt that dress reform would aid the cause of women's rights. The movement was not particularly successful, but as women gained more freedom and rights, changes in dress followed rapidly.

Riesman, D. (1951), *The Lonely Crowd: A Study of the Changing American Character,* Glencoe, Illinois: Free Press, pp. 52, 78, 90, 95, 185, 262. [Also in: Doubleday Anchor Books (1955).]

404   Annotated Bibliography

References made to: zoot suiters, uniforms, fashions, evening dress and sports clothes, and "inconspicuous" dress of the wealthy.

Roach, M. E. (1960), "The Influence of Social Class on Clothing Practices and Orientation at Early Adolescence: A Study of Clothing-Related Behavior of Seventh Grade Girls," unpublished Ph.D. dissertation, Michigan State University.

Clothing-related behavior of adolescent girls studied had no significant associations with social class position.

Robinson, D. E. (1958), "Fashion Theory and Product Design," *Harvard Business Review*, Vol. 36 (November–December, 1958), pp. 126–138.

Author applies fashion theory to changing design of a number of consumer products. Comparisons made with fashion in women's apparel which he cites as the purest and oldest form of fashion expression.

Robinson, D. E. (1959), "The Rules of Fashion Cycles," *Horizon* (March, 1959), pp. 62–67, 113–117.

Fashion is defined as the pursuit of novelty for its own sake. Fashion milks a style to its utmost and then destroys it completely and instantly. Costume variations bounce back and forth between opposite extremes.

Robinson, D. E. (1960), "The Styling and Transmission of Fashions Historically Considered," *Journal of Economic History*, Vol. 20 (December, 1960), pp. 576–587.

Discussion of the fashion process during the Greek Revival period of the second half of the eighteenth century. Some mention made of the carryover of this style change into men's clothing.

Robinson, D. E. (1961), "The Economics of Fashion Demand," *Quarterly Journal of Economics*, Vol. 75 (August, 1961), pp. 376–398.

A socio-economic analysis of fashion with references to clothing. Author concludes that pursuit of demonstrable rarity for its own sake is a principal key to the motivation underlying the demand for luxuries.

Robinson, D. E. (1963A), "The Importance of Fashions in Taste to Business History: An Introductory Essay," *Business History Review*, Vol. 37 (Spring–Summer, 1963), pp. 5–36.

An appraisal of the socio-economic role of fashion. Emphasis on historical perspective. Author notes schism between men's and women's dress in late eighteenth century and the growth of the *haute couture*.

Robinson, D. E. (1963B), "A Note on Fashion Leadership: Reply," *Business History Review*, Vol. 37 (Winter, 1963), pp. 451–455.

Reply to Hollander (1963). Writer defends the trickle-down theory of fashion behavior and restates his position that Balenciago stands pre-eminent among fashion designers. He makes clear, however, that the designer, no matter how great his influence, is still dependent on his own clientele for guidance and support.

Rollinson, B. W. (1930), "Why We Dress," *Practical Home Economics*, Vol. 8 (March, 1930), pp. 72, 90, 91.

Interesting ideas on why man wears clothes. Includes references to several authors' views as to why we dress as we do.

Rollinson, B. W. (1931), "Dame Fashion," *Practical Home Economics,* Vol. 9 (March, 1931), pp. 78, 92.
Author calls fashion a form of "feminine psychology" that rules us all.

Rosencranz, M. L. (1949), "A Study of Women's Interest in Clothing," *Journal of Home Economics,* Vol. 41 (October, 1949), pp. 460–462.
Study of women's interest in clothing. Researcher found interest could be evaluated by measuring the time, money, effort, and attention given to clothing and that a number of factors, such as age and income, showed relationships to clothing interest.

Rosencranz, M. L. (1950), "Sociological Aspects of Clothing Studied," *Journal of Home Economics,* Vol. 42 (March, 1950), pp. 206–207.
Report on a Michigan State College seminar in which theories and studies in social science relevant to the study of clothing were reviewed and social-psychological techniques for research were evaluated.

Rosencranz, M. L. (1958), *Relevance of Occupation to Mothers' Selection of Clothing for Daughters,* Michigan State Agricultural Experiment Station Technical Bulletin No. 268.
Study of extent to which father's occupation and family income were related to: practices in obtaining daughter's clothing, mother's preferences for specific dresses, and dresses worn on selected occasions. Comparisons were drawn between blue-collar and white-collar groups.

Rosencranz, M. L. (1962), "Clothing Symbolism," *Journal of Home Economics,* Vol. 54 (January, 1962), pp. 18–22.
Study in which the researcher considered the degree to which clothing is used as a guide in identifying role and status of unknown persons and the various shades of meaning attached to clothing in particular social situations.

Roshco, B. (1963), *The Rag Race,* New York: Funk and Wagnalls Co.
An account of the intricate workings of the fashion industry, especially Seventh Avenue in New York City.

Ross, E. A. (1923), *Social Psychology,* New York: Macmillan Co., pp. 94–108.
Main thesis of author is that fashion is a series of changes that recur in the choices of people. He points out trends to increasing rapidity of fashion change and an increasing number of fashion items. He also speaks of the need for dress reform, i.e., dress with more utility.

Roth, J. A. (1957), "Ritual and Magic in the Control of Contagion," *American Sociological Review,* Vol. 22 (June, 1957), pp. 310–314. (Also in: Bobbs-Merrill Reprint No. S-492.)
An account of the use of hospital garb ritualistically and as a symbol of status, rather than as logically protective covering.

Rothfeld, O., *Women of India,* Bombay: D. B. Taraporeuata Sons and Co. (no date given), pp. 177–196.

406   Annotated Bibliography

Comment on functions of dress and the quasi-religious sanction of dress in India. Considerable descriptive detail is included.

Rousseau, J. J. (1911), *Émile,* New York: E. P. Dutton and Co., pp. 91–92, 356–357.
Topics discussed include: clothing for the child, the effect of clothing on the body, choice of colors in clothing, clothing in relation to activities of children, and the coquettishness of the dress of girls.

Rudofsky, B. (1947), *Are Clothes Modern?* Chicago: Paul Theobald.
A critical analysis of modern clothing, sharpened by historical and cross-cultural references. Author advocates freedom from conventions of past and subsequent reform in dress.

Ruesch, J., and Kees, W. (1956), *Nonverbal Communication: Notes on the Visual Perception of Human Relations,* Berkeley and Los Angeles: University of California Press, pp. 39–41, 57–75.
Discussion of role of body and appearance in conveying ideas to perceiver. Clothing is a language in itself. Hairdress, masks, or makeup can convey status position or role, as well as other impressions.

Rusling, L. (1905), "Children's Attitude toward Clothes," *Pedagogical Seminary,* Vol. 12 (December, 1905), p. 525.
Short review of a study which suggests that accidents to clothing hurt children because they are made to feel sad and at a loss.

Russell, F. (1892), "A Brief Survey of the American Dress Reform Movements of the Past with Views of Representative Women," *Arena,* Vol. 6 (August, 1892), pp. 325–339.
Summary of points of view of women leaders in dress-reform movement, made on behalf of Dress Reform Committee appointed by Woman's Council. Among those heard from were Mrs. Amelia Bloomer, Mrs. Elizabeth Cady Stanton, Frances E. Willard.

Ryan, M. S. (1951), "Effect on College Girl of Feeling Well Dressed," *Journal of Home Economics,* Vol. 43 (December, 1951), p. 799.
Report of a Cornell University study which revealed factors that lead college girls to have greater confidence in their clothing.

Ryan, M. S. (1952), *Psychological Effects of Clothing, Part I: A Survey of the Opinions of College Girls,* Cornell University Agricultural Experiment Station Bulletin No. 882.
A survey of college girls to determine how and in what way they thought clothing affected them, factors that made them feel well or poorly dressed, degree of their interest in clothing, and their attitudes toward the importance of being well dressed.

Ryan, M. S. (1953A), *Psychological Effects of Clothing, Part II: Comparison of College Students with High School Students, Rural with Urban Students and Boys with Girls,* Cornell University Agricultural Experiment Station Bulletin No. 898.
Comparison of college students with high school students, rural with urban

students, and boys with girls, on basis of same general variables listed in Part I of study.

Ryan, M. S. (1953B), *Psychological Effects of Clothing, Part III: Report of Interviews with a Selected Sample of College Women,* Cornell University Agricultural Experiment Station Bulletin No. 900.

Report of interviews with girls studied in Part I. Certain questions regarding self concepts in relation to clothes and attitudes toward clothing, not fully clarified by the questionnaire method, were probed more deeply.

Ryan, M. S. (1954), *Psychological Effects of Clothing, Part IV: Perception of Self in Relation to Clothing,* Cornell University Agricultural Experiment Station Bulletin No. 905.

A comparison of an individual girl's opinion of her appearance with group opinion. Groups of girls rated themselves and each other. In addition, a personal data sheet was filled out and each girl was given a Personality Inventory. Analysis was made of data drawn from the three sources and comparisons made.

Sanborn, H. C. (1927), "The Function of Clothing and of Bodily Adornment," *American Journal of Psychology,* Vol. 38 (January, 1927), pp. 1–20.

Modesty discussed as a reason for clothing. Author points out that other motives, such as ornament and protection, have been noted throughout history.

Sapir, E. (1931), "Fashion," *Encyclopedia of the Social Sciences,* Vol. 6, New York: Macmillan Co., pp. 139–144. [Also in: Mandelbaum, D. G. (ed.) (1941) *Selected Writings of Edward Sapir in Language, Culture and Personality* and Bobbs-Merrill Reprint No. S-246.]

Author defines fashion as "custom in the guise of departure from custom." He says that the way in which fashions evolve depends upon prevailing culture and social ideals.

Schilder, P. (1950), *The Image and Appearance of the Human Body,* New York: International University Press, pp. 201–206.

Writer discusses functions of clothes. He suggests that as soon as clothes are put on they become part of the body image, symbolic of parts of the body, and of desires of the individuals wearing them.

Schmalhausen, S. D. and Calverton, V. F. (1931), *Woman's Coming of Age,* New York: Horace Liveright, pp. 32–33, 424–446.

Women's dress discussed as an outgrowth of man's wishing her to be as different from him as possible. Comment on fashion and its influence on many aspects of a woman's life; the use of clothing to fight other women; the effect of the fashion industry on women; the cost of fashion in dollars, time, and energy.

Schneider, P. E. (1958), "What Makes Paris Fashion's Capitol," *New York Times Magazine* (July 27, 1958), pp. 18–19, 43, 45.

Discussion of Paris fashion openings. Author says Seventh Avenue buys ideas from Paris. Individuality of French woman compared with American woman's conformity. Mass production described as discouraging personal invention.

Schofield, A. T. (1888), "Dissertation on Dress," *Leisure Hour,* Vol. 37 (1888), pp. 668–671.
A discussion of the relation of dress to health. Comments on both design and fabrics used in clothing.

Schwartz, J. (1963), "Men's Clothing and the Negro," *Phylon,* Vol. 24 (Fall, 1963), pp. 224–231.
Writer seeks other than an economic explanation for differences in clothing consumption of Negroes and Whites. His research suggests that the clothing of Negro men may compensate for inferior social position and also may serve as anthropometric disguise.

Scott, A. C. (1958), *Chinese Costume in Transition,* New York: Theatre Arts Books.
Topics covered include: the development of modern Chinese costume, Western influence on Chinese costume, Chinese influence on Western costume, Communist costume since 1949, and costume of the Chinese theatre.

Scott, C. A. (1896), "Sex and Art," *American Journal of Psychology,* Vol. 7 (January, 1896), pp. 153–226.
Writer develops the following topics: courting in "lower races" and adornment; tattooing for beauty; tattooing and religion; clothing and attraction between the sexes; clothing and shame, jealousy, fear; symbolism and fetishism.

Seeley, J. R., Sim, R. A., and Loosley, E. W. (1956), *Crestwood Heights,* New York: Basic Books. [Also in: Science Editions, John Wiley and Sons (1963), pp. 103–104, 324–325.]
In a study of a metropolitan suburb, clothing found to be an important symbol of changing status at the junior high level. Clothing and general appearances contributed to the adequate playing of sex roles at this age. Conflict in socialization patterns for modesty shown in children's camps.

Service, E. R. (1958), *A Profile of Primitive Culture,* New York: Harper and Bros.
See index for descriptions of dress in many cultures.

Shapiro, H. T. (ed.) (1956), *Man, Culture, and Society,* New York: Oxford University Press, pp. 228–231.
Detailed discussion of the origins of clothing mentioning protection, adornment, social distinction, and shame or modesty.

Silverman, S. S. (1945), *Clothing and Appearance, Their Psychological Implications for Teen-Age Girls,* New York: Teachers College, Columbia University.
Study concerned with the attention adolescent girls give to their appearance, their choice of clothes, and use of cosmetics.

Silverman, S. S. (1947), "Why Girls Are Like That," *Parents' Magazine,* Vol. 22 (March, 1947), p. 29.
Popular report of study of adolescent girls. Deals with use of cosmetics, types of clothes, and psychological satisfactions.

Silverman, S. S. (1960), "Clothing and Appearance," in Seidman, J. M., *The Adolescent,* New York: Holt, Rinehart and Winston, pp. 524–528.

Brief summary of the 1945 Silverman study.

Simmel, G. (1904), "Fashion," *International Quarterly,* Vol. 10 (October, 1904), pp. 137–140. [Also in: *American Journal of Sociology,* Vol. 62 (May, 1957), pp. 541–558.]
Development of theme of paradoxical character of fashion as a means to both conformity and individualism.

Simon, M. S. (1958), "Clothing Expenditure Units: A New Time Series," *Agricultural Economics Research,* Vol. 10 (April, 1958), pp. 37–48.
An attempt to relate decline in percentage of disposable income allotted to apparel items to population shifts, i.e., to the proportionate increase in those of older age. Projection for the future made.

Slotkin, J. S. (1950), *Social Anthropology,* New York: Macmillan Co., pp. 47–51, 64–72, 104–108.
Aspects of dress, adornment, and fashion related to custom, ceremony, ethnocentrism, and social role.

"Soft Suit Seen Safe for Lunar Surface Work," *Science Newsletter,* Vol. 81 (March 10, 1962), p. 150.
Discussion of the adaption of the space suit for moon work. Mention of problems of heat and mobility.

"Space Suit Designed," *Science Newsletter,* Vol. 75 (June 13, 1959), p. 373.
Discussion of the development of the Mark IV space suit which allows freedom of movement and surrounds wearer with an earthlike environment.

"Space Suits for Sick," *Science Newsletter,* Vol. 81 (February 24, 1962), p. 115.
Discussion of use of pressurized suits for victims of strokes and other illnesses affecting blood pressure.

Spears, C. (1959), *How to Wear Colors with Emphasis on Dark Skins,* Minneapolis: Burgess Publishing Co.
Discussion of color choice and clothing design for dark-skinned individuals.

Spencer, H. (1892), *The Principles of Sociology,* Vol. 2, New York: D. Appleton and Co., pp. 174–210.
Under the general topic of ceremonial institutions, author discusses badges and costume, class distinction and sumptuary laws, and fashion.

Spencer, H. (1896), *The Principles of Sociology,* Vol. 3, New York: D. Appleton and Co., pp. 90, 224, 387–389, 519–522, 539.
References to dress under following topics: monasticism, poets and minstrels, clothes as money, Jack of Newbury, factory system, and trade unions.

Starr, F. (1891), "Dress and Adornment," *Popular Science Monthly,* Vol. 39 (October, 1891), pp. 488–502, 787–801; Vol. 40 (December, 1891), pp. 44–57, 194–206.
Topics included are deformations, reasons for dress, origins of ornament, and religious dress.

Starr, F. (1901), *Some First Steps in Human Progress,* Chautauqua, New York: Chautauqua Press, pp. 118–128.
In discussion of the dress and ornament of many cultures, author proposes that

ornamentation is a main function of dress. He illustrates by suggesting that body tattooing came before clothing.

Steiner, R. L. and Weiss, J. (1951), "Veblen Revised in the Light of Counter-Snobbery," *Journal of Aesthetics and Art Criticism,* Vol. 9 (March, 1951), pp. 263–268.

Writers proposed that Veblen's theory of conspicuous consumption is used in reverse by the members of the old elite today in order to distinguish themselves from the new wealthy. They find it paradoxical that the new-wealthy people must not display wealth to be considered as old elite, although they can at last afford the worldly goods that makes display possible.

Sterling, T. (1964), "On Being Naked," *Holiday,* Vol. 36 (August, 1964), pp. 8, 12–15.

A popularly written appraisal of reasons for wearing or not wearing clothes by a writer who has traveled extensively in Africa.

Stewart, G. (1954), *American Ways of Life,* Garden City, New York: Doubleday and Co., pp. 122–131.

An analysis of clothing traditions in America for the purpose of establishing truly American contributions. Although a few frontier costumes were of American inspiration, Americans have in general followed European models in dress. Twentieth-century informality in dress, however, seems to be the product of American leadership.

Stoke, S. M. and West, E. D. (1931), "Sex Differences in Conversational Interests," *Journal of Social Psychology,* Vol. 2 (February, 1931), pp. 120–126.

A study of college men and women in fraternities, sororities, and dormitories showing that clothing ranks high as a topic of conversation.

Stone, G. P. (1962), "Appearance and the Self," in Rose, A. M. (ed.), *Human Behavior and Social Processes: An Interactionist Approach,* New York: Houghton Mifflin Co., pp. 86–118.

A theoretical development of the symbolic interaction approach to the study of appearance and its significance for the self.

Stone, G. P. and Form, W. H. (1955), *Clothing Inventories and Preferences Among Rural and Urban Families,* Michigan State University Agricultural Experiment Station Technical Bulletin No. 246.

A study which confirms the hypothesis that social factors affect both the number of clothing items owned and the preferences people have for their selection and use. Researchers probed the relationships of wardrobe items, price, preferences, and attitudes to rural-urban residence, age, participation, social stratification, urbanization, and residential mobility.

Stone, G. P. and Form, W. H. (1957), *The Local Community Clothing Market: A Study of the Social and Social Psychological Contexts of Shopping,* Michigan State University Agricultural Experiment Station Technical Bulletin No. 262.

A study of economic, social, and social-psychological factors influencing the behavior of homemakers while shopping for clothes.

Stone, G. P., Form, W. H., and Strahan, H. B. (1954), "The Social Climate of Decision in Shopping for Clothes," *Journal of Home Economics,* Vol. 46 (February, 1954), pp. 86–88.

A study of women's preferences in shopping for clothing. Special attention is given to factors that influenced their shopping habits and decisions. Part of study reported in Stone and Form (1957).

Stout, D. R. and Latzke, A. (1958), "Values College Women Consider in Clothing Selection," *Journal of Home Economics,* Vol. 50 (January, 1958), pp. 43–44.

A study of values considered important to college women in selection of clothes. Subjects compared were those who had fashion or retailing courses and those who had not. Some questions asked were concerned with social significance of clothing selections.

Sullivan, K. (1958), "What Ever Happened to the Sunday Suit?" *Catholic Digest,* Vol. 22 (April, 1958), pp. 53–58.

A plea for more formal attire in church. A variety of arguments and rationalizations are set forth to support plea.

Sumner, W. G. (1907), *Folkways,* Boston: Ginn and Co. [Also in: paperback, Mentor Books (1960).]

Classic statements on conventions, fashions, and ideals of beauty. See index for specific pages.

Sybers, R. and Roach, M. E. (1962), "Clothing and Human Behavior," *Journal of Home Economics,* Vol. 54 (March, 1962), pp. 184–187.

Authors trace interest of home economists in research in the sociological aspects of clothing. Examples of research classified under following headings: social status, social mobility, occupation, social control, motivation, attitudes, and methods.

Symonds, E. H. (1933), "The Power of Fashion," *Journal of the Royal Society of Arts,* Vol. 81 (April 21, 1933), pp. 529–545.

A general article on fashion including discussion of fashion in clothing.

Tate, M. T. and Glisson, O. (1961), *Family Clothing,* New York: John Wiley and Sons.

Examination of clothing needs of the family relating changes in needs to stages in the family cycle.

Tax, S. (1963), *Penny Capitalism: A Guatemalan Indian Economy,* Chicago: University of Chicago Press, pp. 93–94, 150–154, 158–163, 201–202. First published as Smithsonian Institution Institute of Social Anthropology Publication No. 16, Washington: U.S. Government Printing Office (1953).

A study of a Guatemalan community. Considerable data are included on production and consumption of textiles and clothing items. Relative costs for clothing for different family members are compared, and class symbolism of costume is noted.

Thomas, W. I. (1899), "Psychology of Modesty and Clothing," *American Journal of Sociology,* Vol. 5 (September, 1899), pp. 246–262.

Discussion of reasons for modesty in clothing. Modesty reactions connected with sexual attraction or protection of sexual organs.

Thomas, W. I (1907), *Sex and Society,* Chicago: University of Chicago Press, pp. 201–220.
Excellent early twentieth-century analysis of the psychology of modesty and clothing. Modesty reactions thought to follow violation of modes of behavior which have become habitual in one way or another. Therefore, when the body has been habitually covered, the taking-off of the covering becomes suggestive because the break-up of a habit calls the act into attention.

Thomas, W. I. (1908), "The Psychology of Woman's Dress," *American Magazine,* Vol. 67 (November, 1908), pp. 66–72.
The author distinguishes clothing from ornament and dress. He states that man is naturally one of the most unadorned of animals and discusses various facets of ornamentation which man uses to rival the "radiance" of animals and flowers.

Thomas, W. I (1909), *Source Book for Social Origins,* Boston: R. G. Badger, pp. 549–558.
Author feels the primary function of clothes is to set off the married woman for sexual reasons. Clothing diminishes her attractions. He also discusses ornament and mentions protection and modesty as functions of clothing.

Thompson, T. (1962), "Fashion Therapy," *Journal of Home Economics,* Vol. 54 (December, 1962), pp. 835–836.
Description of a project of fashion therapy in California mental hospitals carried out by the San Francisco Fashion Group of which the author is a member. Project grew out of recognition of those treating mental patients that personal appearance is one of the clues to mental health.

Thorndike, L. (1931), *A Short History of Civilization,* New York: F. S. Crofts and Co.
See index for references to costume.

"Thoughtfulness in Dress," *Cornhill Magazine,* Vol. 18 (September, 1868), pp. 281–298.
Discussion of the importance of dress and means of achieving appropriate dress.

Titiev, M. (1959), *Introduction to Cultural Anthropology,* New York: Holt, Rinehart and Winston, pp. 3, 234–239, 294–295, 338, 391, 408.
Discussion of functions of clothes and descriptions of cultural variety in dress.

Topping, A. R. (1963), "First in Space—But Not in Femininity," *The New York Times Magazine* (June 30, 1963), pp. 10–11, 44, 46.
A general article on position of women within Russian society. Part of article is devoted to clothing and personal appearance.

Towley, C. (1957), "Manners Improve with Change of Dress," *Minnesota Journal of Education,* Vol. 37 (March, 1957), p. 25.
Brief account of the effect of dress rules on behavior in a senior high school.

Treece, A. J. (1960), "An Interpretation of Clothing Behavior Based on Social-

Psychological Theory," *Journal of Home Economics,* Vol. 52 (March, 1960), pp. 220–221.

An interpretation of clothing behavior based on the following hypotheses: the field of social psychology provides a source of relevant behavioral concepts which could be applied to new data, clothing behavior, and these concepts and their application would provide a basis for the development of learnings fundamental to understanding the function of clothing in behavior.

Trollope, F. (1949), *Domestic Manners of the Americans,* edited by D. Smalley, New York: Alfred A. Knopf, pp. 154, 299–301. [Also in: Vintage Books (1960).]

Observation made in this famous journal that class distinctions in America were based on occupation rather than education, income, and dress. Author speaks in a disparaging way of appearance, dress, taste, and grooming practices of Americans.

Tumin, M. M. (1941), "A Note on Cultural Style," *American Sociological Review,* Vol. 6 (August, 1941), pp. 569–571.

Comment on Kroeber study of women's dress fashions. Writer questions that correlations with general conditions explain the near regularity in the periodicities of dress.

Tumin, M. M. (1952), *Caste in a Peasant Society,* Princeton, New Jersey: Princeton University Press, pp. 84–98.

Study in social structure and function in pueblo of San Luis Jilotepeque. The superordinate Ladinos and subordinate Indians form two castelike groups which are fitted into one social system. Clothing is one index of group identity. See Gillin (1951).

Turner, R. H. and Killian, L. M. (1957), *Collective Behavior,* Englewood Cliffs, New Jersey: Prentice-Hall, pp. 215–217.

Fashion discussed as a process centered around diffusion of changes in taste. Changes in clothing illustrate the cyclical effect of fashion.

Turner, R. H. and Surace, S. J. (1956), "Zoot-Suiters and Mexicans: Symbols in Crowd Behavior," *American Journal of Sociology,* Vol. 62 (July, 1956), pp. 14–20. [Also in Young, K. and Mack, R. W. (eds.) (1960), *Principles of Sociology,* New York: American Book Co., pp. 13–20.]

Researchers tested if the zoot suit were an unambiguous, unfavorable symbol substituted for the more ambiguous symbol Mexican prior to the 1943 riots in Los Angeles. Data consisted of opinions about zoot suiters and Mexicans found in newspaper articles during the period.

Tylor, E. B. (1934), *Anthropology,* New York: D. Appleton and Co., pp. 15, 236.

Author traces development of clothing and adornment. Relates this development to culture.

Underhill, R. (1953), *Here Come the Navaho!* U.S. Office of Indian Affairs, Indian Life and Customs Pamphlet No. 7, pp. 100, 145–146, 224–225.

Comments on clothing of Navaho including descriptions of early costumes and subsequent changes that came with culture contact.

Useem, J., Tangent, P., and Useem, R. H. (1942), "Stratification in a Prairie Town," *American Sociological Review,* Vol. 7 (June, 1942), pp. 331-342.
Description of the stratification pattern of a small community. Clothing is referred to as one of the symbols of class position.

Vanderbie, J. H. and Madnick, H. (1961), *Developmental History of Auxiliary Heating Systems for the Individual Combat Soldier,* Quartermaster Research and Engineering Center, Natick, Massachusetts, Clothing Branch Series Report No. 25.
Summary of research concerned with use of auxiliary heating systems in protective clothing that will make survival possible under extreme environmental conditions.

Van Duzer, A. (1924), "Problems in Teaching Clothing Selection to Young Girls," *Journal of Home Economics,* Vol. 16 (August, 1924), pp. 423-427.
A general discussion of clothing selection in which reference is made to the psychological implications of the fact that mothers often impose on daughters the values of their generation. Practice thought especially true of first generation immigrants.

Van Syckle, C. (1951), *Practices Followed by Consumers in Buying "Large-Expenditure" Items of Clothing, Furniture, and Equipment,* Michigan State College Agricultural Experiment Station Technical Bulletin No. 224.
A study of families. Information was gathered on such items as planning, values wanted in merchandising, investigation preceding buying, labels, place of purchase, method of purchase, satisfaction. Considerable data on clothing included.

Veblen, T. (1894), "The Economic Theory of Woman's Dress," *Popular Science Monthly,* Vol. 46 (December, 1894), pp. 198-205.
Author considers woman a chattel who displays her wealth through dress, a conspicuously unproductive expenditure and a display of waste. He offers three cardinal principles to support his theory of women's dress.

Veblen, T. (1899), *The Theory of the Leisure Class,* New York: Macmillan Co. [Also in: Modern Library (1919 and 1934) and Mentor Books (1953).]
Classic reference on dress as conspicuous consumption. See especially the chapter entitled "Dress as an Expression of the Pecuniary Culture."

Veblen, T. (1934), "The Economic Theory of Woman's Dress," in Ardzrooni, L. (ed.), *Essays in Our Changing Order,* New York: Viking Press, pp. 65-77.
Author distinguishes two elements, dress and clothing. Dress is adornment and originated for that reason. Clothing covers and protects the person and developed as an afterthought. He states that "dress" becomes synonymous with "display of wasteful expenditure" and supports this theory with many examples.

Vener, A. and Hoffer, C. R. (1959), *Adolescent Orientations to Clothing,* Michigan State University Agricultural Experiment Station Technical Bulletin No. 270.
An investigation of the relationship of adolescents' attitudes toward clothing to the following variables: age-grade, social class, peer influence, and parental influence.

Vincent, J. M. (1931), "Sumptuary Legislation," *Encyclopedia of Social Science*, Vol. 14, New York: Macmillan Co., pp. 464–466.
Sumptuary legislation ordinances, which regulate the private expenditures of individuals, are sometimes based on economic reasons. More often, however, they are based on moral and social considerations. Article is a general historical overview of such laws in medieval times, in England, and in New England. Some references are made to dress codes.

Waite, W. C. and Cassady, R., Jr. (1949), *The Consumer and the Economic Order*, New York: McGraw-Hill Book Co., pp. 208–209, 223–231.
The authors consider clothing expenditure in relation to income and discuss the influence of fashion on consumption. They see fashion in America as an important source of human waste.

Warden, J. A. (1957), "Some Desires or Goals for Clothing of College Women," *Journal of Home Economics*, Vol. 49 (December, 1957), p. 795.
Study at Southern Illinois University to ascertain the relationship which college women believe exists between their clothing desires or goals and the clothing they own.

Warning, M. (1960), "Future Explorations in Home Economics," *Journal of Home Economics*, Vol. 52 (October, 1960), pp. 646–651.
Discussion of need for further study of patterns of clothing behavior, especially in the economic and socio-psychological areas. Many suggestions for research in these areas.

Wax, M. (1957), "Themes in Cosmetics and Grooming," *American Journal of Sociology*, Vol. 62 (May, 1957), pp. 588–593.
Commentary on meaning of cosmetics and related ways of manipulating physical appearance. Social functions of such grooming practices also examined.

Wax, M., Wax, R., and Robert V. Dumont, Jr., *Formal Education in an American Indian Community*, Report of Cooperative Research Project No. 1361, Cooperative Research Program, U.S. Office of Education, published as a supplement to *Social Problems* (Spring, 1964), pp. 49–53.
Authors show how attitudes toward school and education are closely tied to feelings of clothing deprivation among the Sioux Indians.

Webb, W. M. (1907), *The Heritage of Dress*, London: E. G. Richards.
Book covers many facets of the subject of clothing and dress. Topics included are: dress for special occasions, dress for certain types of persons, evolution and origin of dress, specific articles of dress, effects of fashion, rise and fall of fashion, and hair and cosmetics.

Welch, P. and Havemann, E. (1964), "Homosexuality," *Life*, Vol. 56 (June 26, 1964), pp. 66–80.
A report on homosexuality in America, including description of clothing habits of homosexuals.

West, J. (1945), *Plainville, U.S.A.*, New York: Columbia University Press, pp. 37–40, 176–178.

Discussion of kinds of clothing worn by the people of a farm community and their patterns of modesty.

Westermarck, E. A. (1921), *The History of Human Marriage,* London: Macmillan Co., pp. 534–571.

Discussion of functions of clothing, including use of clothing to attract the opposite sex. Remarks on clothing of many different cultures include references to origins and functions.

Weyer, E., Jr. (1959), *Primitive Peoples Today,* Garden City, New York: Doubleday and Co.

Text includes descriptions and excellent photographs of the clothing of many primitive societies. See index for specific references.

"Wherewithal Shall We Be Clothed?" *Journal of Home Economics,* Vol. 17 (March, 1925), pp. 156–157.

A discussion of implications of Heard's *Narcissus,* stressing fact that men as well as women are concerned with clothes, that clothing, therefore, is a natural aspect of human development.

Whetten, N. L. (1948), *Rural Mexico,* Chicago: University of Chicago Press.

Discussion of fiesta costume and other types of dress worn in various sections of Mexico. See index for specific references to clothing.

White, G. H. (1930), "A Marken Island Custom," *Notes and Queries,* Vol. 158 (April 19, 1930), pp. 273–275.

Description of Marken Island custom of dressing boys and girls the same until about age seven. Author rejects psychoanalytic explanations and suggests that Marken Island dress is simply an isolated survival of a once universal custom.

Whiting, B. B. (1963), *Six Cultures,* New York: John Wiley and Sons.

See index for references to modesty. Clothing is not indexed but there are descriptive references in the studies of the separate cultures.

Williams, F. M. (1959), "Clothing and Personal Care," *How American Buying Habits Change,* U.S. Department of Labor, Washington: U.S. Government Printing Office, pp. 127–148.

Discussion of changes in clothing during the first half of twentieth century. According to writer, manners and dress have become more and more informal. Reasons for this change are explored as well as trends in clothing expenditures for men, women, and children.

Williams, L. (1931), "The Philosophy of Clothes," *Spectator,* Vol. 147 (October 10, 1931), pp. 9–11.

Discussion of conflict between modesty and display.

Williams, W. M. (1885), "The Philosophy of Clothing," *Knowledge,* Vols. 7 and 8.

A series of articles concerned with hygienic qualities of clothing. See indexes for specific references.

Winakor, G. (1955), "Time Lag Between High Fashion and Accepted Fashion," *Journal of Home Economics,* Vol. 47 (May, 1955), pp. 343–344.

Magazines used as a source of data for analysis of time lag between high fashion and accepted fashion. The two classifications of magazines used in study were found not as discriminating as expected for tracing the fashion cycle of garments.

Winakor, G. (1962), "Consumer Expenditures for Clothing, 1929–1958," *Journal of Home Economics,* Vol. 54 (February, 1962), pp. 115–118.
Study of Illinois farm families' expenditures for clothing in 1930's versus present. Actual percentage of income spent for clothing has declined, although amount has increased.

Winakor, G. and Martin, M. (1963), "Used-Clothing Sales in a Small City," *Journal of Home Economics,* Vol. 55 (May, 1963), pp. 357–359.
Report of a consumer survey done to find out who buys used clothing, what kinds of garments are bought, and how much is paid for them. Study shows what goods are easy or hard to sell and the total receipts of such sales.

Windhorst, M. M. and Latzke, A. C. (1943), "What College Women Spend on Clothes," *Journal of Home Economics,* Vol. 35 (November, 1943), pp. 555–559.
A study concerned with evaluation of spending patterns at various social and economic levels. College girls' expenditures exceeded those of their age-peers not in college.

Winick, C. (1963), "Dear Sir or Madam, as the Case May Be," *Antioch Review,* Vol. 23 (Spring, 1963), pp. 35–49.
An analysis of the current trend toward similar clothing for both men and women. Discussion of many of the adoptions and adaptations of men's clothing which have been made by women within the last thirty years. Suggestion made that these changes are related to change in the whole social pattern of our country.

Wissler, C. (1945), *Indians of the United States,* New York: Doubleday, Doran and Co.
See index for reference to dress of specific tribes. Comment made that the stereotype for Indian dress is actually the dress of the Dakotas only (see p. 157).

Wolfe, B. (1954), *The Late Risers,* New York: Random House, pp. 136–142, 217–218.
Novelistic description of clothing for the New York Negro.

Woolworth, C. B. (1930), "Clothes and the Young Idea," *Practical Home Economics,* Vol. 8 (August, 1930), pp. 227, 245.
Discussion of the influence of clothing on behavior.

Wright, J. F. C. (1940), *Slava Bohu,* New York: Farrar and Rinehart, pp. 244–249, 311–312.
Discussion of incidents in which Doukhobors have used the removal of clothing to protest controls imposed upon them by government or other authority.

Wykes-Joyce, M. (1961), *Cosmetics and Adornment: Ancient and Contemporary Usage,* New York: Philosophical Library.

Summary of origin and development of cosmetics and adornment. Also comment on hair, beards, tattooing, perfumes, and cosmetic surgery.

Young, A. B. (1937), *Recurring Cycles of Fashion,* New York: Harper and Bros. Presentation of theory that a definite cyclical pattern exists for fashions and therefore, to some extent, fashions can be predicted. Establishes cycles for back fullness, tubular, and bell-shaped silhouettes. Cycles in men's fashions as well as in women's are analyzed.

Young, K. (1927), *Source Book for Social Psychology,* New York: Alfred A. Knopf, pp. 658–660.
Fashion discussed as a form of crowd behavior. Attention given to the means used to get designers' work accepted and to the transmittal of fashion to the people.

Young, K. (1960), *Handbook of Social Psychology,* New York: Appleton-Century-Crofts, pp. 310–329.
Thorough discussion of fashion and its relation to culture. Excellent sections on fashion and mores and fashion and men. Suggestion that the strength of fashion lies in feelings and emotions.

Zachry, C. B. (1940), *Emotion and Conduct in Adolescence,* New York: D. Appleton Century Co., pp. 62–65.
Brief discussion of adolescent dress and appearance, and its relation to physical and emotional development.

Zimmerman, C. C. (1936), *Consumption and Standards of Living,* New York: D. Van Nostrand Co., pp. 232–275.
Clothing discussed in relation to function, fashion, social role, physical compensation, fixation of age, sex patterns, and sartorial classification.

Zweig, F. (1952), *The British Worker,* Harmondsworth, Middlesex: Penguin Books, pp. 157–165.
Comment on clothing standards and behavior of the male worker in Britain.

Index

Abeokuta, 92, 96
Academic costume, 141, 280, 364
Acceptance, social, 44, 83, 113, 368
Adolescent girl, 408
　manipulation of appearance, 42
Adolescents, 77, 83, 85, 86, 365, 384, 387, 395, 396, 397, 403
　attitudes toward clothing, 414
　clothing awareness, 79
　dress of, 58, 67–68, 260, 368, 369, 418
　motives for clothing, 375
Adornment, 1, 2, 3, 38, 65, 374, 378, 382, 398, 408; *see also* Dress
Adults, 85
Advertisements, for men's clothes, 171–173
Aesthetic aspects of clothing, 367
Aesthetic sensitivity, 385
Aesthetic standards, for dress, 13, 372, 402
African cosmetics, 35
Age, 81, 364, 377, 410
　dress for, 57, 58, 77–78, 111, 360, 414, 416
Aged, dress for, *see* Elderly
Alb, 141
Albuquerque, New Mexico, 272
Alexandra, Queen of England, 348
Ames, Iowa, 106, 108, 110
Amies, H., 324
Amish, 378, 386, 394
Andaman Islanders, 9
Anthropometry, 399, 408
　of Negro, 169
　size of clothing, 394
Aphrodite, Cnidian, 45
Appearance, 34, 42, 44, 217, 220, 229, 244, 266, 268, 368, 410

Appearance, class difference, 160, 162
　as communication, 406
　meanings of, 187, 373
　modification of, 16, 36, 42, 377
　physical, 247
　preferences for, 380
　Russian women, 137
　standards for, 267, 379, 393
Archaeological data, on clothing, 5, 371
Architecture, related to clothing, 383, 392, 393, 399
Armor, 371
Army service, effect on clothing, 115
Art, definition of, 13
　portrayal of dress, 361
Artificial silk, 97
Ascetic dress, ancient India, 138
Astronauts, 213
Attitudes, 86, 229, 361, 376, 407, 410, 411
　toward clothing, 77, 115, 360, 385, 395
　moral, 364
　toward overweight, 396
Attractiveness, facial, 385
　male, effects of clothes on, 254, 257
　physical, 370, 401
　standards for, 393
Aurignacian Period, 22
Australian aborigines, 9, 18, 26, 205, 372

Badges, 124, 127, 409
Bagandas, 26
Balenciago, 404
Bantus, 25
Bark cloth, processing of, 30–31
Baronga, 46
Bathing, 36, 39

419

Bathonga, 46
Beards, 147, 418
Beauty, dieting, 34
　fatness, 34–35
　ideals of, 73, 137, 334, 356, 360, 367, 375, 387, 389, 390, 393, 411
　　Africa, 34–35
　　America, 34, 40
　　effect of Hollywood on, 35
　　Russia, 136
Beauty aids, 35; *see also* Cosmetics
Beauty salons, Russian, 137
Bengali, 46
Bernreuter Personality Inventory, 247
Binding, 26
Biological organism, effects of clothing on, 185
Blackmarket, Russian, 136
Black shirts, 125
Blankets, 30
　Indian, 18
Bloomer, Amelia, 406
Body, care, 397
　concealing of, 36, 66
　deodorizing, 36, 39
　modification of, permanent, 13
　　temporary, 13
　molding of, 36, 37, 42
　scenting of, 36, 39
　comfort, 205, 206, 363, 395, 399, 402
　of fabrics, 360
　perspiration, 206
　exposure, 14, 50, 51, 66, 75, 176, 178, 380; *see also* Nudity
　image, 393, 407
Boots, 21, 30, 310
Bosom, 36, 38, 39
Botocudo, 17
Bowerman, C. E., 84
Boy, clothing of, 109
　role of, 69–71
　rural-urban differences, 69
　social role of, 69
Brassieres, 38
Bridal dress, 53–55
Bridal veil, 55
Brown shirts, 125
Brummel, Beau, 285, 352
Budgets, 367

Burke, K., 226, 229
Burmese, 26
Bushman, 35
Buttons, 33, 292
Buying of dresses, 388

Cameroon tribes, 56
Capes, fur, 18
Caps, 112
Carlyle, T., 244, 368
Cossack, 141
Caste, 61, 165, 174, 375, 378, 413
　clothing symbolism, 62, 183
Castes, dress of, India, 369, 377
Castle, Irene, 356
Catholic priests, dress of, 66
Celestinus, Pope, 140
Ceremony, 14, 15, 409
　clothes for, 125
　see also Ritual
Change, in clothing, 370, 381
　social, 279
Charles I, King of England, 351
Charles VII, King of France, 348, 351
Charles IX, King of France, 298
Chemise, 327, 394
Children, 85, 388, 396
　dress of, 64, 363, 388, 406
　　Sioux, 258
　stability of, 64
　interest in clothing, 387
　Victorian ideal of, 70
Chinese, 30, 33, 60
　costume of, 127–137, 408
Church, dress for, 411
Church vestments, 280; *see also* Religious dress
Cicatrization, *see* Scarification
Circumcision, 26
Class, social, 61, 81, 82, 86, 117, 342, 392, 393, 401, 404, 413, 414
　determination of, 158
　middle, 340, 343, 402
　upper, 160–161, 341, 345
Class distinctions in dress, 117, 409
Classes, social, clothing of, 60, 62, 77–78, 163, 164, 414
　Hasidic, 142–149
Claude, Queen of France, 349

Index

Cleanliness, 259
Climate, effect on clothing, 104, 379
Clinard, M., 272
Clique, 86
Clo, 186, 205
Cloak, 28
Clothing, as adaptation to climate, 379
  to conserve energy, 206
  as heat insulation, 206
  properties of, 207–208
  restraint of, 388
  symbol of authority, 124; *see also* Uniforms
  thermal comfort, 207
  see also Adornment, Consumption, Dress, Functions of clothing, Origins of clothing, Status, Symbolism
Clothing awareness, 77, 79, 85
Clothing habits, 1879 vs. 1909, 367
Codpiece, 74
Coiffure, 22, 44; *see also* Hair, dressing of
Collars, paper, 116
  ringed brass, 26
College students, 369, 406
  women, 406, 411, 415, 417
Colonial dress, 384
Color preferences, 370, 401, 406, 409
Comanches, 16
Comfort, 399; *see also* Body, comfort
Communication, 219, 244
  by clothing, 223
Communism, 60
Communist dress, in China, 127–130
  as symbol, 130
Concept of others, 247; *see also* Perception of others
Conformity, 38, 44, 70, 115, 330, 338, 360, 364, 379, 382, 388, 397, 398, 402, 409
Conspicuous consumption, 170, 295, 399, 410, 414
Conspicuous expenditure, 93
Consumer credit, 105
Consumer preference, 361
Consumption, 376, 415
  of clothing, 105–106, 342, 363, 376, 378
  in America, 59
  in Nigeria, 59
Conventions, 411
Cooley, C. H., 217, 222, 229, 238, 250

Coolidge, Mrs. Calvin, 355
Cooper, J. M., 19
Cope, 141
Corset, 73, 348, 349
Cosmetics, 36–45, 130, 133, 182, 188, 246, 269, 310, 352, 364, 371, 377, 394, 406, 408, 415, 418
  expenditure for, 24
  functions of, 24
  male use of, 349
  Russia, 136
Cosmetic surgery, 418
Cotton, 30, 31, 91, 92, 97, 175, 312
Courtesans, 44, 73
Craze, 344, 366, 367
Crinoline, 73, 348, 351
Cro-Magnon man, 22, 37
Cultural pattern, 330
  variety in dress, 361
Culture contact, 19, 282, 391, 397, 413
Custom, 280, 330, 360, 368, 395, 399, 407, 409
Customs, of Amish, 378

Darwin, G., 287
Decision making, 388
Decoration, 10, 364, 376, 388
  of body, Andaman Islanders, 9
    Australian aborigines, 9
    Melanesian, 9
Deformation, 26, 409
  cranial, 26
Delinquency, 271
Delinquents, 368
De Medici, Catherine, Queen of France, 349
Demi-mondes, 346, 363
Deno, E. D., 85
Deodorants, 39
De Pompadour, Madame, 351
Deprivation, clothing, 77, 79, 85, 188, 258, 260–261, 382, 384, 415
  status, 403
Designers, 363, 383, 418
Deviance, in dress, 362
  personal, 188
  subcultural, 189
Dewey, John, 229
Dhoti, 76
Diet consciousness, 161, 356

Diet consciousness, Russian, 137
Dieting, 34, 43
Differentiation, 65, 66, 339–340, 360, 368, 416
Dior, Christian, 324
Discourse, 217, 220
Doukhobors, 361, 383, 399, 417
Douty, H. I., 84
Dress, as communication, 164
  definition of, 1
  as extension of body, 49
  as extension of self, 374
  as material goods, 2, 3
  meaning of, 49
  reasons for, 44
  as social habit, 46, 47
  in social interaction, 2
  symbol of alienation, 52
  symbol of economic position, 59–60
  See also Adornment, Clothes, Functions of clothing, Origins of clothing
Dress codes, 368, 374, 395, 412
  reform, 28, 128, 281, 315, 360, 374, 376, 382, 389, 399, 403, 405, 406
  Communist, 128
  for men, 302
  regulations, 47, 365
  of Mennonites, 374
Dropouts, Sioux Indians, 261
Drug users, dress of, 376
Du Barry, Madame, 351
Dunlap, K., 65, 66
Dyeing, Japanese, 317

Ebony, 171–172
Economic factors, effect on clothing, 59–60, 67
Economic trends, 375
Edward III, King of England, 296, 298
Effemininity in men's dress, 315
Ego, 222
Egypt, 33, 37
Elderly, clothes of, 58, 90, 361, 374, 385, 400
  clothing problems of, 365
  number of, 102
  preferences of, 363
Elizabeth I, Queen of England, 298, 348, 350
Elizabeth II, Queen of England, 324
Ellis, H., 49, 65

Emulation in dress, 81
Environment, and dress, 113
Erikson, E., 222
Eskimos, 20, 21, 25, 28, 32, 47, 66, 282, 396, 308
Gambell, 387
Ethnocentrism, 409
Etiquette, in dress, 14, 395
Evening dress, 404
Evolution of dress, 364, 383
Expenditure for clothing, 86–90, 98, 367, 409, 415, 416
  farm families, 103
  Negro, 116, 170
  Nigeria, 93
  regional, 103
  urban families, 103
  whites, 170
Expenditure for cosmetics, 24

Fabrics, 373
Fad, 344, 360, 364, 366, 367, 373, 389, 390, 392, 393, 397, 399
  and the adolescent girl, 42
  as differentiation from, 345
  as identification with, 345
  See also Fashion
Family, as reference group, 86
  as socializing agent, 82
  clothing of, 365, 367, 373, 381, 390, 391, 400, 411, 414, 417
  cycle, 59, 86–90, 394, 411
  farm, 99–100
  income of, 97–98
  influence on clothing, 58–59
  size, 88, 102
  urban, 99–100
Farm community, 69, 406, 410, 416
Farthingale, 73
Fashion, 162, 322, 367, 369, 372, 373, 374, 376, 378, 379, 380, 381, 382, 383, 385, 387, 389, 390, 391, 392, 393, 394, 395, 396, 397, 399, 400, 403, 404, 405, 407, 409, 411, 415, 418
  adolescent follower, 42
  as acculturative agent, 391
  aesthetic aspect, 327
  bandwagon effect, 328
  as collective behavior, 323, 364

Fashion, as differentiation, 339–340, 360
  diffusion of, 334, 337, 341, 360, 392, 413
  extremes, 403
  functions of, 362, 364
  high, 416
  in history, 366
  as identification, 339–340
  nature of, 366
  in ornaments, 366
  relation to economy, 380
  resistance to, 325
  in Russia, 60–61, 137, 380
  San Carlos, 18
  as social movement, 282–283, 330, 365
  trickle down theory, 341, 404
  see also Fad
Fashion change, 325, 329, 367, 373, 393, 403
  controls, 388
  cycles, 332, 399, 413, 418
  designer, 284, 363, 383, 418
  industry, 340, 371, 381, 405, 407
  leadership, 283, 324, 343, 346, 363, 364, 377, 410
    cinema, 356
    congressmen, 380
    designers, 363, 404
    legal, 389
    local community, 390
    mistresses, 351
    presidents, 354, 380, 389
    royal, 347–353
    sportsmen, 357
    stage, 355
  show, Peking, 133
  therapy, 269–270, 397, 412
Fashions, 1915, 361
  1960, 369
Fatting house, 34
Felt, 29–30
Femininity, 395, 401
  in males, 214
  in Russia, 135
Feminist, in China, 130–131
Fibers, vegetable, 9, 30, 31
Fiesta costume, 416
Finery, 260, 400
Flax, 9, 31
Flint, Michigan, 78
Flugel, J. C., 64, 65, 66

Folk costume, 134–135, 280, 300, 402
Folk society, 279
Folkways, and dress, 14
Foot binding, 37
Footwear, 176, 182, 372, 398
Form, W. H., 84
Foundation garments, 182, 360
Frock coat, 141
Fuegians, 17, 19, 372
Functions of clothing, 9, 10, 17, 65, 164, 363, 367, 368, 371, 383, 388, 393, 398, 406, 407, 410, 412, 413, 416, 418
  expressive, 6–7, 186
  instrumental, 6–7, 186, 366
  see also Differentiation
Fur, 29, 32

Gambell, 308
Gender, 220; *see also* Sex
George IV, King of England, 352
Gestures, 212, 217
Gimbel, Sophie, 324
Girls' clothing, 109
Gold Coast, 92, 97
Gorer, G., 234
Government, 124
Greenland, 33
Gregory the Great, Pope, 140
Grooming, 36–45, 415
G-string, 16
Guatemala, 378, 411
Gujarat, 46

Hair, 415, 418
  animal, 30
  dressing of, 10, 16, 22–23, 36, 40, 41, 43, 54, 176, 182–183, 360, 401
  symbol of age status, 23
  symbol of sex status, 23
Harding, Mrs. Warren, 355
Hartmann, G. W., 256
Hasidim, dress of, 146–157
  social classes, 142–149
Hats, 173, 180
  protection, 20
  status symbol, 20
Head, covering of, 150, 181
Headgear, Yoruba, 92

Index

Head shaping, 37
Health, 399; *see also* Hygiene of clothing
Heard, G., 416
Heat insulation, of clothing, 205
Hemp, 31
Henequen, 31
Hennin, 348
Henry II, King of France, 349
Henry VIII, King of England, 298, 350
Herero, 36, 56
Herrick, R., 49
Hitler, Adolf, 125
Hollywood, 396
Homosexuality, 375, 415
Hong Kong, China, 133
Hoop skirts, 73, 348, 351
Hospital dress, 372, 405
Hoult, T. F., 84
Housing, 105
Huizinga, J., 237
Hurlock, E. B., 78
Hygiene of clothing, 186, 304–307, 360, 362, 366, 373, 379, 389, 390, 399, 408, 416

Identification, 219, 339, 340
Identity, 222, 225, 238, 241, 246
Imitation, 370
Immodesty, 16, 368, 374
Incas, 26
Income, 367, 409, 415
India, costume of, 138, 360, 369, 375, 378, 406
Indians, Dakotas, 417
  Flatheads of Idaho, 26
  Fuegian, 205
  North American, 21, 22, 374
  of British Columbia, 30
  San Carlos, 174–184
  Sioux, 257–264, 415
Indigo, 92
Individuality, and dress, 247, 364, 385, 409
Infant, 233–234, 388
  dress of, 109, 234
  effect of clothing on, 191–203, 381
Influentials on dress, 81
Informality, trend to, 360, 365
Innovations in clothing, acceptance of, 67
Insignia, 66, 124
Interaction, social, 187, 189, 379

Interaction, and dress, 81
Interest in clothing, 249, 405
Isabella of Bavaria, Queen of France, 348
Islam, 26, 96, 138
Ivy League look, 166

James I, King of England, 298, 351
Japan, tattooing, 25
Japanese costume, 139, 311, 397
Jeans, 259
Jewelry, 130, 176, 310, 371
Jews, 26, 142–157, 301
Job getting, effect of clothes, 113
Johnson, H. H., 48
Judicial robes, 280

Kabui, 46
Kennedy, Jacqueline, 285
Kimono, 311, 314, 316, 399
Kinch, J. W., 84
Koryak, 32
Knickers, symbol of role, 64–72
Kroeber, A. L., 332

Laboring class, 116; *see also* Working class
Labret, 16, 17, 26
Ladinos, clothing of, 174–180
Lagos, Nigeria, 96
Langtry, Lily, 355
Lansing, Michigan, 79
Latif, I., 234
Leisure time, and dress, 112
Lenglen, Mlle., 357
Life, 171–172
Life cycle, 85
Lindesmith, A. R., 232
Linen, 313
Lip plugs, 16, 17, 26
  stretching, 37
Loango, 75
Loincloth, 76
Longhose, 74
Louis XI, King of France, 348
Louis XIII, King of France, 348
Louis XIV, King of France, 347
Louis XV, King of France, 351
Louis XVI, King of France, 349
Lynd, Helen, 226, 227, 228
Lynes, R., 343

Mackintosh 115
Madras, 92
Magical use of clothing, 17, 121–122, 184
Malay, 46
Manchu costume, 128
Manners, 14, 393, 395, 416
Mao Tse-Tung, 128
Marie Antoinette, 349
Married men's dress, 112
Mary Queen of Scots, 349
Masculinity, 395, 401
Masks, 375
Mass production, 407
Material objects, and social interaction, 2
    as symbols, 187
Materials, for clothing, 12
Mead, G. H., 82, 217, 221, 222, 223, 229, 232, 236, 238, 243
Meaning, 218
Melanesia, 23
Meller, Raquel, 356
Men, dress of, 74, 91, 109, 111–117, 251–257, 365, 395, 401
    China, 130
    class difference, 162
    evolution in, 287–292
    Negro, 164–174
    San Carlos, 178–179
    stability of, 64, 68
Mennonites, dress regulations of, 374
Mental-health movement, 70
Mental illness, and dress, 189, 268, 269–271, 370, 397
    and nudity, 403
Middle Ages, 73, 74
Middle-class values, 70
Mobility, social, 104, 143, 410, 411
Moccasin, 21
Mode, 399
Modesty, 10, 14, 15, 47–48, 360, 362, 364, 368, 369, 373, 374, 375, 376, 382, 384, 389, 395, 398, 399, 407, 408, 412, 416
    Arab, 48
    Christian, 47–48
    Hasidic, 150
    Moslem, 48
    Roman Catholic, 48
    social habit, 16, 17
Mods, 276–278, 361, 369, 395, 397

Monasticism, 409
Mongols, 29
Mood, 226
Moore, O. K., 233
Moral criticism of grooming and dress, 43
    in Bible, 37–38
Morality of dress, 388
Moral precepts, 227
Moral standards for dress, 14
Mother Hubbard, 20
Motives, for clothing choice, 362
    for dress and adornment, 5, 376, 382, 390, 392, 394, 405, 409, 411
    for fashion change, 67, 386, 387
Mourning dress, 10, 386
Mufflers, 112
Muslims, 26, 96, 138
Mussolini, Benito, 125
Mutilation of body, 26

Nāga, 75
Nakedness, 47, 48, 392, 410; *see also* Body exposure, Nudity
Napoleon, 350
National costume, 280, 300
    China, 134–135
Navajo, dress of, 391, 413
Neatness, 258
Needle, eyed, 8, 12, 32, 33, 371
Needs, clothing, 97
Negro, clothing for, 23, 62, 164–174, 393, 398, 408, 417
    expenditure for clothing, 116
Negroes, as caste, 62
Neolithic period, 30
Newcomb, T. M., 86
New Guinea, 47, 75
New Look, 323–329
Nigeria, 91–97, 281, 283, 378, 399
Nonconformity, 379
Norms, social, 189, 227
Nude infants, 192–200
Nudity, 361, 377, 383, 384, 388, 389, 392, 399, 403, 410
    and health, 49, 367
    as negation of social habit, 46
    as social movement, 49
    ceremonial, 14, 46–47
    magical, 48

Index

Nudity, sexual appeal, 48
 see also Body exposure

Occupation, and dress, 100, 104, 113, 411
 and social class, 413
Occupational dress, 168, 364
 businessman, 384
 China, 129–130
 white collar, 377
 worker, 377, 383, 405
 see also Working class, dress of
Ochre, 8, 18, 24, 35, 37
Omahas, 23
Ondo, 93, 96
Origins of clothing, 6, 8, 65, 364, 365, 371, 374, 408, 415, 416
Origins of ornament, 8, 409
Ornament, 13, 368, 407
 as insurance, 360
Orwell, George, 326
Overcoats, Japanese, 317

Painting, body, 10, 16, 18, 35, 36, 402
 ritual, 24
 for war, 24
Pakistani dress, 386, 397
Paleolithic period, 29, 32–33
Pallium, 140
Pannier, 352
Papyrus, 31
Parasols, 352
Parataxic distortion, 240
Paris, 396, 407
Parkas, 310
Participation, social, 249, 367, 373, 410
Patagonians, 21
Peer groups, 84–86, 241, 258, 261, 414
Perception of others, 188, 247, 373, 376, 407
Permanent waving, 40–41
Peron, Juan, 125
Personality, 222, 382, 387, 392
 and dress, 364, 401
 measurement of, 247, 249
Peru, 33, 297
Philippe le Bel, King of France, 296, 298
Physical environment, and clothing, 20–21
Physiological adaptation, 19, 370
Physiology, and clothes, 186, 302, 363, 372, 401

Piaget, J., 240, 243
Pickford, Mary, 356
Pius XI, Pope, 361, 368
Polish workers, 116
Political system, and dress, 60
Polynesians, 25, 66
Pompadour, Madame de, 351
Poor, dress of, 163
Popularity, 370
Population changes, decrease in farm, 101–103
Pregnancy, clothing for, 55–56, 88
Pressurized suit, 186, 210–212, 377, 389, 409
Priest, dress of, 61, 140, 372
Printing, Japanese, 317
Prison clothes, 246, 398
Prostitutes, 246
Protection, 9, 362, 364, 374, 376, 382, 384, 398, 407, 408, 412
Protective clothing, 9, 17, 65, 375, 388, 414
 in hospital, 118–123
 magical charm, 17, 121
 rainwear, 183
 symbol of status, 118–121
Protestant ministers, dress of, 67
Psychosis, 370
 and appearance, 268
 see also Mental illness

Quaker costume, 381

Raincoat, 115
Raleigh, Sir Walter, 352
Rank, social, related to dress, 125
Rationing of clothes, 117, 329
Rayon, 97
Reference groups, 82, 86
Referents, for clothing, 80, 81, 84
Reform, dress, see Dress reform
Regional dress, 113; see also National costume
Religion, effect on dress, 61
Religious dress, 42, 61, 66, 140, 246, 280, 372, 376, 378, 386, 401, 409
 functions of, 141, 146
 see also Amish, Hasidim, Sacred dress
Research, clothing, 68, 361, 367, 405, 411, 415
Retailers, 402

Rites, of intensification, 15
  of passage, 15, 69
Ritual, 142, 150, 397
  and dress, 15, 60, 123
  see also Ceremony and Painting, body
Roach, M. E., 85
Robes, skin, 29
Rockers, 276–278, 361, 369, 395, 397
Role, 395, 409, 418
  and appearance, 42
  and clothing, 66–69, 71–72, 368, 371, 405
Role playing, 236, 243
  and costume, 237, 239
Roles, female, 42, 187, 285
  male, 187, 285
Role-taking, 219
Roman dress, 372
Roosevelt, Alice, 354
Rosen, B. C., 84
Rouge, 24
Royalty, 346, 373
  dress of, 189, 265–266
  as fashion leaders, 265, 363
Ruff, 348–349
Rural residence, and dress, 69, 406, 410
Russia, 60, 136
  position of women, 412
Russian dress, 135
Ryan, M. S., 78

Sacred dress, 138–141
Safety clothing, 114, 369
Sales, of used clothing, 107–110
Samoa, 396
Sandals, 22, 96
Sapir, E., 327
Sarong, 20, 31
Scarification, 10, 16, 25, 37, 402
Scars, dueling, German, 25
Scents, for body, 39
Second-hand clothing, 114, 184; see also Used clothing
Self, 218, 219, 232–233, 246, 379, 410
Self and appearance, 230
Self-concept, 42, 188, 236, 241, 244, 247, 271, 362, 370, 376, 381, 387, 393, 407
  and clothing, 66–67, 71–72, 222, 368
  relation to tattooing, 368
Self-confidence, 247

Self-confidence, effect of clothes on, 387
Senators, dress of, 125
Sentiments, 229
Seventh Avenue, 405, 407
Sewing, 8, 29
Sex, attraction of dress and grooming, 17, 44, 45, 47, 371, 372, 373, 383, 384, 387, 408, 412, 416
  differences in muscle tonus of infants, 195, 201
  distinction, in dress, 72, 130, 214, 234, 236, 360
  role, and dress, 14, 57–58, 74, 214, 364, 401, 417
Shoes, 94, 95, 173, 179
  as protection, 20
  as status symbol, 20
Shopping, 410, 411
Siberia, 21, 33
Significant other, 235
Silk, 313, 371
Silverman, S. S., 78, 85
Simmel, G., 339
Size, of ready-made clothing, 399, 402
Skin, painting of, 35, 36
  color of, 169, 372, 409
Skins, curing of, 28–29
  used as clothing, 8, 9, 17
Slacks, banning of, 260
  women's, 184, 310, 365, 383
Slaves, Negro, dress of, 166–169
Slavonia, South, 56
Slums and dress, 113
Social control, 371
Social distance, 248, 253, 256–257, 379, 386
Social distinction, 408; see also Status
Social habit, 330
Socialization, 82–86, 187–188, 241, 243–244
  anticipatory, 237, 243
  fantastic, 237, 243
  by mother, 235
Social order, 2, 279
Social pressure, 360
Socio-economic group, 382
Sociometric tests, 368
Sollas, W. J., 32
Sons of Freedom, 399
Sorel, Agnes, 351
Space suit, medical use, 210–212

Index

Space suits, 186, 377, 389, 409
Spinning, 175
Spock, B., 70
Sports clothes, 404
Standards, clothing, 111, 258–259, 260
    male workers, 418
    minimum, 387
Stanton, Elizabeth Cady, 406
Status, 84, 113, 402, 406, 411
    and dress, 37, 43, 60, 165, 405
Status identification, 398
    rating, and clothing, 250, 386
    symbols, 158–159, 276, 341
        clothing, 251
        Hasidic, 143, 149
Stereotypes, 66, 401
Stone, G. P., 84
Stratification, 342, 410; *see also* Class, social
Stratification symbols, 125; *see also* Class, social
Strauss, A. L., 232
Student dress, 138
Style, 332, 391, 399
Style change, 369
Style of life symbols, 62, 343
Subculture, youth, 81
Subgroups, 83
Subincision, 26
Sudanese, 23
Suit, business, 187
Sullivan, H. S., 217, 222, 230, 240, 243
Sumner, W. G., 335
Sumptuary law, 281, 295–301, 315, 362, 364, 375, 377, 391, 397, 401, 409, 415
    America, 299
    England, 298
    France, 298
    Greece, 297
    Ireland, 298
    Japan, 299
    purposes of, 296–297
    resistance to, 300–301
    Rome, 297
Sunday suit, 114
Sun Yat-sen, 132
Surgical cap, 118–122
    gown, 118–122
    mask, 118–122
Surplice, 141

Survivals in dress, 280, 288–292, 363, 372
Swaddling, 380
Swanson, Gloria, 356
Swiss Lake Dwellers, 9, 33
Symbolic interaction theory, 216, 410; *see also* Social interaction theory
Symbolism, 218, 371
    class, 402, 411
    nonverbal, 220
    status, 250, 400
Symbolism of dress, 10, 76, 84, 130, 280, 282, 368, 371, 372, 376, 377, 378, 379, 390
    caste, 62, 183
    class, 62
    occupation, 10
    ritual condition, 10
    sexual, 10, 360, 382
    status, 10, 55–56, 158, 159, 362, 366, 384, 405, 408

Taboos, 10
Tailoring, 18, 19, 29, 32, 33, 314, 371, 373
    Aurignacian, 8
    barbarian, 9
    Chinese, 9, 133
    diffusion of, 20
    Japanese, 314
    Mongol, 9
    Roman, 9
Tapa, 31
Tasmanians, 18
Taste, 327, 332, 333, 334, 340, 343, 383, 387, 392, 393, 394, 395, 399
Tattooing, 10, 16, 25, 37, 271–276, 368, 371, 375, 408, 410, 418
Technology and clothing production, 12, 383
Teenage dress, 58, 189–190, 361, 395, 396; *see also* Adolescents, Mods, Rockers
Teeth, cleansing of, 36
    coloring of, 16, 36
    filing of, 16, 26, 36
    removal of, 16, 26
Textiles of Swiss Lake Dwellers, 9
Therapy, clothing, in low blood pressure, 186, 210–212, 389
    for mental illness, 269–270, 397, 412
Tierra del Fuego, 17, 19, 372
Toga, 141

Topless dress, 15
Traditional dress, 280
Transvestitism, 364, 375, 384
Transylvania, 46
Trousers, 329
 for women, 369
Turks, 301

Uganda, 48
Unconscious, 364
Underwear, 92, 95, 182, 319
Uniforms, 66, 125–126, 223, 241, 314–315, 329, 404
 army, 126, 129, 132, 320
 functions of, 60, 124–127
 German, 125, 126
 Japanese, 314
 school, 315, 319, 320
 workers', 383
Urban residence and dress, 69, 406, 410
Used clothing, 60, 105–106, 107–110, 114, 168–169, 184, 260, 417
Utility of clothing, 378

Values, 226
Veblen, T., 66, 221, 337, 410
Vener, A. M., 78, 85
Vertugadine, 349; *see also* Farthingale
Victoria, Queen of England, 351
Vogue, 369

Wa-chaga, 48
Wardrobe, minimum, 208, 396
Warrior, dress of, 125, 346
Wa-taveita, 48, 56
Weaving, 30, 31, 174, 371, 396
 origin of, 9
Weber, M., 284, 342
Wedding dress, 15, 53, 55, 176, 375
 symbolism of, 54–55

Weight, body, 396
 of clothing, 367
 see also Diet consciousness
Westermarck, E., 65
Western dress, influence of, 96, 396
 in Orient, 131, 134, 311, 313, 316, 408
White men's dress, 309; *see also* Western dress
Wigs, 150, 167, 348, 373
Willard, Frances E., 406
Willendorf, Venus of, 22
William Rufus, King of England, 348
Wills, Helen, 357
Wirth, L., 225
Wissler, C., 20, 22
Women, dress of, 67–68, 109, 363
 in China, 130
 and class difference, 161, 162
 in Guatemala, 175–176, 181
 in manual work, 369
 in Middle Ages, 73
 in Russia, 136
 in Wales, 126
 Yoruba, 92
 education of, 100
 employment of, 98–99
Wool, 30
Woolen industry, 312
Work clothes, 260
Working class, dress of, 129–130
 female, 402
 male, 111–117, 418
 see also Occupational dress
World War II, 70
Wrist watch, 96, 182

Yoruba, 91–97, 378, 399

Zemchugyna, Pauline, 136
Zoot-suit, 311, 404, 413
Zulu, 35